MASAHIRO HIKOKUBO

Yusei has taken his duel with Roman to heart and is racing through the courses on Seibal's field at full throttle with all his heart and soul, betting on the draw of destiny. Tear apart the darkness with Sect!!

MASASHI SATO

At Chapter 60, which is collected in this volume, the series hit the five-year mark!! I'll join Yusei in boosting my Sense and do my best as we head for the climax!!

YU-GI-OH! 5D's

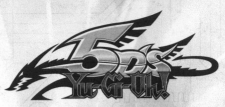

Volume 8
SHONEN JUMP Manga Edition

Story by **MASAHIRO HIKOKUBO**
Art by **MASASHI SATO**
Production Assistance **STUDIO DICE**

Translation & English Adaptation **TAYLOR ENGEL AND IAN REID, HC LANGUAGE SOLUTIONS**
Touch-up Art & Lettering **JOHN HUNT**
Designer **SHAWN CARRICO**
Editor **MIKE MONTESA**

Printed in the U.S.A.

Published by VIZ Media, LLC
P.O. Box 77010
San Francisco, CA 94107

10 9 8 7 6 5 4 3 2 1
First printing, October 2015

viz media
www.viz.com

RATED T FOR TEEN

PARENTAL ADVISORY
YU-GI-OH! 5D's is rated T for Teen and is recommended for ages 13 and up. This volume contains fantasy violence.
ratings.viz.com

SHONEN JUMP
www.shonenjump.com

5D's
Yu-Gi-Oh!

VOLUME 8
LIGHT SENSE!!

Story by **MASAHIRO HIKOKUBO**
Art by **MASASHI SATO**
Production Assistance **STUDIO DICE**

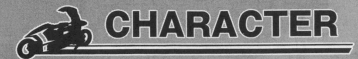

CHARACTER

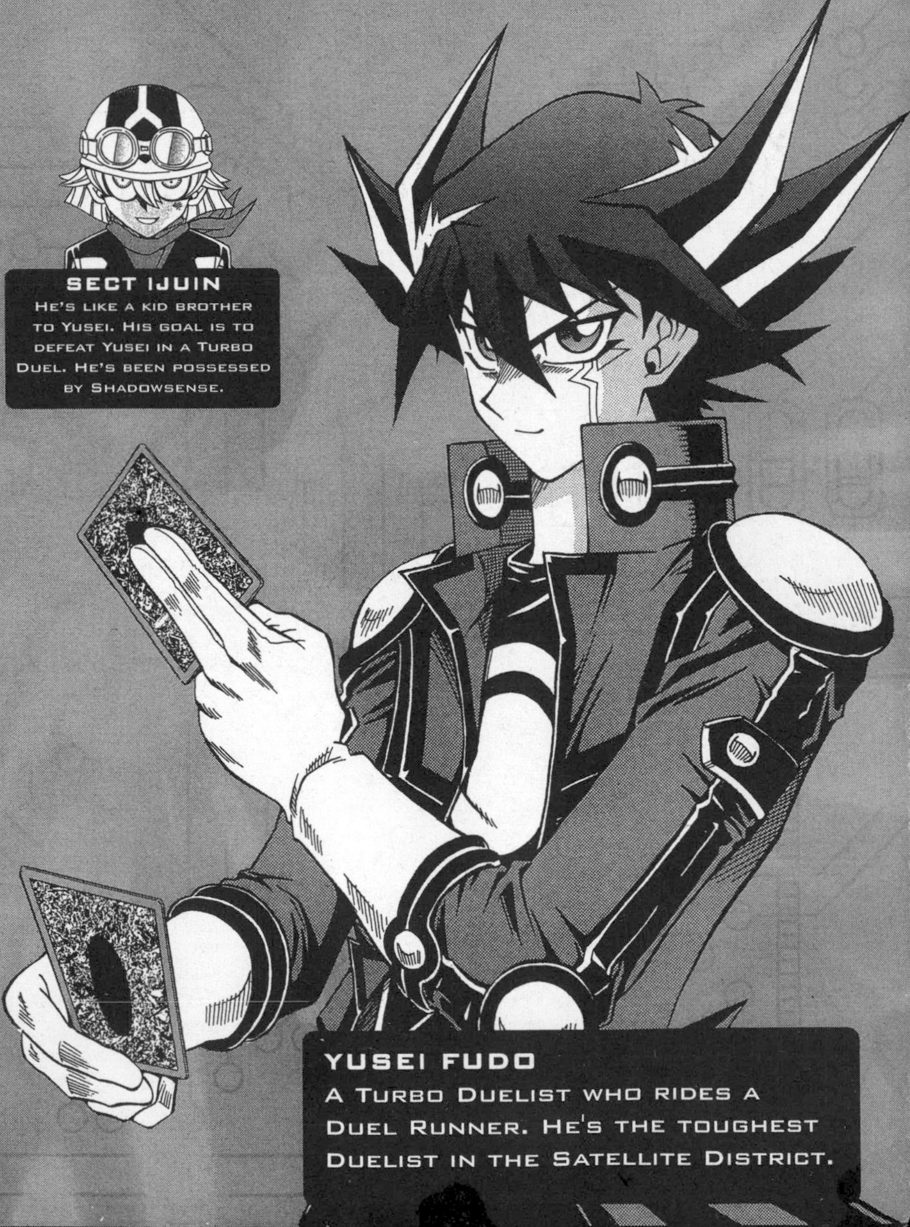
SECT IJUIN
HE'S LIKE A KID BROTHER TO YUSEI. HIS GOAL IS TO DEFEAT YUSEI IN A TURBO DUEL. HE'S BEEN POSSESSED BY SHADOWSENSE.
YUSEI FUDO
A TURBO DUELIST WHO RIDES A DUEL RUNNER. HE'S THE TOUGHEST DUELIST IN THE SATELLITE DISTRICT.

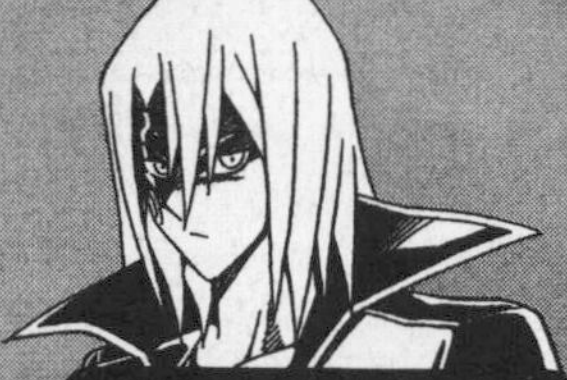

KALIN KESSLER

A fiendishly strong Turbo Duelist whose specialty is his "handless combo."

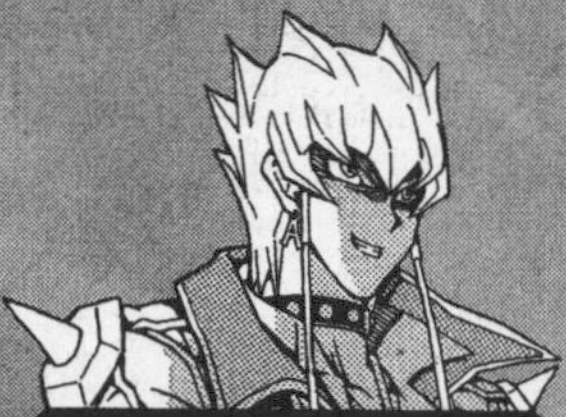

JACK ATLAS

A Turbo Duelist known as "the King," and feared by all around him.

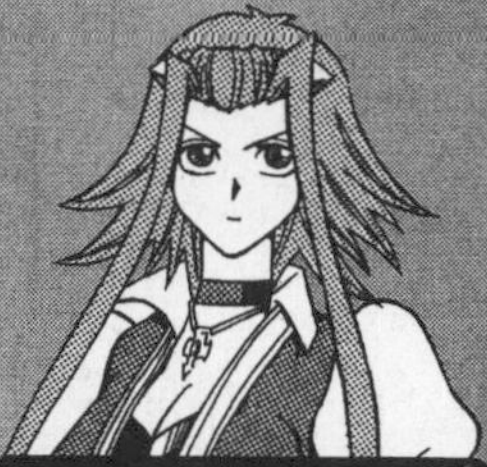

AKIZA IZINSKI

A turbo duelist who holds the title "Queen of Queens."

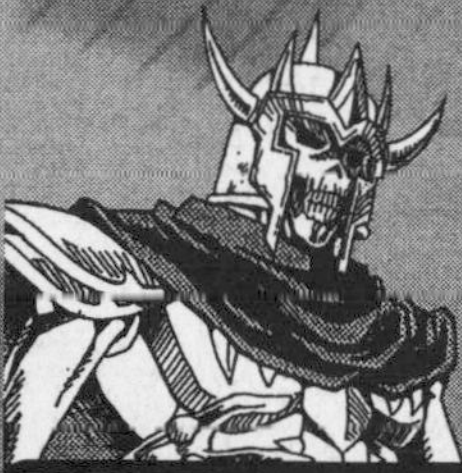

SKELETON KNIGHT

A mysterious turbo duelist who possesses Shadow power and gave some to Sect.

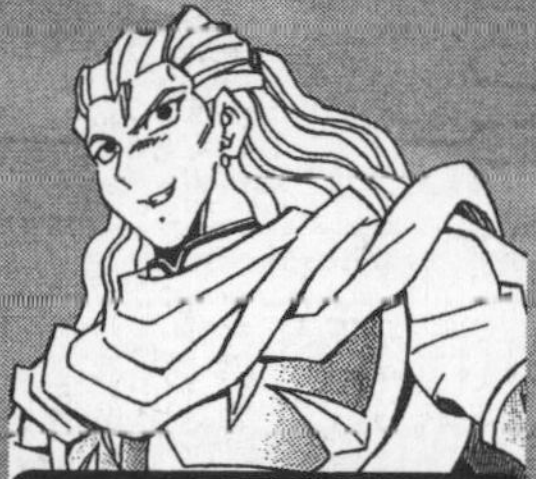

REX GOODWIN

The host of the D1 Grand Prix. He's trying to get his hands on the ultimate god.

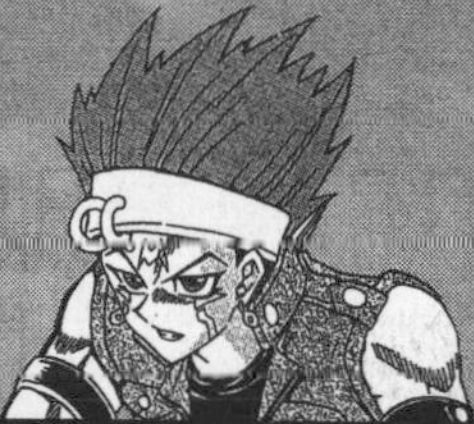

CROW HOGAN

A super high-speed synchro-user, nicknamed "The Black Whirlwind."

STORY

In New Domino City, in the year 20XX, Turbo Duels fought from the seats of motorcycle-shaped duel disks called "Duel Runners," are the hottest game in town.

Yusei Fudo, the toughest duelist in Satellite, suffered a painful loss to Jack Atlas. In order to duel Jack again, Yusei entered the D1 Grand Prix, the battle to determine the toughest duelist in the world!! As the strongmen of the dueling world slugged it out, Yusei fought his way into the second round, where he beat Crow, Leo and Luna, and won his own Duel Dragon, Stardust Spark Dragon! In the Corridor of the Northern Sky, Yusei connected to the Skeleton Knight's feelings and became the King of Sky's Lock, but Sect has fallen into darkness and become the King of Earth's Lock. In an attempt to take back Sect's soul, Yusei challenges him to a Turbo Duel...!!

Yu-Gi-Oh! 5D's

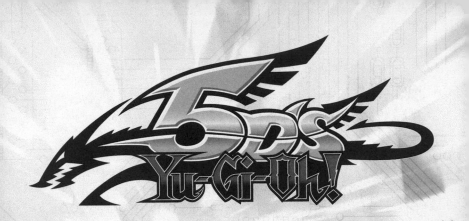

VOLUME 8

LIGHT SENSE!!

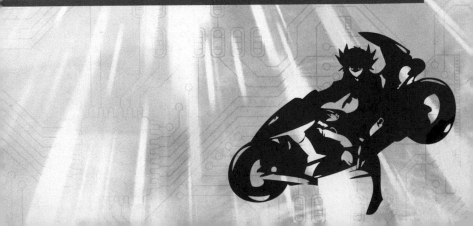

RIDE-54

THOUGHTS FOR A FRIEND...!!

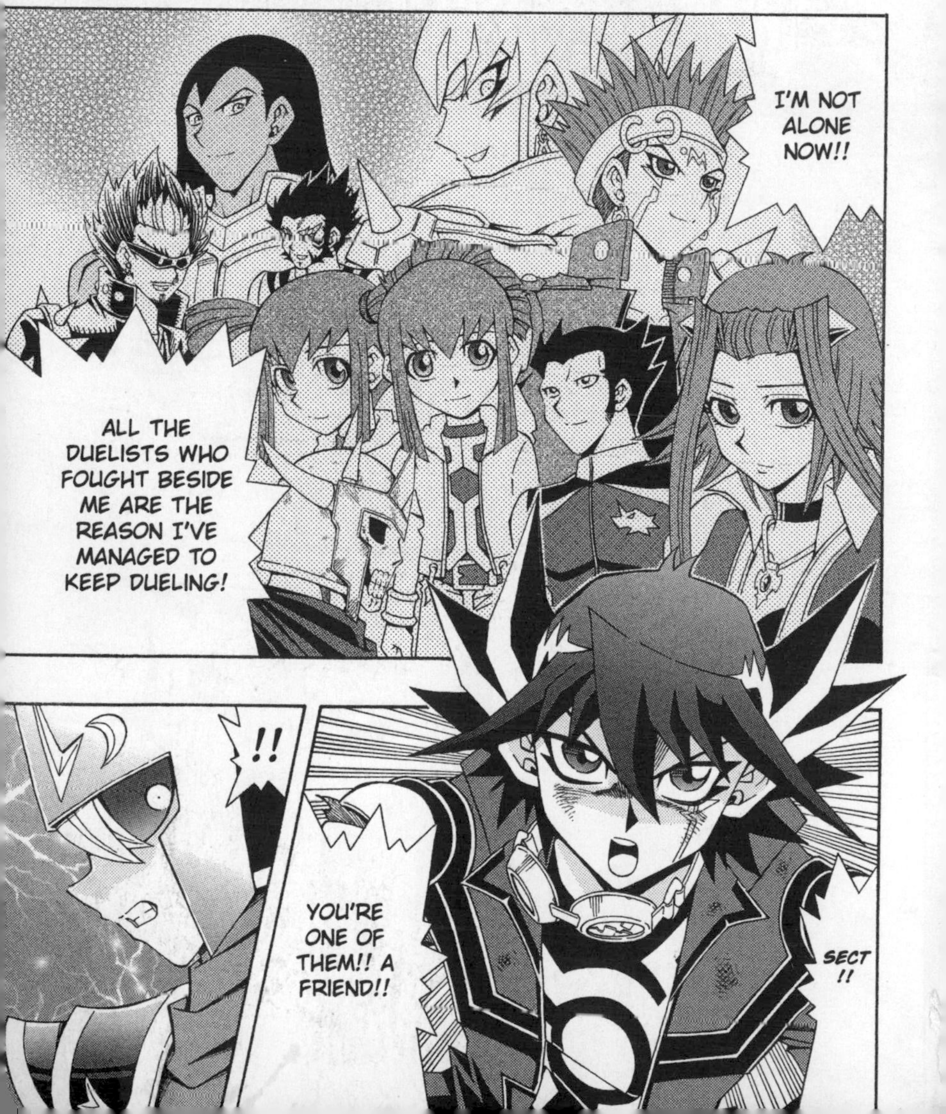
I'M NOT ALONE NOW!!
ALL THE DUELISTS WHO FOUGHT BESIDE ME ARE THE REASON I'VE MANAGED TO KEEP DUELING!
YOU'RE ONE OF THEM!! A FRIEND!!
SECT !!
!!

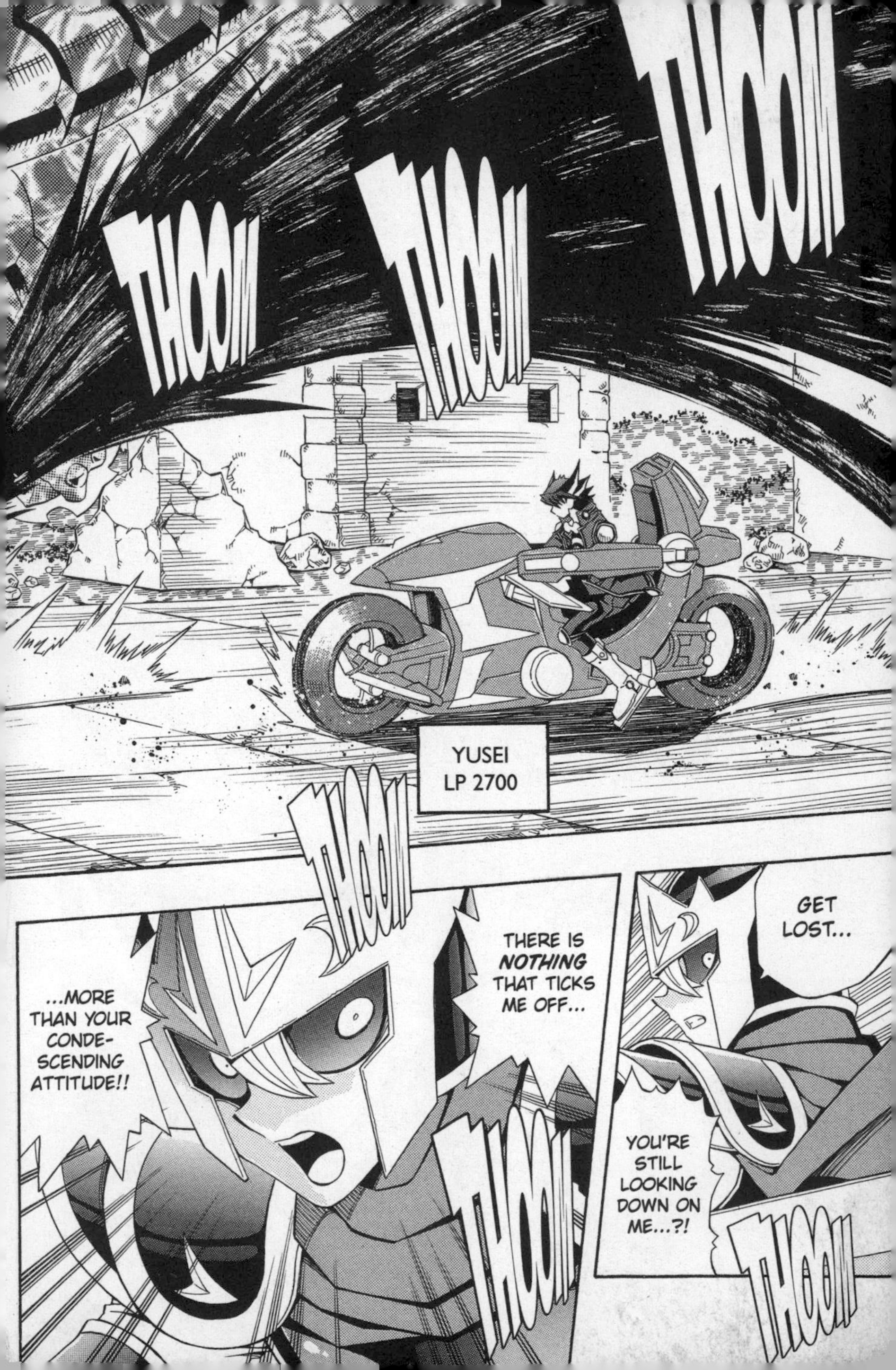
THOOM
THOOM
THOOM
YUSEI
LP 2700
THOOM
GET LOST...
YOU'RE STILL LOOKING DOWN ON ME...?!
THOOM
THERE IS *NOTHING* THAT TICKS ME OFF...
...MORE THAN YOUR CONDE-SCENDING ATTITUDE!!
THOOM

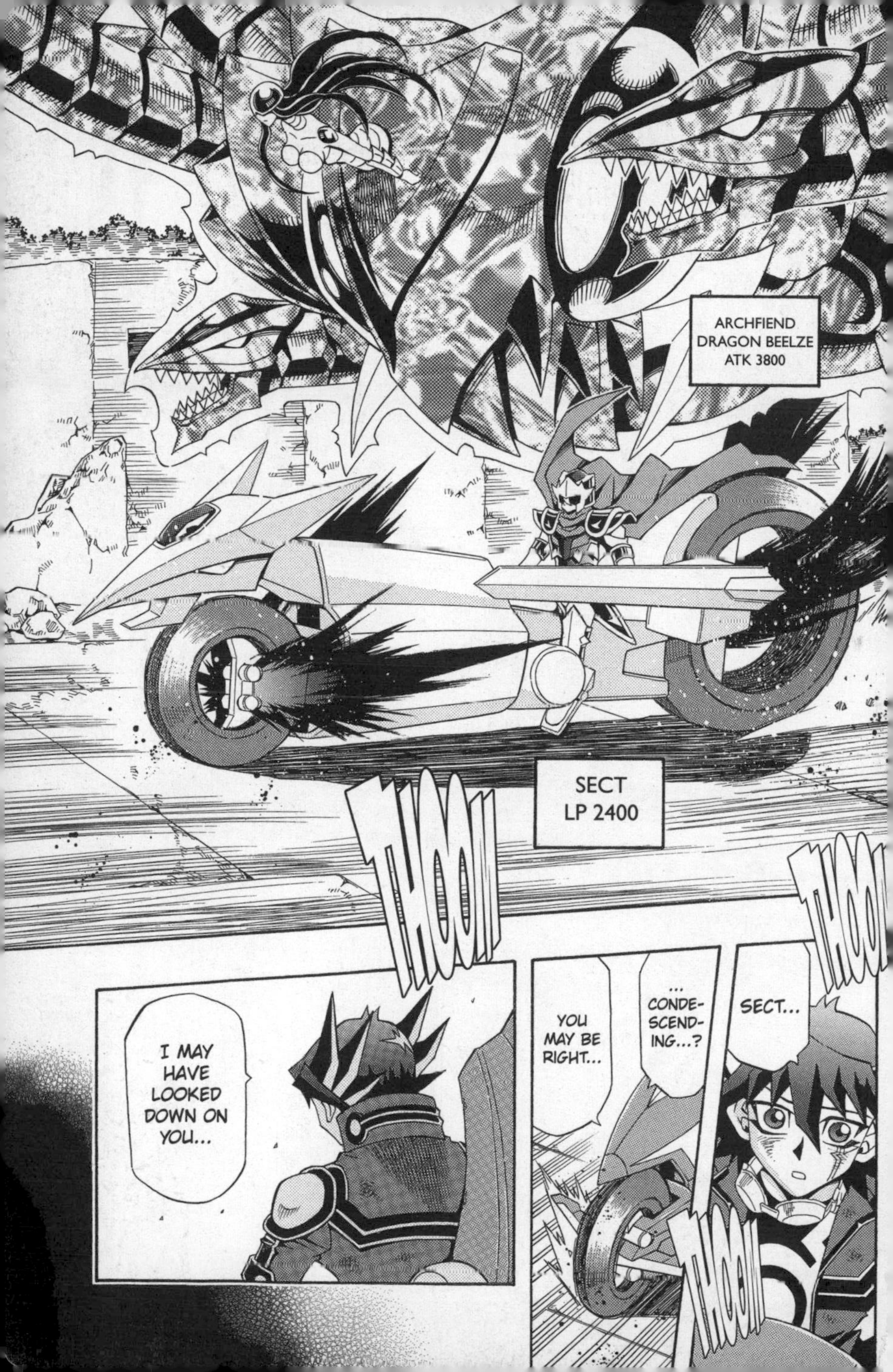
ARCHFIEND DRAGON BEELZE ATK 3800
SECT LP 2400
THOOM
THOOM
SECT...
...CONDESCENDING...?
YOU MAY BE RIGHT...
THOOM
I MAY HAVE LOOKED DOWN ON YOU...

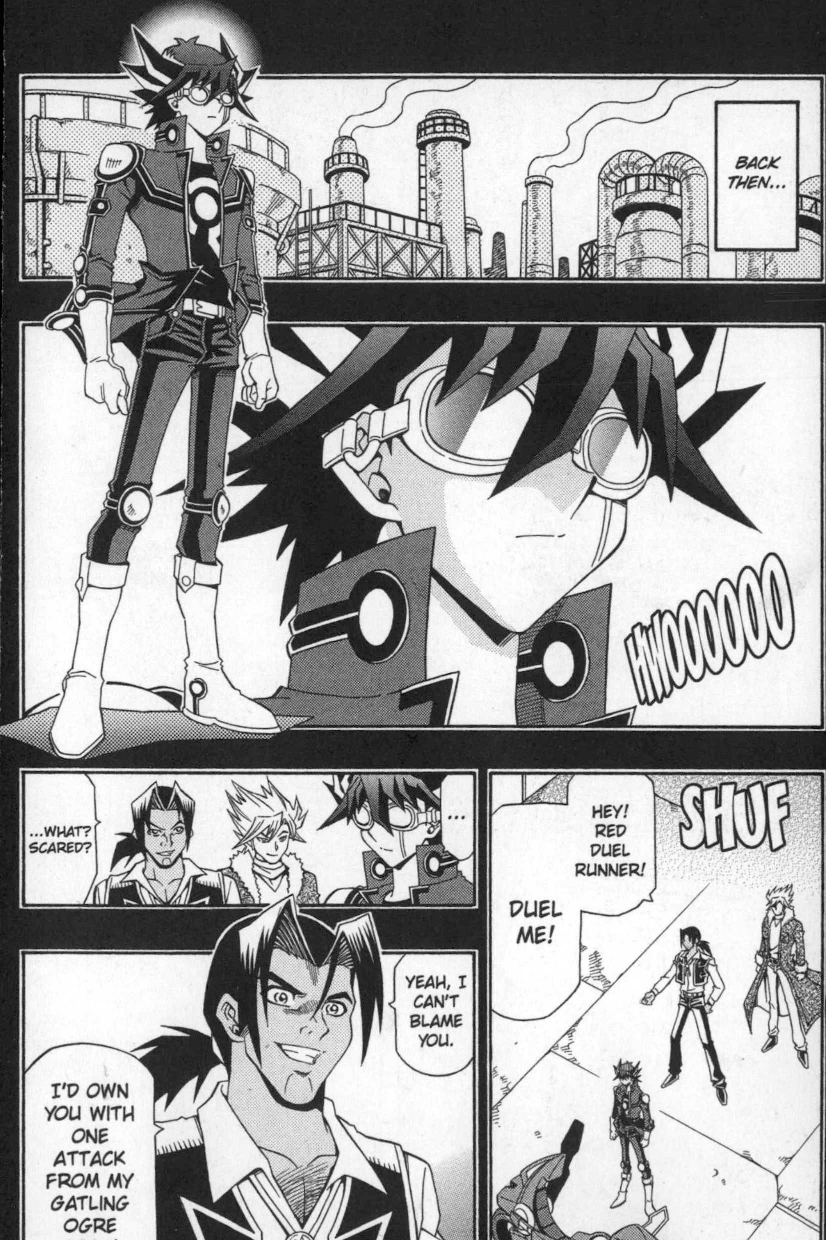
BACK THEN...
HWOOOOOO
SHUF
HEY! RED DUEL RUNNER!
DUEL ME!
...
...WHAT? SCARED?
YEAH, I CAN'T BLAME YOU.
I'D OWN YOU WITH ONE ATTACK FROM MY GATLING OGRE DECK!

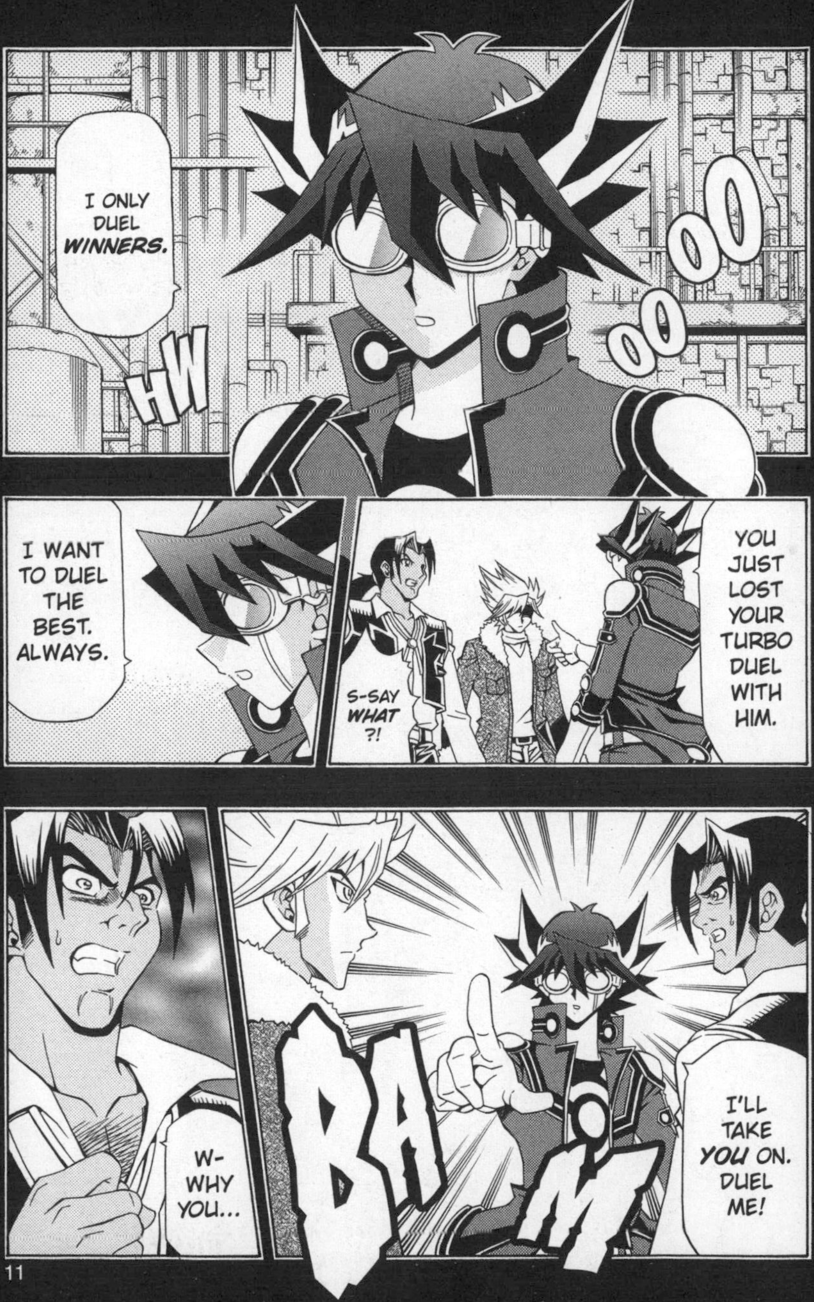

I ONLY DUEL WINNERS.
HWOOOOOO
YOU JUST LOST YOUR TURBO DUEL WITH HIM.
S-SAY WHAT?!
I WANT TO DUEL THE BEST. ALWAYS.
I'LL TAKE YOU ON. DUEL ME!
BAM
W-WHY YOU...

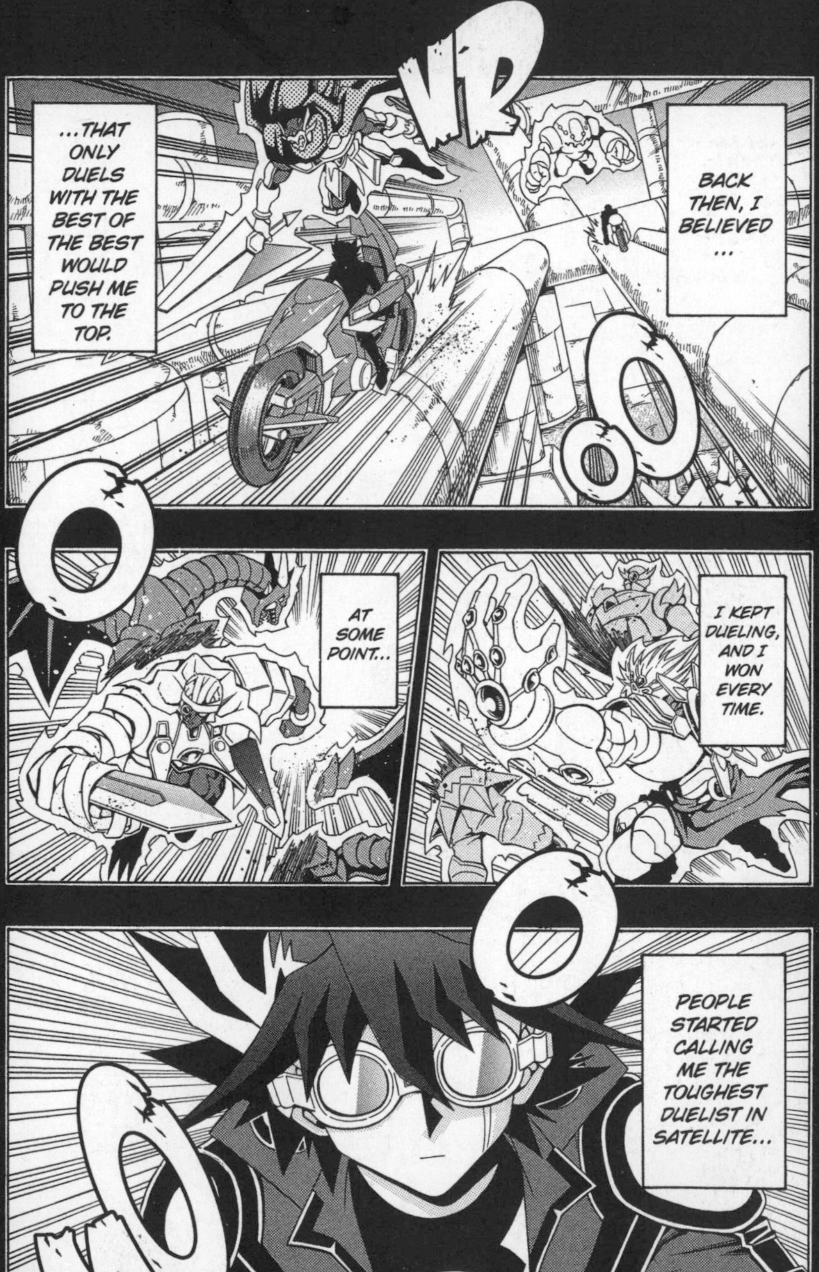
VR
BACK THEN, I BELIEVED...
...THAT ONLY DUELS WITH THE BEST OF THE BEST WOULD PUSH ME TO THE TOP.
I KEPT DUELING, AND I WON EVERY TIME.
AT SOME POINT...
PEOPLE STARTED CALLING ME THE TOUGHEST DUELIST IN SATELLITE...
M

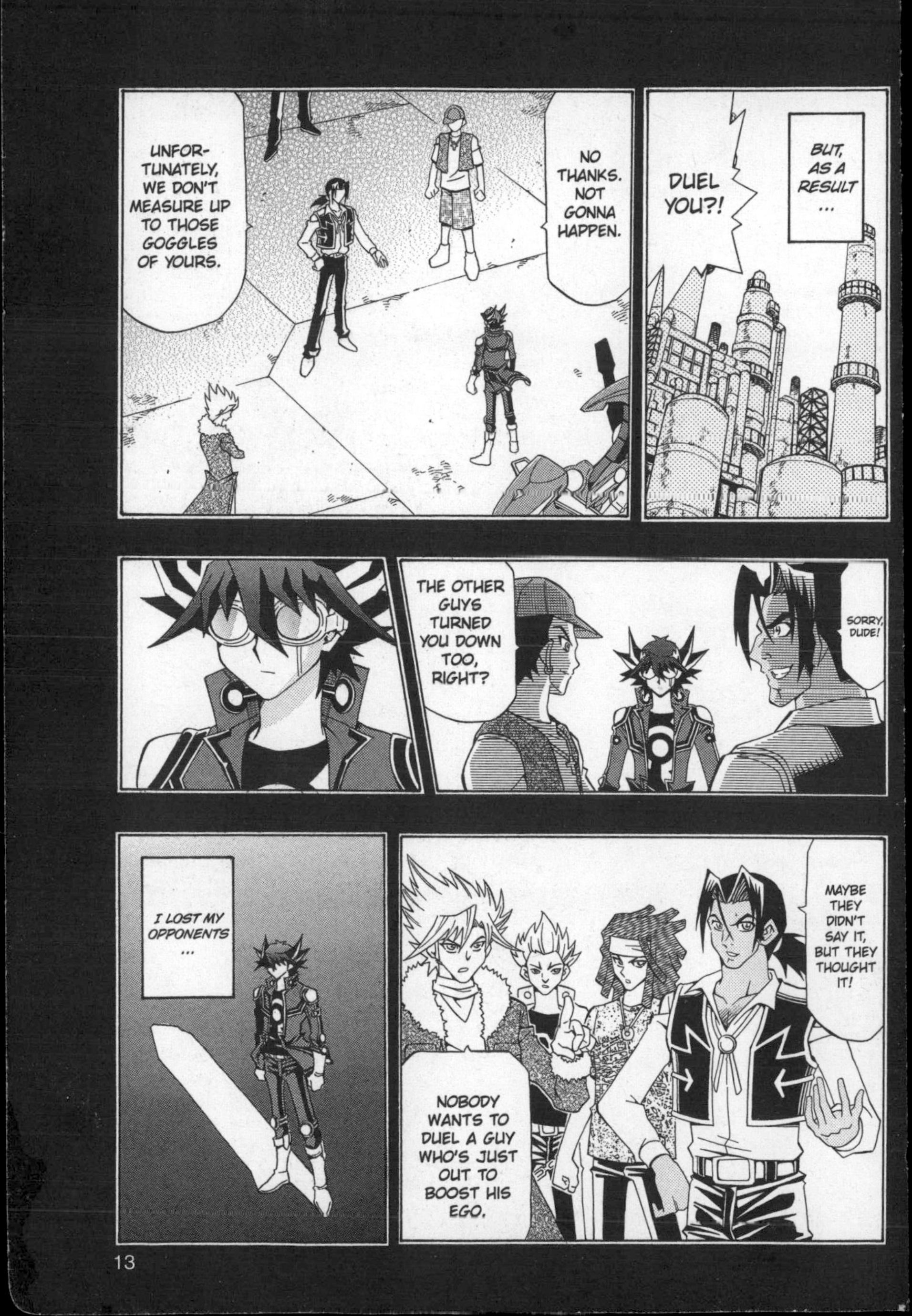
BUT, AS A RESULT ...
DUEL YOU?!
NO THANKS. NOT GONNA HAPPEN.
UNFOR-TUNATELY, WE DON'T MEASURE UP TO THOSE GOGGLES OF YOURS.
THE OTHER GUYS TURNED YOU DOWN TOO, RIGHT?
SORRY, DUDE!
MAYBE THEY DIDN'T SAY IT, BUT THEY THOUGHT IT!
NOBODY WANTS TO DUEL A GUY WHO'S JUST OUT TO BOOST HIS EGO.
I LOST MY OPPONENTS ...

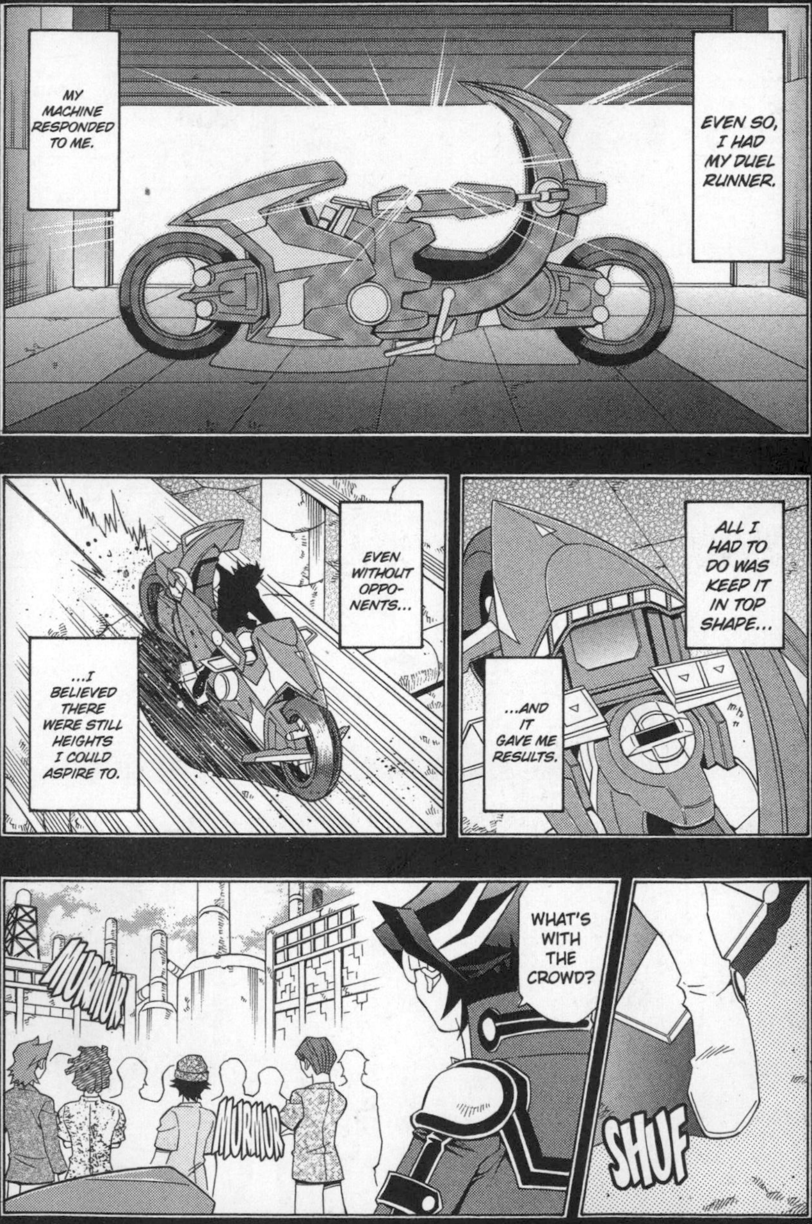
EVEN SO, I HAD MY DUEL RUNNER.
MY MACHINE RESPONDED TO ME.
ALL I HAD TO DO WAS KEEP IT IN TOP SHAPE...
...AND IT GAVE ME RESULTS.
EVEN WITHOUT OPPONENTS...
...I BELIEVED THERE WERE STILL HEIGHTS I COULD ASPIRE TO.
SHUF
WHAT'S WITH THE CROWD?
MURMUR
MURMUR

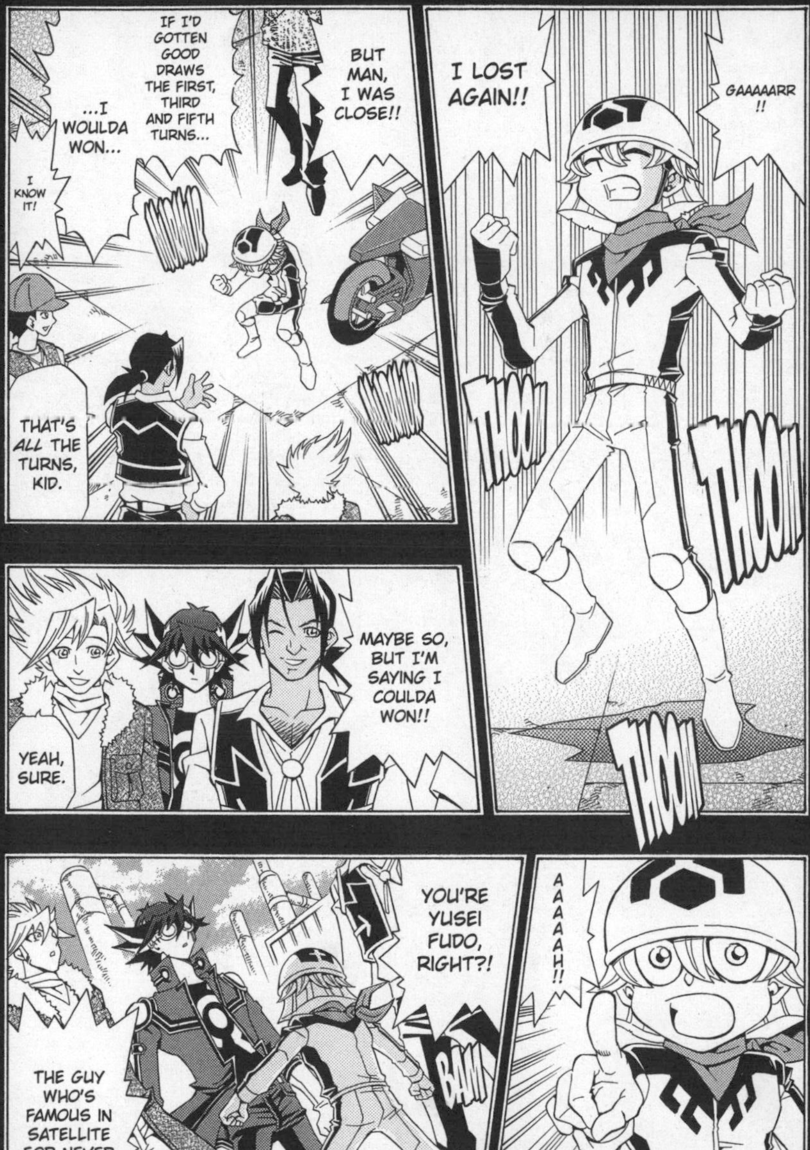
I LOST AGAIN!!
GAAAAARR!!
THOOM
THOOM
THOOM
BUT MAN, I WAS CLOSE!!
IF I'D GOTTEN GOOD DRAWS THE FIRST, THIRD AND FIFTH TURNS...
...I WOULDA WON...
I KNOW IT!
THAT'S *ALL* THE TURNS, KID.
MAYBE SO, BUT I'M SAYING I COULDA WON!!
YEAH, SURE.
AAAAAAH!!
YOU'RE YUSEI FUDO, RIGHT?!
BAM
THE GUY WHO'S FAMOUS IN SATELLITE FOR NEVER LOSING...

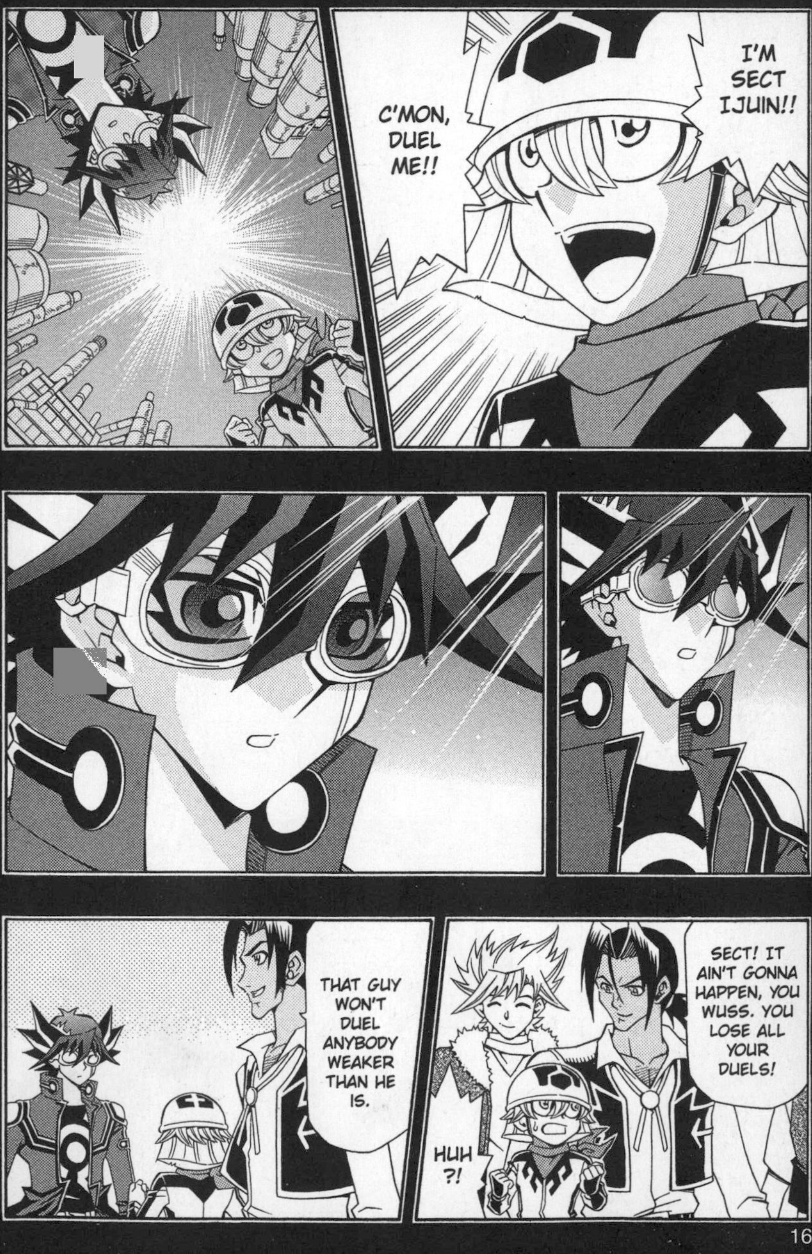
I'M SECT IJUIN!!
C'MON, DUEL ME!!
SECT! IT AIN'T GONNA HAPPEN, YOU WUSS. YOU LOSE ALL YOUR DUELS!
HUH ?!
THAT GUY WON'T DUEL ANYBODY WEAKER THAN HE IS.

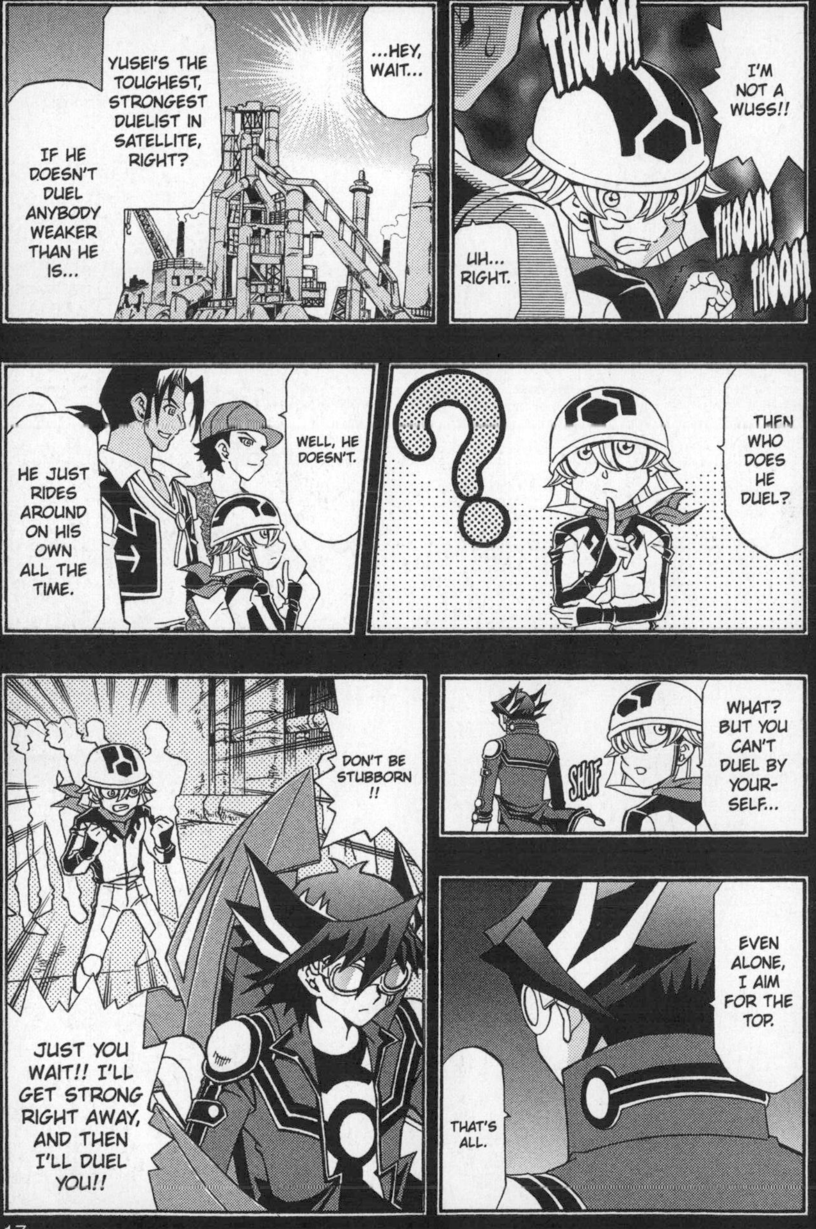
THOOM
I'M NOT A WUSS!!
THOOM THOOM
UH... RIGHT.
...HEY, WAIT...
YUSEI'S THE TOUGHEST, STRONGEST DUELIST IN SATELLITE, RIGHT?
IF HE DOESN'T DUEL ANYBODY WEAKER THAN HE IS...
THEN WHO DOES HE DUEL?
WELL, HE DOESN'T.
HE JUST RIDES AROUND ON HIS OWN ALL THE TIME.
WHAT? BUT YOU CAN'T DUEL BY YOURSELF...
SHUF
EVEN ALONE, I AIM FOR THE TOP.
THAT'S ALL.
DON'T BE STUBBORN!!
JUST YOU WAIT!! I'LL GET STRONG RIGHT AWAY, AND THEN I'LL DUEL YOU!!

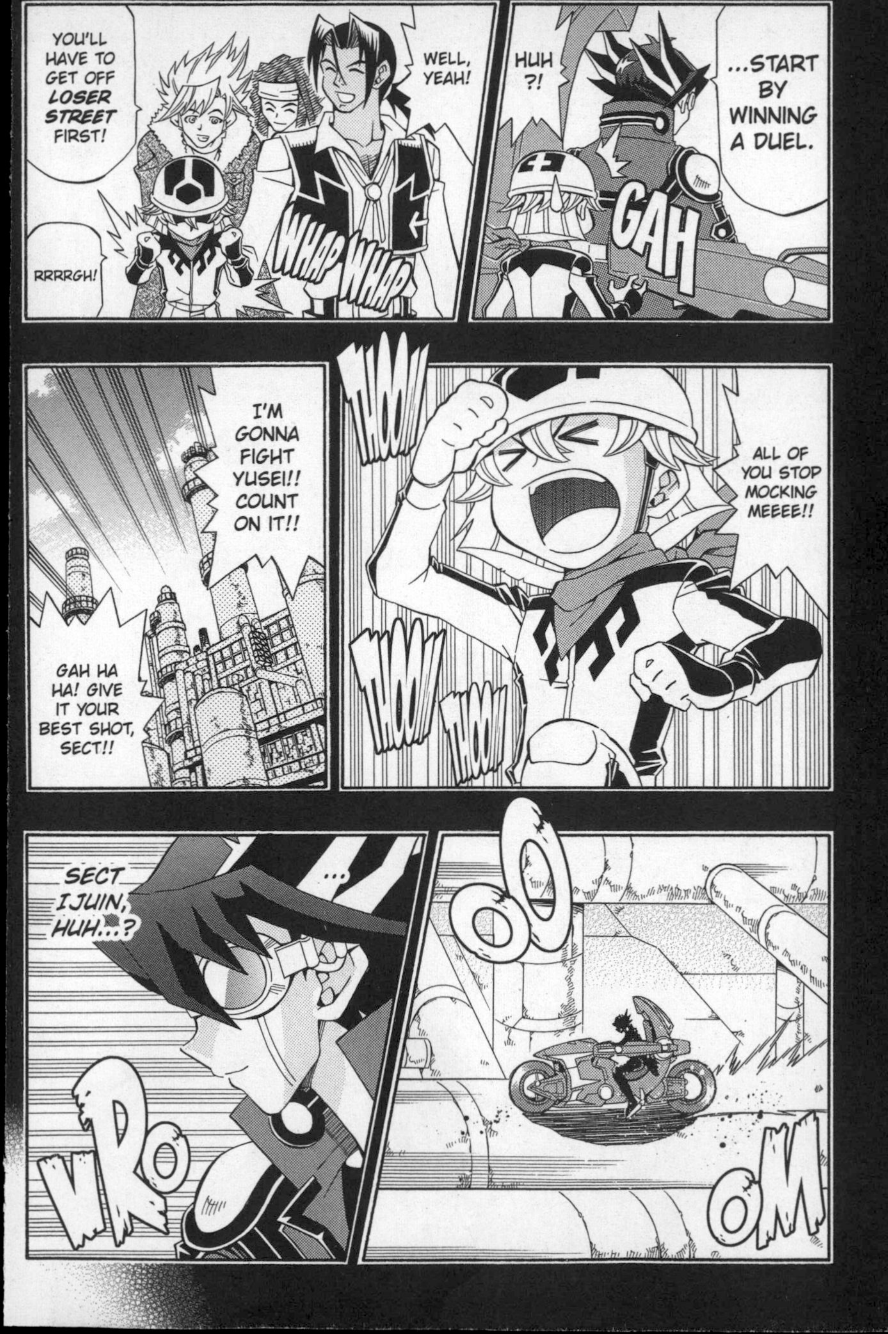
...START BY WINNING A DUEL.
HUH ?!
GAH
WELL, YEAH!
YOU'LL HAVE TO GET OFF LOSER STREET FIRST!
WHAP WHAP
RRRRGH!
THOOM
ALL OF YOU STOP MOCKING MEEEE!!
THOOM
THOOM
I'M GONNA FIGHT YUSEI!! COUNT ON IT!!
GAH HA HA! GIVE IT YOUR BEST SHOT, SECT!!
OO
OM
...
SECT IJUIN, HUH...?
VRO

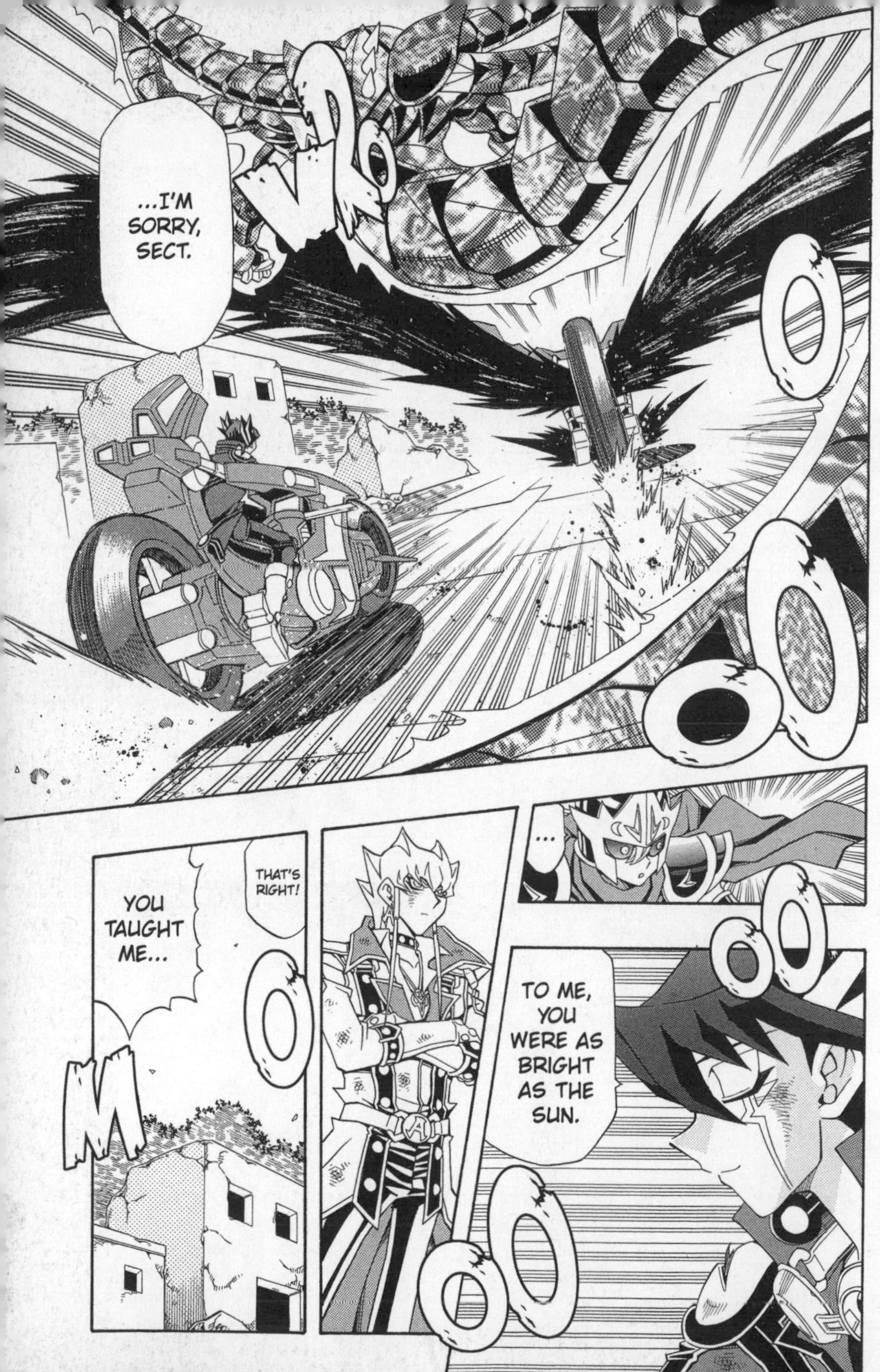
...I'M SORRY, SECT.
...
TO ME, YOU WERE AS BRIGHT AS THE SUN.
THAT'S RIGHT!
YOU TAUGHT ME...

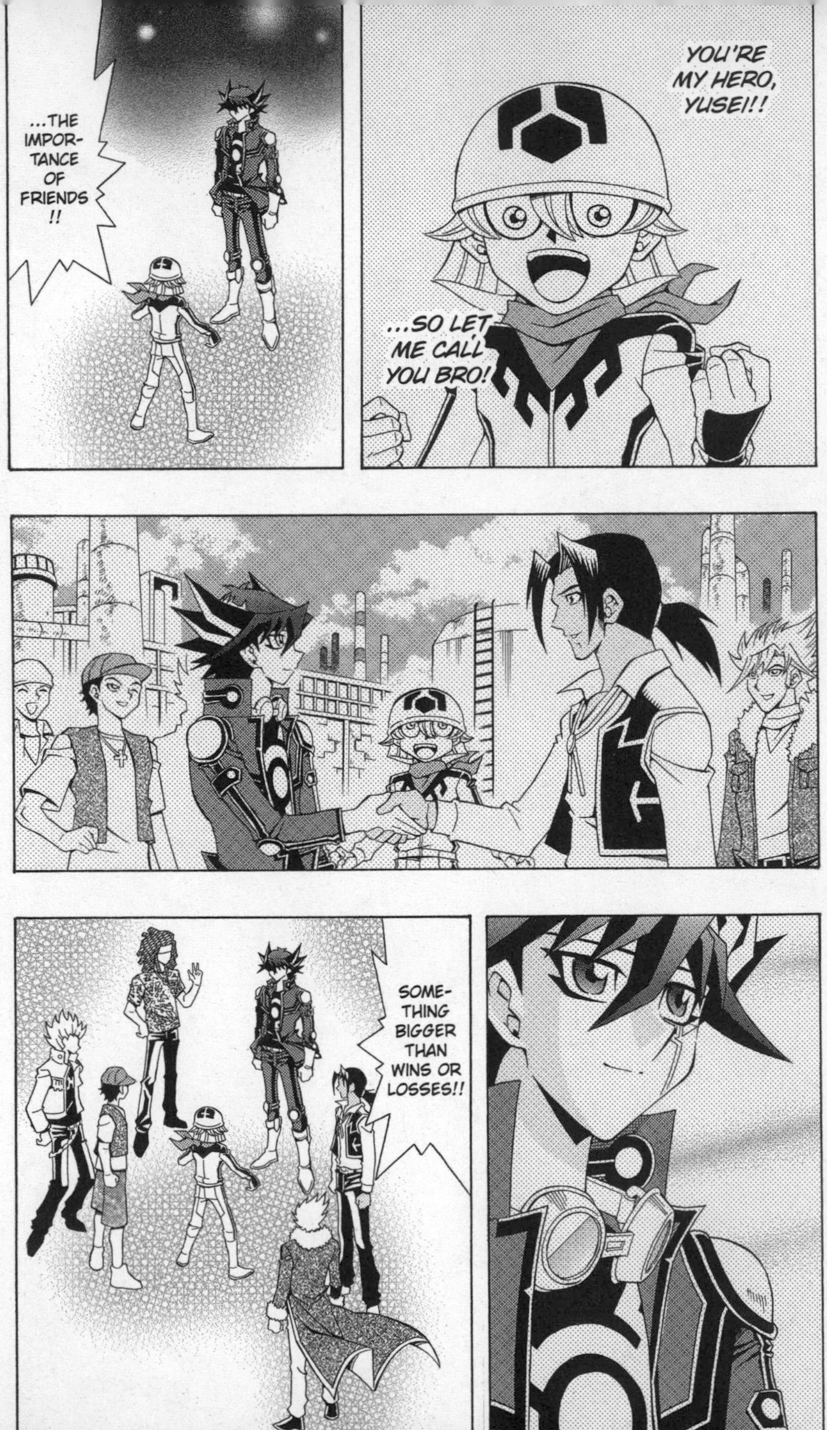
YOU'RE MY HERO, YUSEI!!
...SO LET ME CALL YOU BRO!
...THE IMPORTANCE OF FRIENDS!!
SOMETHING BIGGER THAN WINS OR LOSSES!!

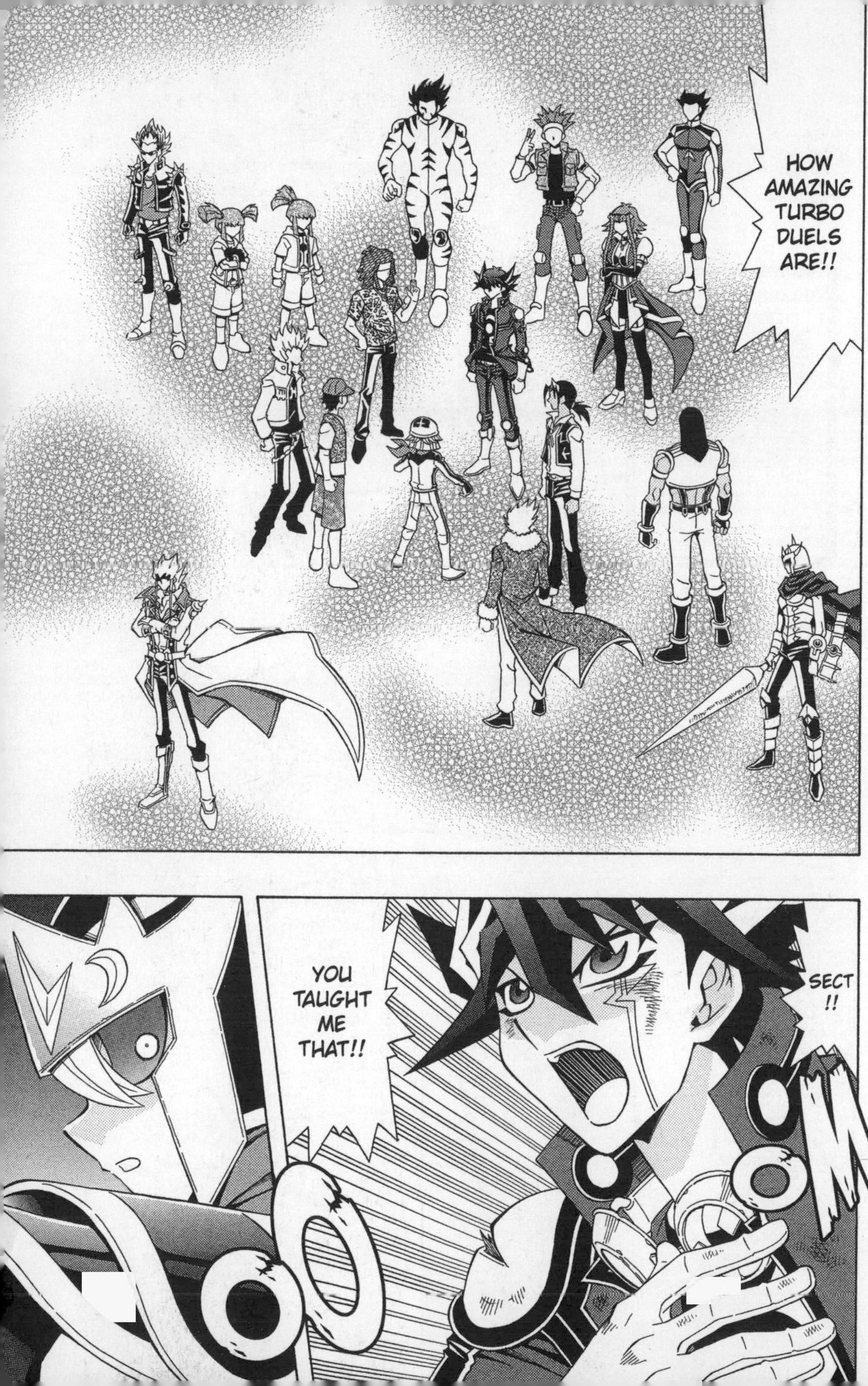
HOW AMAZING TURBO DUELS ARE!!
SECT !!
YOU TAUGHT ME THAT!!

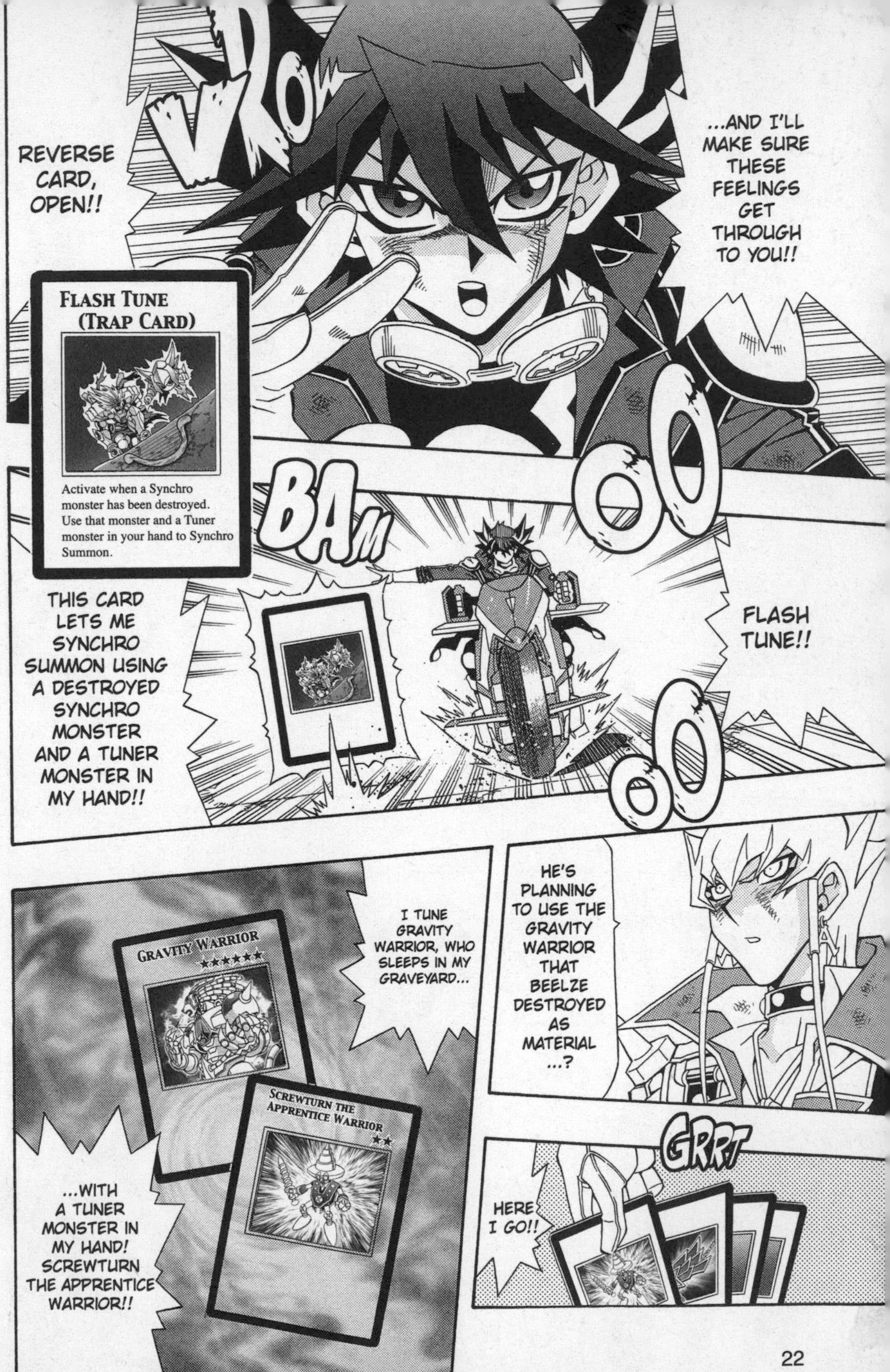
...AND I'LL MAKE SURE THESE FEELINGS GET THROUGH TO YOU!!
VROOM
REVERSE CARD, OPEN!!
FLASH TUNE (TRAP CARD)
Activate when a Synchro monster has been destroyed. Use that monster and a Tuner monster in your hand to Synchro Summon.
FLASH TUNE!!
BAM
THIS CARD LETS ME SYNCHRO SUMMON USING A DESTROYED SYNCHRO MONSTER AND A TUNER MONSTER IN MY HAND!!
HE'S PLANNING TO USE THE GRAVITY WARRIOR THAT BEELZE DESTROYED AS MATERIAL ...?
GRRT
HERE I GO!!
I TUNE GRAVITY WARRIOR, WHO SLEEPS IN MY GRAVEYARD...
GRAVITY WARRIOR
SCREWTURN THE APPRENTICE WARRIOR
...WITH A TUNER MONSTER IN MY HAND! SCREWTURN THE APPRENTICE WARRIOR!!

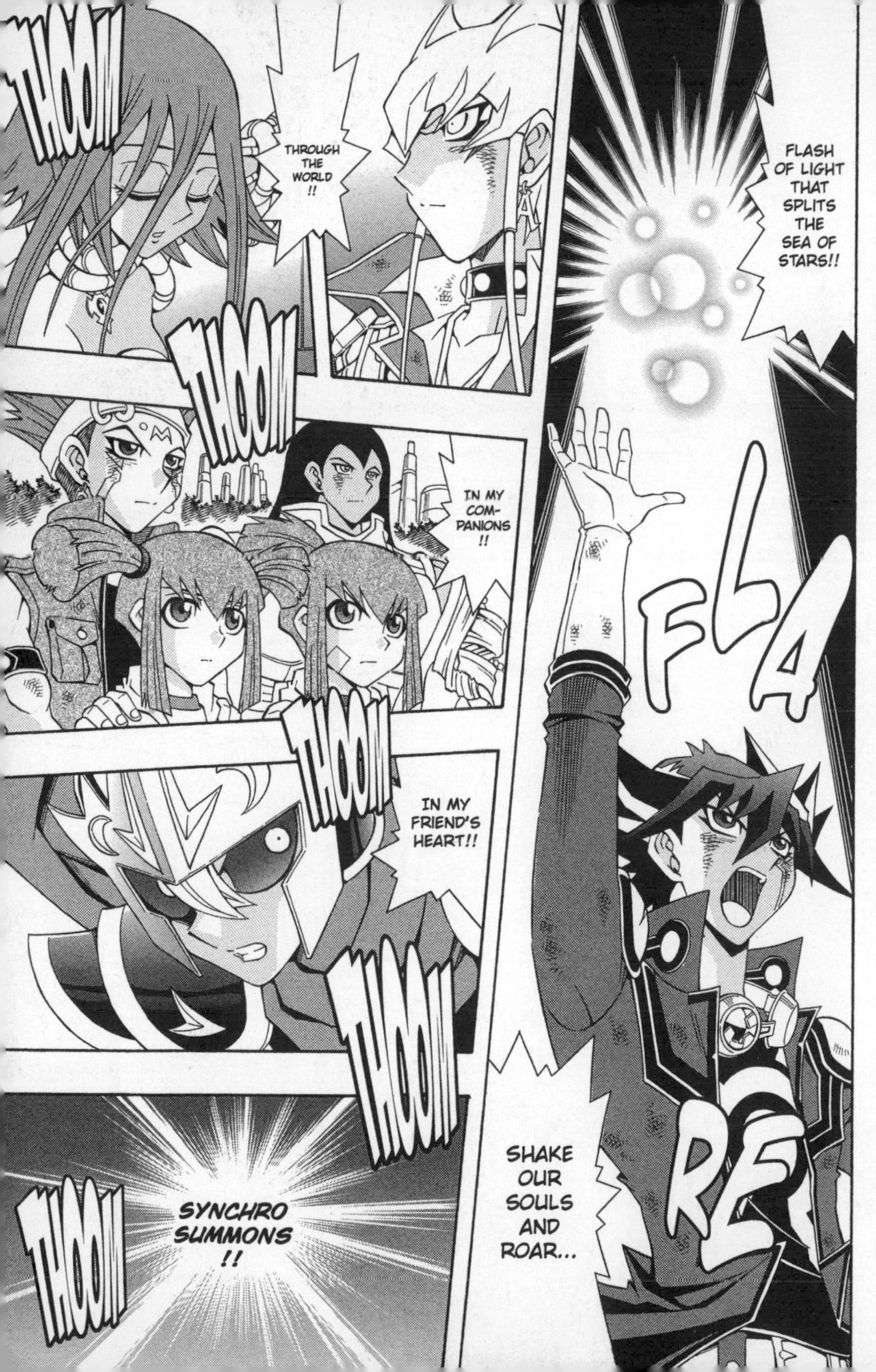

FLASH OF LIGHT THAT SPLITS THE SEA OF STARS!!
FLA
RE
SHAKE OUR SOULS AND ROAR...
THROUGH THE WORLD!!
THOOM
THOOM
IN MY COMPANIONS!!
THOOM
IN MY FRIEND'S HEART!!
THOOM
SYNCHRO SUMMONS!!
THOOM

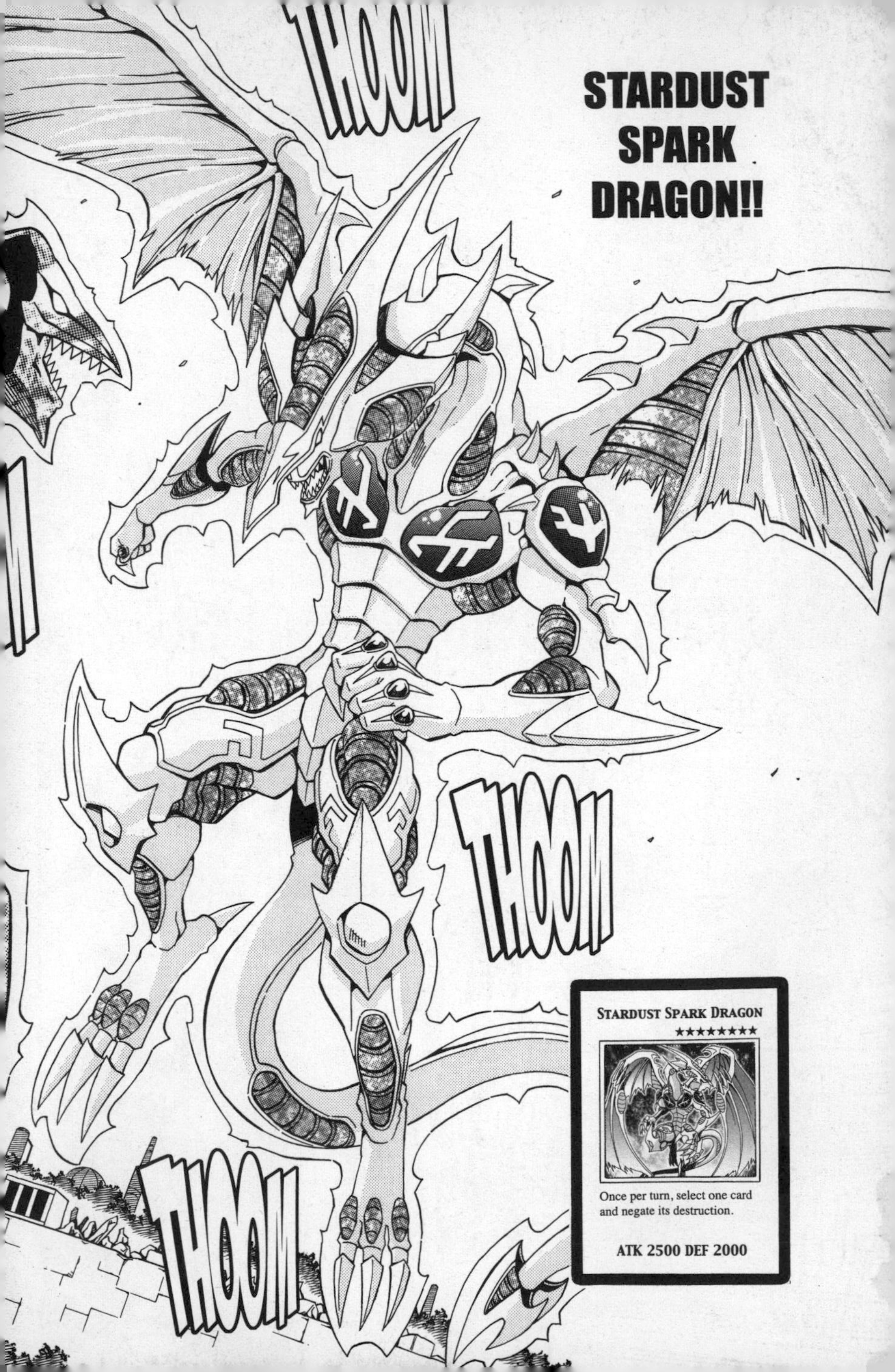
STARDUST SPARK DRAGON!!
THOOM
THOOM
STARDUST SPARK DRAGON
Once per turn, select one card and negate its destruction.
ATK 2500 DEF 2000
THOOM

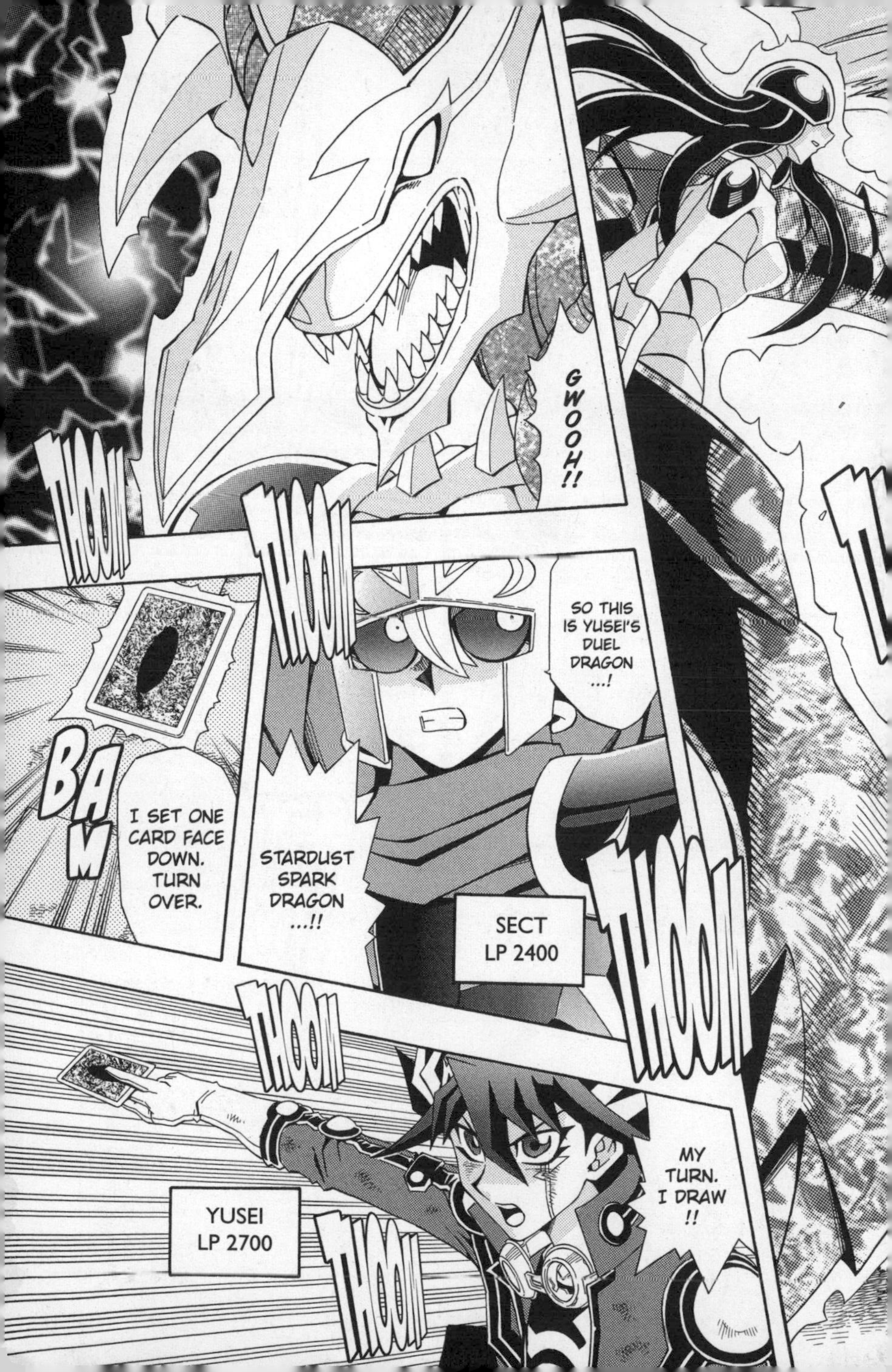
GWOOOH!!
THOOM
THOOM
SO THIS IS YUSEI'S DUEL DRAGON ...!
STARDUST SPARK DRAGON ...!!
SECT LP 2400
THOOM
BAM
I SET ONE CARD FACE DOWN. TURN OVER.
THOOM
MY TURN. I DRAW !!
YUSEI LP 2700
THOOM

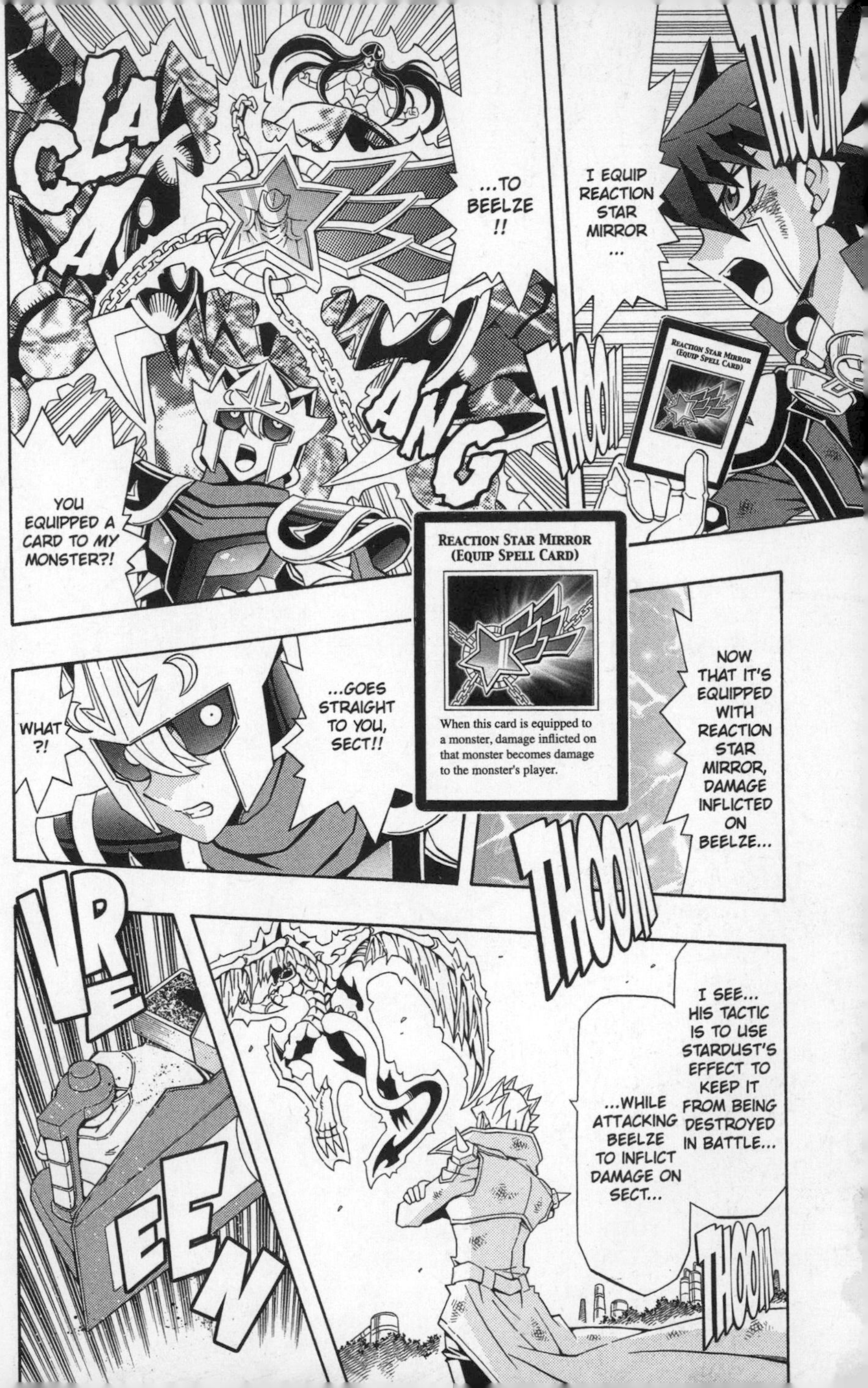
THOOM
I EQUIP REACTION STAR MIRROR ...
THOOM
REACTION STAR MIRROR (EQUIP SPELL CARD)
...TO BEELZE !!
YOU EQUIPPED A CARD TO MY MONSTER?!
NOW THAT IT'S EQUIPPED WITH REACTION STAR MIRROR, DAMAGE INFLICTED ON BEELZE...
REACTION STAR MIRROR
(EQUIP SPELL CARD)
When this card is equipped to a monster, damage inflicted on that monster becomes damage to the monster's player.
THOOM
...GOES STRAIGHT TO YOU, SECT!!
WHAT ?!
I SEE... HIS TACTIC IS TO USE STARDUST'S EFFECT TO KEEP IT FROM BEING DESTROYED IN BATTLE...
...WHILE ATTACKING BEELZE TO INFLICT DAMAGE ON SECT...
THOOM

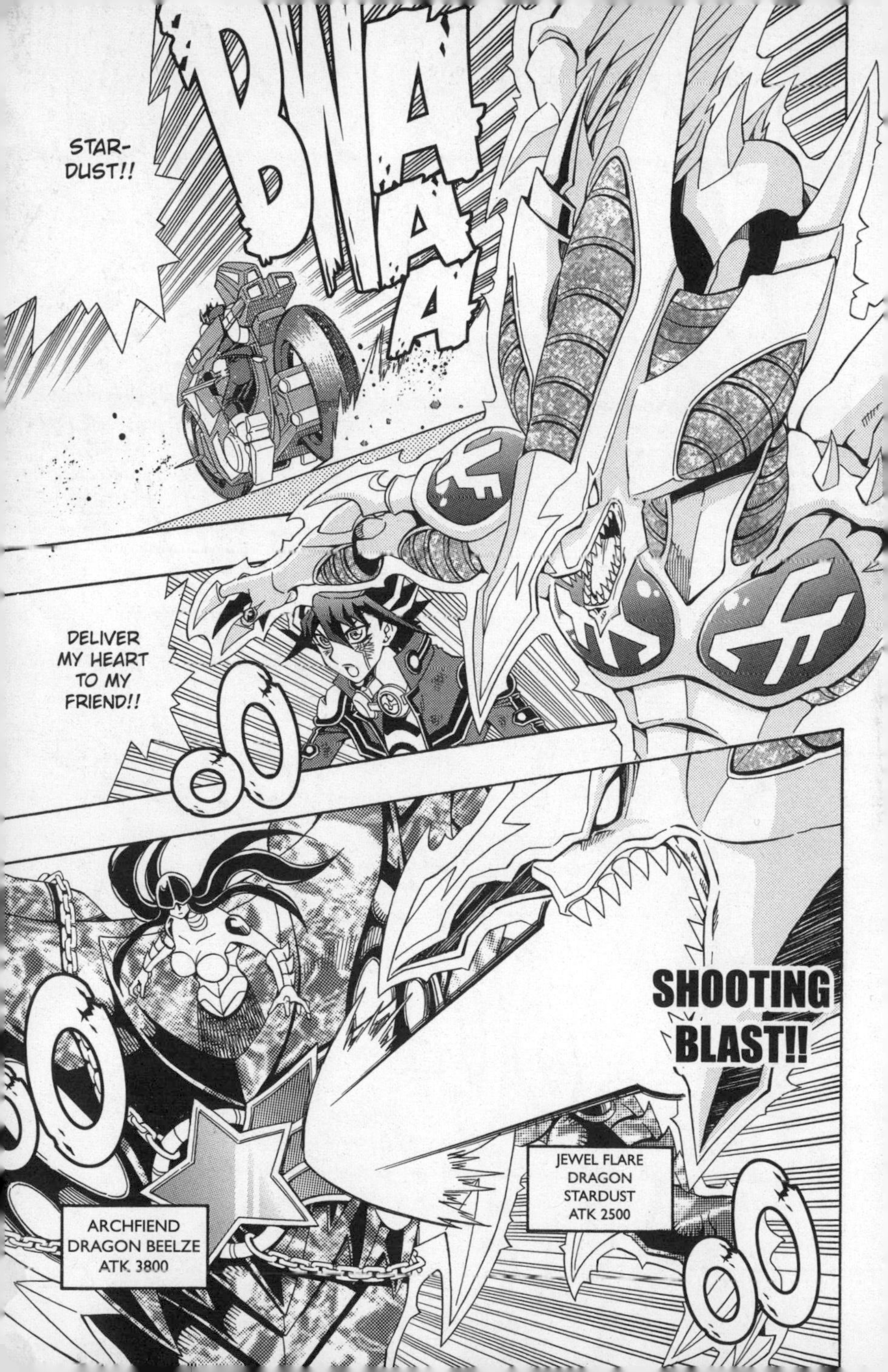
BWAAA
STAR-
DUST!!
DELIVER
MY HEART
TO MY
FRIEND!!
SHOOTING
BLAST!!
JEWEL FLARE
DRAGON
STARDUST
ATK 2500
ARCHFIEND
DRAGON BEELZE
ATK 3800

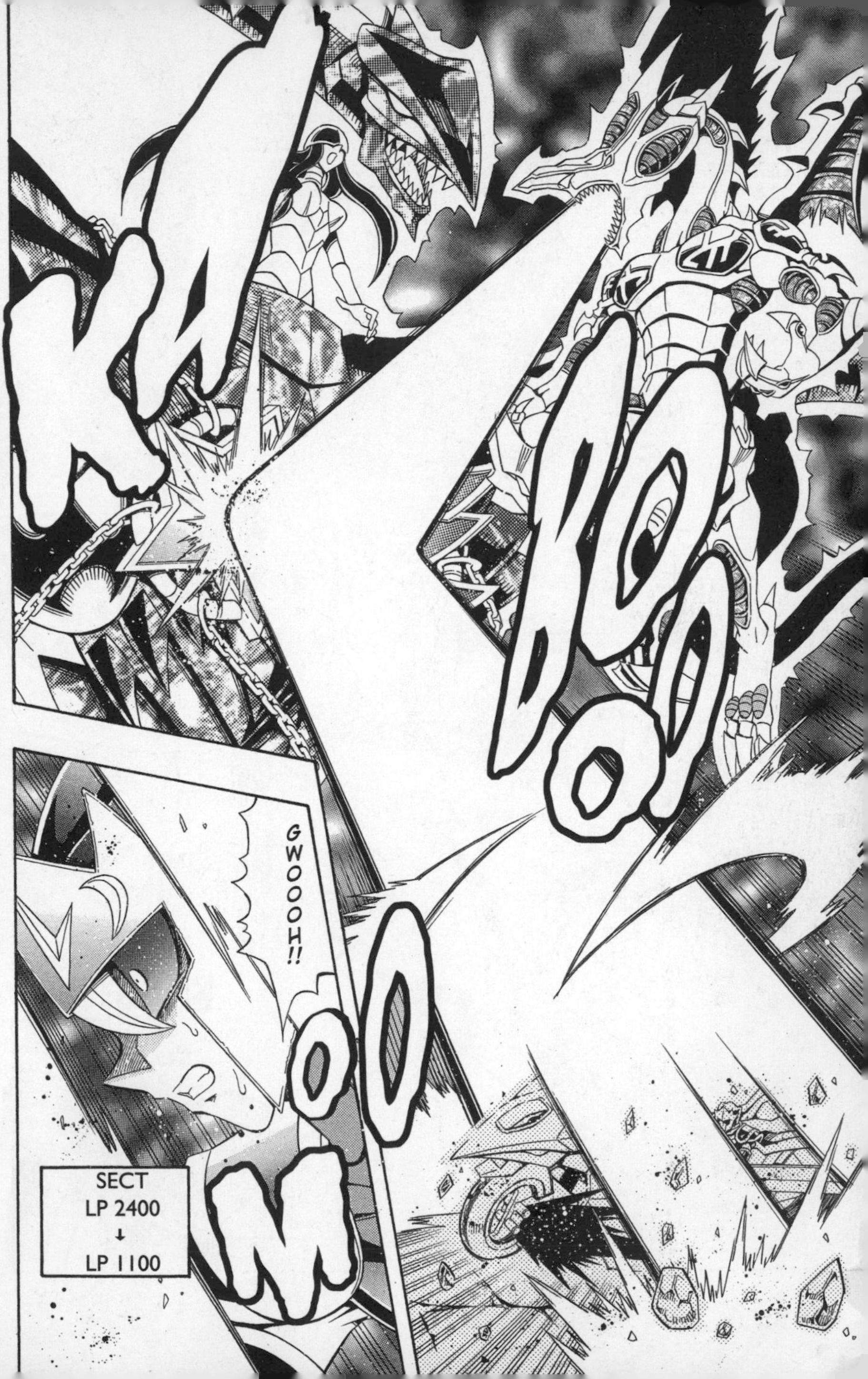
GWOOOOH!!
SECT
LP 2400
↓
LP 1100

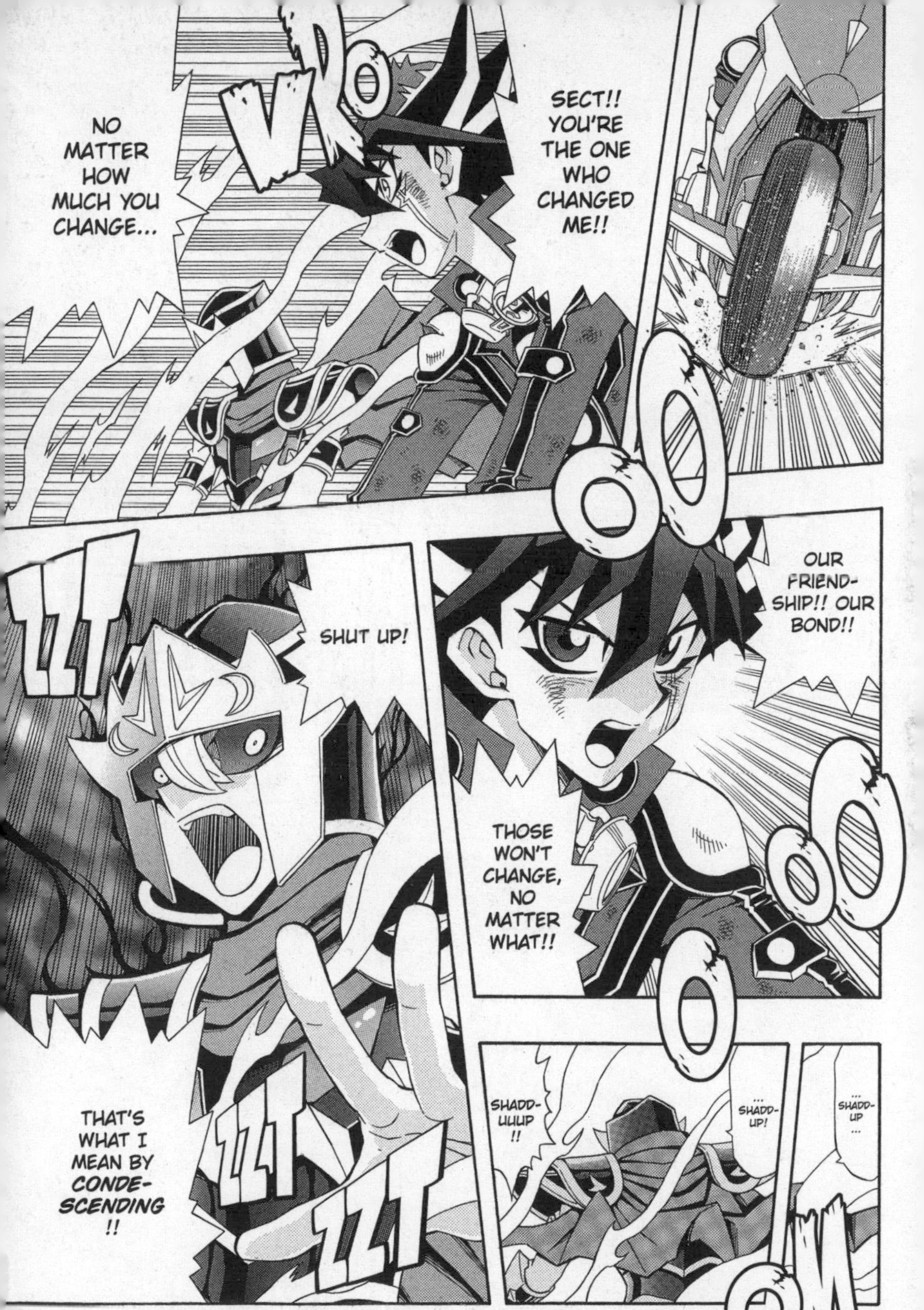
SECT!! YOU'RE THE ONE WHO CHANGED ME!!
NO MATTER HOW MUCH YOU CHANGE...
OUR FRIEND-SHIP!! OUR BOND!!
THOSE WON'T CHANGE, NO MATTER WHAT!!
... SHADD-UP ...
... SHADD-UP!
SHADD-UUUP !!
SHUT UP!
ZZT
THAT'S WHAT I MEAN BY CONDE-SCENDING !!
ZZT
ZZT

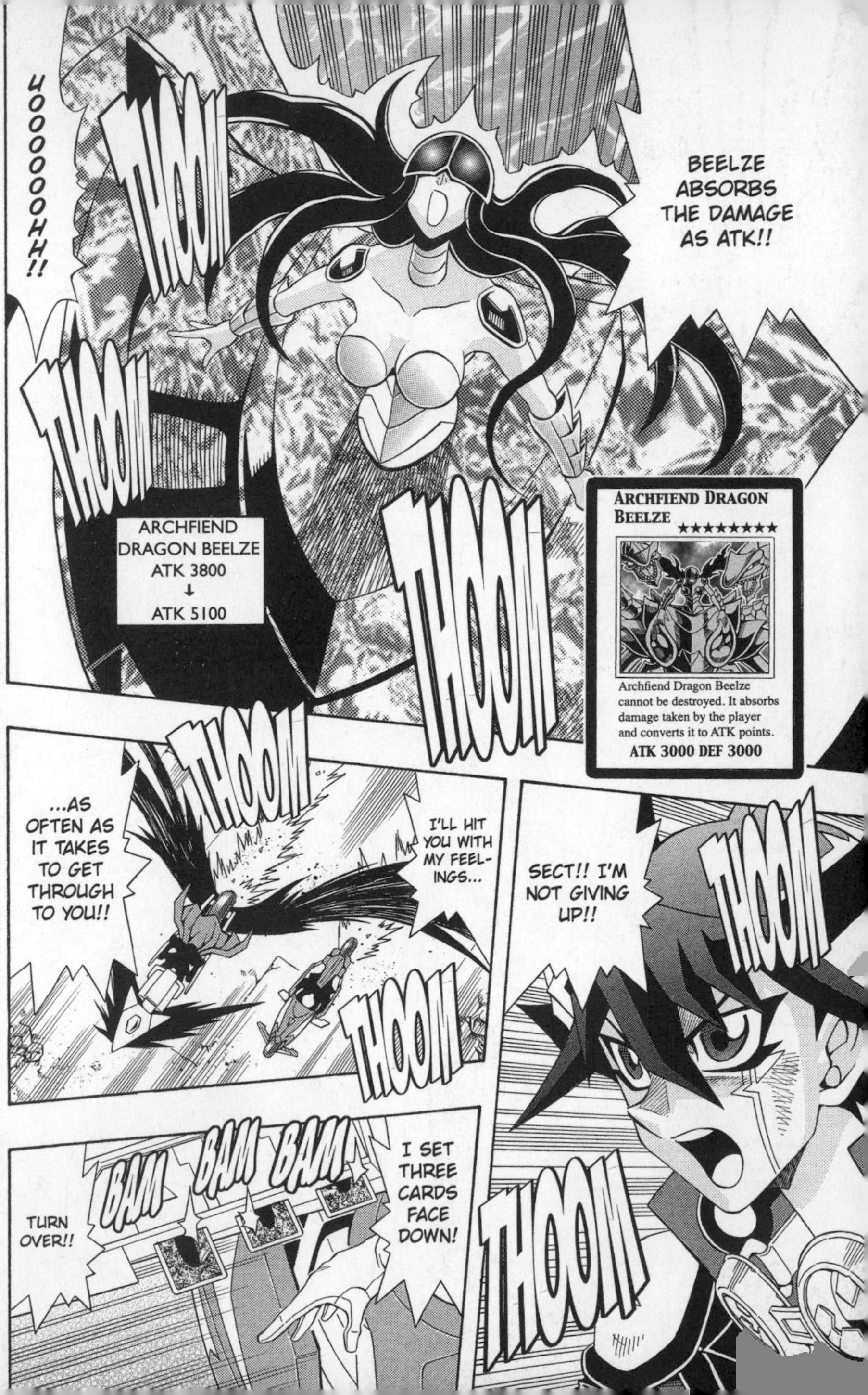
BEELZE ABSORBS THE DAMAGE AS ATK!!
ARCHFIEND DRAGON BEELZE
★★★★★★★★
Archfiend Dragon Beelze cannot be destroyed. It absorbs damage taken by the player and converts it to ATK points.
ATK 3000 DEF 3000
THOOM
ARCHFIEND DRAGON BEELZE ATK 3800 ↓ ATK 5100
THOOM
THOOM
UOOOOOOOHH!!
SECT!! I'M NOT GIVING UP!!
THOOM
THOOM
I'LL HIT YOU WITH MY FEEL-INGS...
THOOM
...AS OFTEN AS IT TAKES TO GET THROUGH TO YOU!!
THOOM
I SET THREE CARDS FACE DOWN!
BAM BAM BAM
TURN OVER!!

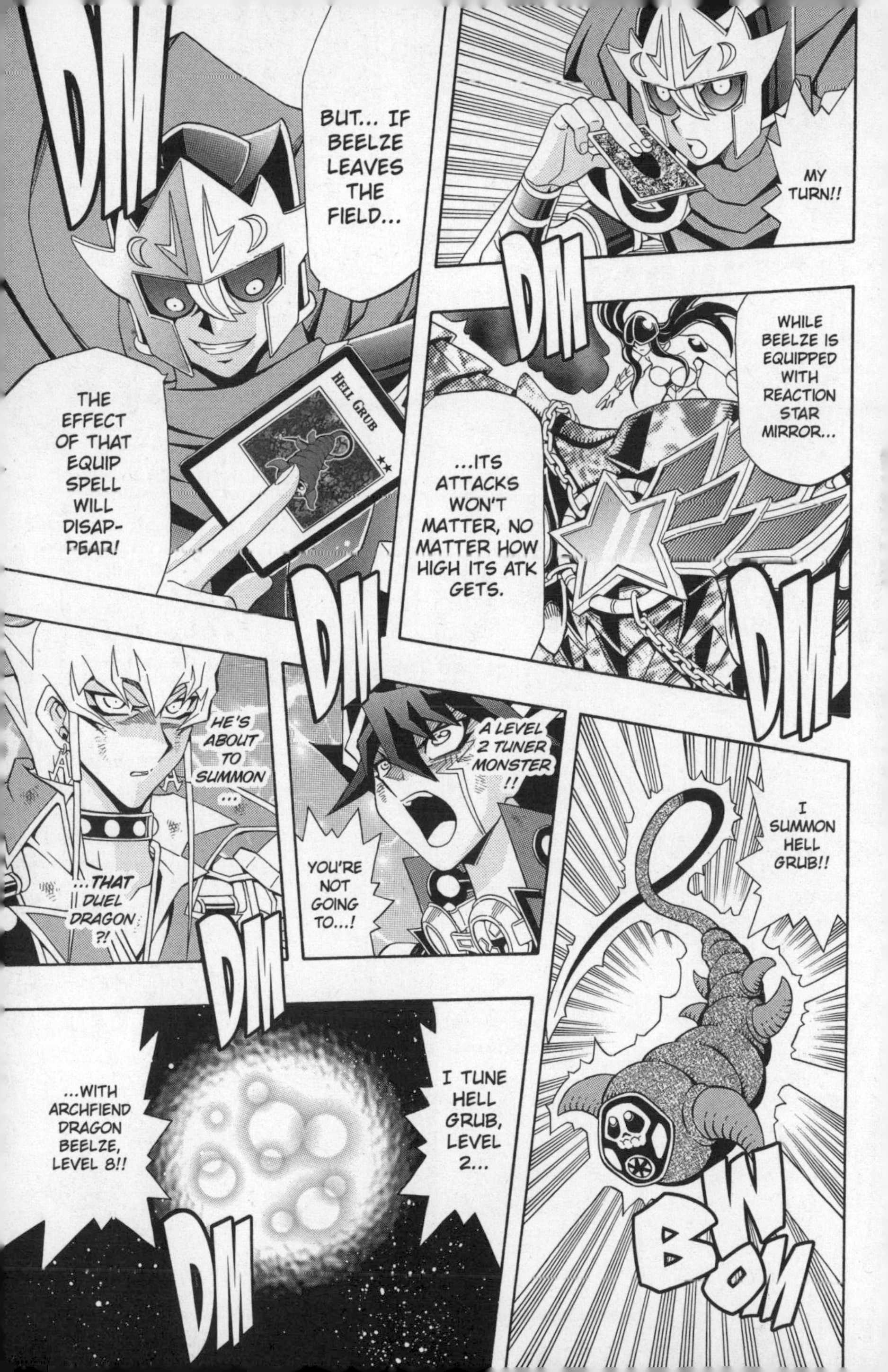
MY TURN!!
DM
WHILE BEELZE IS EQUIPPED WITH REACTION STAR MIRROR...
...ITS ATTACKS WON'T MATTER, NO MATTER HOW HIGH ITS ATK GETS.
DM
DM
BUT... IF BEELZE LEAVES THE FIELD...
HELL GRUB
THE EFFECT OF THAT EQUIP SPELL WILL DISAP-PEAR!
DM
I SUMMON HELL GRUB!!
A LEVEL 2 TUNER MONSTER!!
YOU'RE NOT GOING TO...!
HE'S ABOUT TO SUMMON...
...THAT DUEL DRAGON?!
DM
I TUNE HELL GRUB, LEVEL 2...
...WITH ARCHFIEND DRAGON BEELZE, LEVEL 8!!
DM

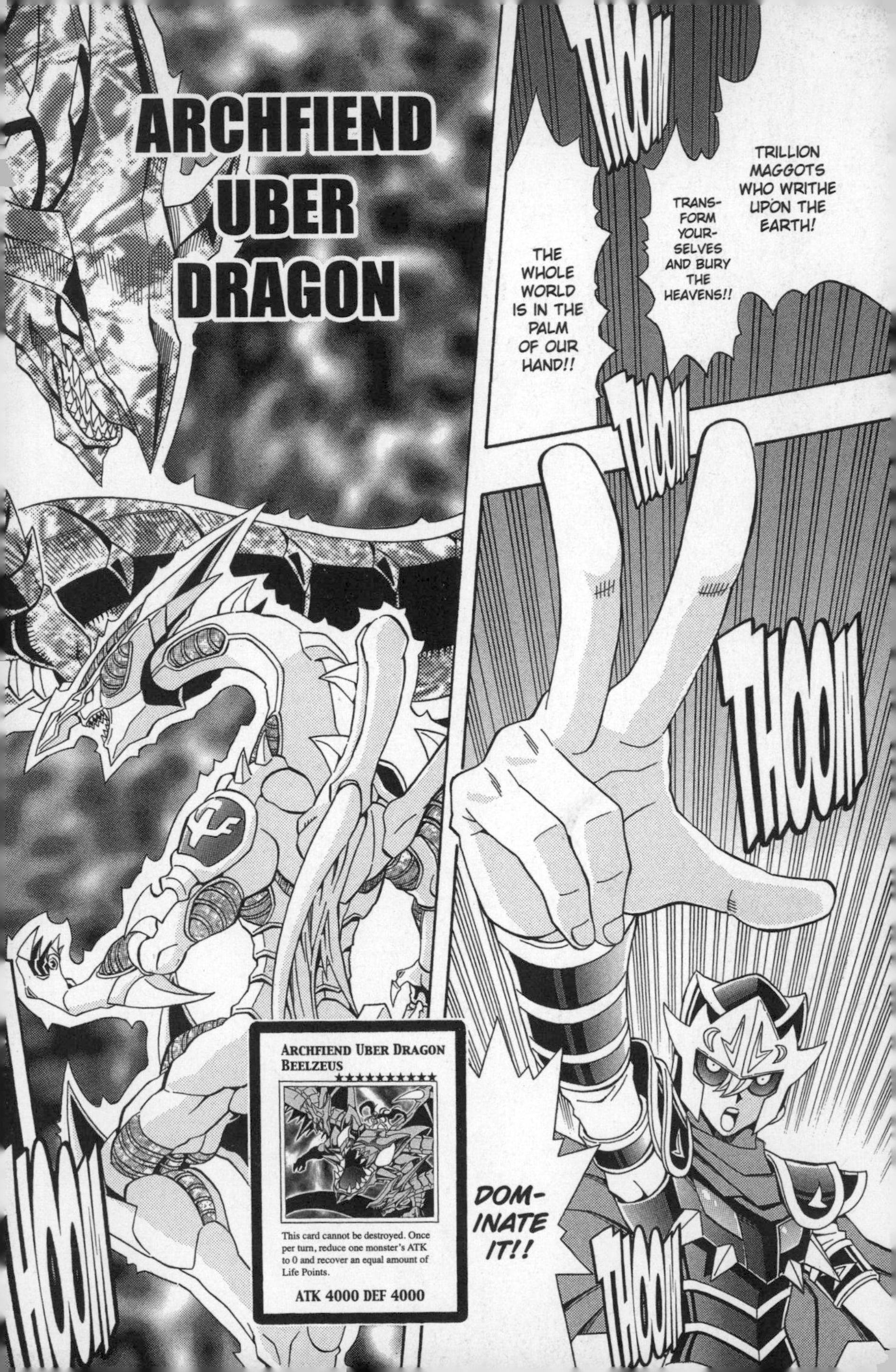
THOOM
TRILLION MAGGOTS WHO WRITHE UPON THE EARTH!
TRANSFORM YOURSELVES AND BURY THE HEAVENS!!
THE WHOLE WORLD IS IN THE PALM OF OUR HAND!!
THOOM
THOOM
DOMINATE IT!!
THOOM
ARCHFIEND UBER DRAGON
ARCHFIEND UBER DRAGON BEELZEUS
This card cannot be destroyed. Once per turn, reduce one monster's ATK to 0 and recover an equal amount of Life Points.
ATK 4000 DEF 4000
THOOM

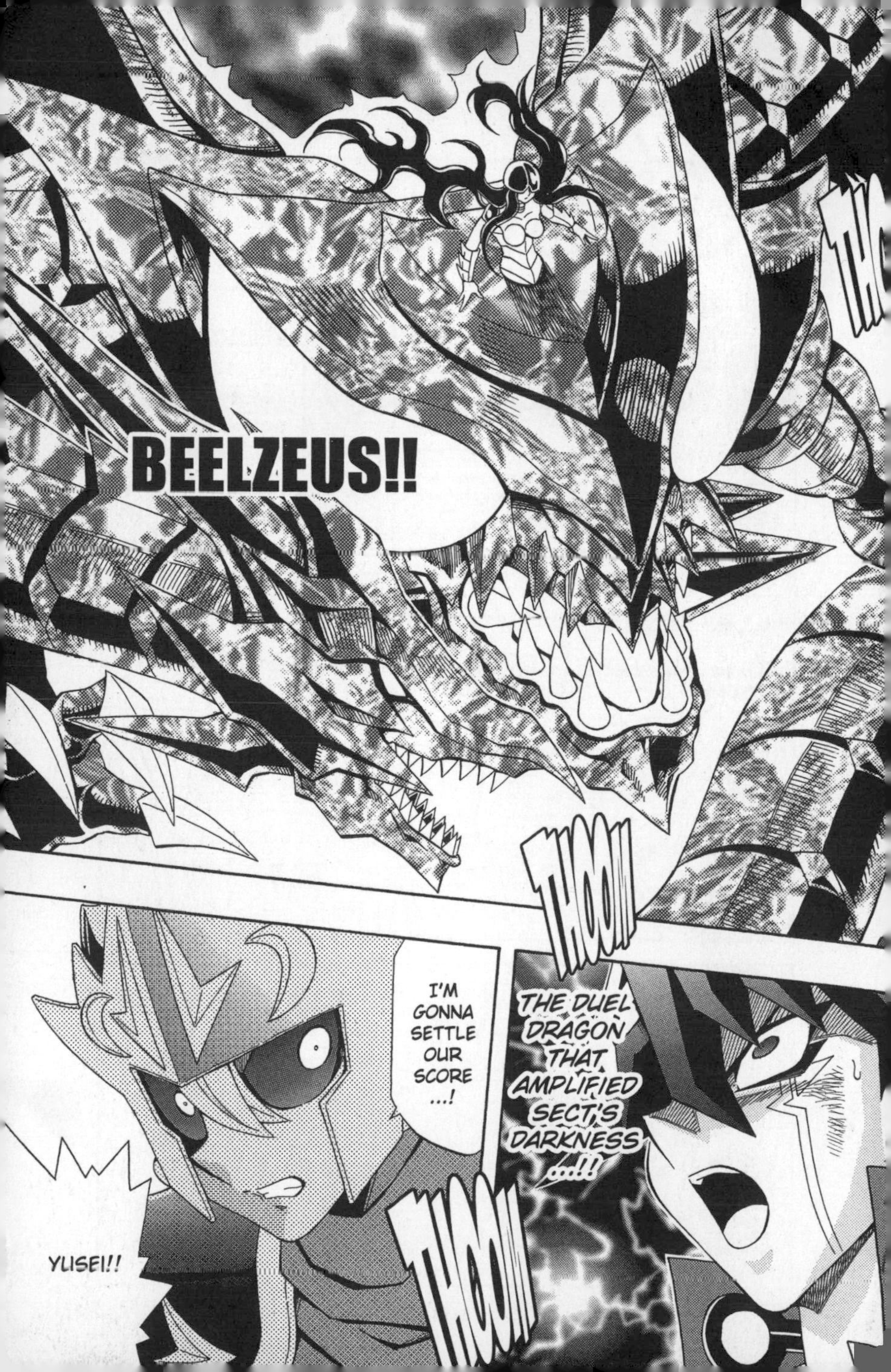
THO
BEELZEUS!!
THOOM
THE DUEL DRAGON THAT AMPLIFIED SECT'S DARKNESS ...!!
THOOM
I'M GONNA SETTLE OUR SCORE ...!
YUSEI!!

5D's TRACKS

THE 53RD

BY SATOMASA

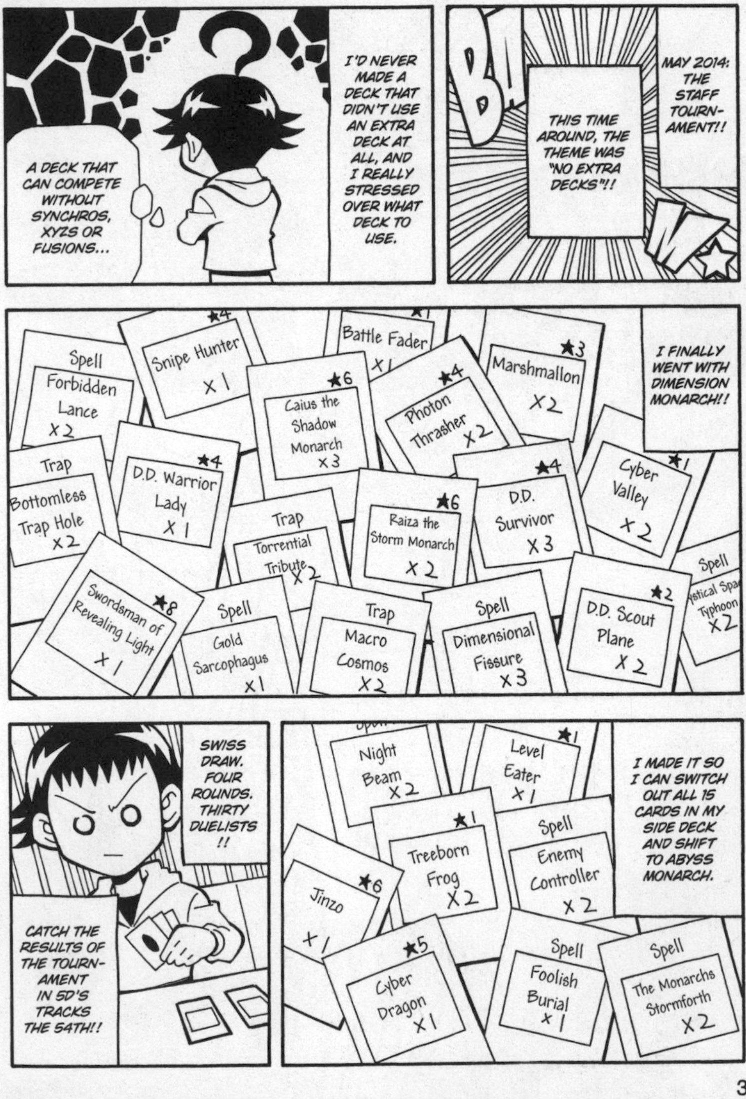

MAY 2014: THE STAFF TOURNAMENT!!
THIS TIME AROUND, THE THEME WAS "NO EXTRA DECKS"!!
I'D NEVER MADE A DECK THAT DIDN'T USE AN EXTRA DECK AT ALL, AND I REALLY STRESSED OVER WHAT DECK TO USE.
A DECK THAT CAN COMPETE WITHOUT SYNCHROS, XYZS OR FUSIONS...
I FINALLY WENT WITH DIMENSION MONARCH!!
Marshmallon ×2
Battle Fader
Snipe Hunter ×1
Spell Forbidden Lance ×2
Caius the Shadow Monarch ×3
Photon Thrasher ×2
Cyber Valley ×2
D.D. Survivor ×3
Raiza the Storm Monarch ×2
Trap Torrential Tribute ×2
D.D. Warrior Lady ×1
Trap Bottomless Trap Hole ×2
Spell Mystical Space Typhoon ×2
D.D. Scout Plane ×2
Spell Dimensional Fissure ×3
Trap Macro Cosmos ×2
Spell Gold Sarcophagus ×1
Swordsman of Revealing Light ×1
I MADE IT SO I CAN SWITCH OUT ALL 15 CARDS IN MY SIDE DECK AND SHIFT TO ABYSS MONARCH.
Level Eater ×1
Night Beam ×2
Spell Enemy Controller ×2
Treeborn Frog ×2
Jinzo ×1
Spell The Monarchs Stormforth ×2
Spell Foolish Burial ×1
Cyber Dragon ×1
SWISS DRAW. FOUR ROUNDS. THIRTY DUELISTS!!
CATCH THE RESULTS OF THE TOURNAMENT IN 5D'S TRACKS THE 54TH!!

RIDE-55
BOND'S REWARD!!

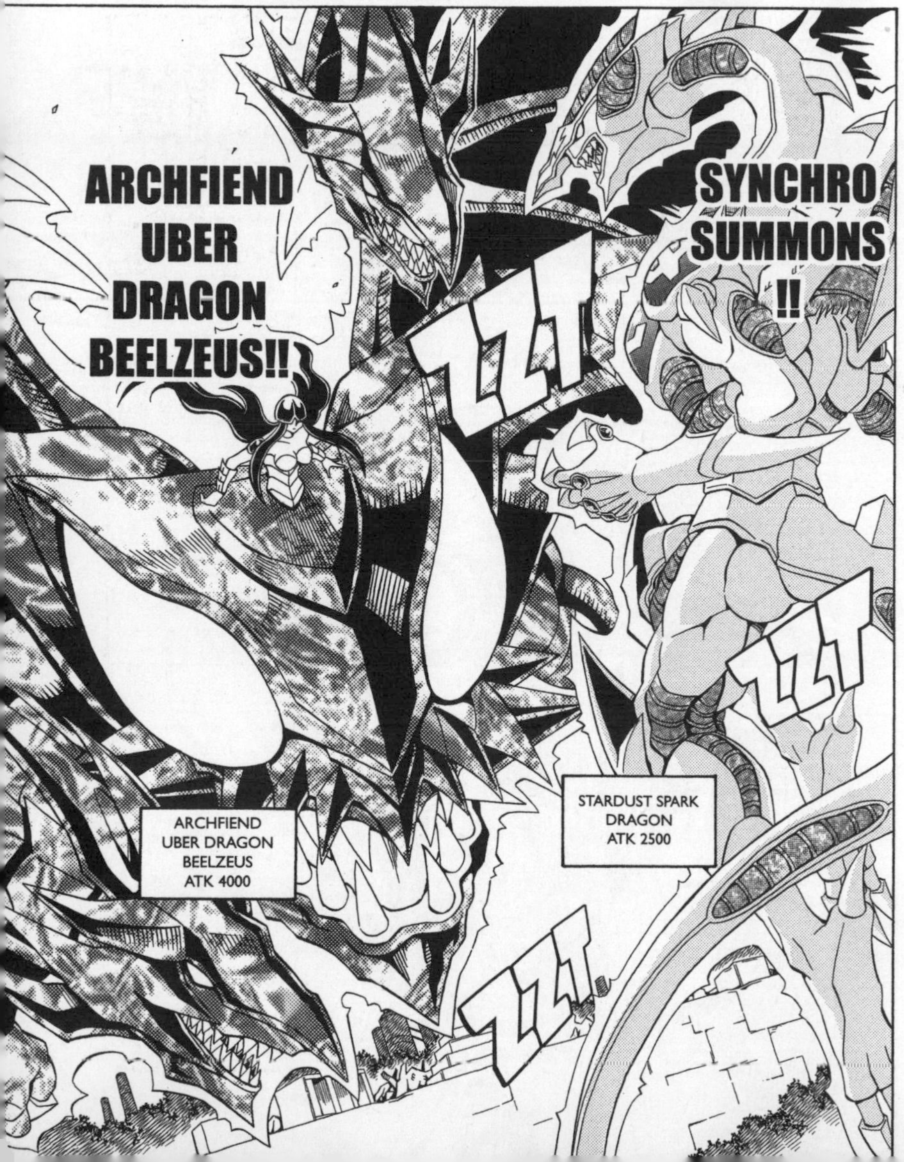
SYNCHRO SUMMONS!!
ARCHFIEND UBER DRAGON BEELZEUS!!
ZZZT
ZZZT
STARDUST SPARK DRAGON ATK 2500
ARCHFIEND UBER DRAGON BEELZEUS ATK 4000
ZZZT

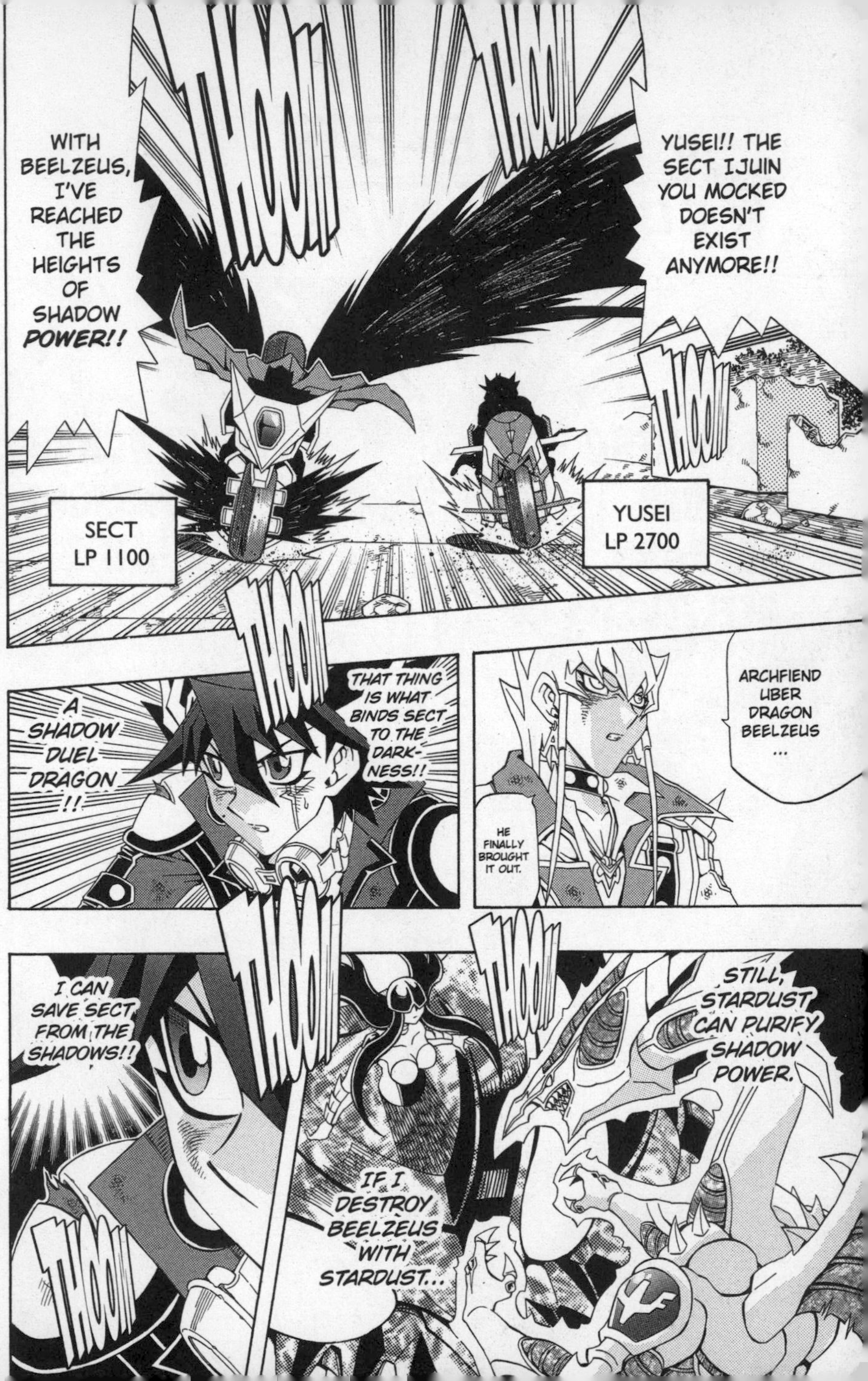
THOOM
THOOM
YUSEI!! THE SECT IJUIN YOU MOCKED DOESN'T EXIST ANYMORE!!
WITH BEELZEUS, I'VE REACHED THE HEIGHTS OF SHADOW POWER!!
THOOM
YUSEI LP 2700
SECT LP 1100
ARCHFIEND UBER DRAGON BEELZEUS ...
HE FINALLY BROUGHT IT OUT.
THOOM
THAT THING IS WHAT BINDS SECT TO THE DARKNESS!!
A SHADOW DUEL DRAGON!!
THOOM
THOOM
STILL, STARDUST CAN PURIFY SHADOW POWER.
I CAN SAVE SECT FROM THE SHADOWS!!
IF I DESTROY BEELZEUS WITH STARDUST...
THOOM

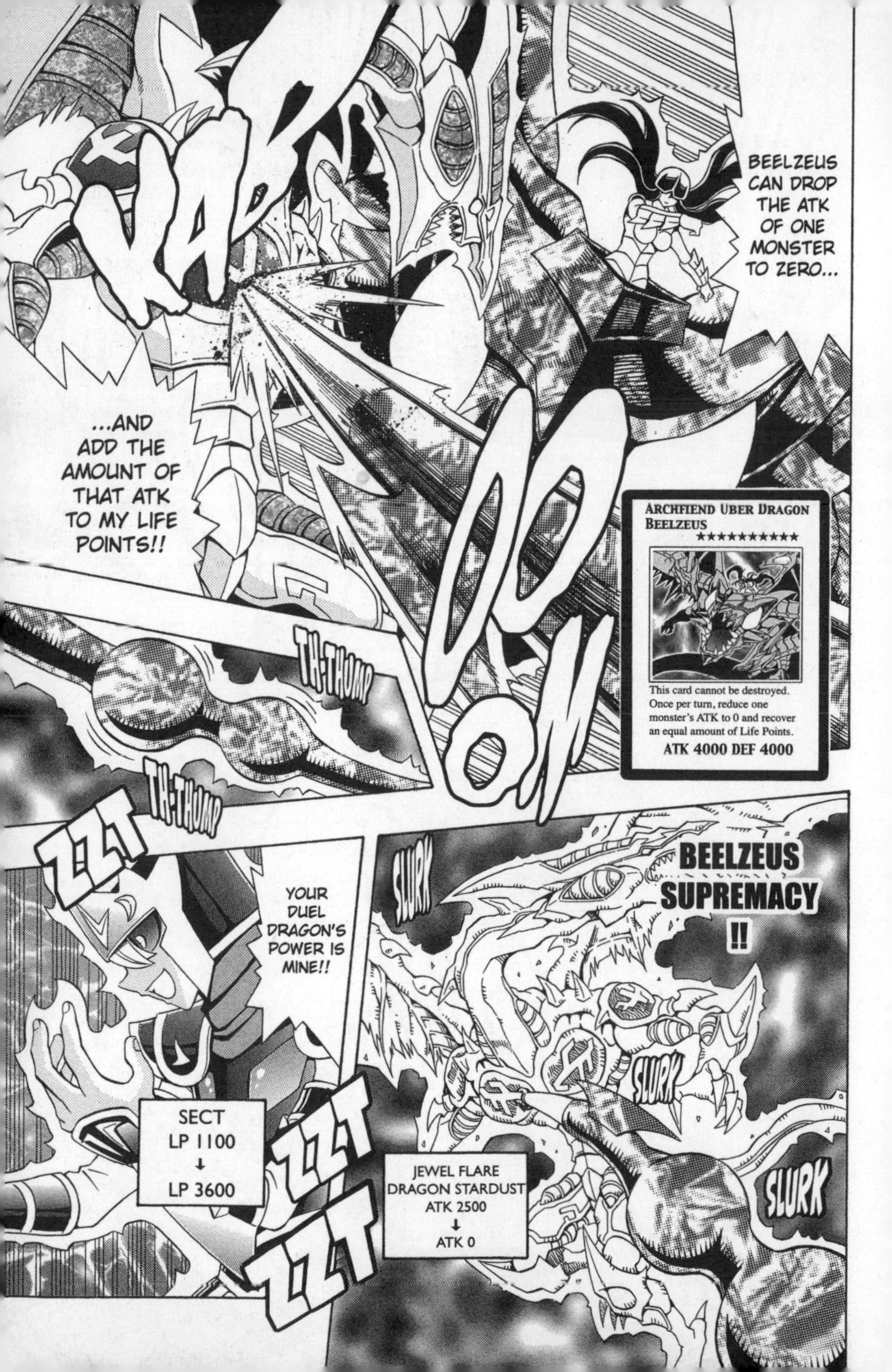
BEELZEUS CAN DROP THE ATK OF ONE MONSTER TO ZERO...
...AND ADD THE AMOUNT OF THAT ATK TO MY LIFE POINTS!!
ARCHFIEND UBER DRAGON BEELZEUS
★★★★★★★★★★
This card cannot be destroyed. Once per turn, reduce one monster's ATK to 0 and recover an equal amount of Life Points.
ATK 4000 DEF 4000
TH-THUMP
TH-THUMP
Z-Z-T
SLURK
BEELZEUS SUPREMACY!!
SLURK
SLURK
JEWEL FLARE DRAGON STARDUST ATK 2500 ↓ ATK 0
YOUR DUEL DRAGON'S POWER IS MINE!!
Z-Z-T
Z-Z-T
SECT LP 1100 ↓ LP 3600

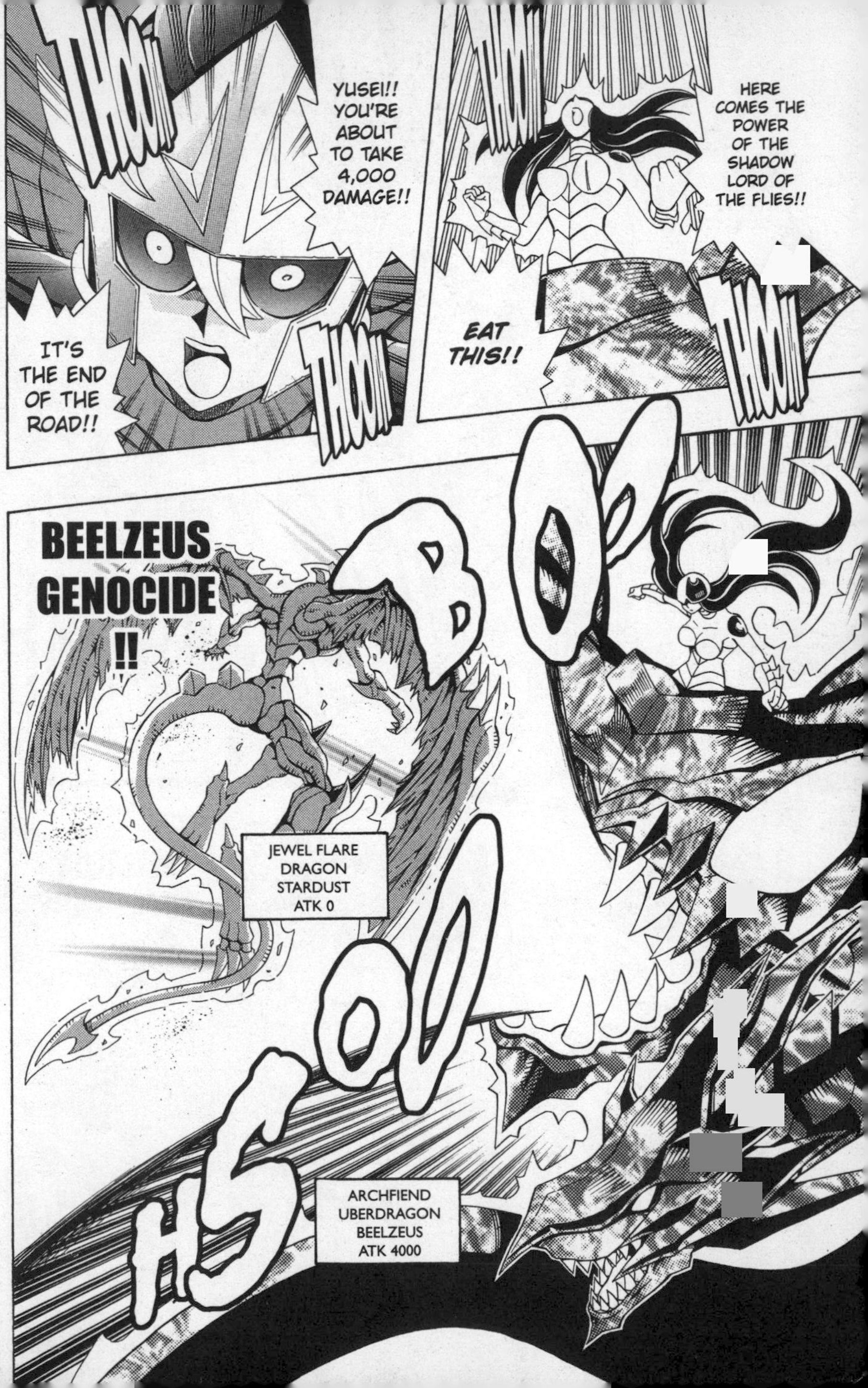
HERE COMES THE POWER OF THE SHADOW LORD OF THE FLIES!!
THOOM
EAT THIS!!
THOOM
THOOM
YUSEI!! YOU'RE ABOUT TO TAKE 4,000 DAMAGE!!
IT'S THE END OF THE ROAD!!
THOOM
BOOM
BEELZEUS GENOCIDE !!
JEWEL FLARE DRAGON STARDUST ATK 0
HSOOO
ARCHFIEND UBERDRAGON BEELZEUS ATK 4000

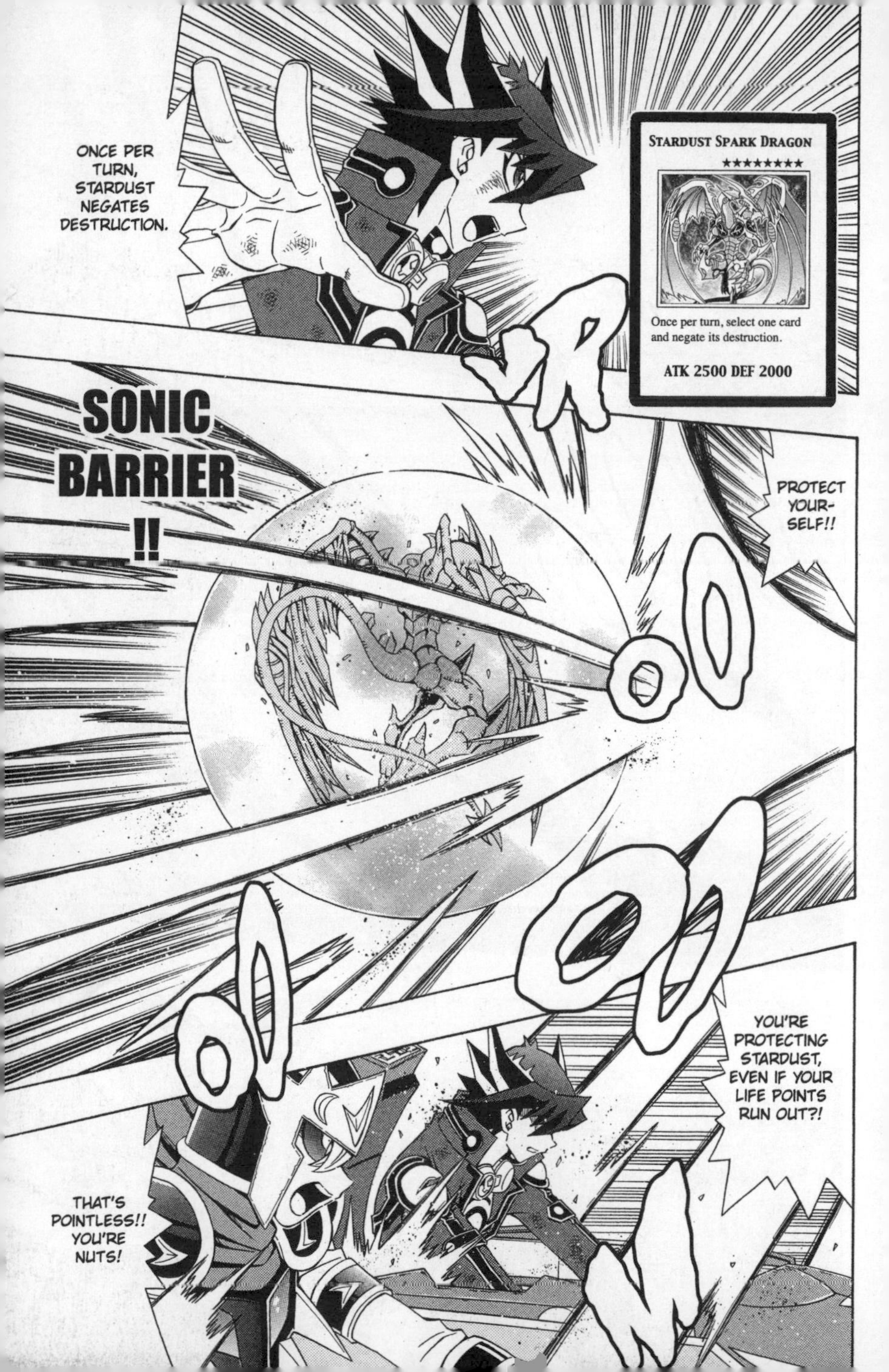
STARDUST SPARK DRAGON
★★★★★★★★
Once per turn, select one card and negate its destruction.
ATK 2500 DEF 2000
ONCE PER TURN, STARDUST NEGATES DESTRUCTION.
PROTECT YOURSELF!!
SONIC BARRIER!!
YOU'RE PROTECTING STARDUST, EVEN IF YOUR LIFE POINTS RUN OUT?!
THAT'S POINTLESS!! YOU'RE NUTS!

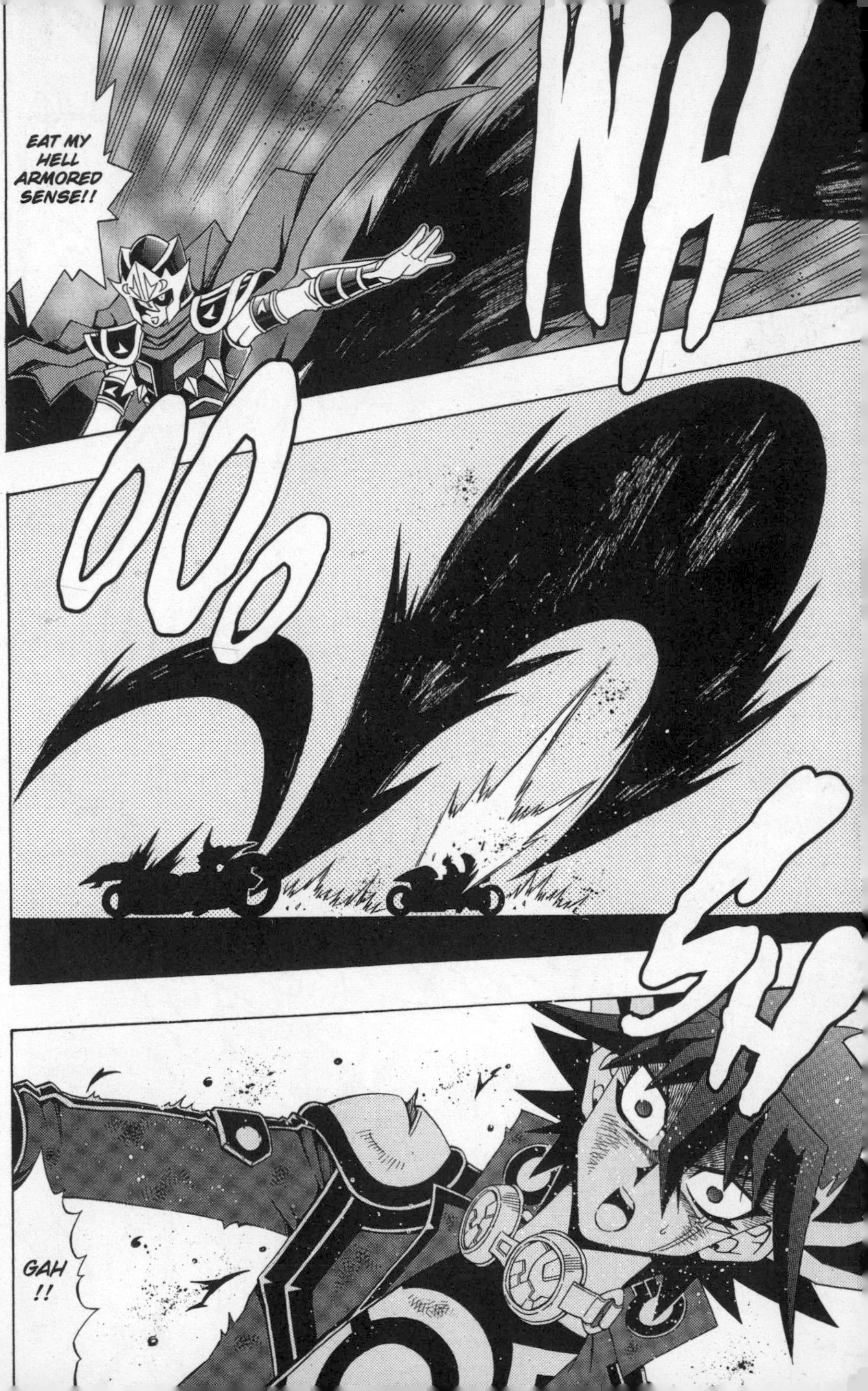
EAT MY HELL ARMORED SENSE!!
WHOOOSH
GAH!!

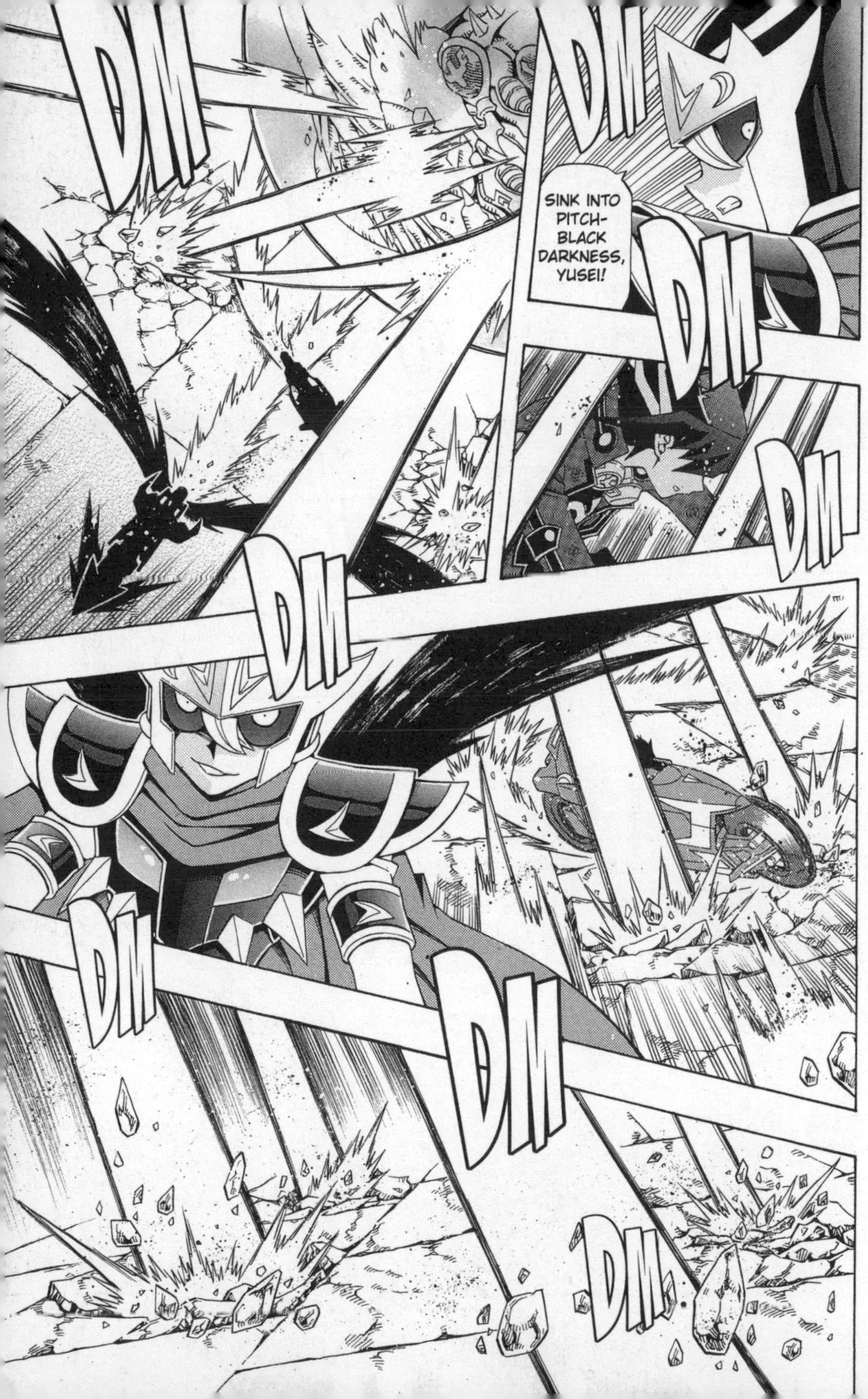
DM
SINK INTO PITCH-BLACK DARKNESS, YUSEI!
DM
DM
DM
DM
DM
DM
DM
DM

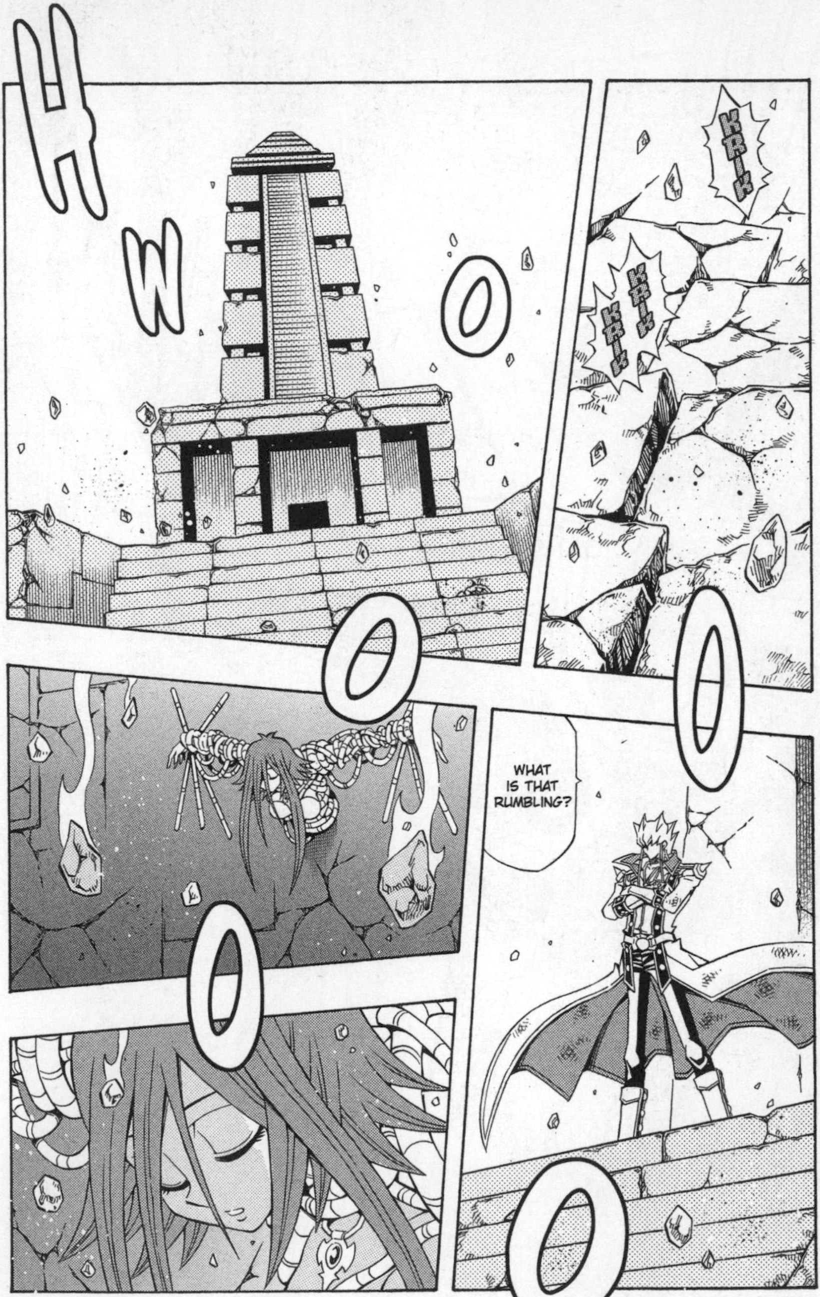
KRIK
KRIK KRIK
HWOOOOO
WHAT IS THAT RUMBLING?

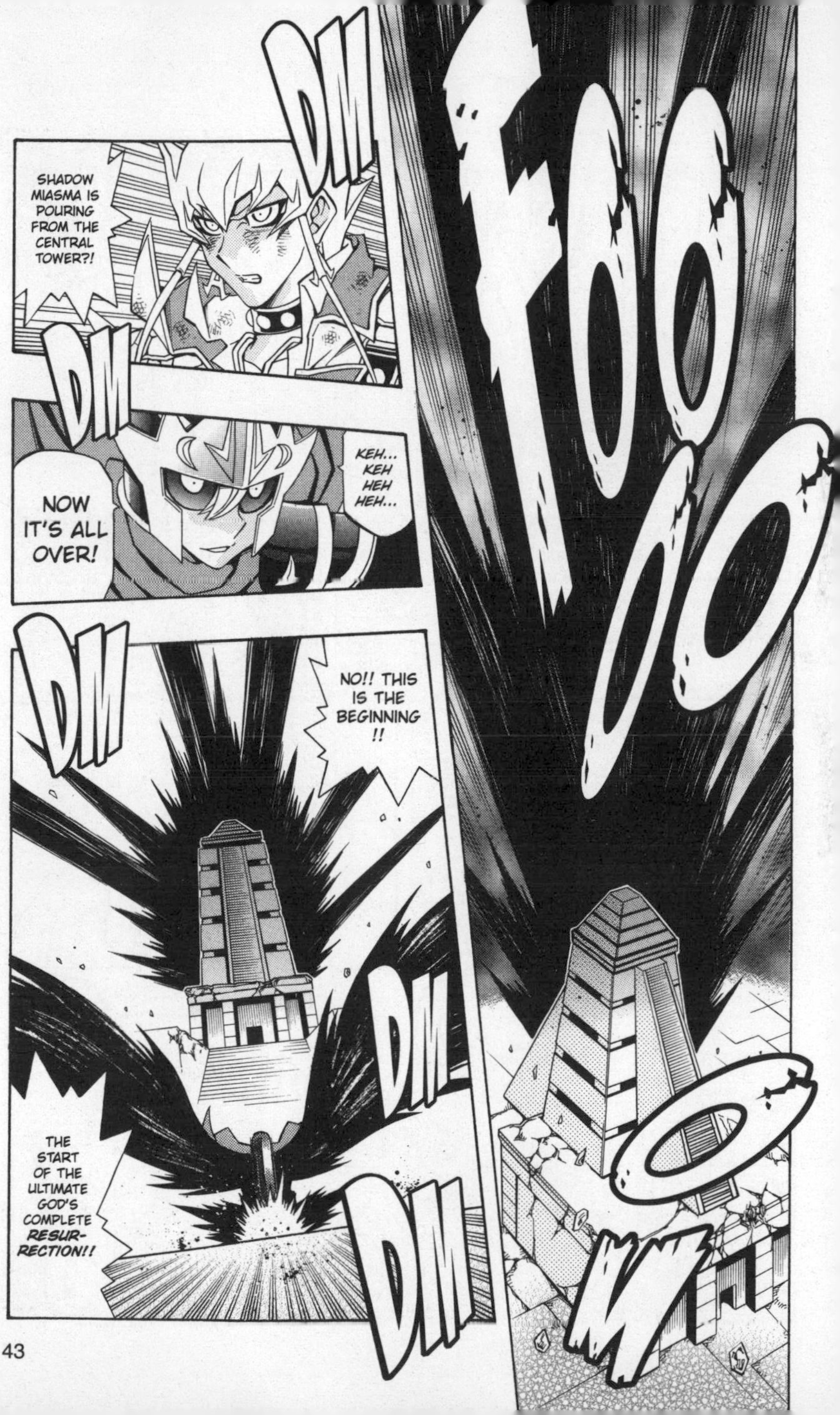
FOOOO
DM
SHADOW MIASMA IS POURING FROM THE CENTRAL TOWER?!
DM
KEH... KEH HEH HEH...
NOW IT'S ALL OVER!
DM
NO!! THIS IS THE BEGINNING!!
DM
DM
THE START OF THE ULTIMATE GOD'S COMPLETE *RESURRECTION!!*

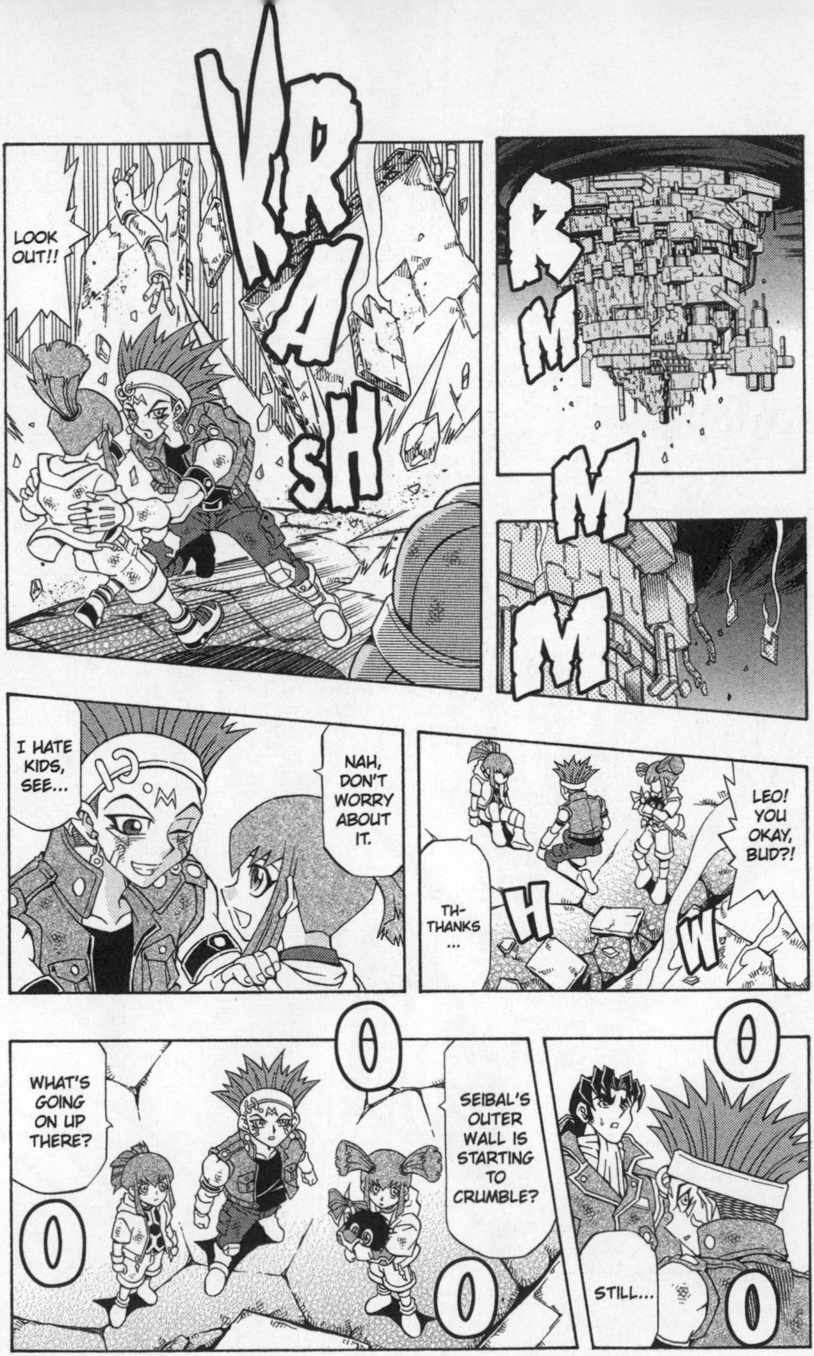
RMMM
VRASH
LOOK OUT!!
LEO! YOU OKAY, BUD?!
TH-THANKS ...
NAH, DON'T WORRY ABOUT IT.
I HATE KIDS, SEE...
STILL...
SEIBAL'S OUTER WALL IS STARTING TO CRUMBLE?
WHAT'S GOING ON UP THERE?

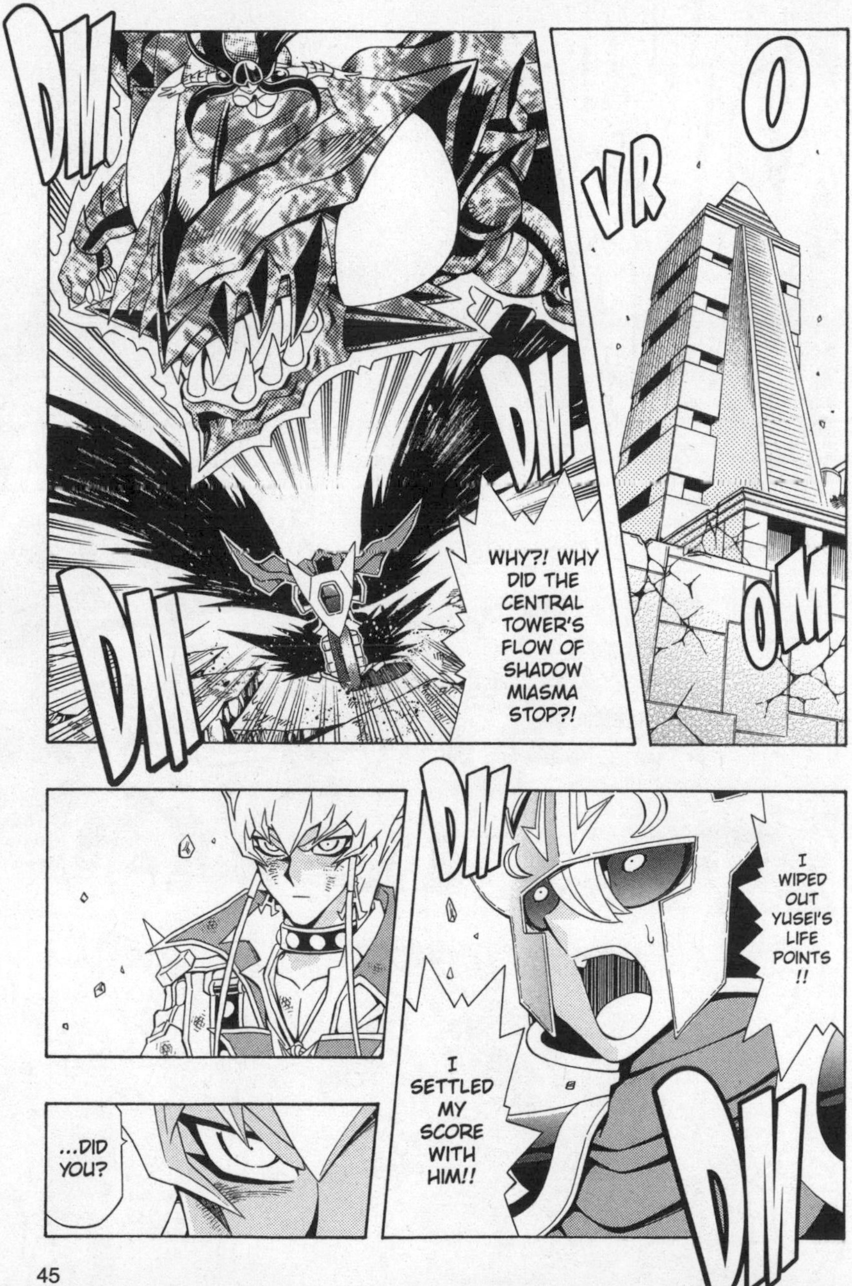
VR
O
OM
DM
DM
DM
WHY?! WHY DID THE CENTRAL TOWER'S FLOW OF SHADOW MIASMA STOP?!
DM
I WIPED OUT YUSEI'S LIFE POINTS!!
I SETTLED MY SCORE WITH HIM!!
DM
...DID YOU?

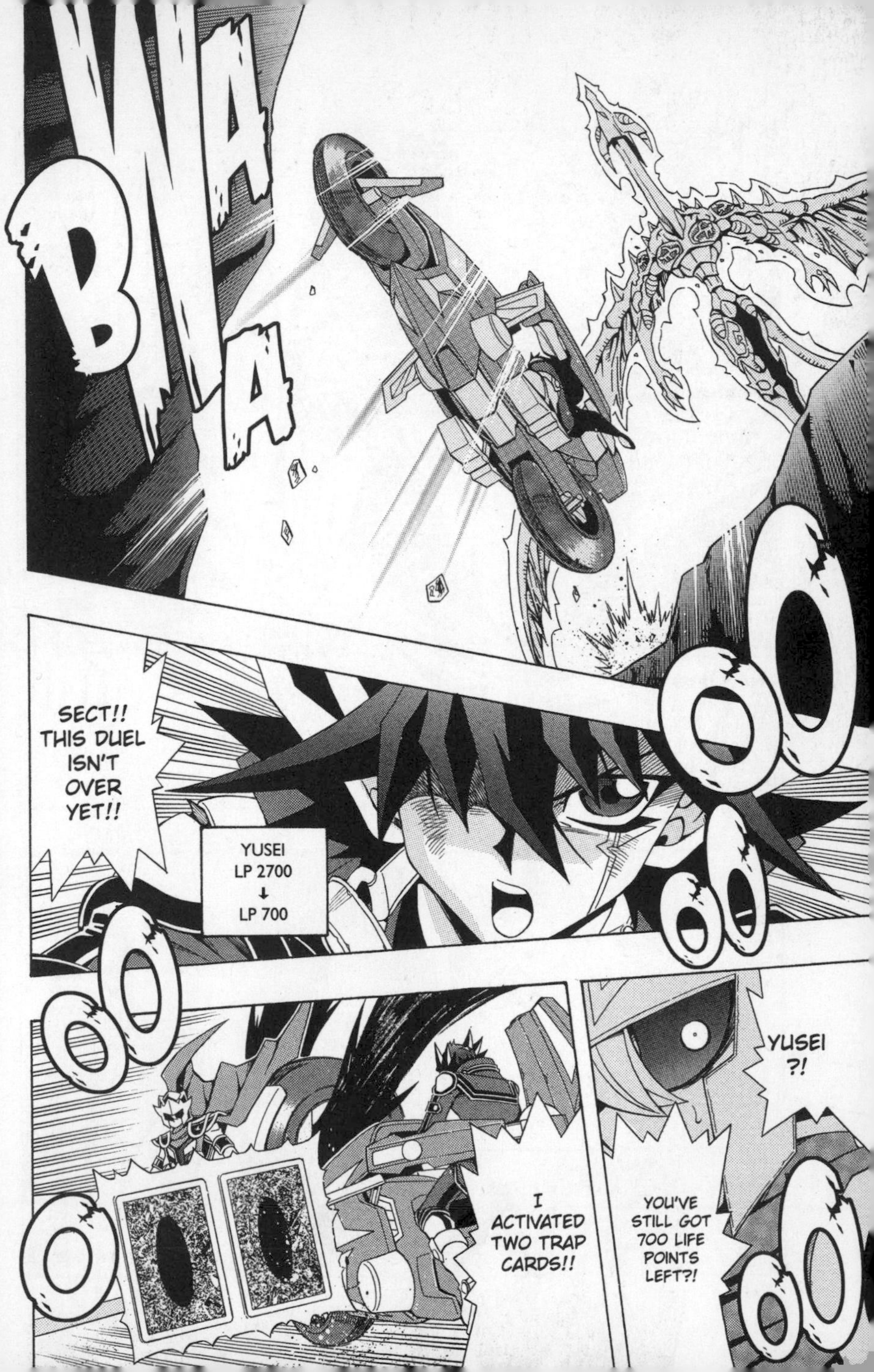
YUSEI
LP 2700
↓
LP 700
SECT!! THIS DUEL ISN'T OVER YET!!
YUSEI ?!
YOU'VE STILL GOT 700 LIFE POINTS LEFT?!
I ACTIVATED TWO TRAP CARDS!!

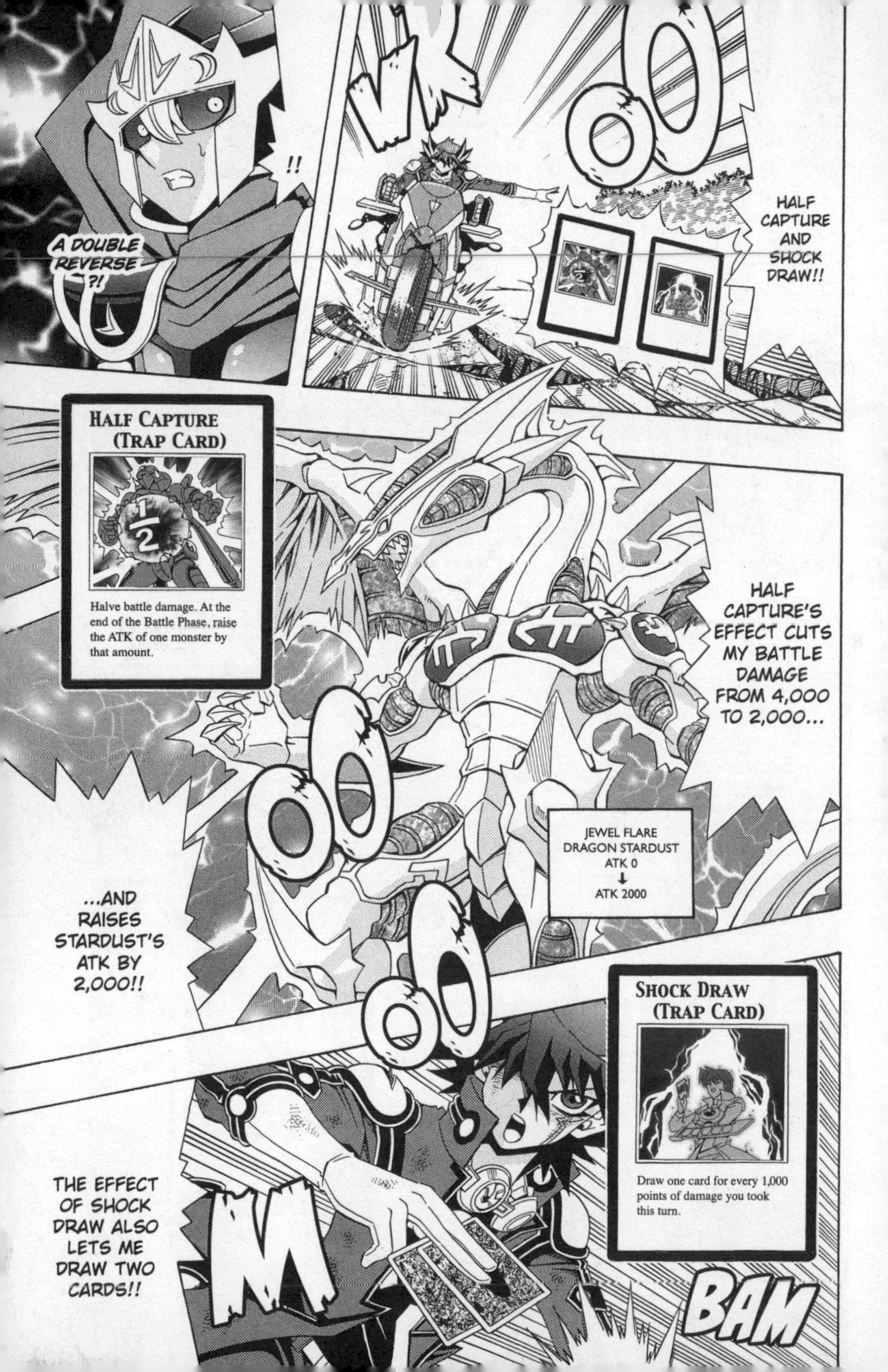

HALF CAPTURE AND SHOCK DRAW!!
!!
A DOUBLE REVERSE ?!
HALF CAPTURE'S EFFECT CUTS MY BATTLE DAMAGE FROM 4,000 TO 2,000...
HALF CAPTURE (TRAP CARD)
Halve battle damage. At the end of the Battle Phase, raise the ATK of one monster by that amount.
JEWEL FLARE DRAGON STARDUST ATK 0 ↓ ATK 2000
...AND RAISES STARDUST'S ATK BY 2,000!!
SHOCK DRAW (TRAP CARD)
Draw one card for every 1,000 points of damage you took this turn.
BAM
THE EFFECT OF SHOCK DRAW ALSO LETS ME DRAW TWO CARDS!!

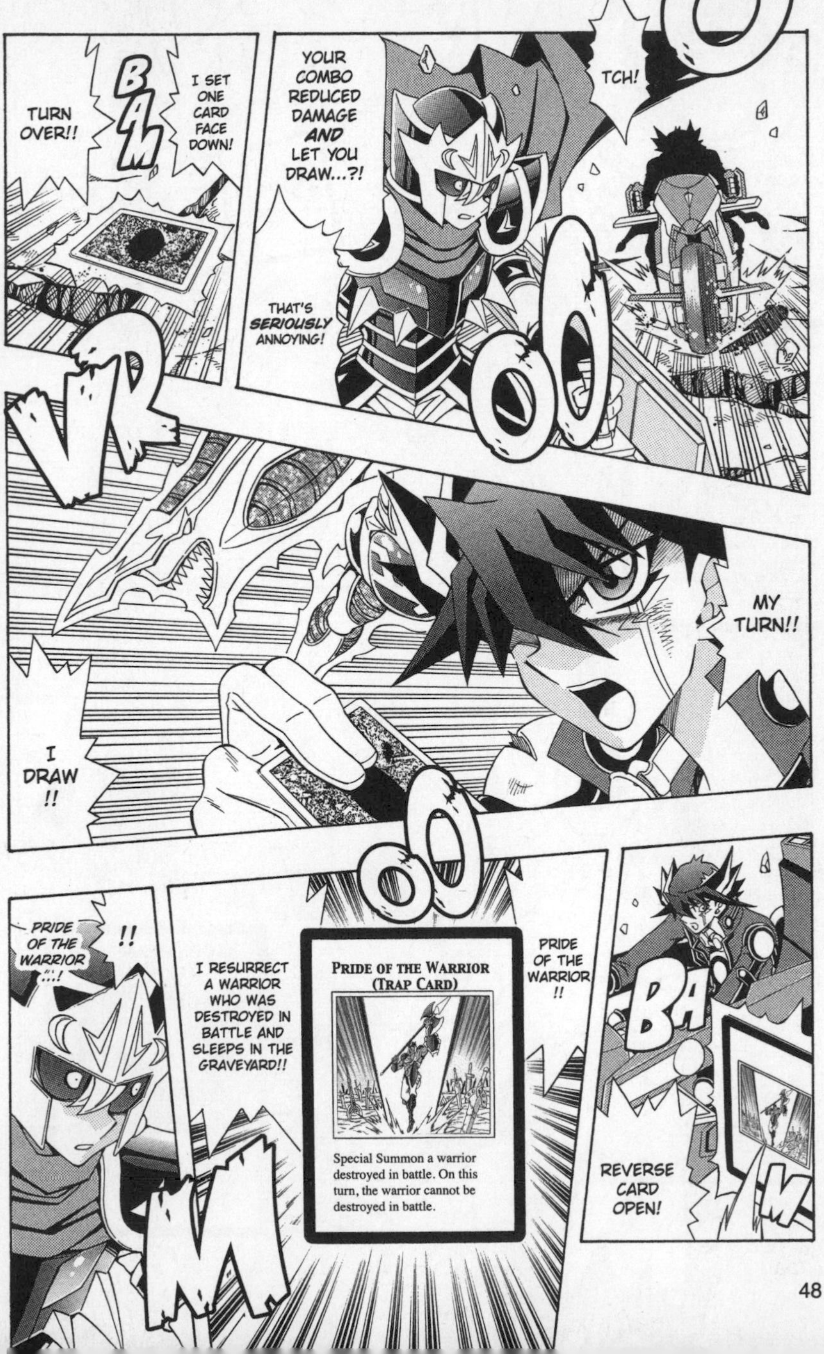
TCH!
YOUR COMBO REDUCED DAMAGE AND LET YOU DRAW...?!
THAT'S SERIOUSLY ANNOYING!
I SET ONE CARD FACE DOWN!
BAM
TURN OVER!!
VR
MY TURN!!
I DRAW!!
REVERSE CARD OPEN!
BAM
PRIDE OF THE WARRIOR!!
PRIDE OF THE WARRIOR (TRAP CARD)
Special Summon a warrior destroyed in battle. On this turn, the warrior cannot be destroyed in battle.
I RESURRECT A WARRIOR WHO WAS DESTROYED IN BATTLE AND SLEEPS IN THE GRAVEYARD!!
PRIDE OF THE WARRIOR...!
!!

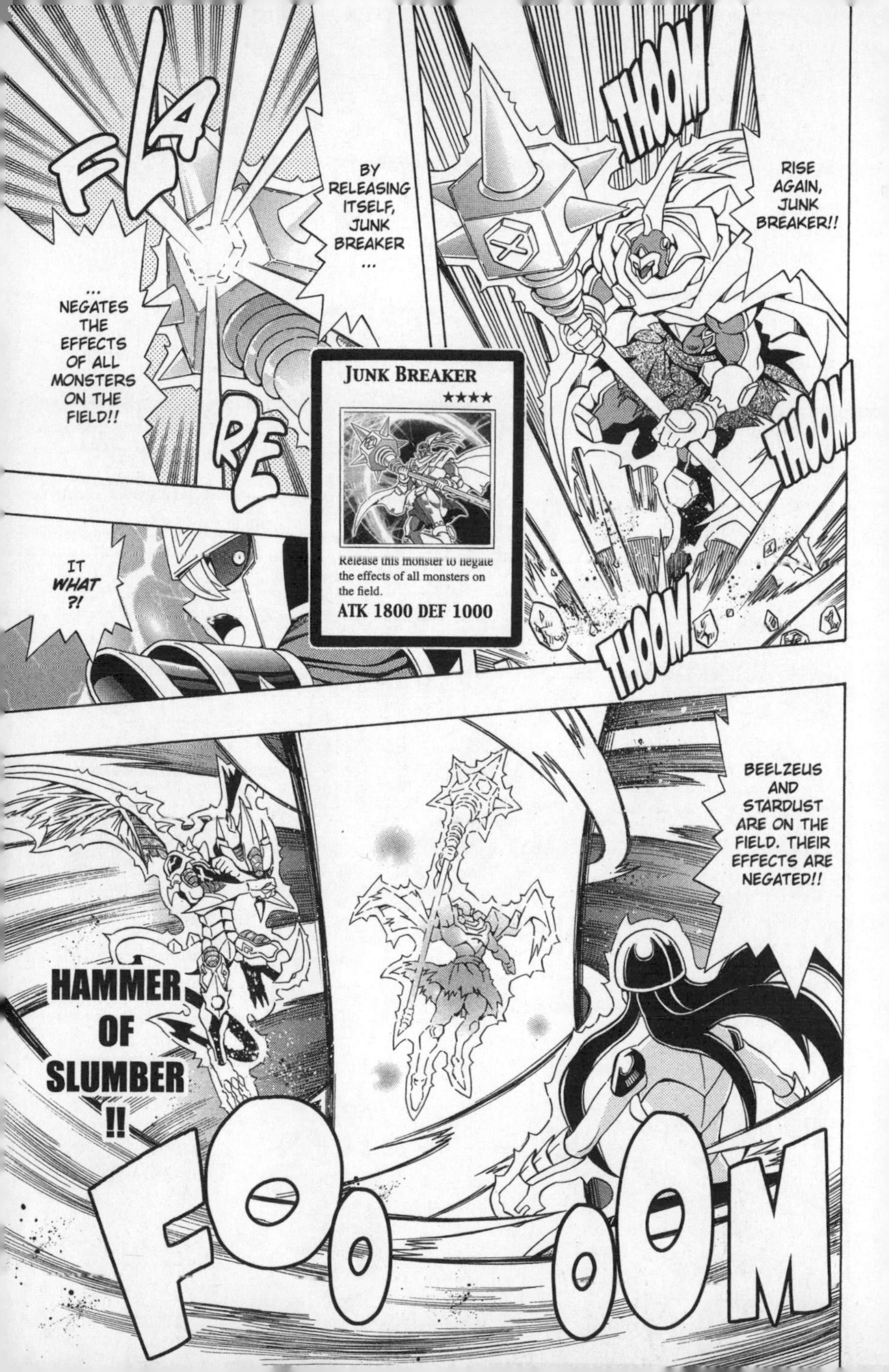
THOOM
RISE AGAIN, JUNK BREAKER!!
THOOM
THOOM
BY RELEASING ITSELF, JUNK BREAKER ...
FLA
RE
... NEGATES THE EFFECTS OF ALL MONSTERS ON THE FIELD!!
JUNK BREAKER
★★★★
Release this monster to negate the effects of all monsters on the field.
ATK 1800 DEF 1000
IT *WHAT* ?!
BEELZEUS AND STARDUST ARE ON THE FIELD. THEIR EFFECTS ARE NEGATED!!
HAMMER OF SLUMBER !!
FOOOOOM

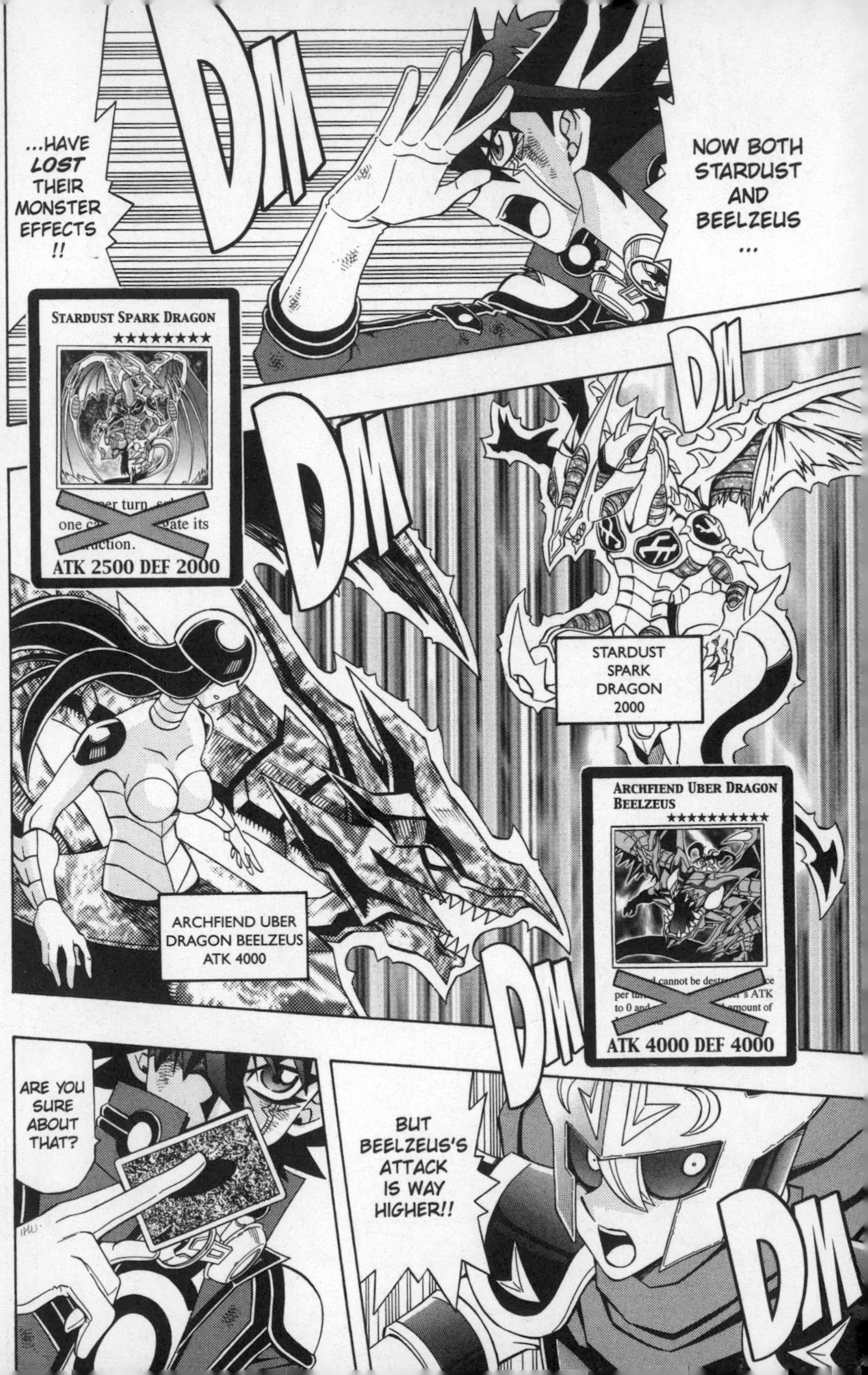
DM
NOW BOTH STARDUST AND BEELZEUS ...
...HAVE LOST THEIR MONSTER EFFECTS!!
DM
STARDUST SPARK DRAGON 2000
ARCHFIEND UBER DRAGON BEELZEUS
ATK 4000 DEF 4000
DM
STARDUST SPARK DRAGON
ATK 2500 DEF 2000
ARCHFIEND UBER DRAGON BEELZEUS ATK 4000
DM
DM
BUT BEELZEUS'S ATTACK IS WAY HIGHER!!
ARE YOU SURE ABOUT THAT?

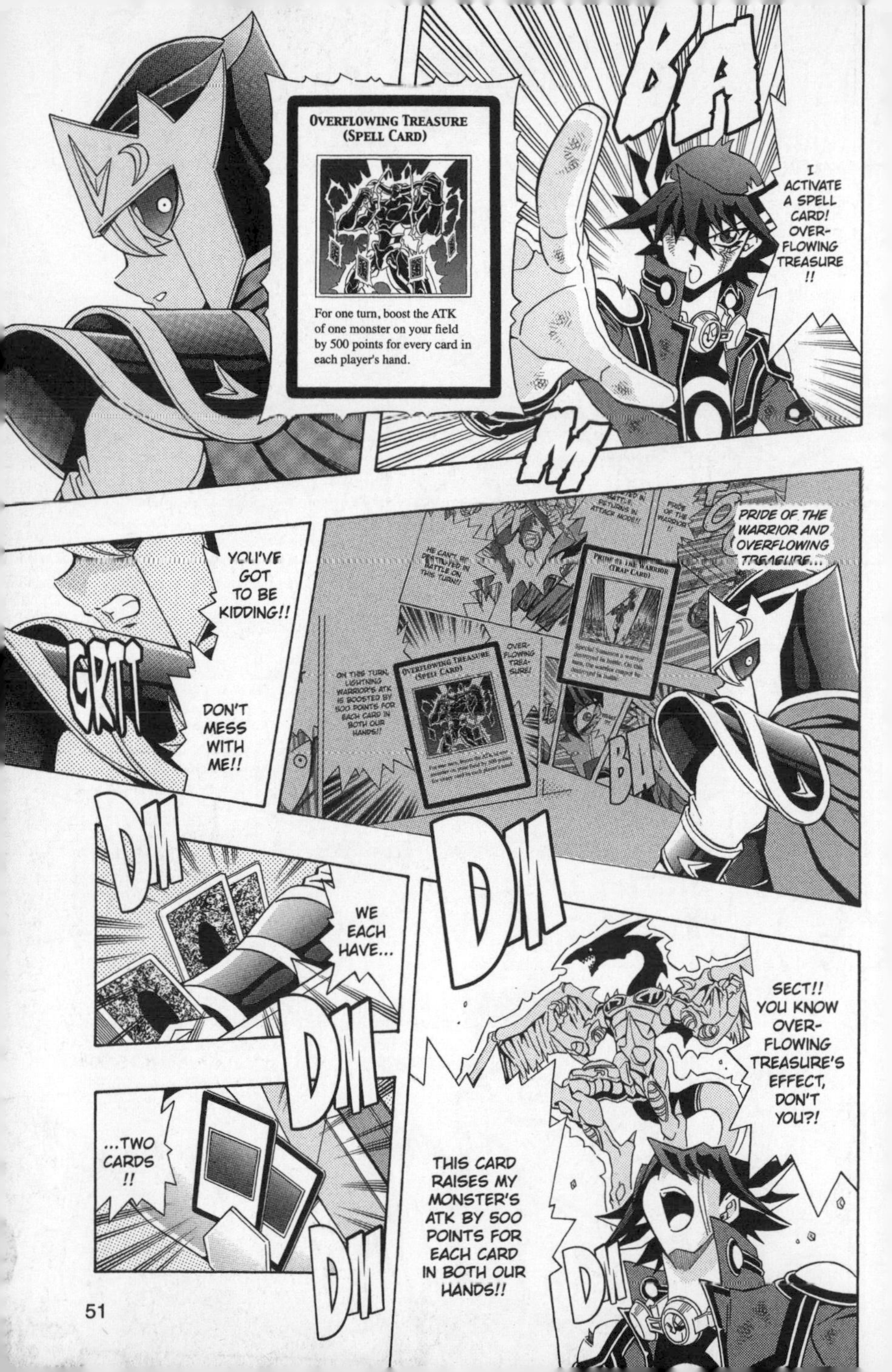
BA
I ACTIVATE A SPELL CARD! OVER-FLOWING TREASURE !!
M
OVERFLOWING TREASURE
(SPELL CARD)
For one turn, boost the ATK of one monster on your field by 500 points for every card in each player's hand.
PRIDE OF THE WARRIOR AND OVERFLOWING TREASURE...
PRIDE OF THE WARRIOR !!
OVER-FLOWING TREA-SURE!
ON THIS TURN, LIGHTNING WARRIOR'S ATK IS BOOSTED BY 500 POINTS FOR EACH CARD IN BOTH OUR HANDS!!
BA
YOU'VE GOT TO BE KIDDING!!
GRTT
DON'T MESS WITH ME!!
DM
SECT!! YOU KNOW OVER-FLOWING TREASURE'S EFFECT, DON'T YOU?!
THIS CARD RAISES MY MONSTER'S ATK BY 500 POINTS FOR EACH CARD IN BOTH OUR HANDS!!
DM
DM
WE EACH HAVE...
DM
...TWO CARDS !!
DM

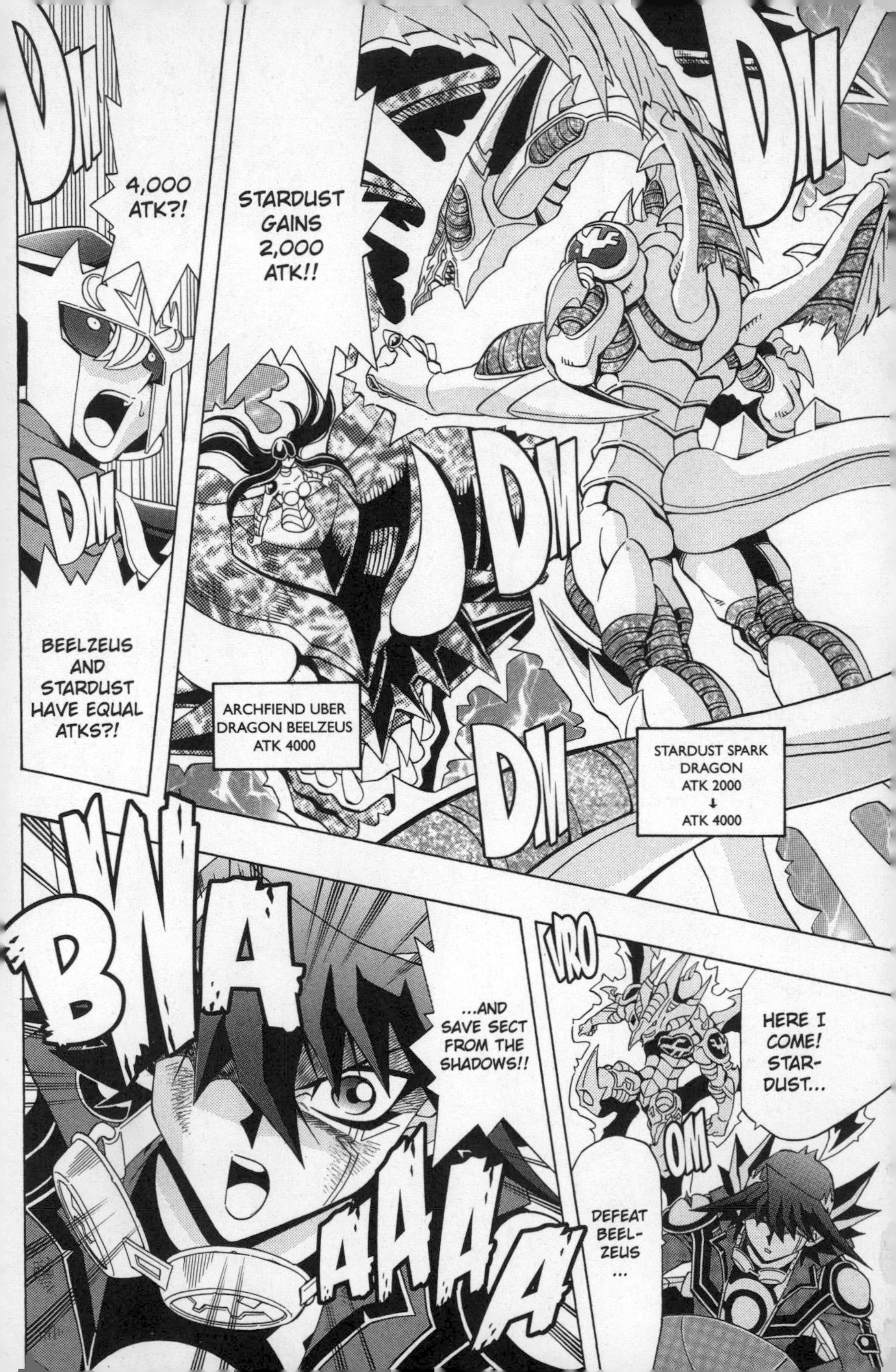

DM
STARDUST GAINS 2,000 ATK!!
DM
STARDUST SPARK DRAGON ATK 2000 ↓ ATK 4000
DM
ARCHFIEND UBER DRAGON BEELZEUS ATK 4000
DM
DM
4,000 ATK?!
DM
BEELZEUS AND STARDUST HAVE EQUAL ATKS?!
VRO
HERE I COME! STAR-DUST...
OM
DEFEAT BEEL-ZEUS ...
...AND SAVE SECT FROM THE SHADOWS!!
BWA
AAAA

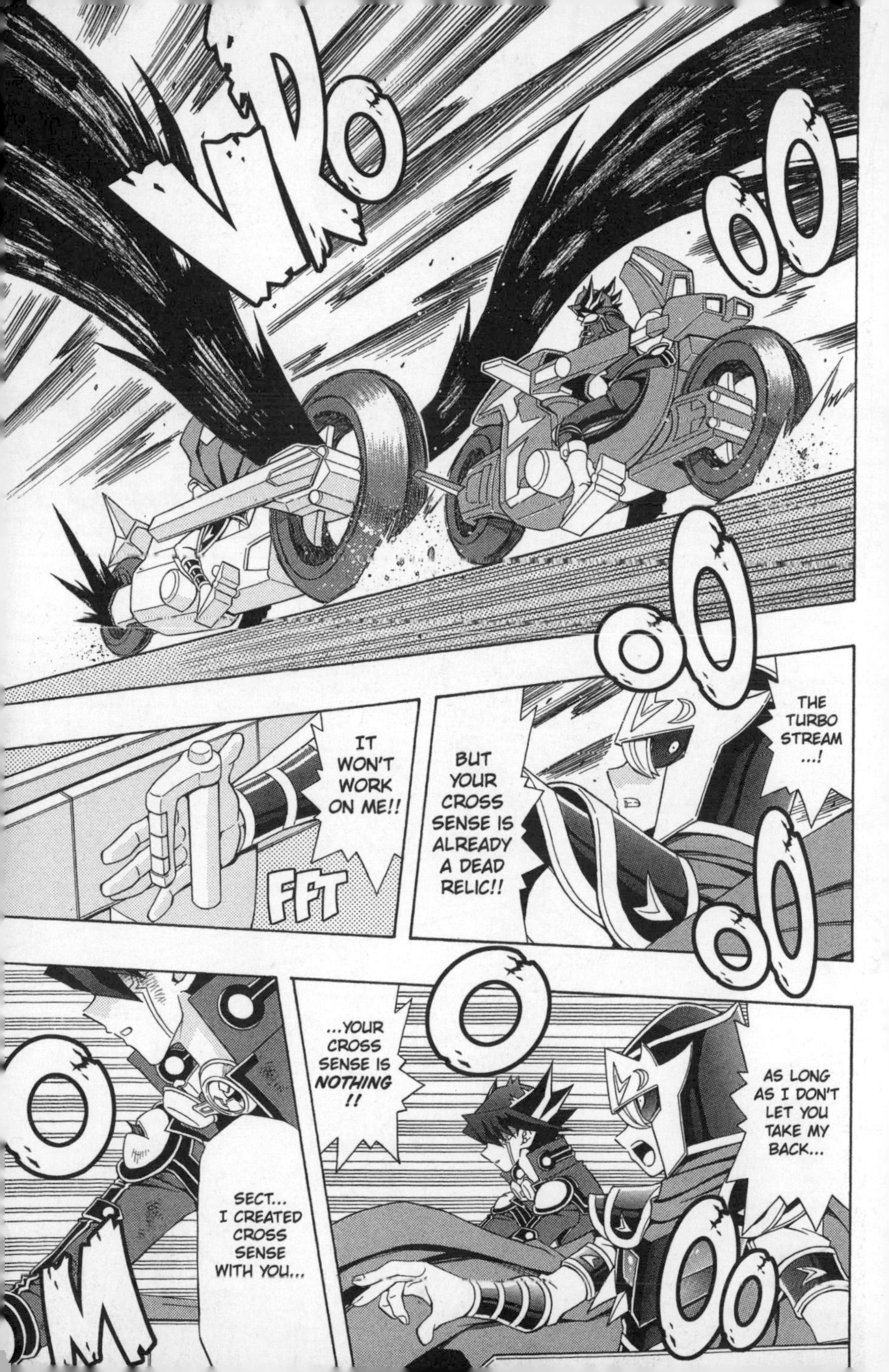
THE TURBO STREAM ...!
BUT YOUR CROSS SENSE IS ALREADY A DEAD RELIC!!
IT WON'T WORK ON ME!!
FFT
AS LONG AS I DON'T LET YOU TAKE MY BACK...
...YOUR CROSS SENSE IS *NOTHING* !!
SECT... I CREATED CROSS SENSE WITH YOU...

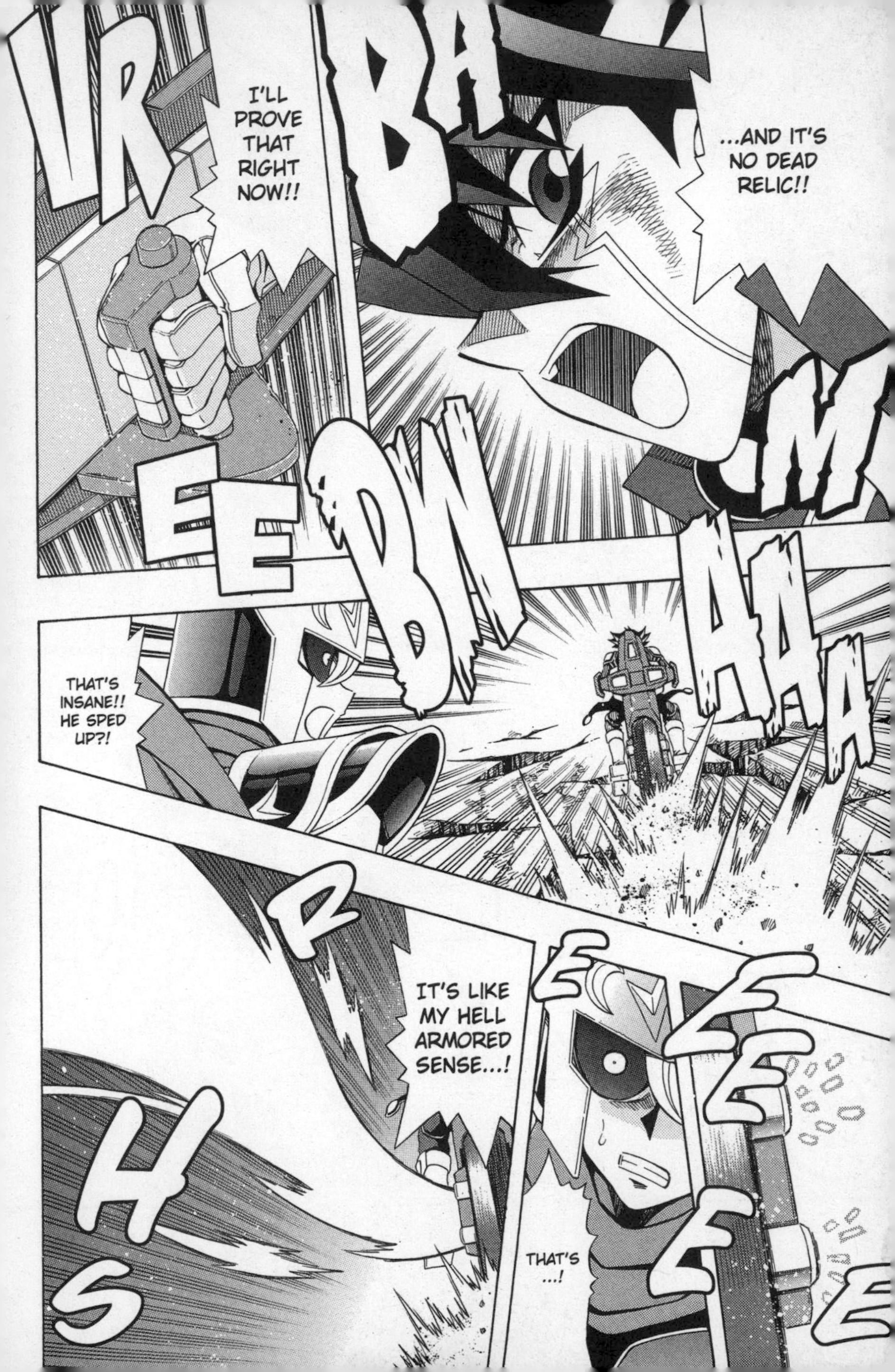
BA
...AND IT'S NO DEAD RELIC!!
VR
I'LL PROVE THAT RIGHT NOW!!
M
AAA
BW
EE
THAT'S INSANE!! HE SPED UP?!
EEEEE
R
IT'S LIKE MY HELL ARMORED SENSE...!
THAT'S ...!
H
S

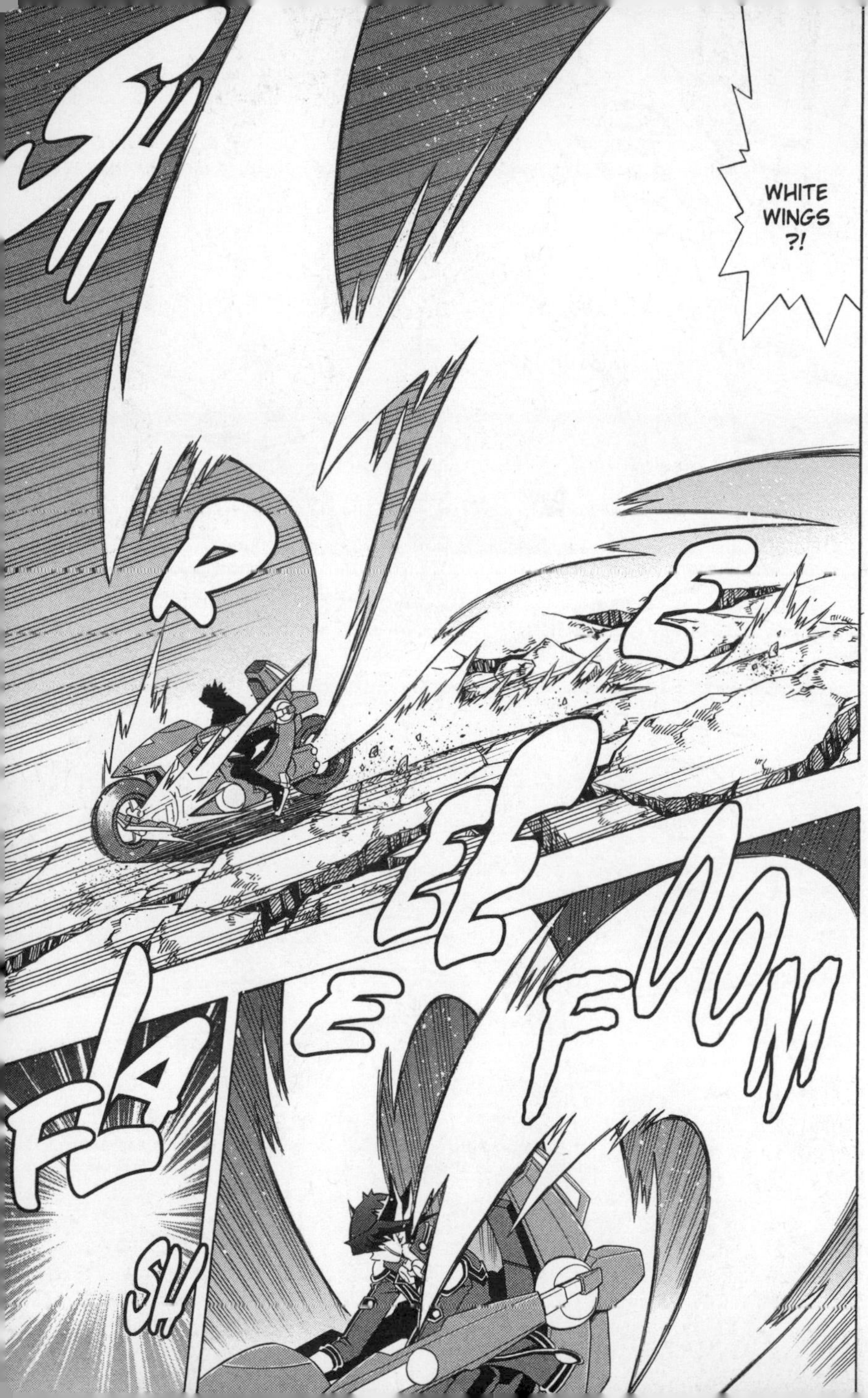
WHITE WINGS ?!

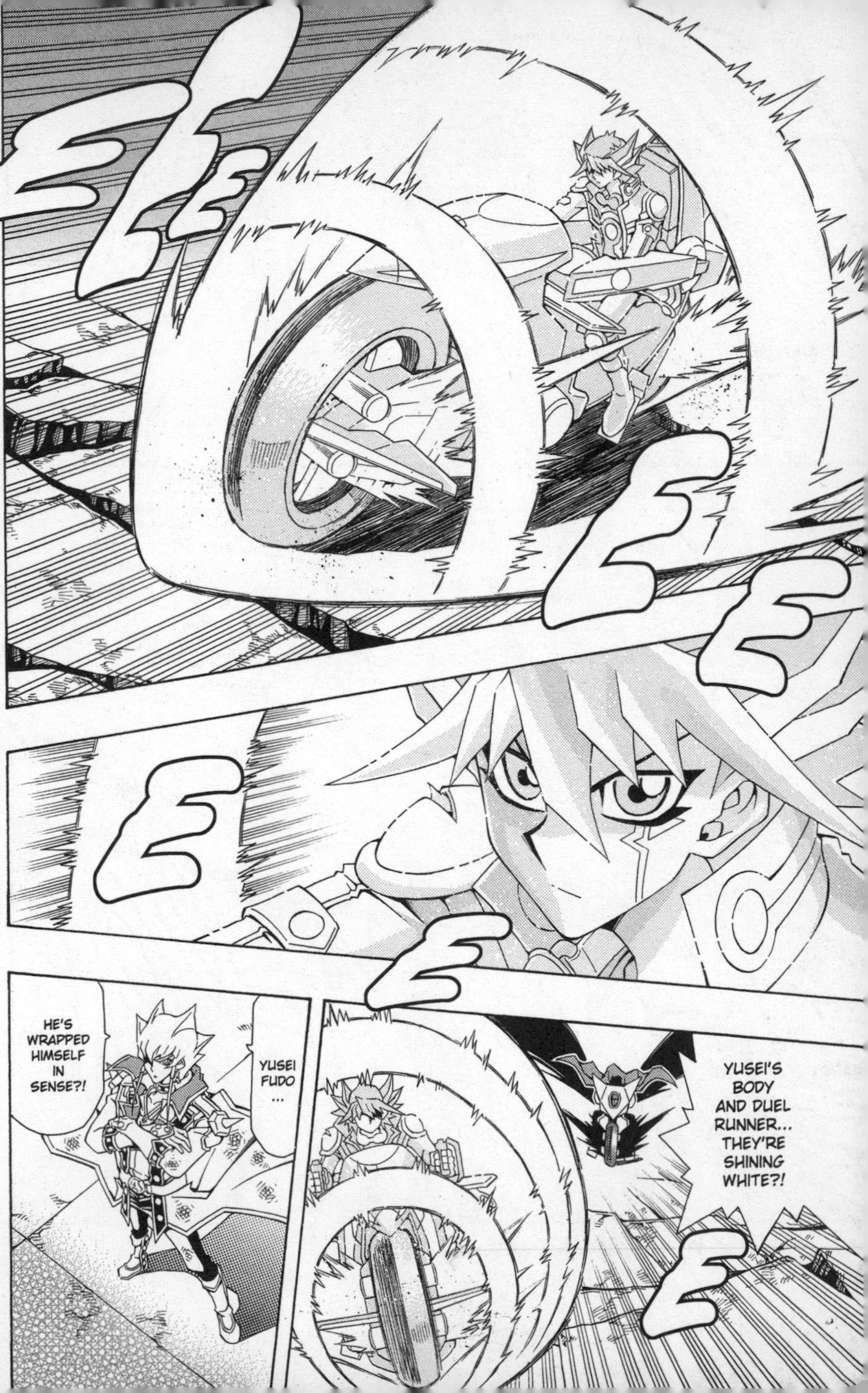
EEEEEE
EE
YUSEI'S BODY AND DUEL RUNNER... THEY'RE SHINING WHITE?!
E
YUSEI FUDO ...
HE'S WRAPPED HIMSELF IN SENSE?!

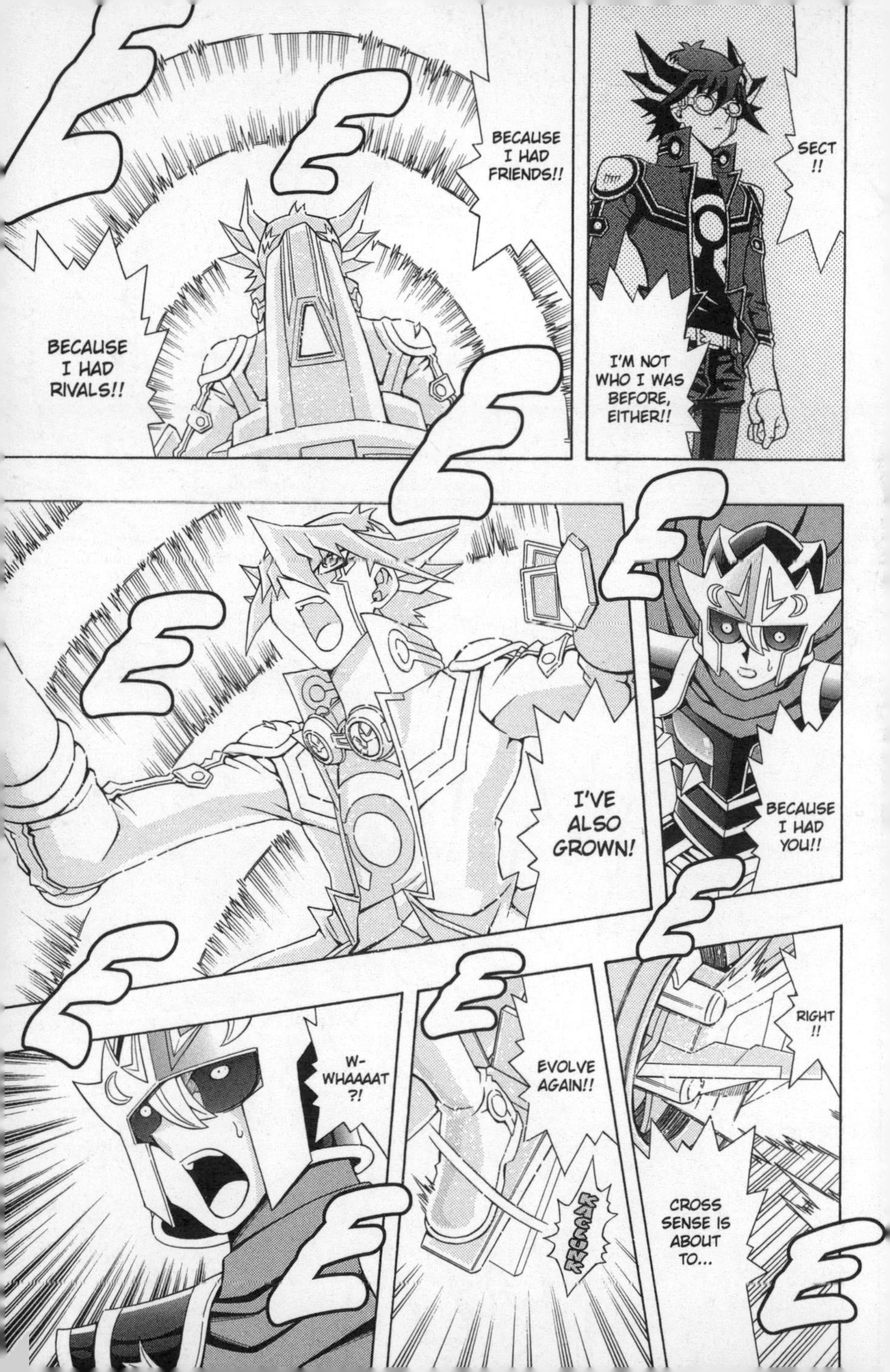
SECT !!
I'M NOT WHO I WAS BEFORE, EITHER!!
BECAUSE I HAD FRIENDS!!
BECAUSE I HAD RIVALS!!
BECAUSE I HAD YOU!!
I'VE ALSO GROWN!
RIGHT !!
CROSS SENSE IS ABOUT TO...
EVOLVE AGAIN!!
KACHUNK
W-WHAAAAT ?!

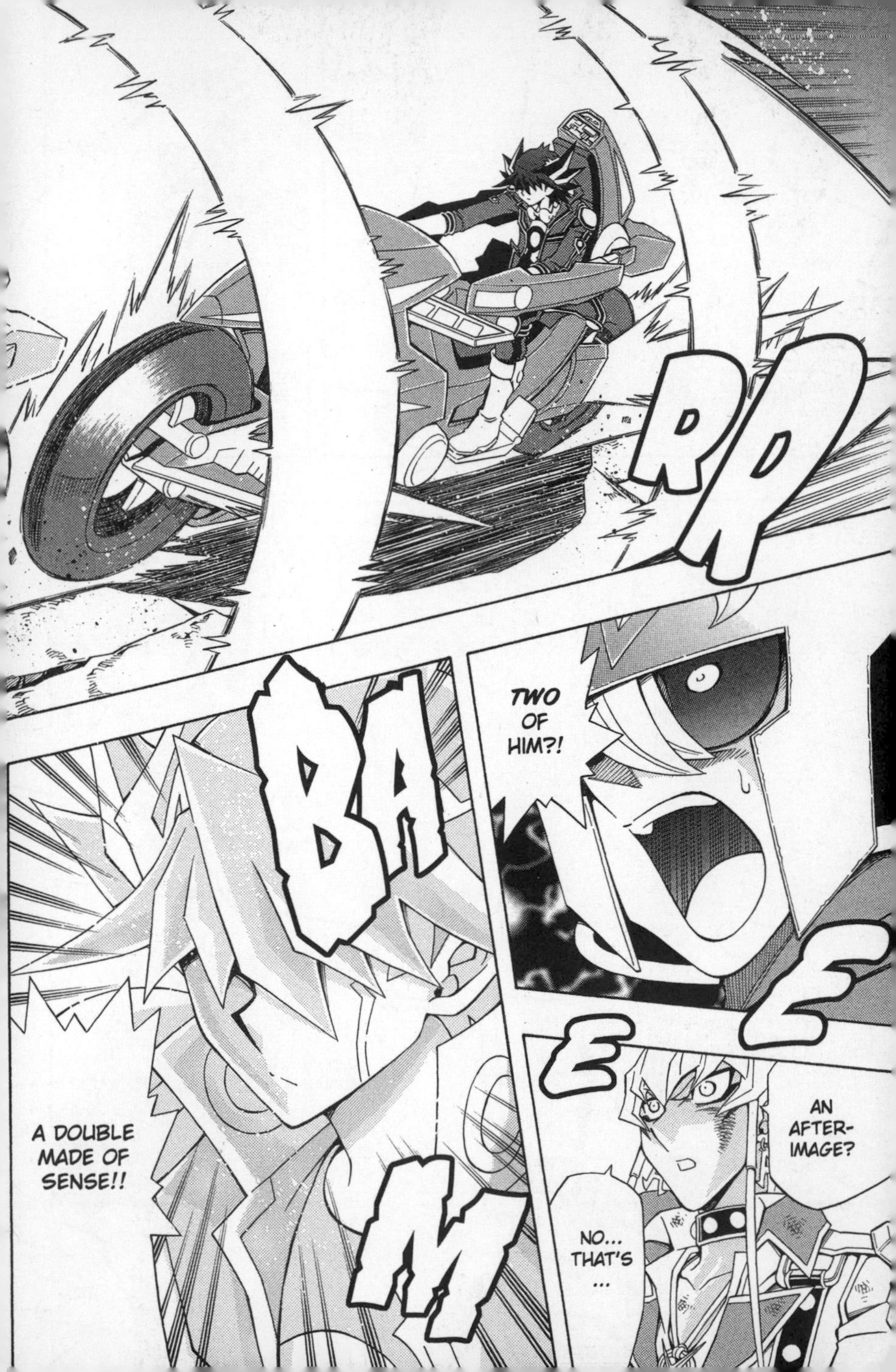
RR
TWO OF HIM?!
E E
AN AFTER-IMAGE?
NO... THAT'S ...
BA
M
A DOUBLE MADE OF SENSE!!

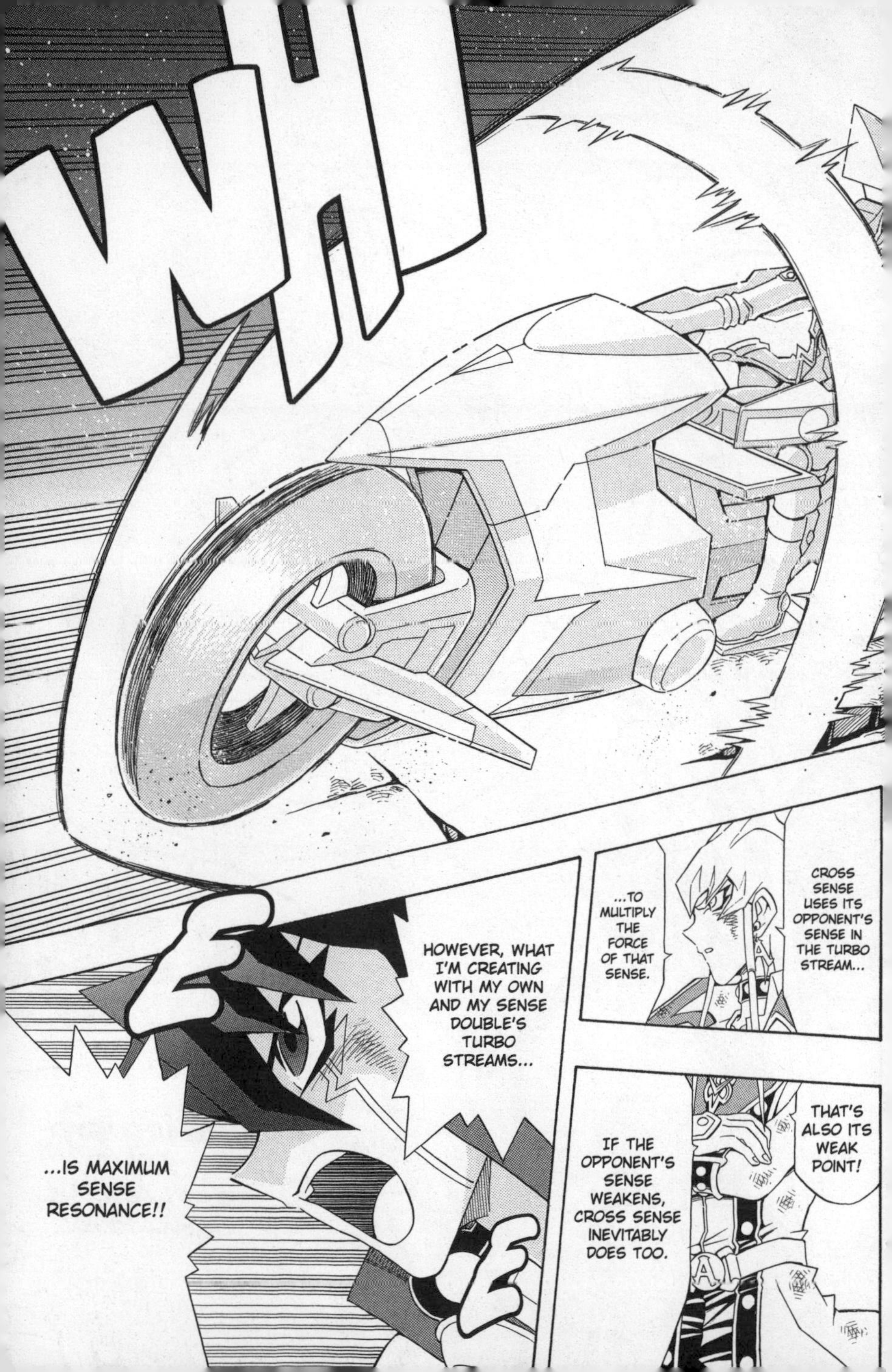
WH!
CROSS SENSE USES ITS OPPONENT'S SENSE IN THE TURBO STREAM...
...TO MULTIPLY THE FORCE OF THAT SENSE.
THAT'S ALSO ITS WEAK POINT!
IF THE OPPONENT'S SENSE WEAKENS, CROSS SENSE INEVITABLY DOES TOO.
HOWEVER, WHAT I'M CREATING WITH MY OWN AND MY SENSE DOUBLE'S TURBO STREAMS...
...IS MAXIMUM SENSE RESONANCE!!

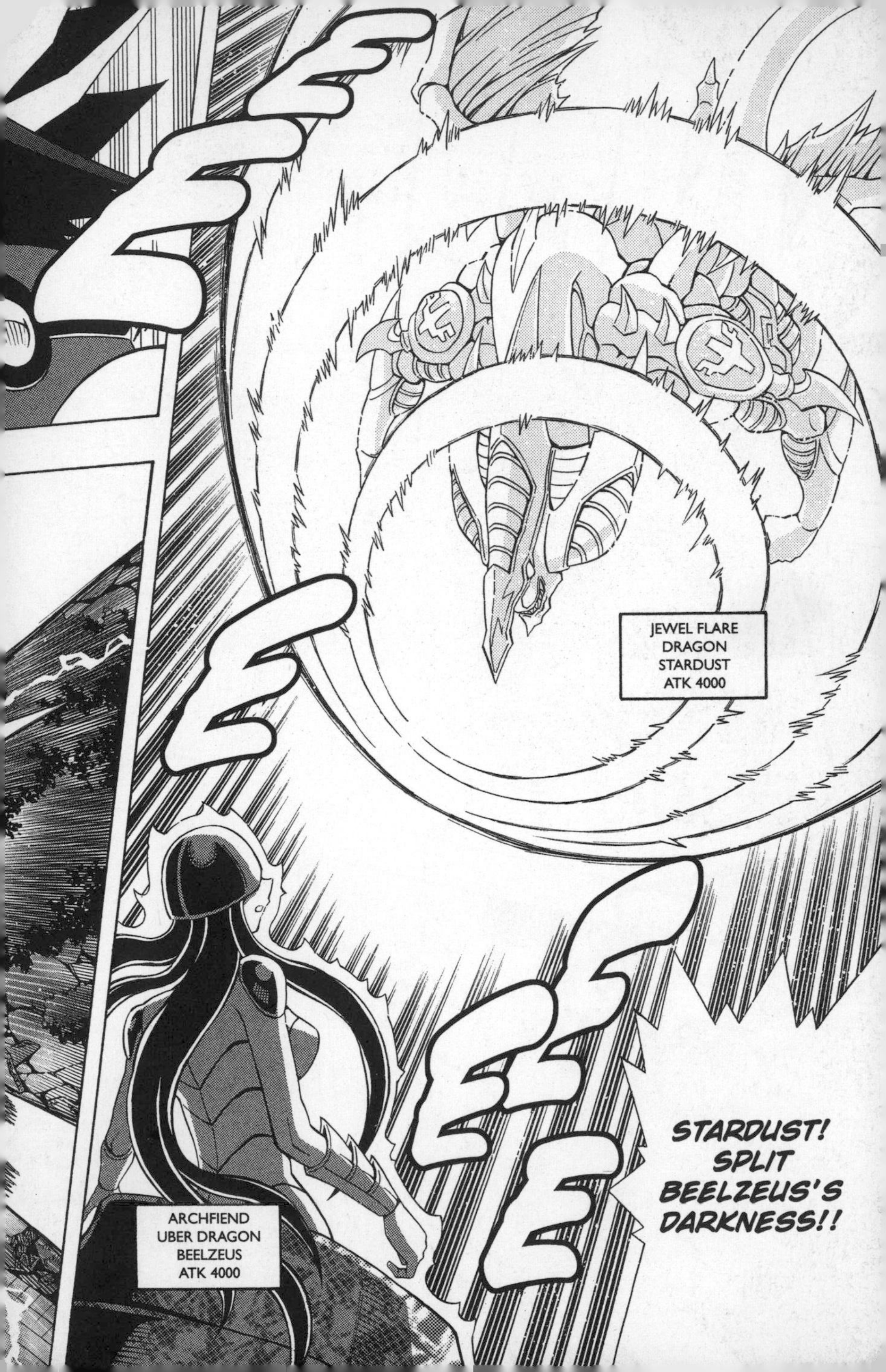
JEWEL FLARE DRAGON STARDUST ATK 4000
STARDUST! SPLIT BEELZEUS'S DARKNESS!!
ARCHFIEND UBER DRAGON BEELZEUS ATK 4000

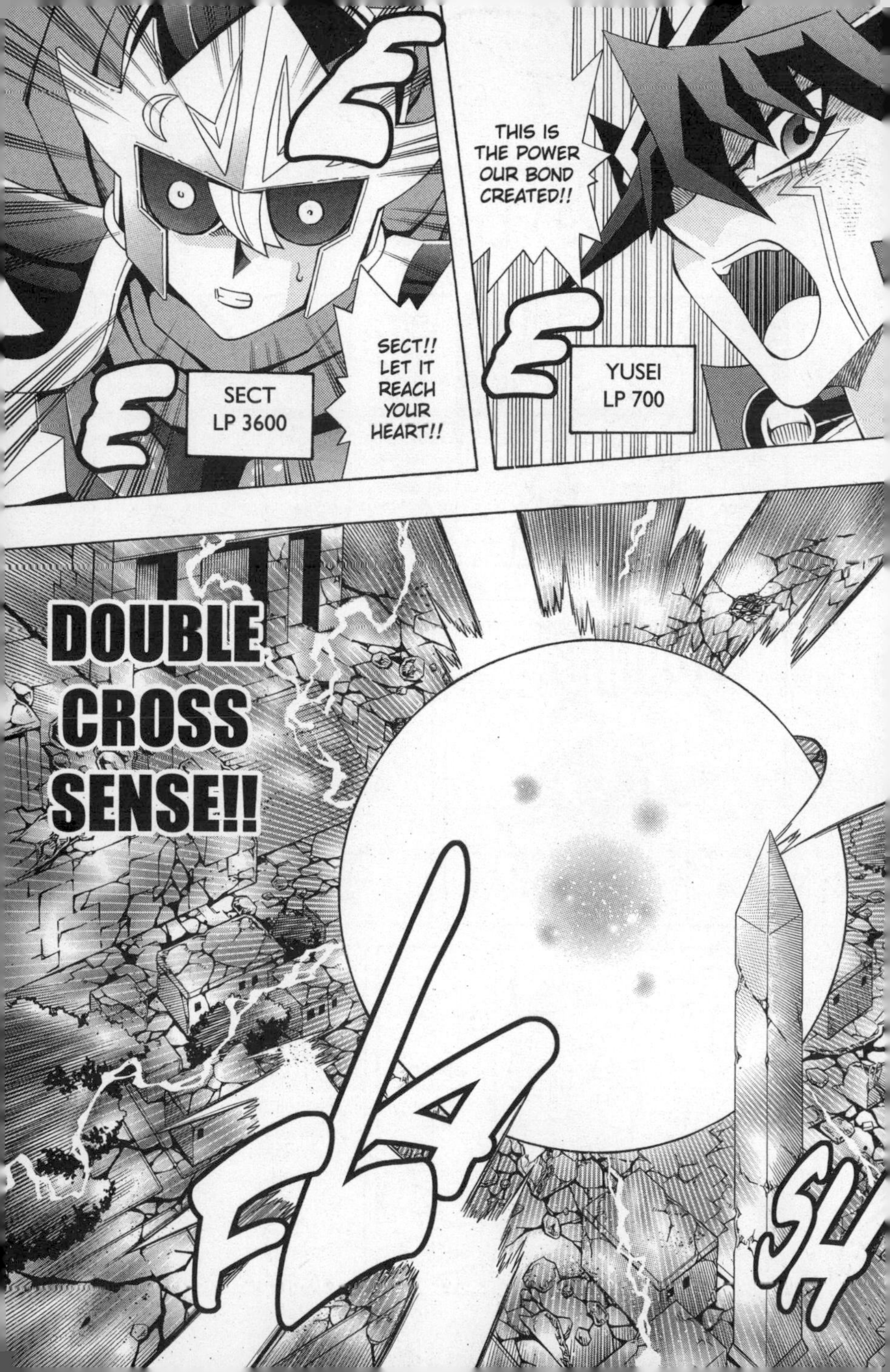
THIS IS THE POWER OUR BOND CREATED!!
YUSEI LP 700
SECT!! LET IT REACH YOUR HEART!!
SECT LP 3600
DOUBLE CROSS SENSE!!
SH
FLA

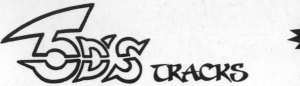

5D's TRACKS

THE 54TH

BY SATOMASA

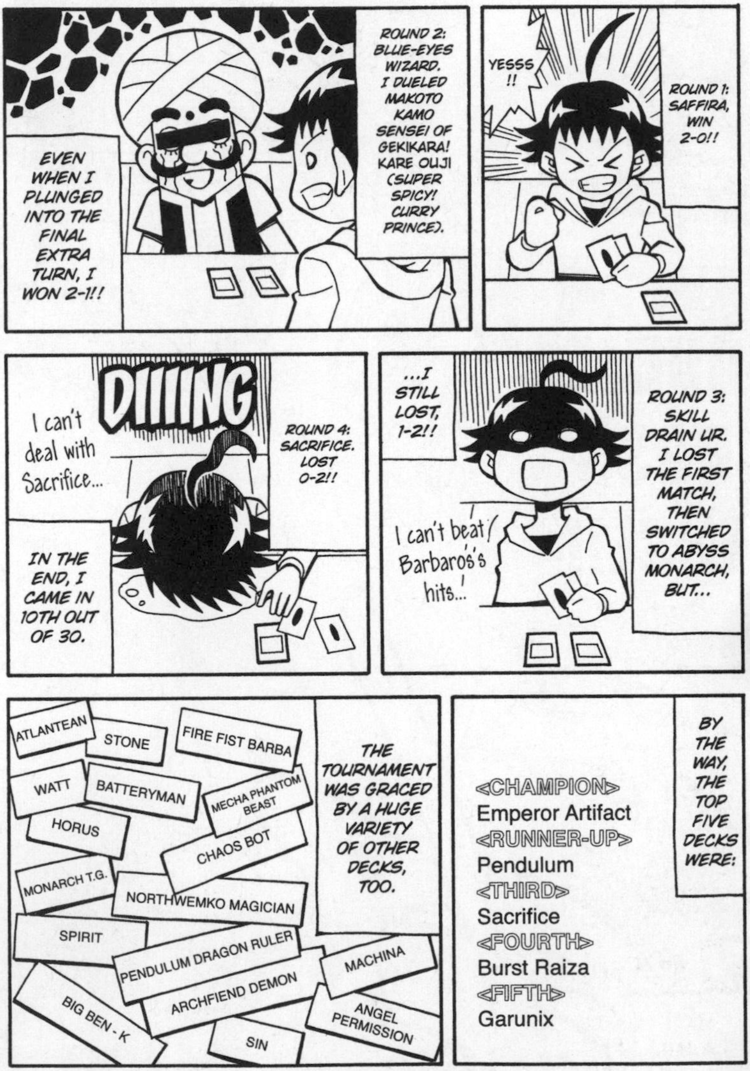
ROUND 1: SAFFIRA, WIN 2-0!!
YESSS !!
ROUND 2: BLUE-EYES WIZARD. I DUELED MAKOTO KAMO SENSEI OF GEKIKARA! KARE OUJI (SUPER SPICY! CURRY PRINCE).
EVEN WHEN I PLUNGED INTO THE FINAL EXTRA TURN, I WON 2-1!!
ROUND 3: SKILL DRAIN UR. I LOST THE FIRST MATCH, THEN SWITCHED TO ABYSS MONARCH, BUT...
...I STILL LOST, 1-2!!
I can't beat Barbaros's hits...
ROUND 4: SACRIFICE. LOST 0-2!!
DIIIING
I can't deal with Sacrifice...
IN THE END, I CAME IN 10TH OUT OF 30.
BY THE WAY, THE TOP FIVE DECKS WERE:
<CHAMPION>
Emperor Artifact
<RUNNER-UP>
Pendulum
<THIRD>
Sacrifice
<FOURTH>
Burst Raiza
<FIFTH>
Garunix
THE TOURNAMENT WAS GRACED BY A HUGE VARIETY OF OTHER DECKS, TOO.
ATLANTEAN
STONE
FIRE FIST BARBA
WATT
BATTERYMAN
MECHA PHANTOM BEAST
HORUS
CHAOS BOT
MONARCH T.G.
NORTHWEMKO MAGICIAN
SPIRIT
PENDULUM DRAGON RULER
MACHINA
ARCHFIEND DEMON
BIG BEN - K
ANGEL PERMISSION
SIN

RIDE-56

BEYOND THE FLASH...!!

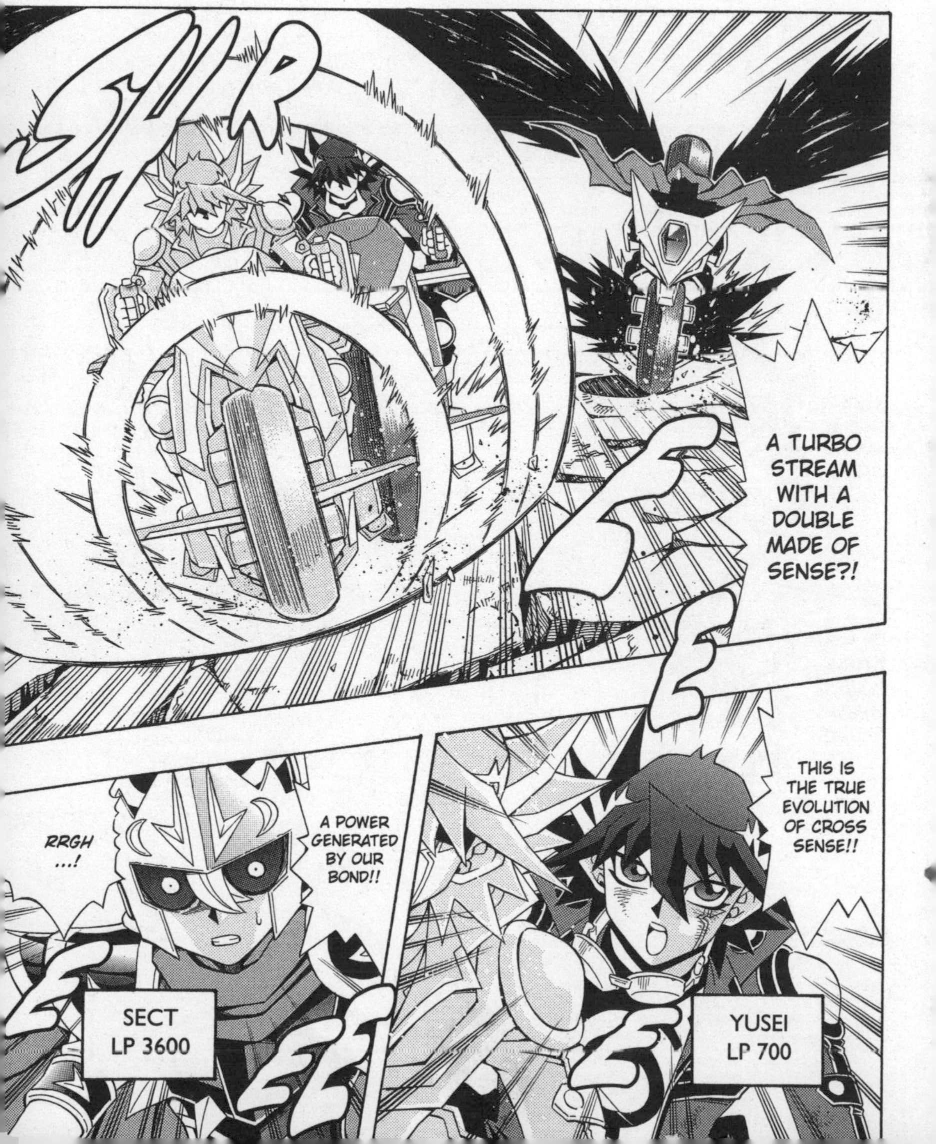
SHIR
A TURBO STREAM WITH A DOUBLE MADE OF SENSE?!
THIS IS THE TRUE EVOLUTION OF CROSS SENSE!!
YUSEI LP 700
A POWER GENERATED BY OUR BOND!!
RRGH ...!
SECT LP 3600

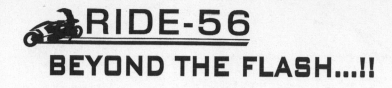

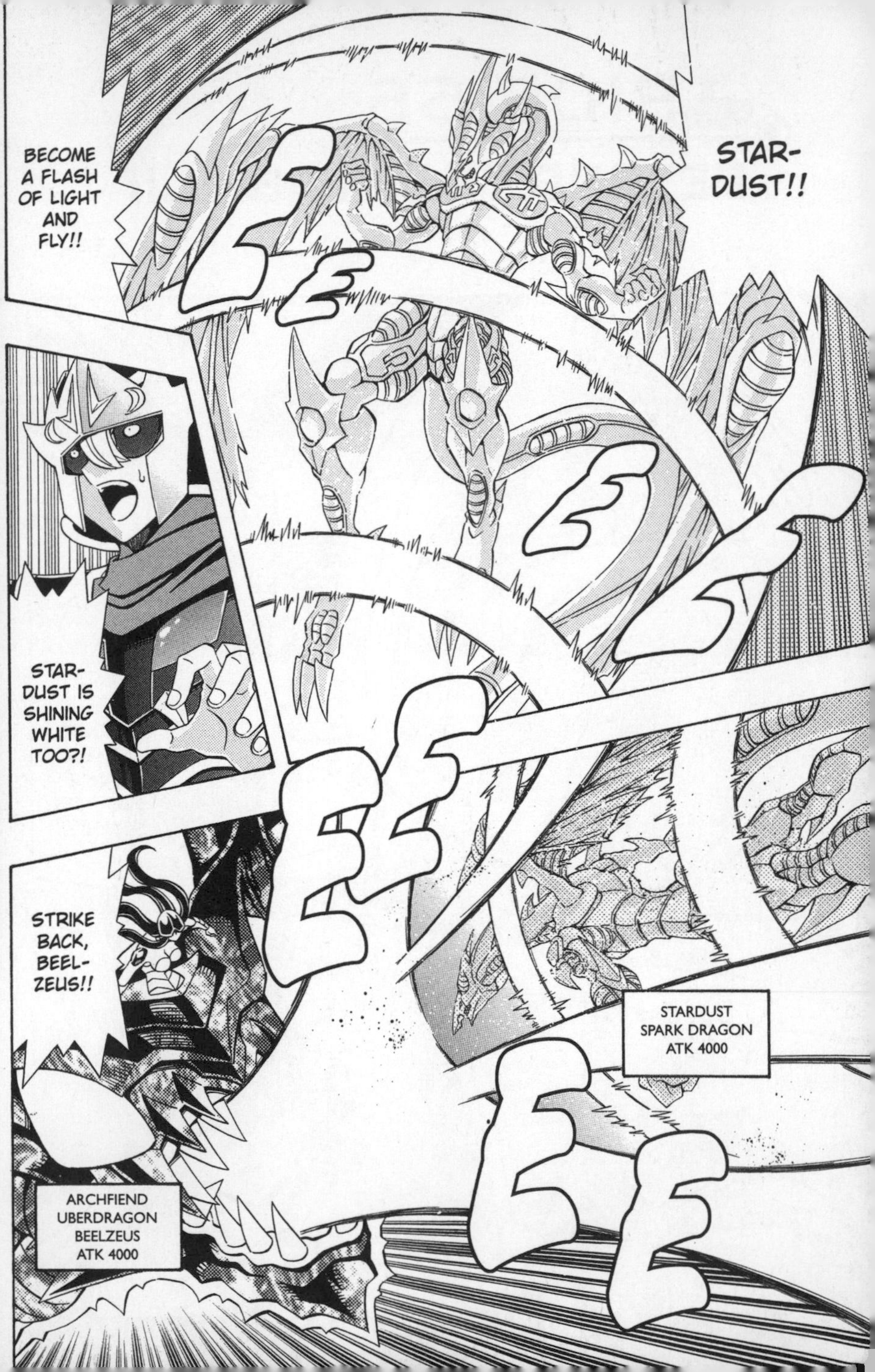
STAR-DUST!!
BECOME A FLASH OF LIGHT AND FLY!!
STAR-DUST IS SHINING WHITE TOO?!
STARDUST SPARK DRAGON ATK 4000
STRIKE BACK, BEEL-ZEUS!!
ARCHFIEND UBERDRAGON BEELZEUS ATK 4000

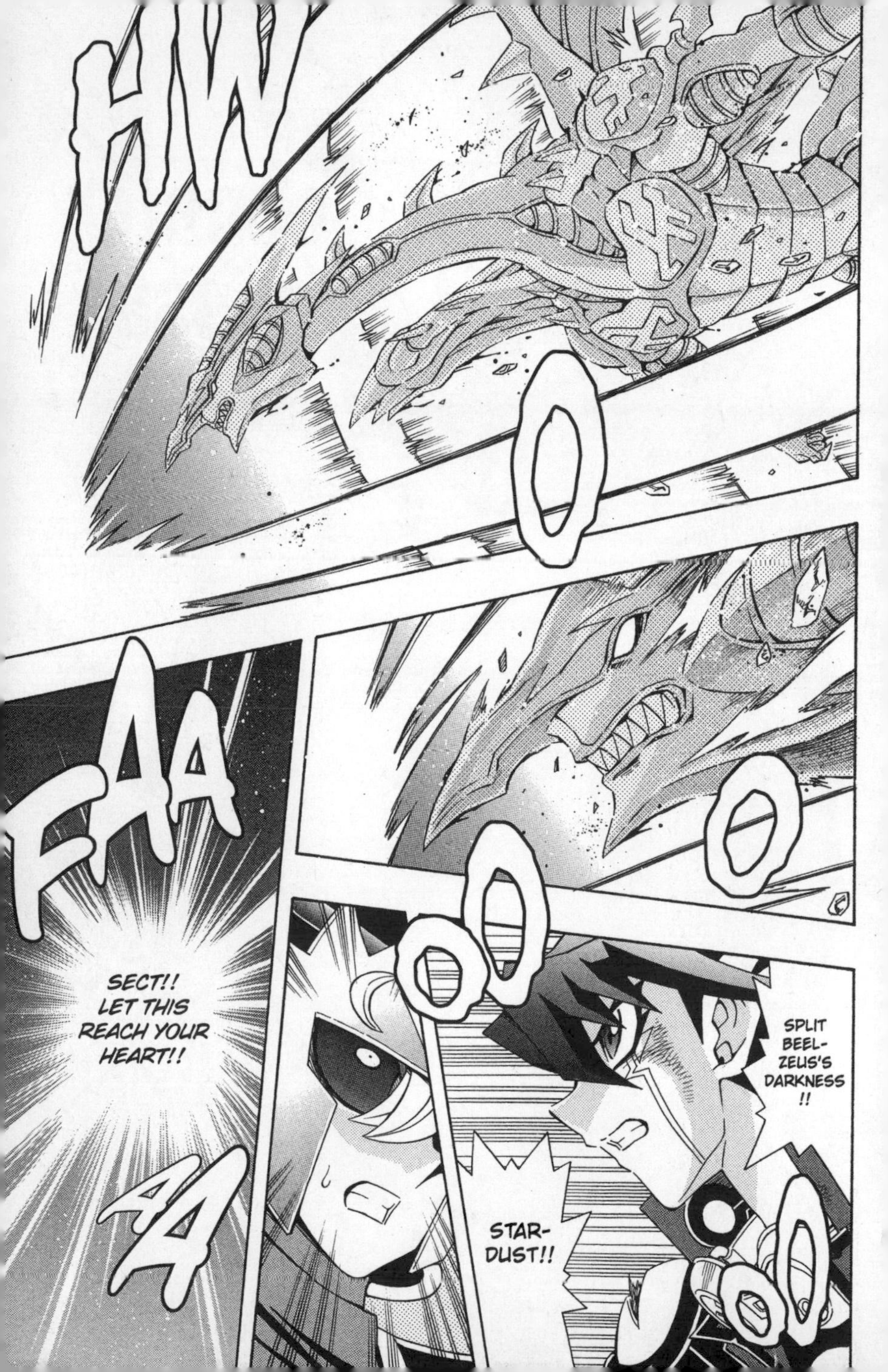
HW
SPLIT BEEL-ZEUS'S DARKNESS!!
STAR-DUST!!
FAA
SECT!! LET THIS REACH YOUR HEART!!
AA

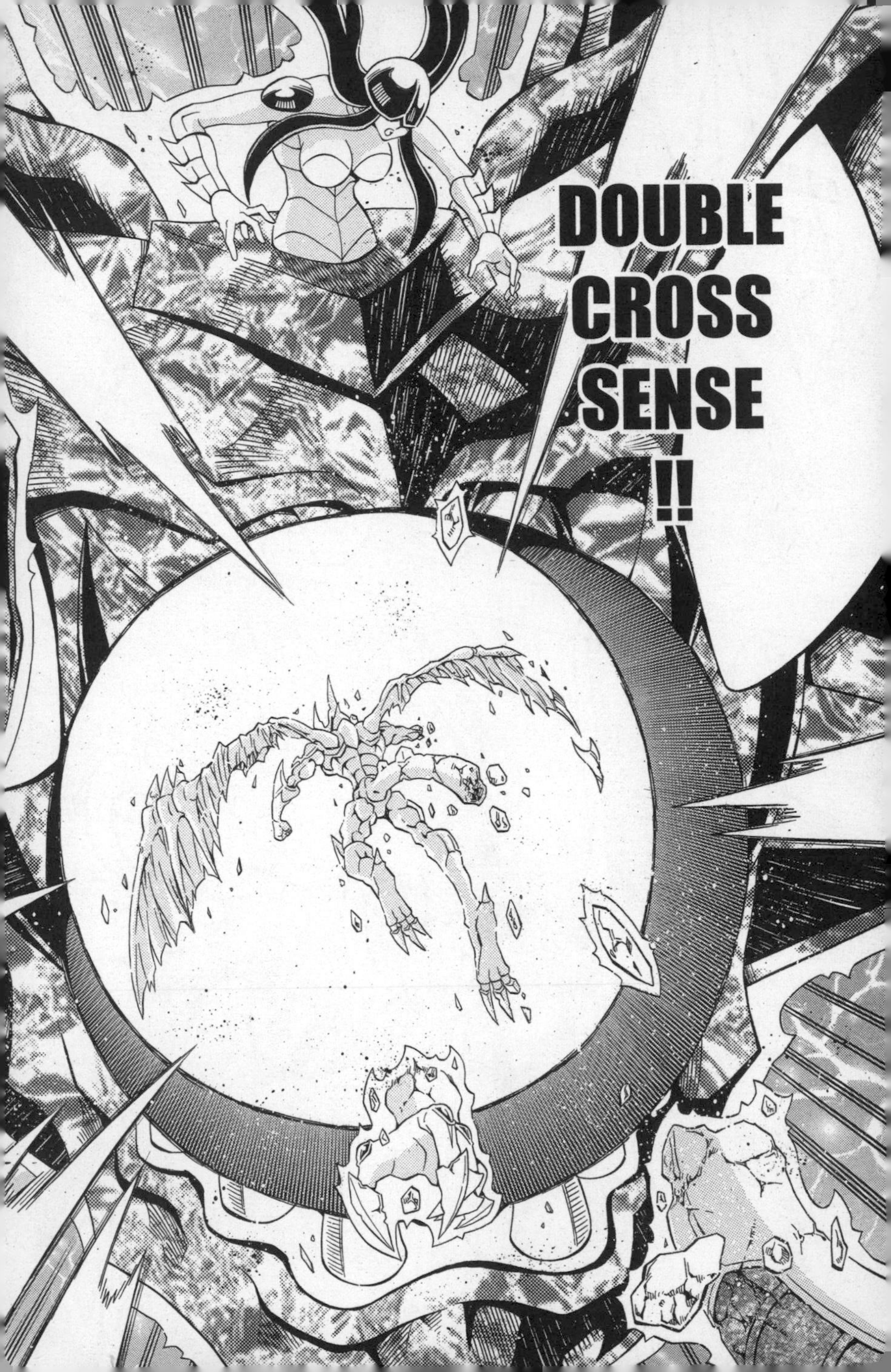
DOUBLE CROSS SENSE!!

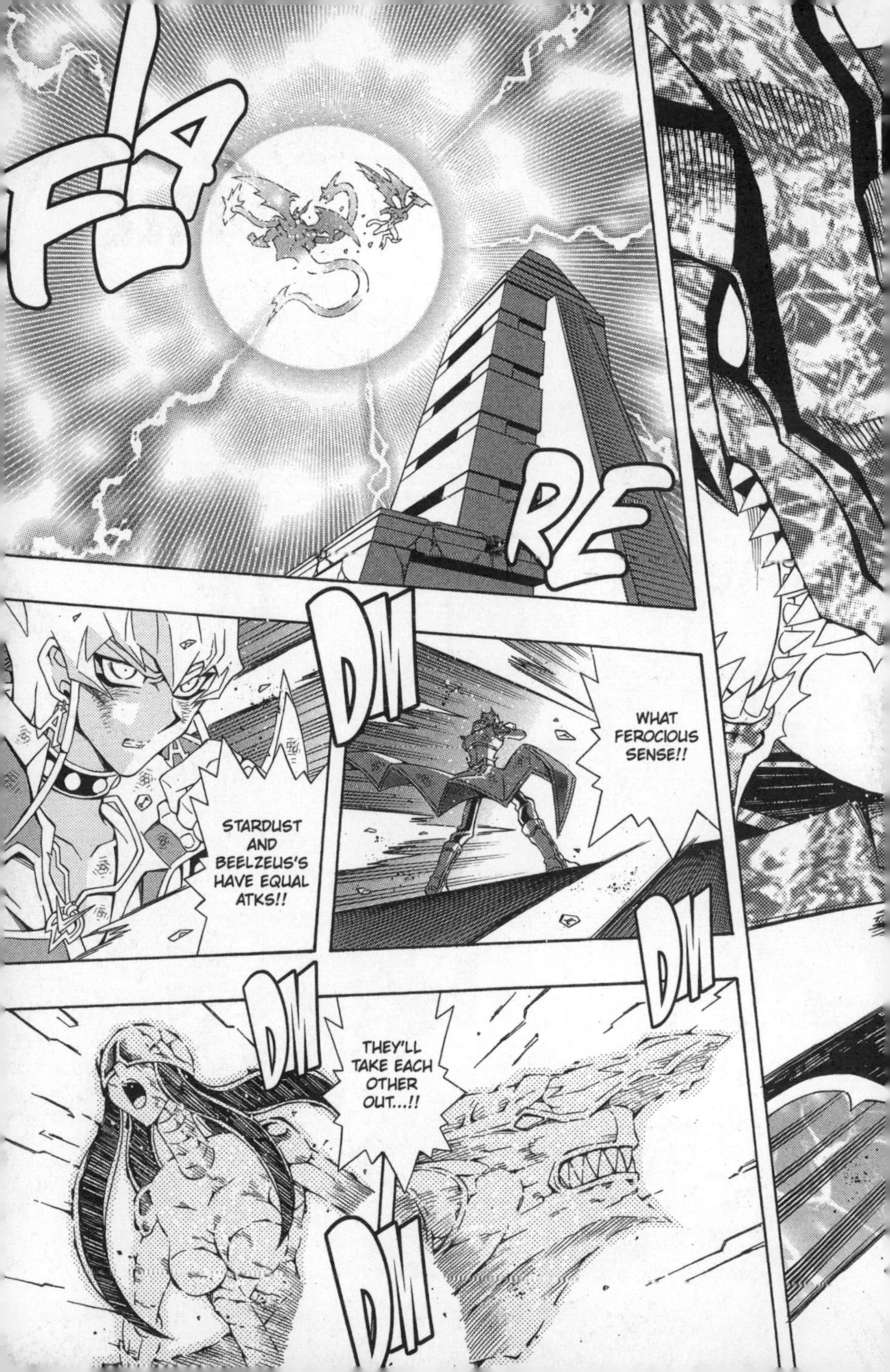
FLA
RE
DM
WHAT FEROCIOUS SENSE!!
STARDUST AND BEELZEUS'S HAVE EQUAL ATKS!!
DM
DM
THEY'LL TAKE EACH OTHER OUT...!!
DM

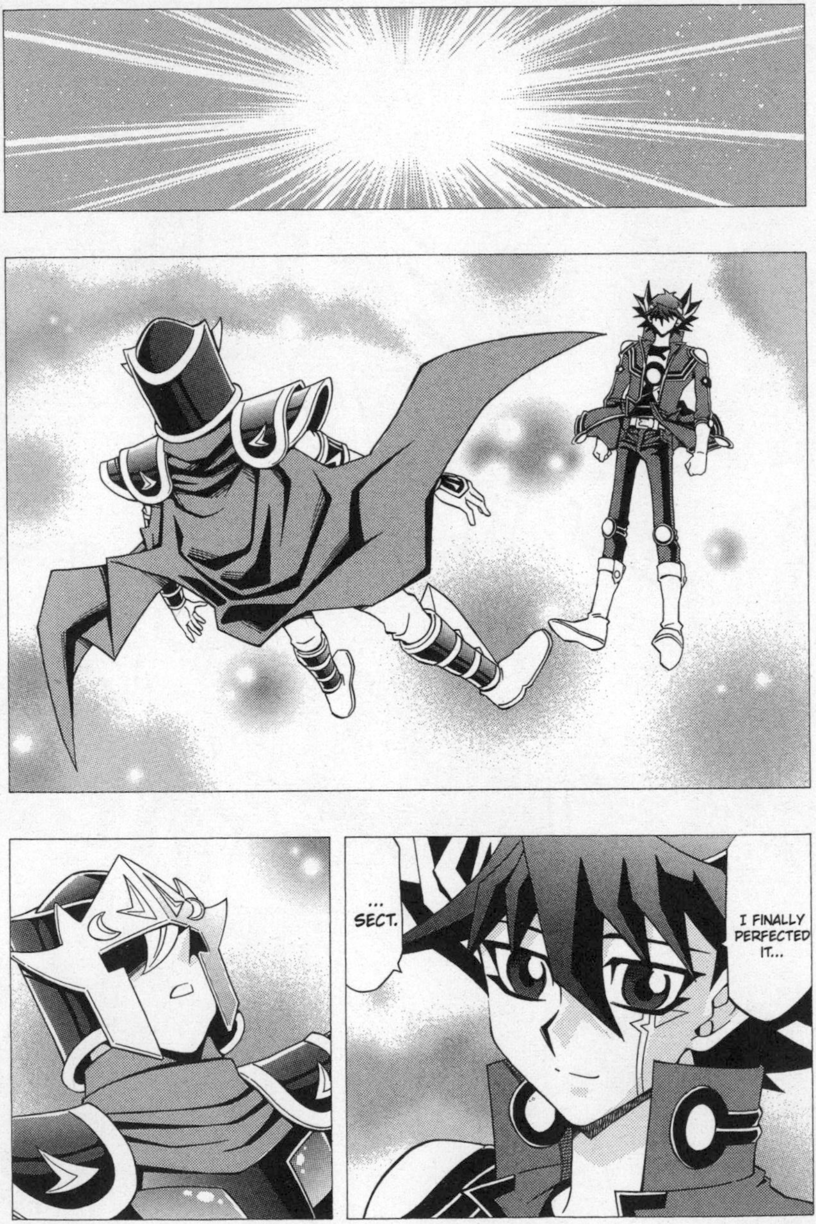
I FINALLY PERFECTED IT...
... SECT.

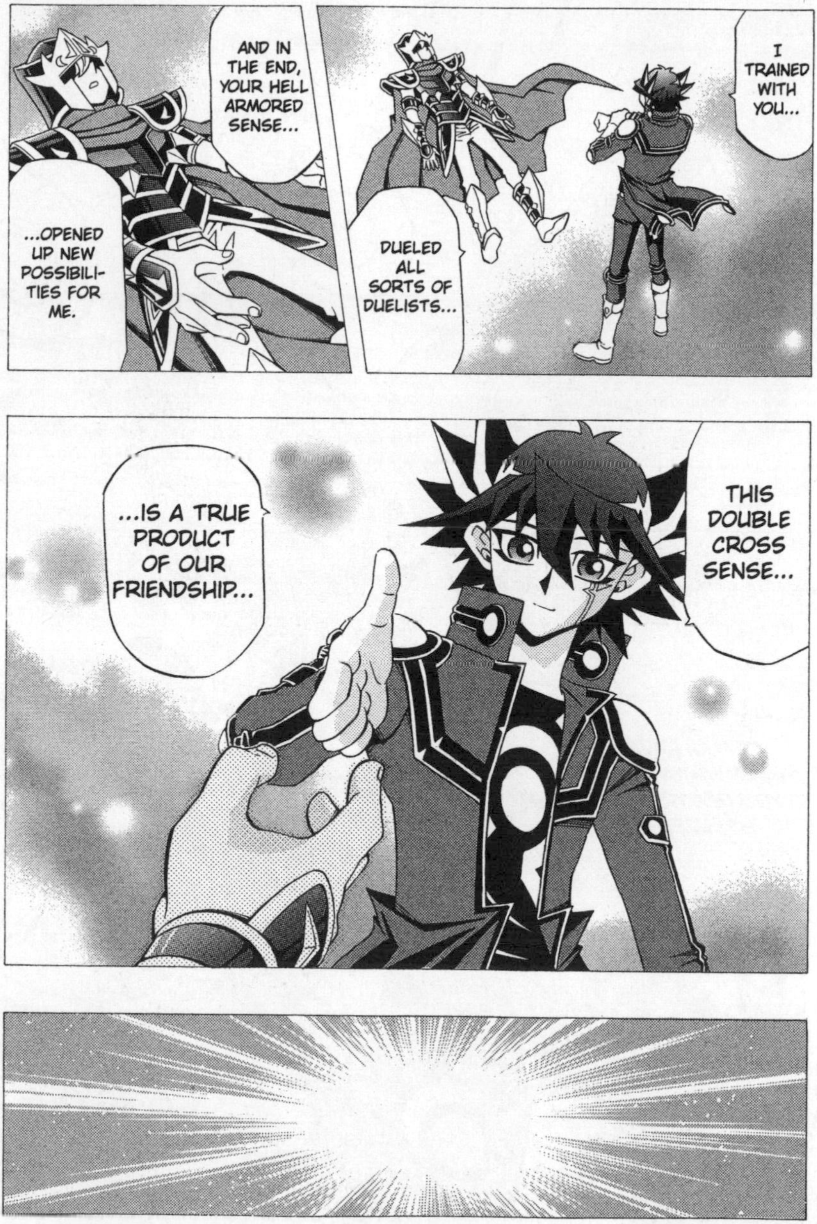
I TRAINED WITH YOU...
DUELED ALL SORTS OF DUELISTS...
AND IN THE END, YOUR HELL ARMORED SENSE...
...OPENED UP NEW POSSIBILI-TIES FOR ME.
THIS DOUBLE CROSS SENSE...
...IS A TRUE PRODUCT OF OUR FRIENDSHIP...

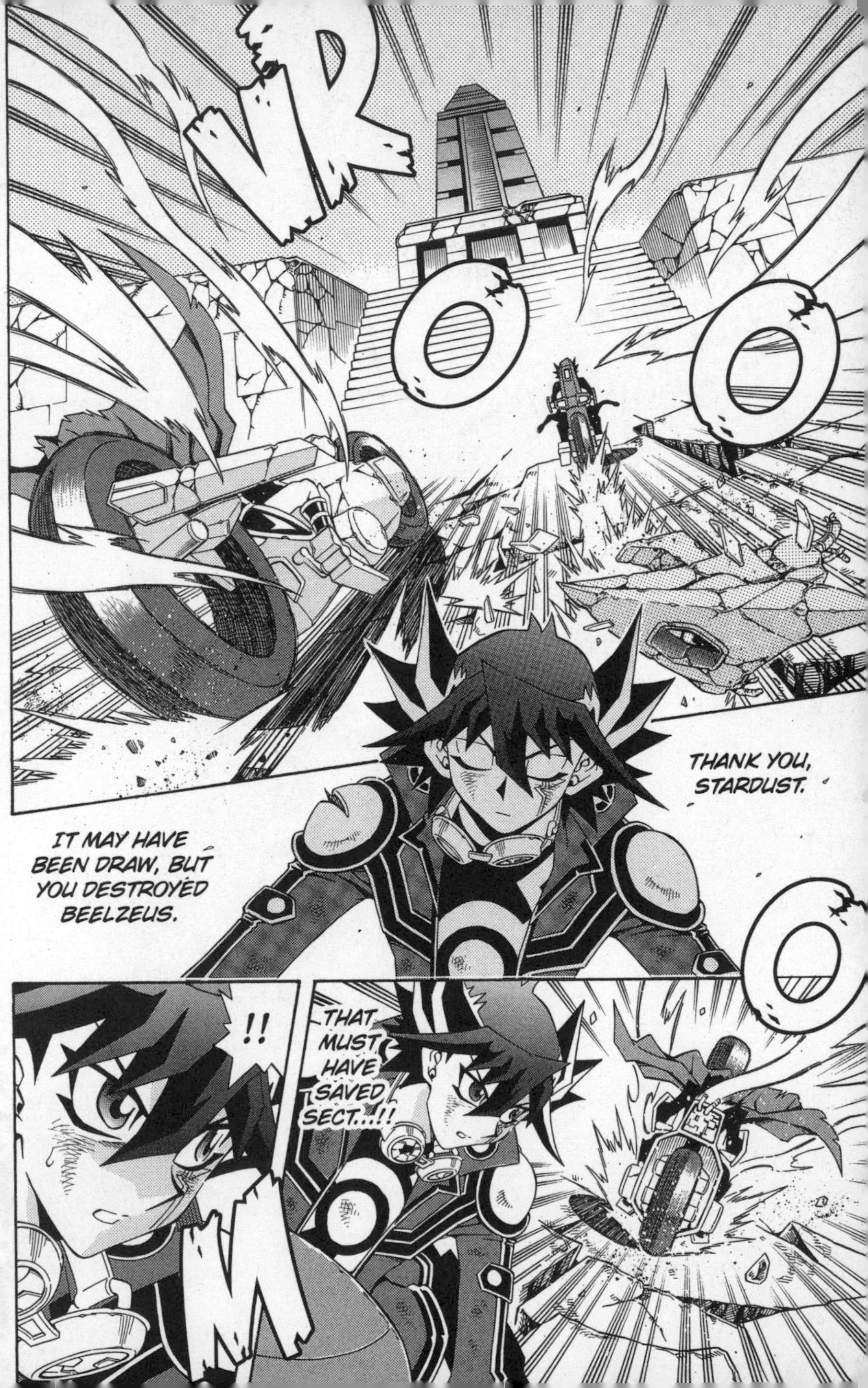
VROOOM
THANK YOU, STARDUST.
IT MAY HAVE BEEN DRAW, BUT YOU DESTROYED BEELZEUS.
THAT MUST HAVE SAVED SECT...!!
!!

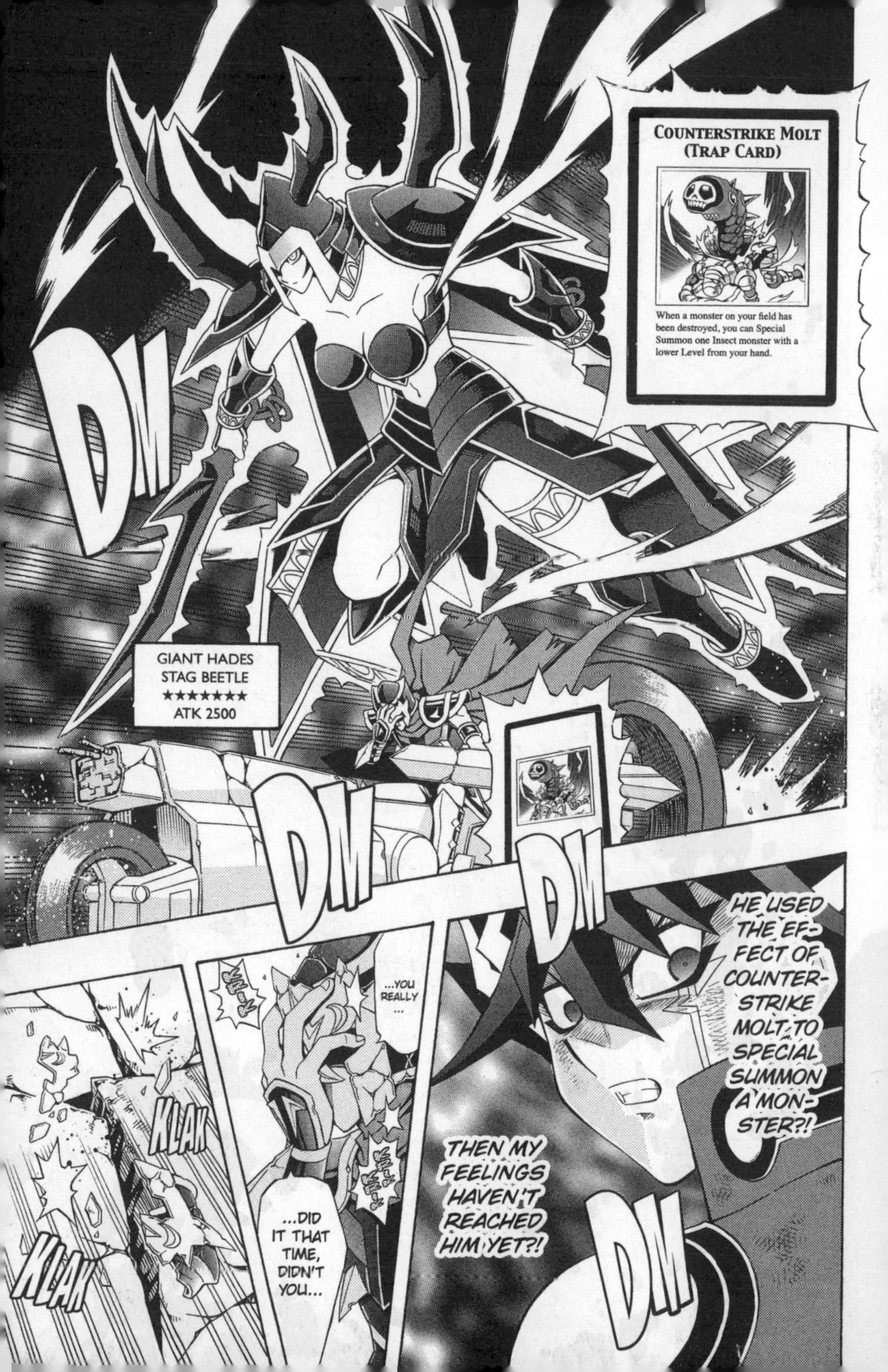
COUNTERSTRIKE MOLT
(TRAP CARD)
When a monster on your field has been destroyed, you can Special Summon one Insect monster with a lower Level from your hand.
DM
GIANT HADES
STAG BEETLE
★★★★★★★
ATK 2500
DM
DM
HE USED THE EF-FECT OF COUNTER-STRIKE MOLT TO SPECIAL SUMMON A MON-STER?!
THEN MY FEELINGS HAVEN'T REACHED HIM YET?!
DM
...YOU REALLY ...
...DID IT THAT TIME, DIDN'T YOU...
KLAK
KLAK

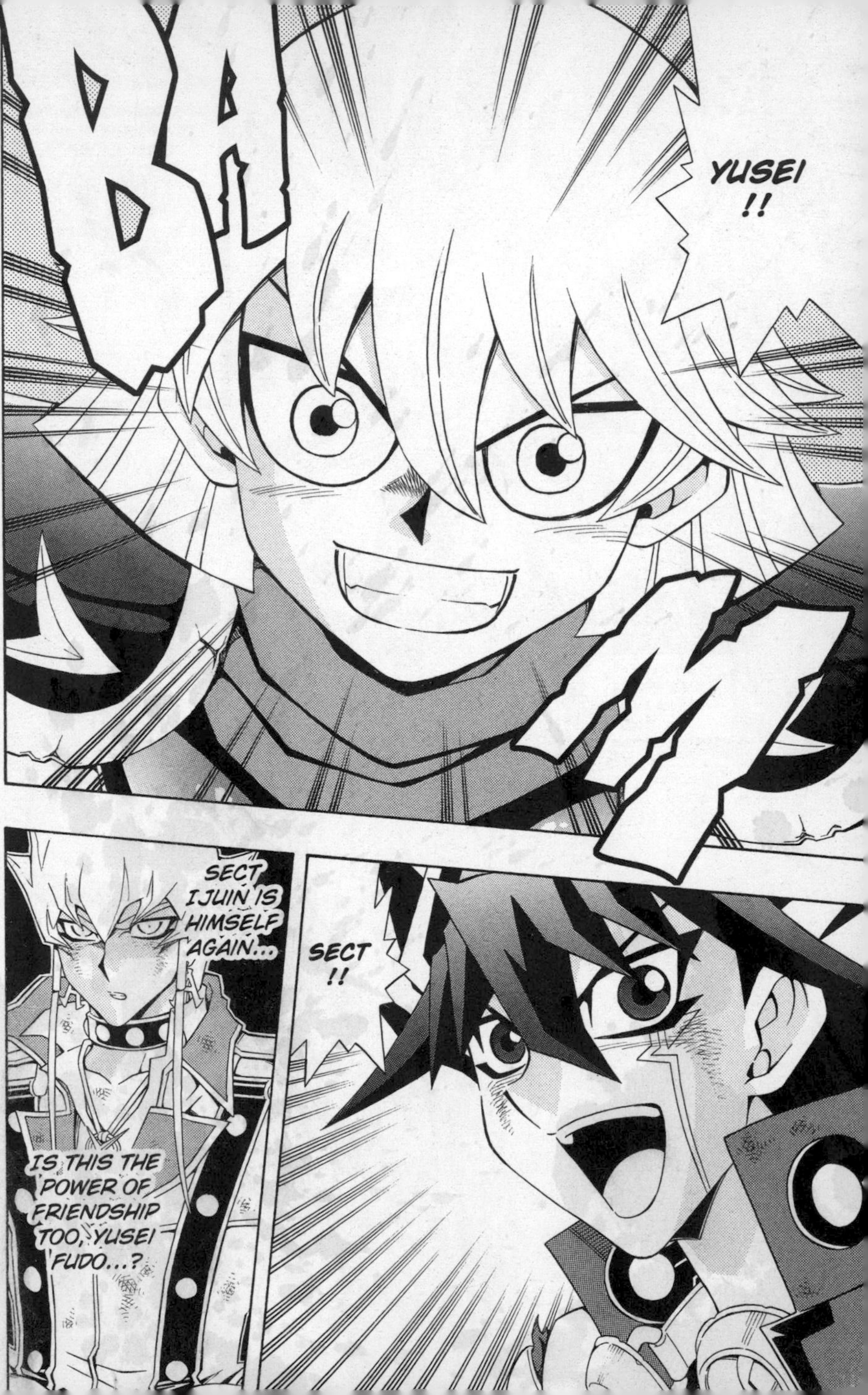
YUSEI !!
BAM
SECT !!
SECT IJUIN IS HIMSELF AGAIN...
IS THIS THE POWER OF FRIENDSHIP TOO, YUSEI FUDO...?

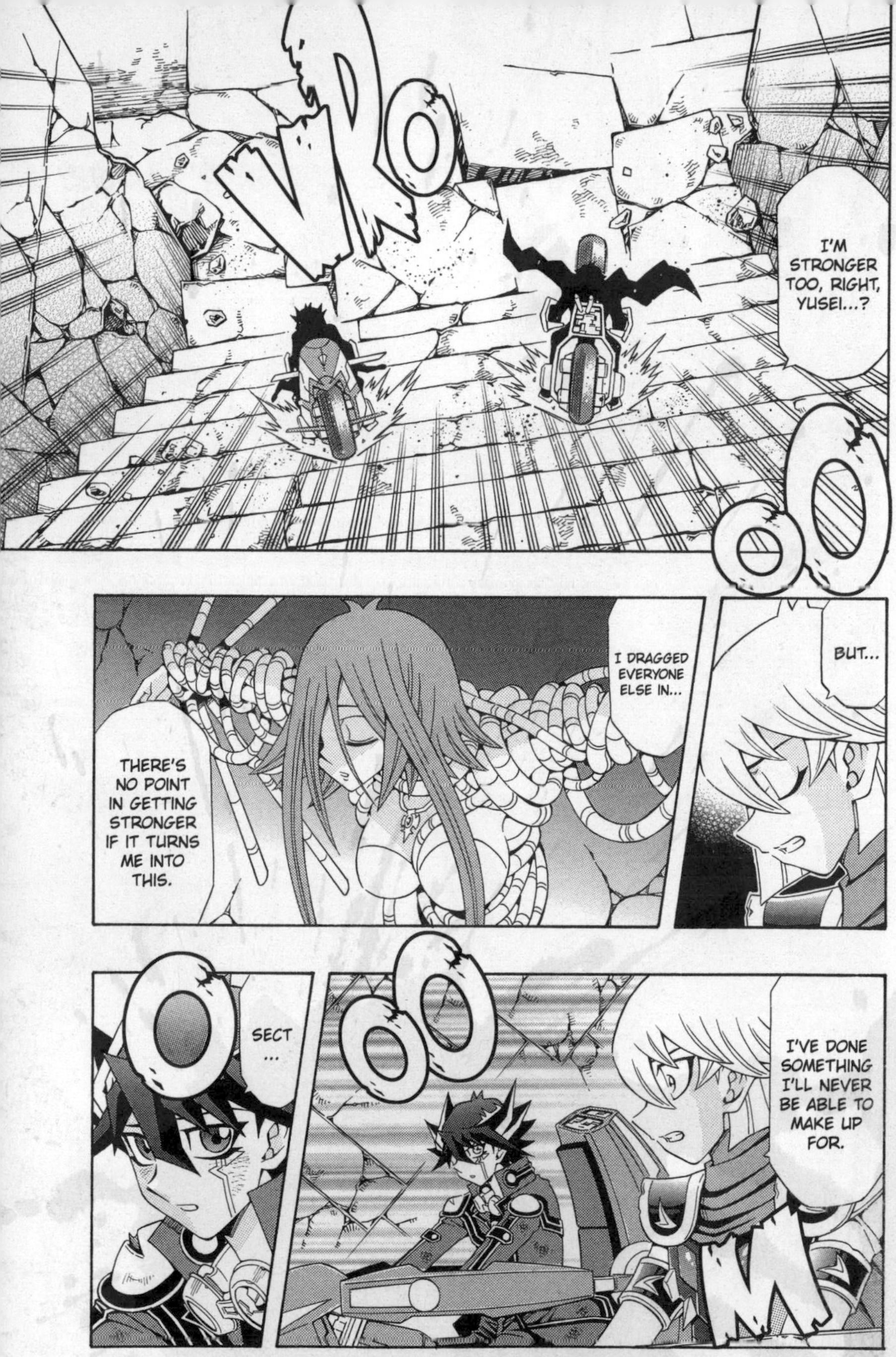
VROOOO
I'M STRONGER TOO, RIGHT, YUSEI...?
BUT...
I DRAGGED EVERYONE ELSE IN...
THERE'S NO POINT IN GETTING STRONGER IF IT TURNS ME INTO THIS.
I'VE DONE SOMETHING I'LL NEVER BE ABLE TO MAKE UP FOR.
SECT...

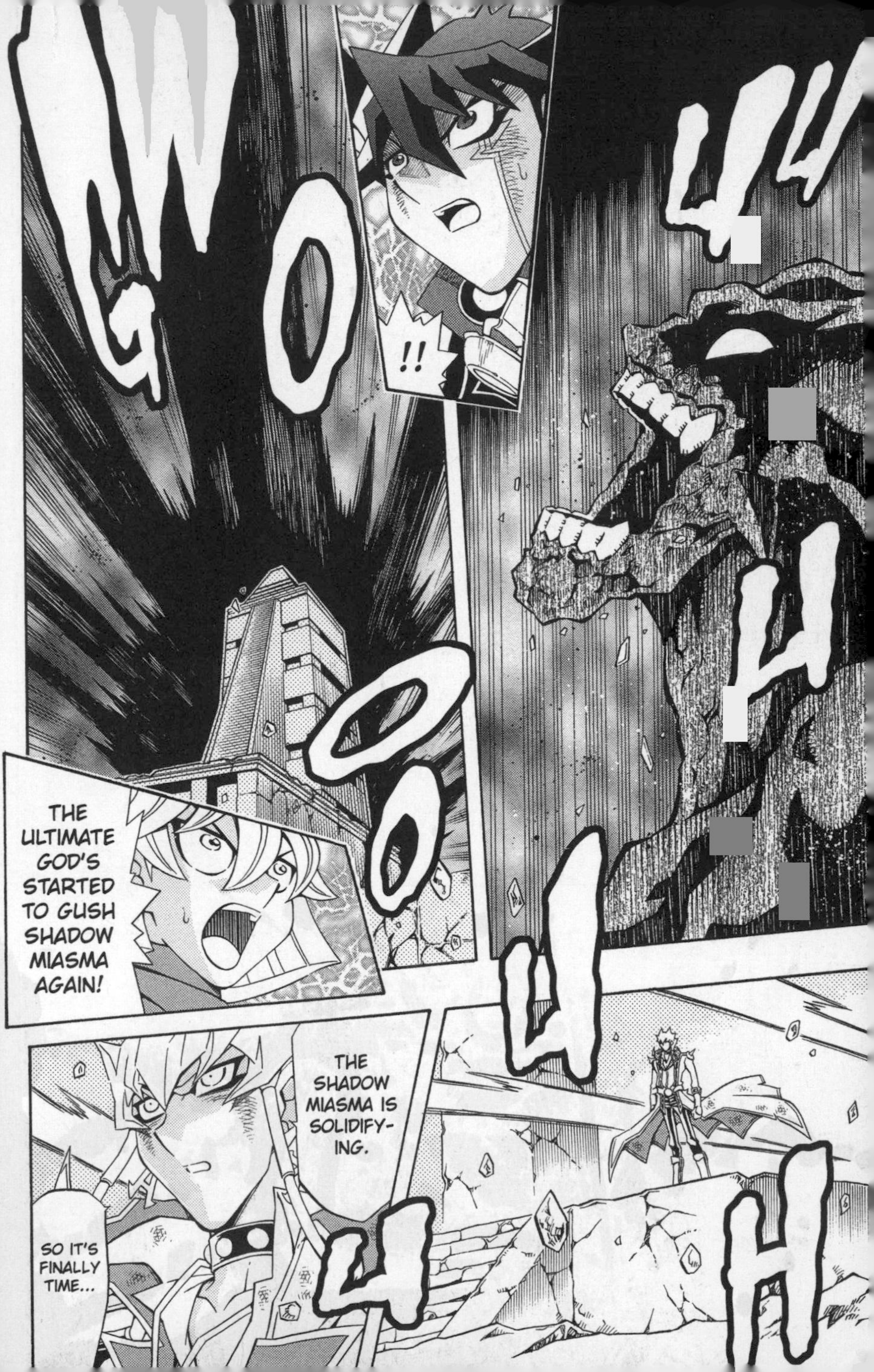
GWOOOOUUUUH
!!
THE ULTIMATE GOD'S STARTED TO GUSH SHADOW MIASMA AGAIN!
THE SHADOW MIASMA IS SOLIDIFY-ING.
SO IT'S FINALLY TIME...

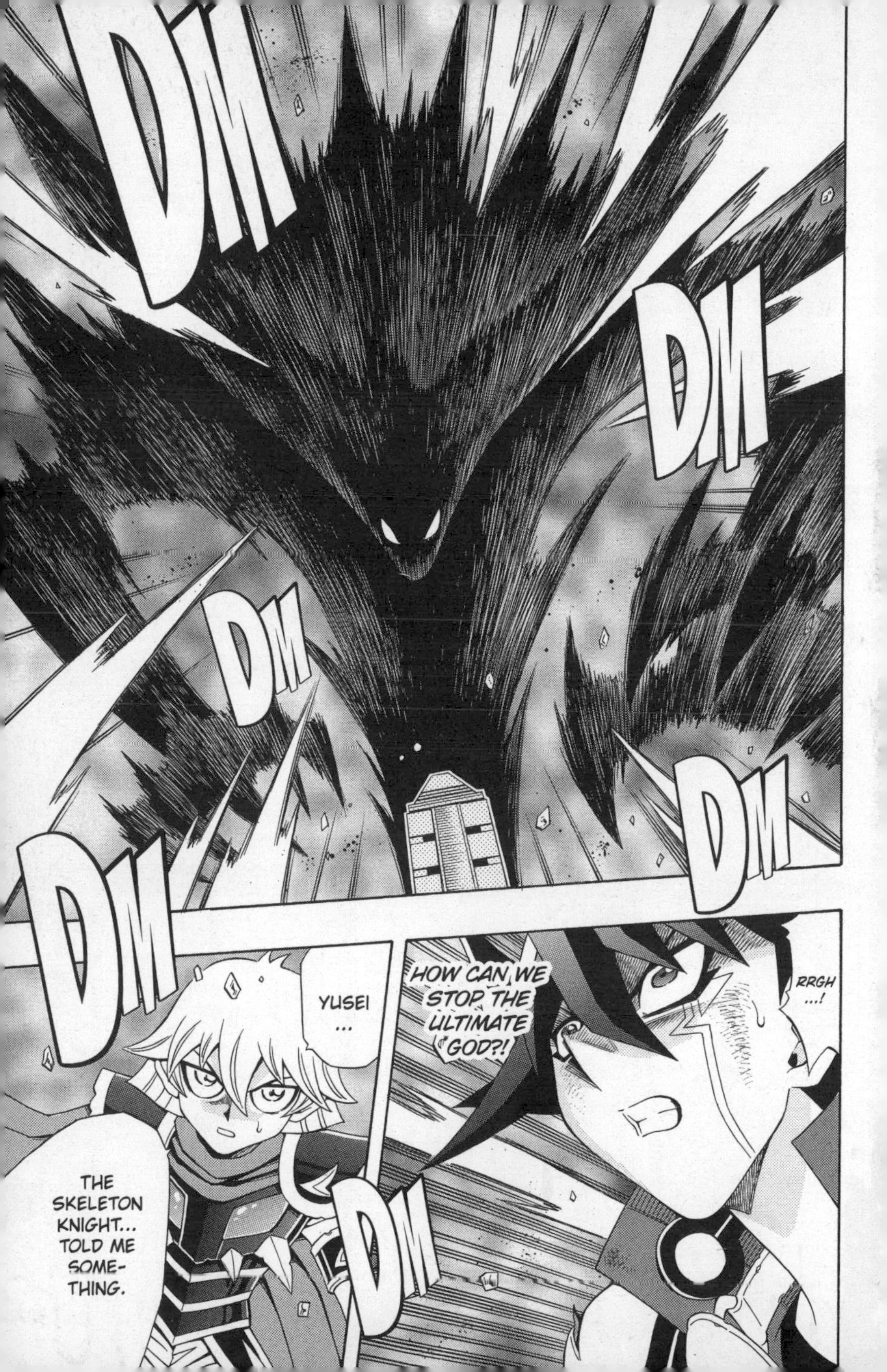
DM
DM
DM
DM
DM
DM
RRGH ...!
HOW CAN WE STOP THE ULTIMATE GOD?!
YUSEI ...
DM
THE SKELETON KNIGHT... TOLD ME SOME-THING.

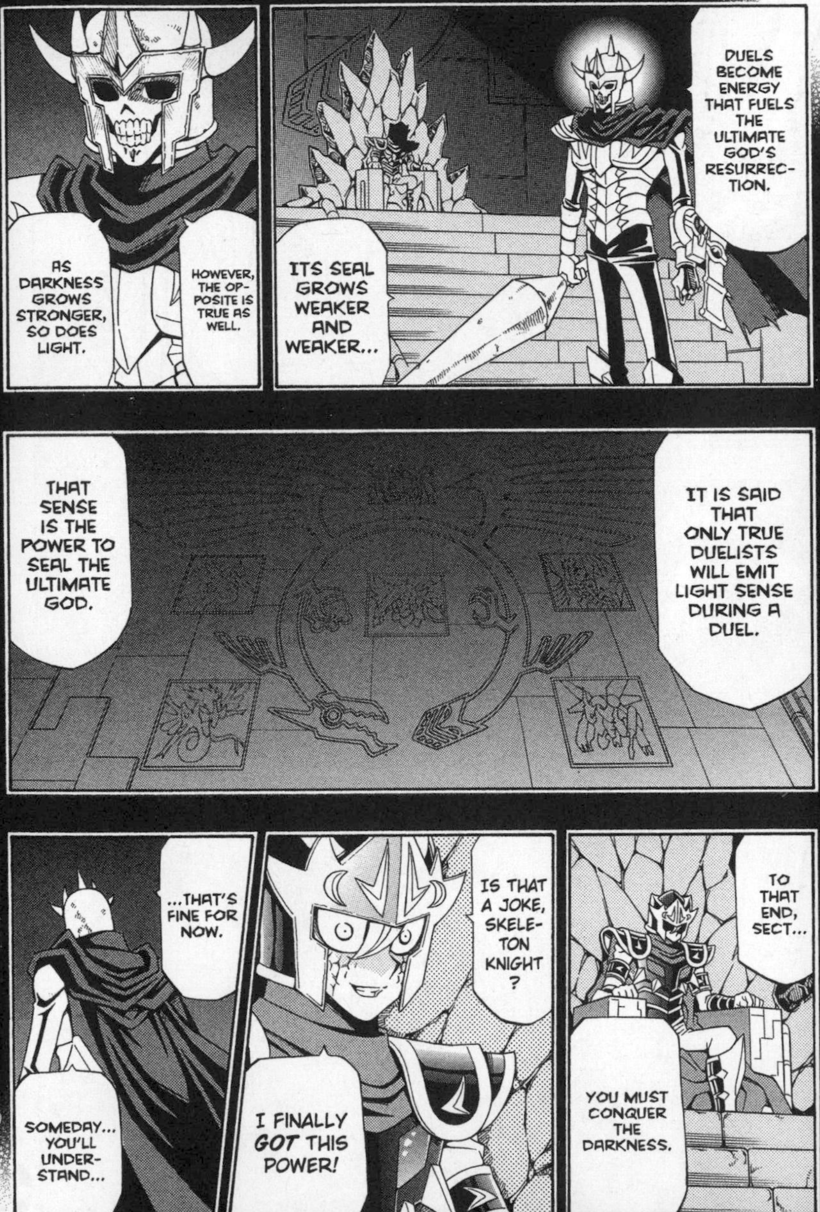
DUELS BECOME ENERGY THAT FUELS THE ULTIMATE GOD'S RESURREC-TION.
ITS SEAL GROWS WEAKER AND WEAKER...
HOWEVER, THE OP-POSITE IS TRUE AS WELL.
AS DARKNESS GROWS STRONGER, SO DOES LIGHT.
IT IS SAID THAT ONLY TRUE DUELISTS WILL EMIT LIGHT SENSE DURING A DUEL.
THAT SENSE IS THE POWER TO SEAL THE ULTIMATE GOD.
TO THAT END, SECT...
YOU MUST CONQUER THE DARKNESS.
IS THAT A JOKE, SKELE-TON KNIGHT?
I FINALLY *GOT* THIS POWER!
...THAT'S FINE FOR NOW.
SOMEDAY... YOU'LL UNDER-STAND...

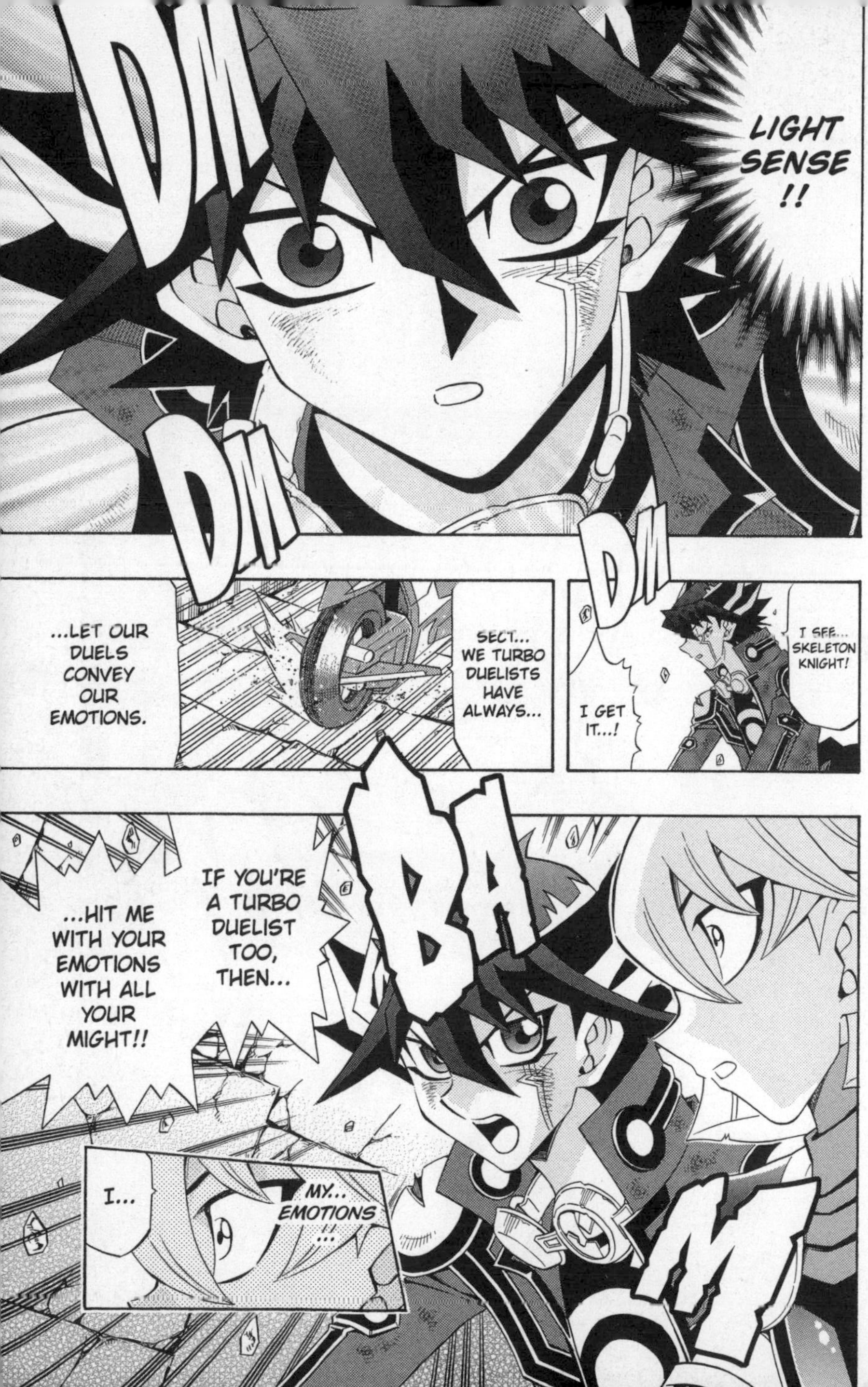
LIGHT SENSE !!
DM
DM
DM
I SEE... SKELETON KNIGHT!
I GET IT...!
SECT... WE TURBO DUELISTS HAVE ALWAYS...
...LET OUR DUELS CONVEY OUR EMOTIONS.
BA
IF YOU'RE A TURBO DUELIST TOO, THEN...
...HIT ME WITH YOUR EMOTIONS WITH ALL YOUR MIGHT!!
M
MY... EMOTIONS !! ...
I...

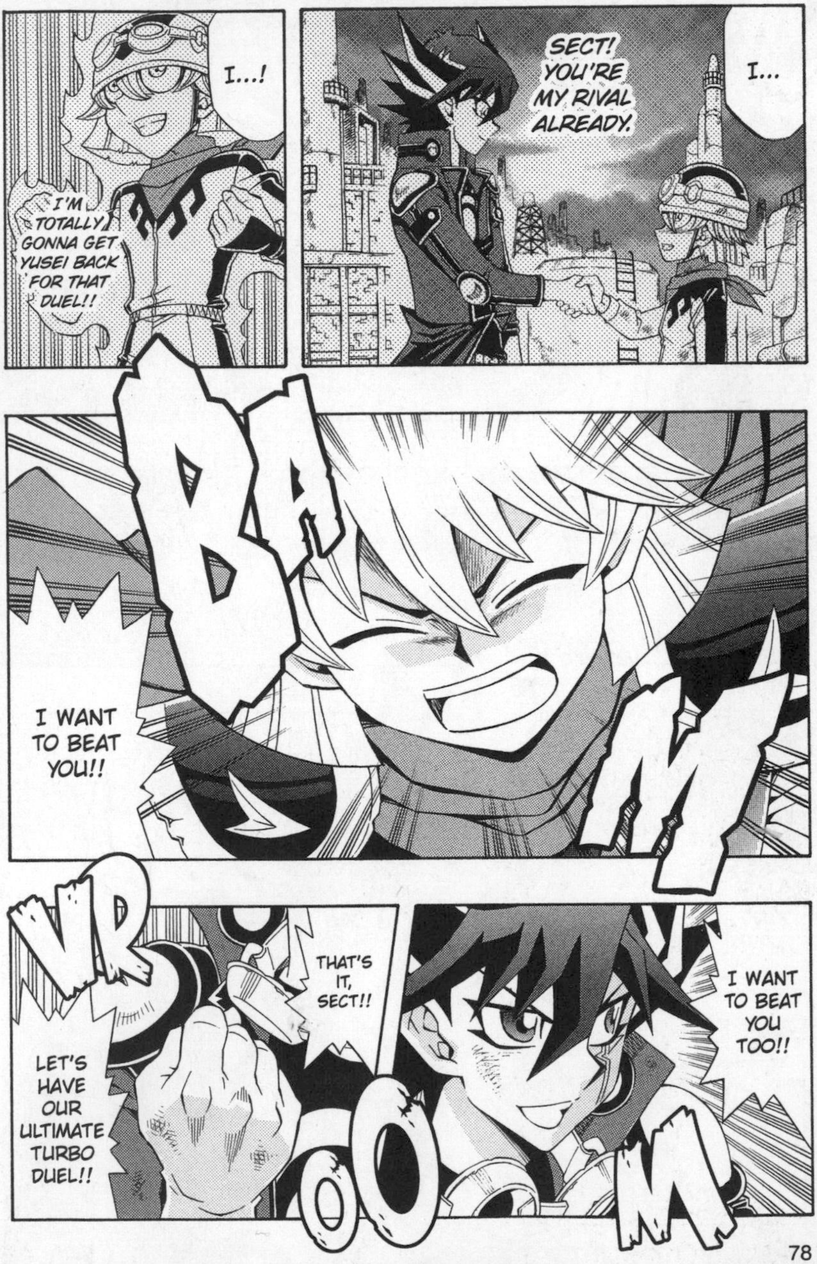
I...
SECT! YOU'RE MY RIVAL ALREADY.
I...!
I'M TOTALLY GONNA GET YUSEI BACK FOR THAT DUEL!!
BAM
I WANT TO BEAT YOU!!
I WANT TO BEAT YOU TOO!!
THAT'S IT, SECT!!
LET'S HAVE OUR ULTIMATE TURBO DUEL!!

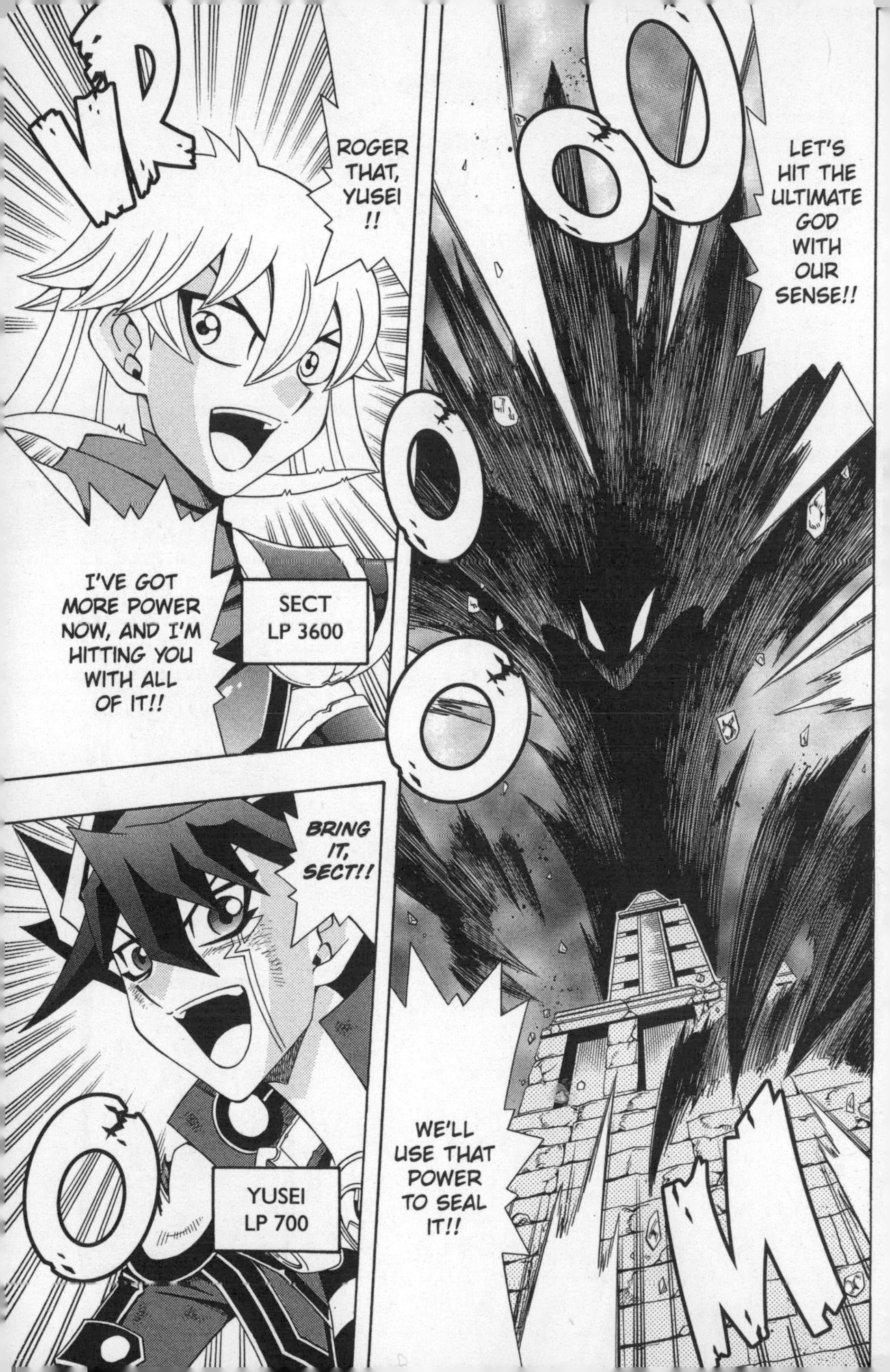
LET'S HIT THE ULTIMATE GOD WITH OUR SENSE!!
WE'LL USE THAT POWER TO SEAL IT!!
ROGER THAT, YUSEI!!
I'VE GOT MORE POWER NOW, AND I'M HITTING YOU WITH ALL OF IT!!
SECT
LP 3600
BRING IT, SECT!!
YUSEI
LP 700

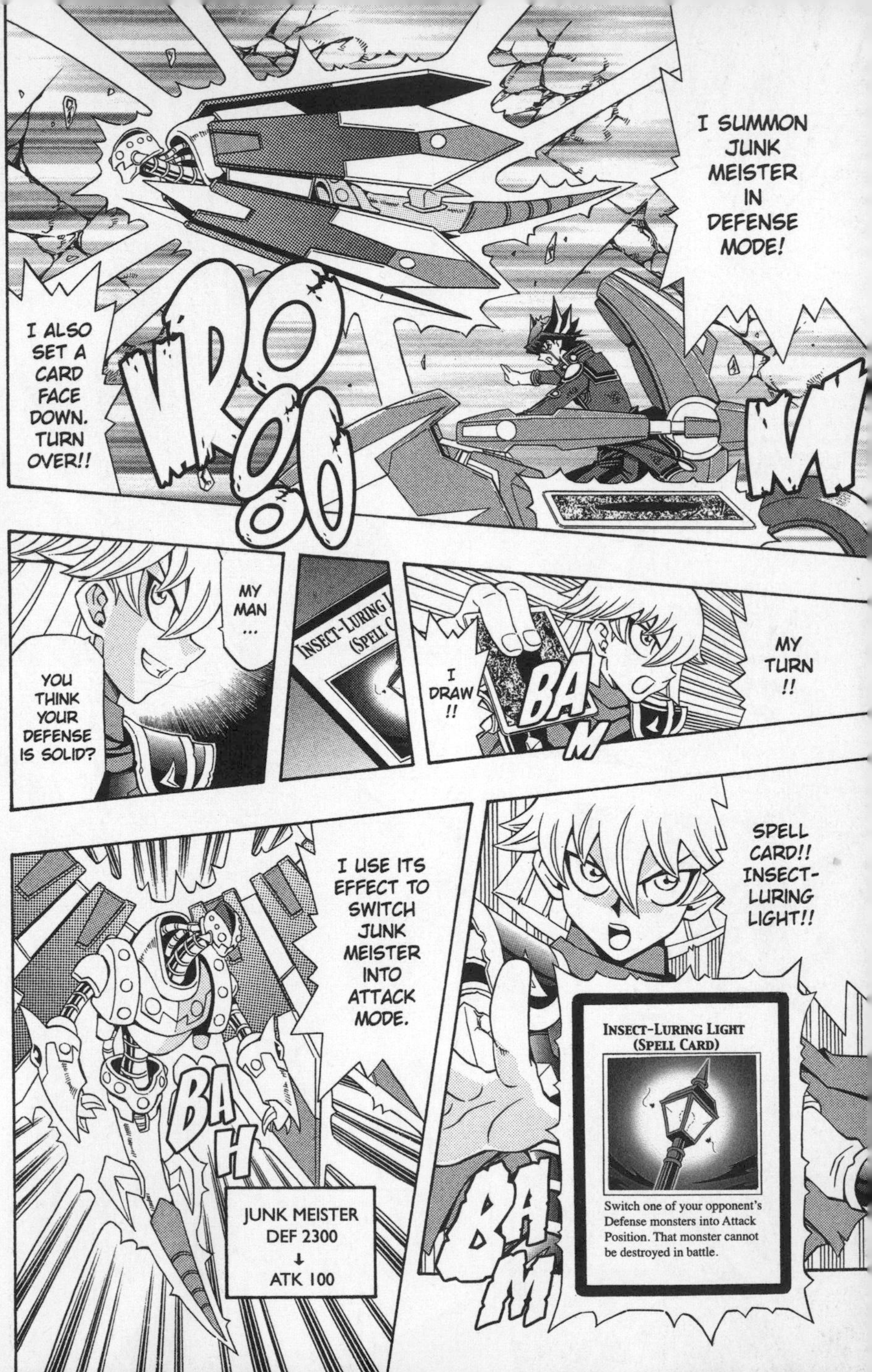
I SUMMON JUNK MEISTER IN DEFENSE MODE!
VROOOOM
I ALSO SET A CARD FACE DOWN. TURN OVER!!
MY TURN!!
BAM
I DRAW!!
MY MAN...
YOU THINK YOUR DEFENSE IS SOLID?
SPELL CARD!! INSECT-LURING LIGHT!!
INSECT-LURING LIGHT (SPELL CARD)
Switch one of your opponent's Defense monsters into Attack Position. That monster cannot be destroyed in battle.
BAM
I USE ITS EFFECT TO SWITCH JUNK MEISTER INTO ATTACK MODE.
BAH
JUNK MEISTER DEF 2300 ↓ ATK 100

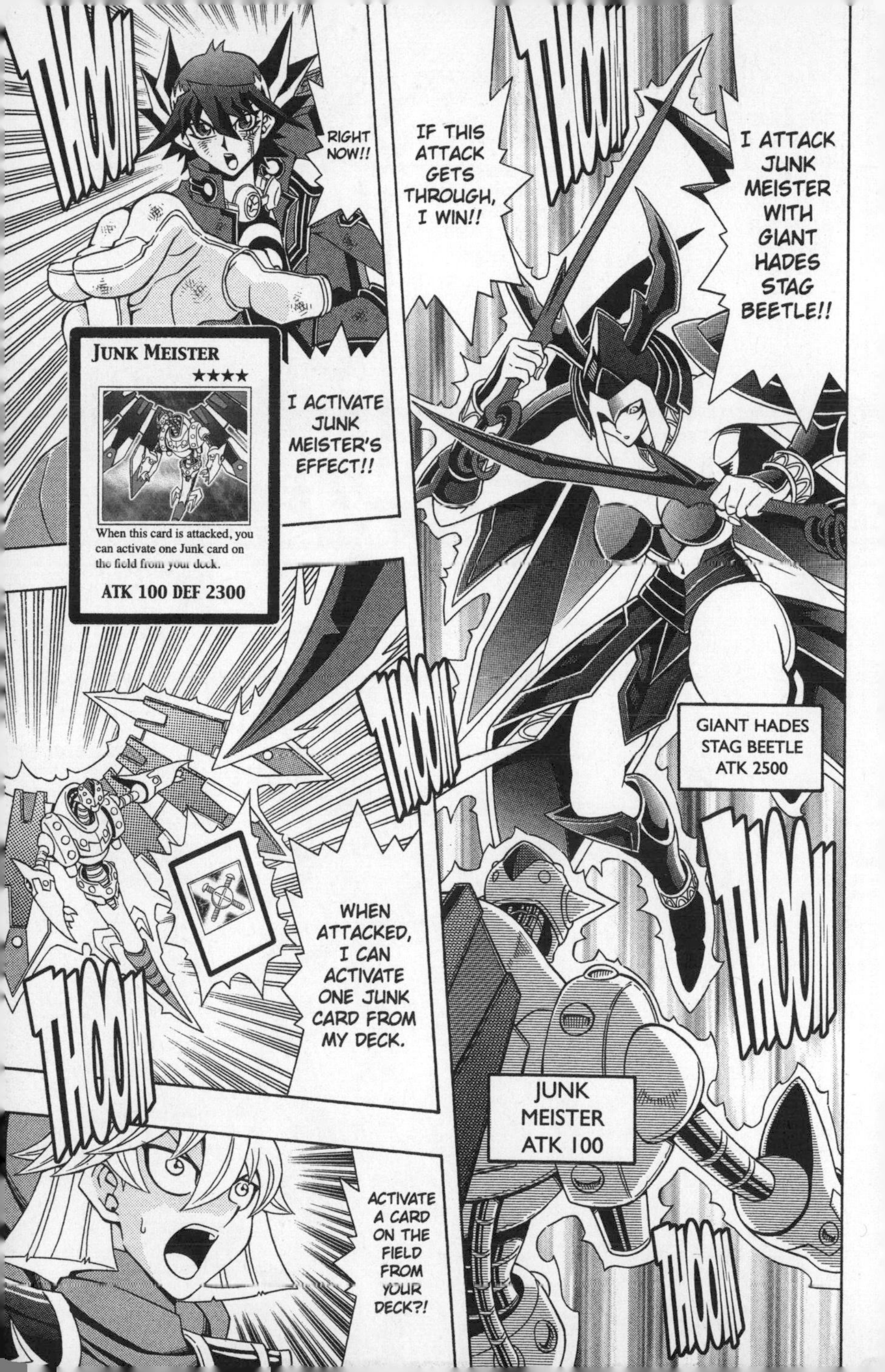
THOOM
I ATTACK JUNK MEISTER WITH GIANT HADES STAG BEETLE!!
IF THIS ATTACK GETS THROUGH, I WIN!!
GIANT HADES STAG BEETLE ATK 2500
THOOM
JUNK MEISTER ATK 100
THOOM
THOOM
RIGHT NOW!!
I ACTIVATE JUNK MEISTER'S EFFECT!!
JUNK MEISTER
★★★★
When this card is attacked, you can activate one Junk card on the field from your deck.
ATK 100 DEF 2300
THOOM
WHEN ATTACKED, I CAN ACTIVATE ONE JUNK CARD FROM MY DECK.
THOOM
ACTIVATE A CARD ON THE FIELD FROM YOUR DECK?!

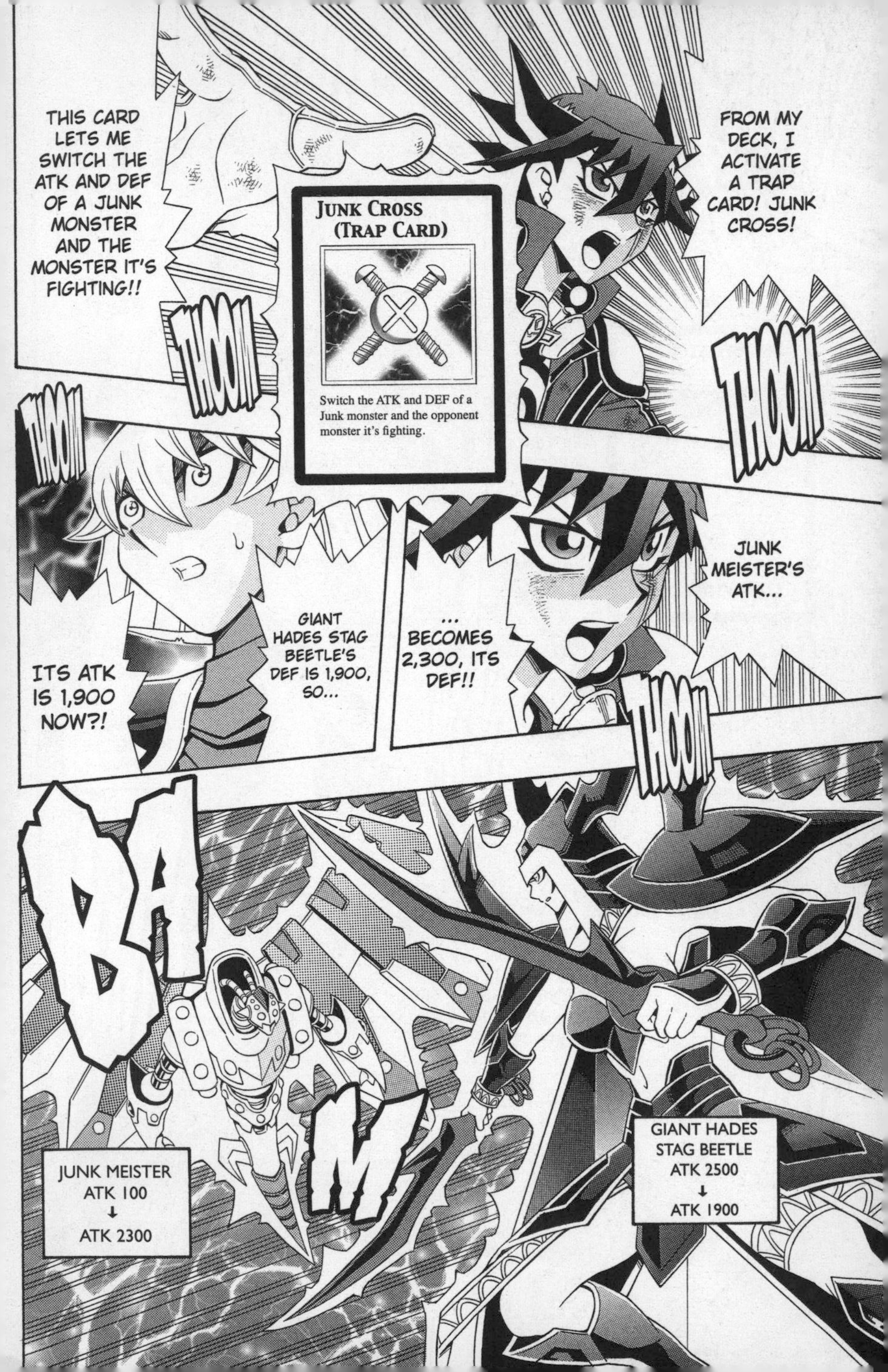
FROM MY DECK, I ACTIVATE A TRAP CARD! JUNK CROSS!
THOOM
JUNK CROSS (TRAP CARD)
Switch the ATK and DEF of a Junk monster and the opponent monster it's fighting.
THIS CARD LETS ME SWITCH THE ATK AND DEF OF A JUNK MONSTER AND THE MONSTER IT'S FIGHTING!!
THOOM
JUNK MEISTER'S ATK...
... BECOMES 2,300, ITS DEF!!
THOOM
GIANT HADES STAG BEETLE'S DEF IS 1,900, SO...
ITS ATK IS 1,900 NOW?!
THOOM
GIANT HADES STAG BEETLE ATK 2500 ↓ ATK 1900
JUNK MEISTER ATK 100 ↓ ATK 2300
BAM

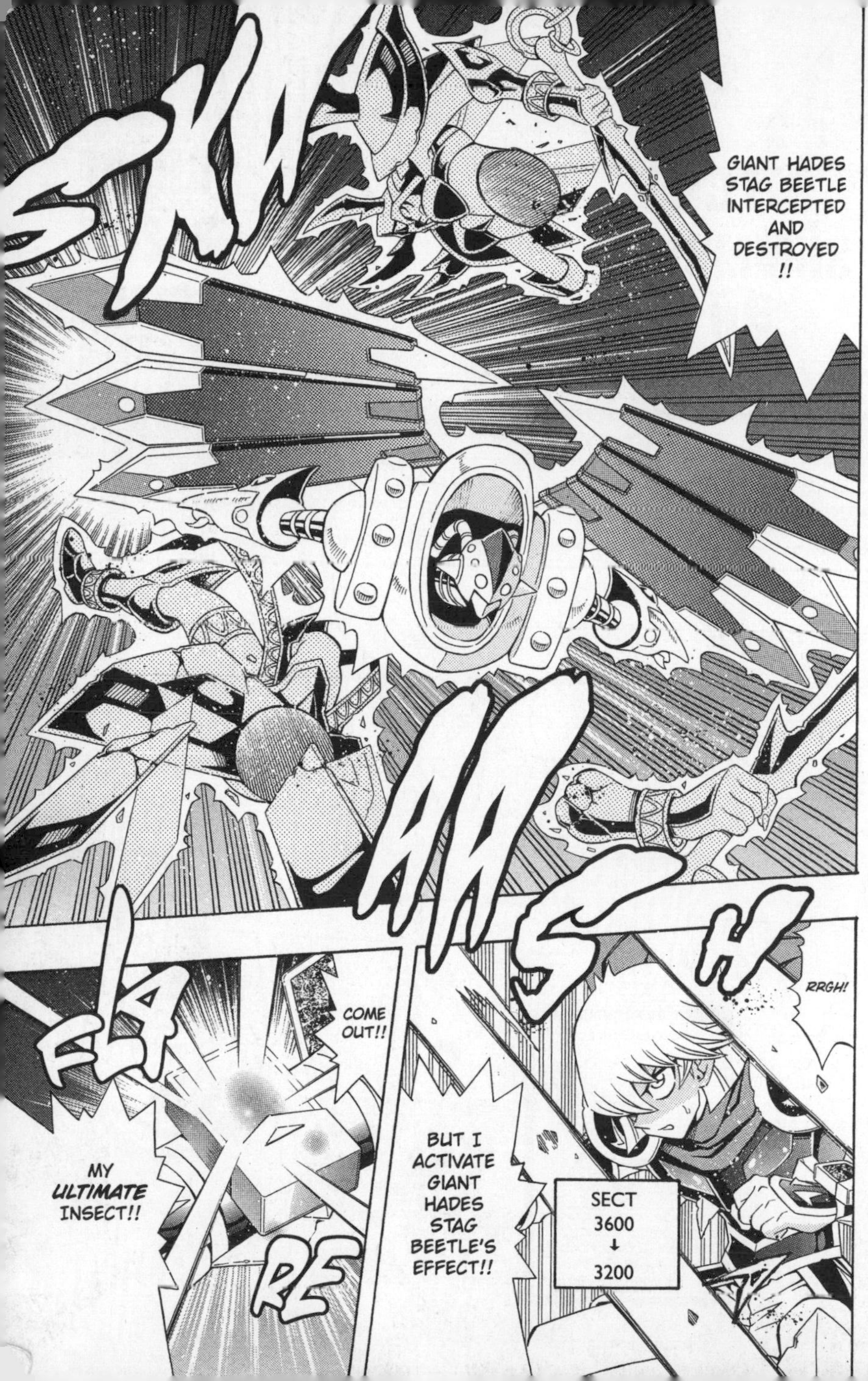
GIANT HADES STAG BEETLE INTERCEPTED AND DESTROYED!!
RRGH!
BUT I ACTIVATE GIANT HADES STAG BEETLE'S EFFECT!!
SECT
3600
↓
3200
COME OUT!!
MY ULTIMATE INSECT!!
FLARE

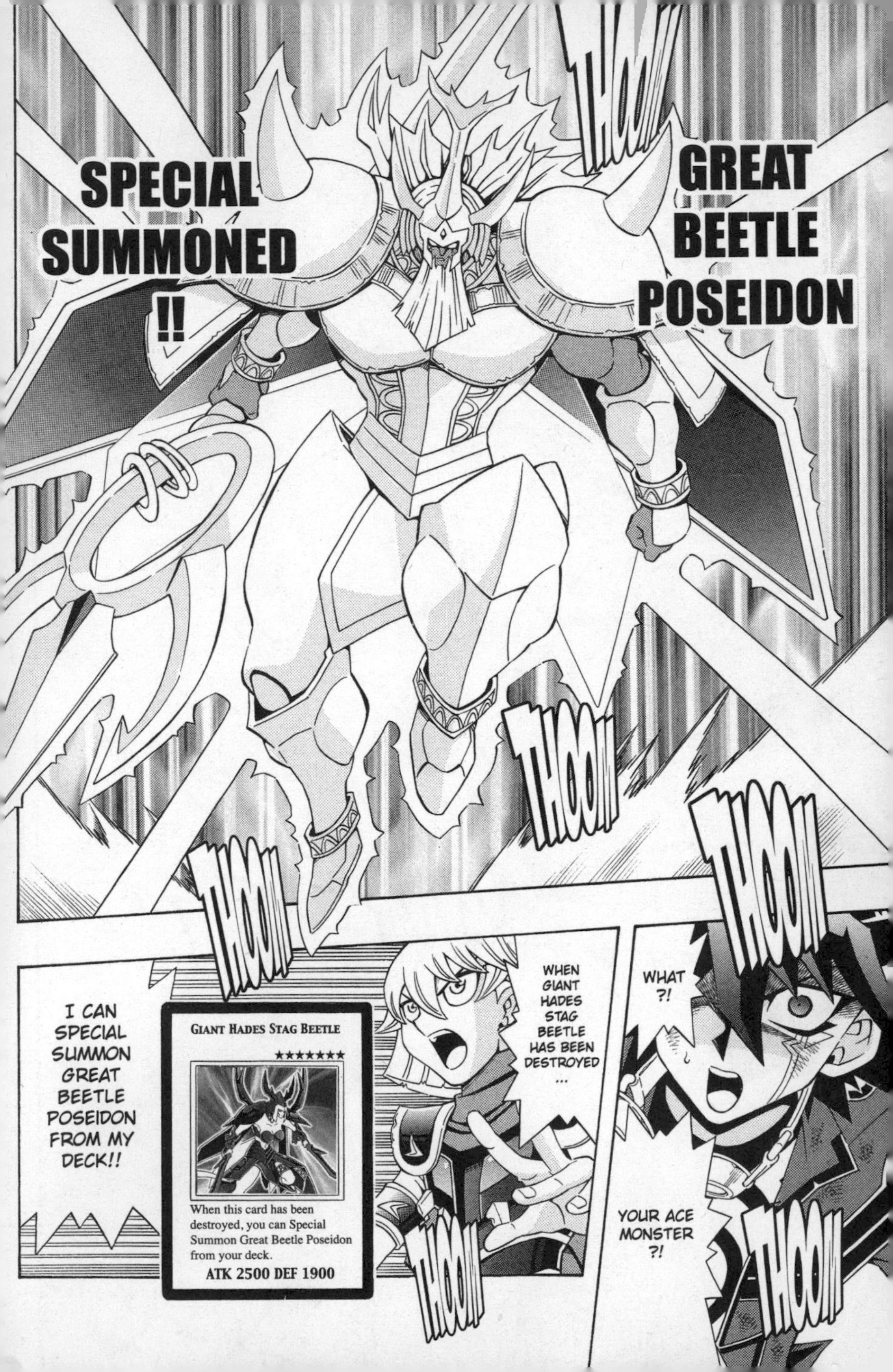
GREAT BEETLE POSEIDON
THOOM
SPECIAL SUMMONED !!
THOOM
THOOM
THOOM
WHAT ?!
YOUR ACE MONSTER ?!
THOOM
WHEN GIANT HADES STAG BEETLE HAS BEEN DESTROYED ...
THOOM
I CAN SPECIAL SUMMON GREAT BEETLE POSEIDON FROM MY DECK!!
GIANT HADES STAG BEETLE
★★★★★★★
When this card has been destroyed, you can Special Summon Great Beetle Poseidon from your deck.
ATK 2500 DEF 1900

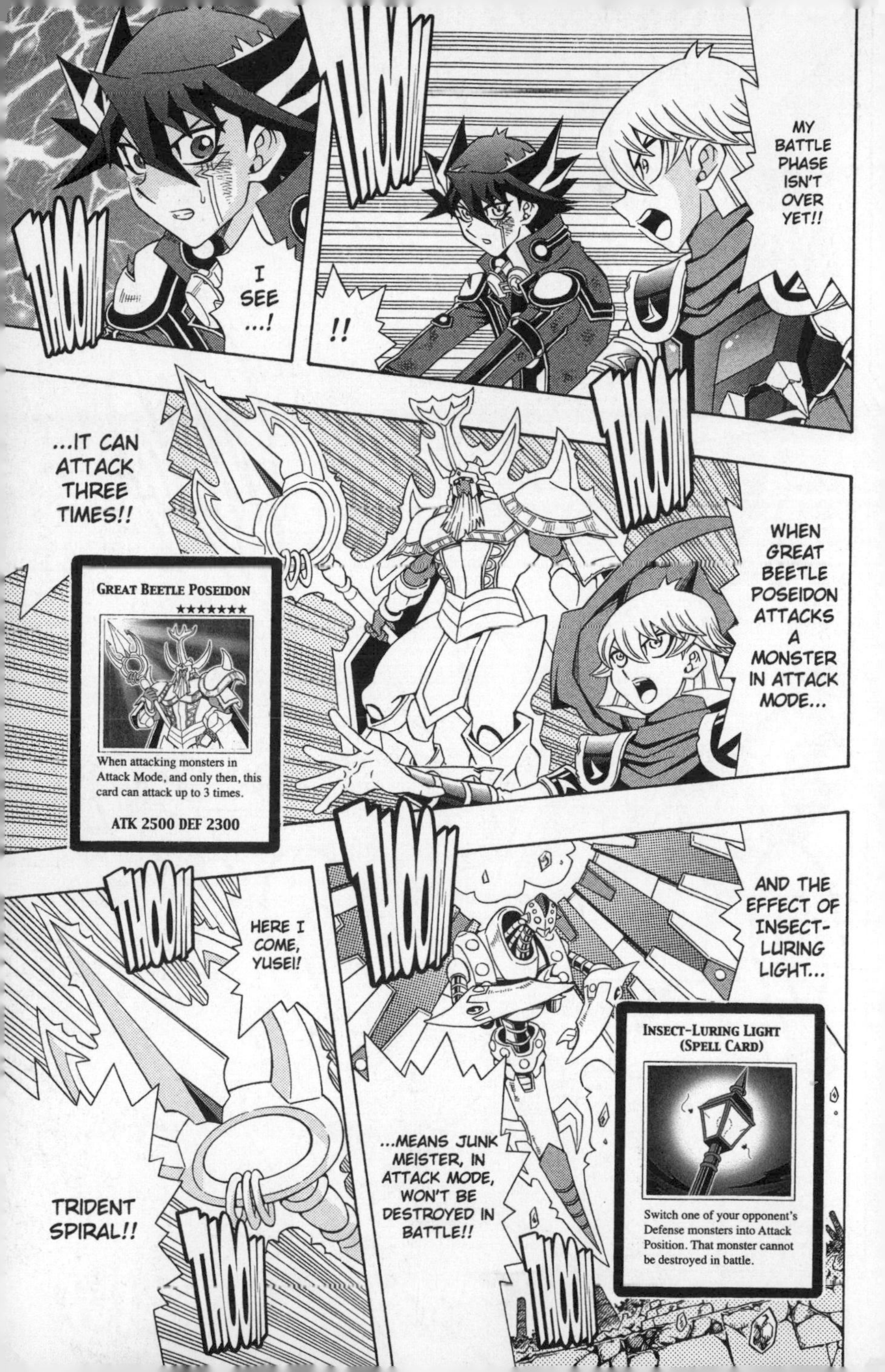
MY BATTLE PHASE ISN'T OVER YET!!
THOOM
!!
I SEE ...!
THOOM
THOOM
WHEN GREAT BEETLE POSEIDON ATTACKS A MONSTER IN ATTACK MODE...
...IT CAN ATTACK THREE TIMES!!
GREAT BEETLE POSEIDON
★★★★★★★
When attacking monsters in Attack Mode, and only then, this card can attack up to 3 times.
ATK 2500 DEF 2300
THOOM
AND THE EFFECT OF INSECT-LURING LIGHT...
INSECT-LURING LIGHT (SPELL CARD)
Switch one of your opponent's Defense monsters into Attack Position. That monster cannot be destroyed in battle.
...MEANS JUNK MEISTER, IN ATTACK MODE, WON'T BE DESTROYED IN BATTLE!!
THOOM
THOOM
HERE I COME, YUSEI!
TRIDENT SPIRAL!!
THOOM

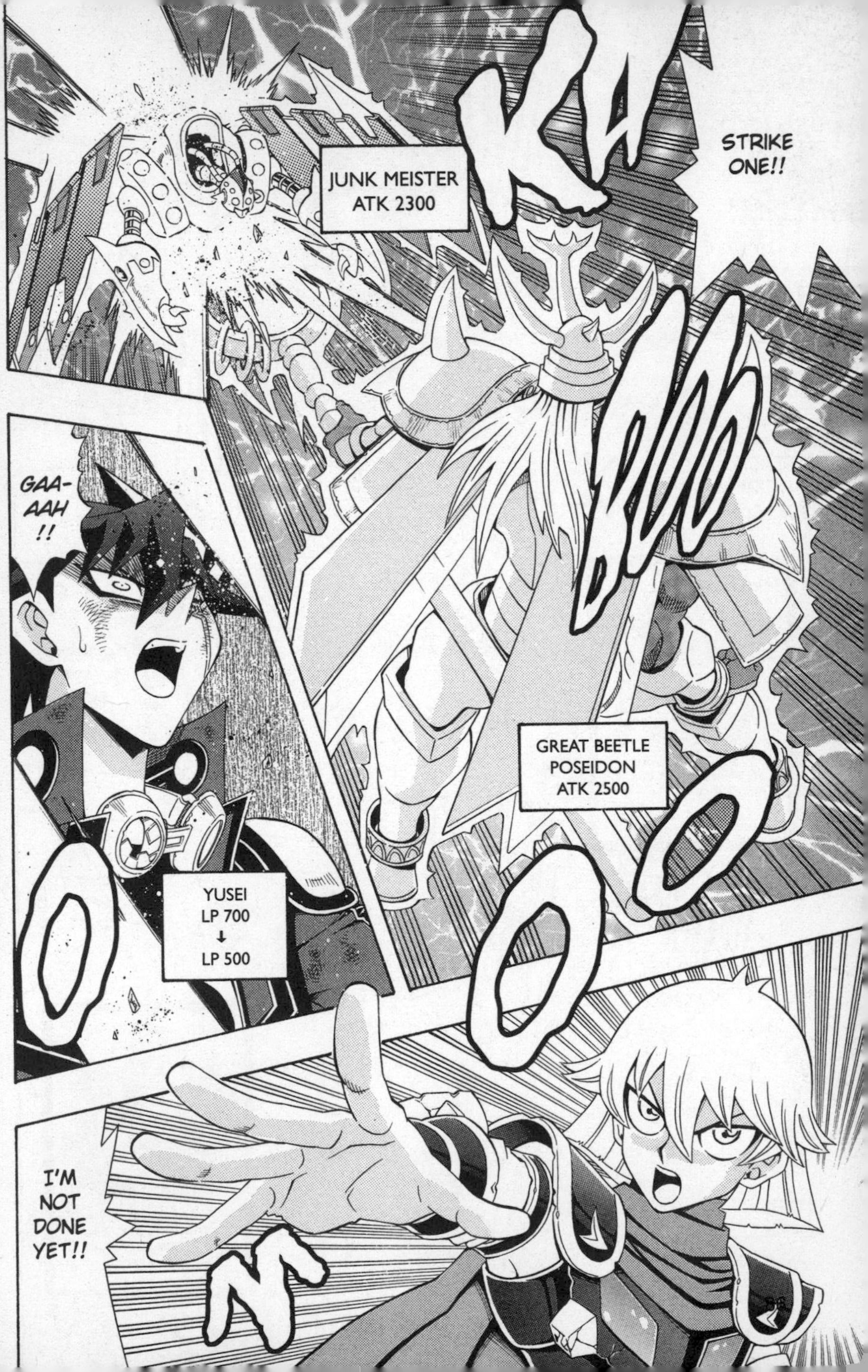
STRIKE ONE!!
JUNK MEISTER ATK 2300
GREAT BEETLE POSEIDON ATK 2500
GAA-AAH!!
YUSEI LP 700 ↓ LP 500
I'M NOT DONE YET!!

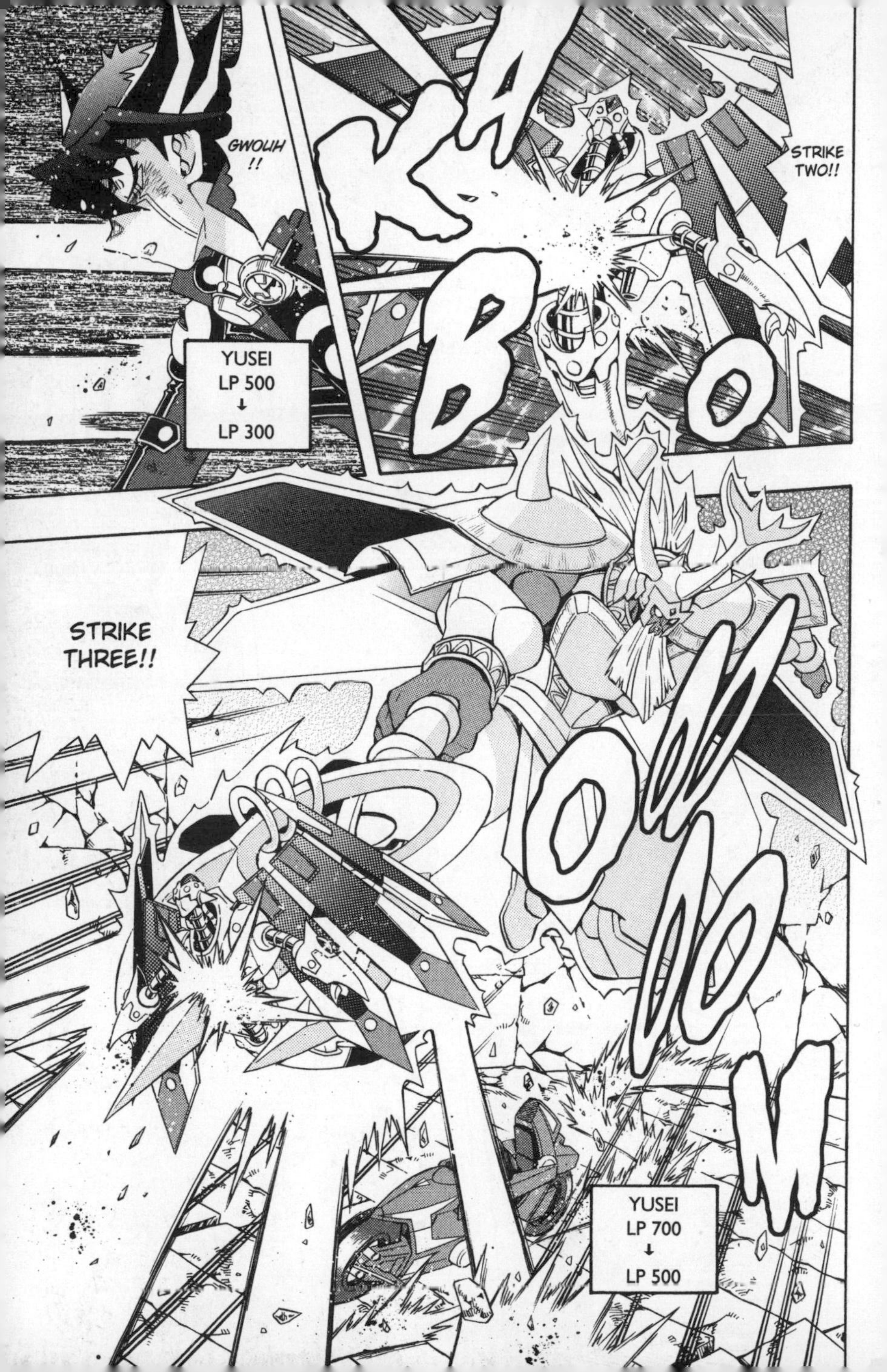
STRIKE TWO!!
GWOUH !!
YUSEI
LP 500
↓
LP 300
STRIKE THREE!!
YUSEI
LP 700
↓
LP 500

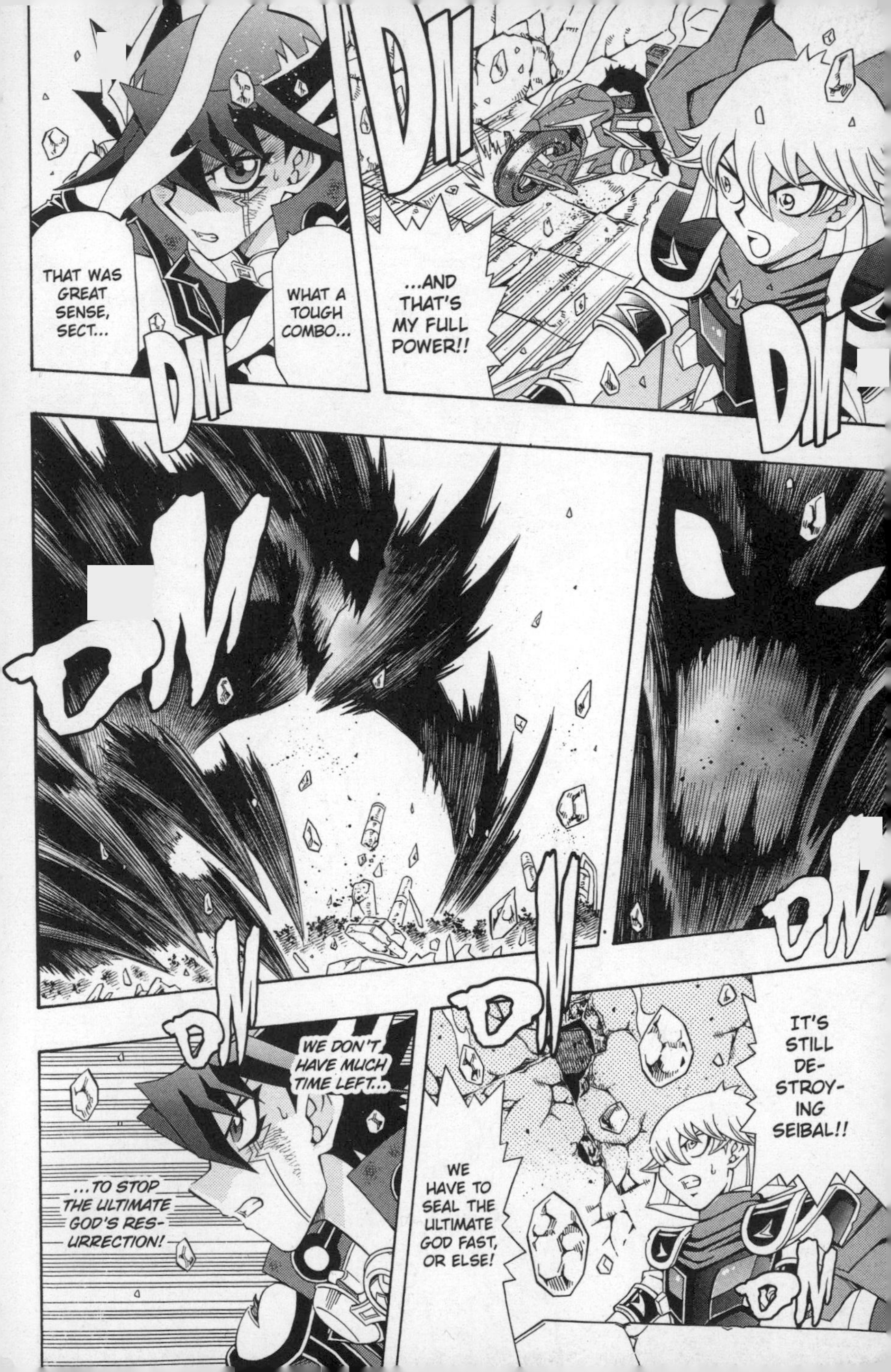
DM
...AND THAT'S MY FULL POWER!!
DM
WHAT A TOUGH COMBO...
THAT WAS GREAT SENSE, SECT...
DM
DM
DM
DM
IT'S STILL DE-STROY-ING SEIBAL!!
WE HAVE TO SEAL THE ULTIMATE GOD FAST, OR ELSE!
DM
WE DON'T HAVE MUCH TIME LEFT...
...TO STOP THE ULTIMATE GOD'S RES-URRECTION!
DM

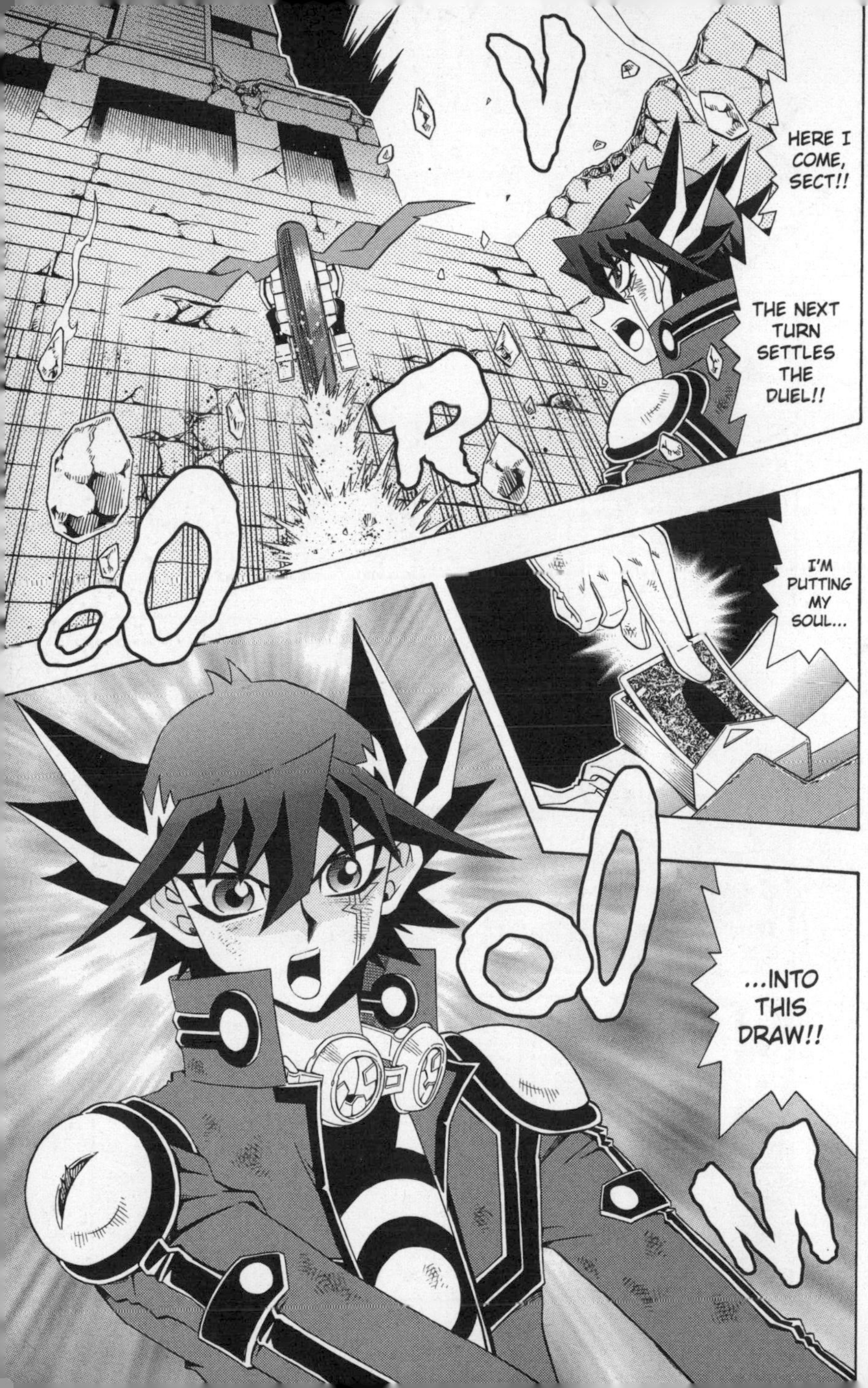
HERE I COME, SECT!!
THE NEXT TURN SETTLES THE DUEL!!
VROOOOM
I'M PUTTING MY SOUL...
...INTO THIS DRAW!!

5D's TRACKS

THE 55TH

BY SATOMASA

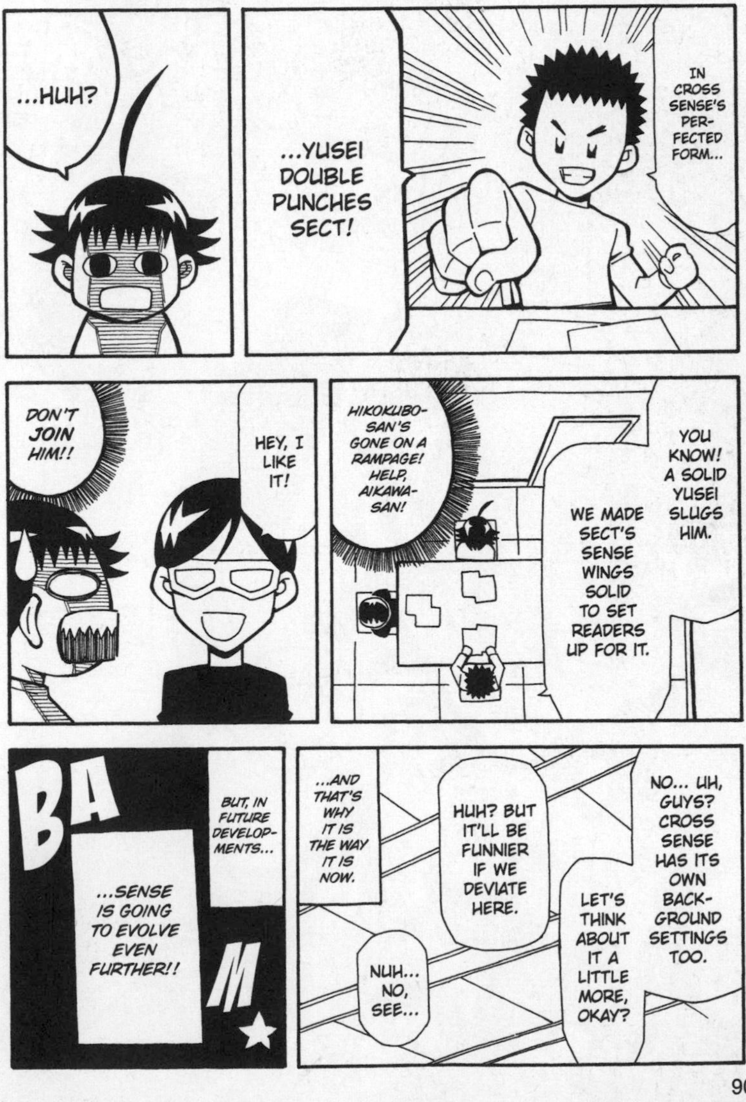
IN CROSS SENSE'S PER-FECTED FORM...
...YUSEI DOUBLE PUNCHES SECT!
...HUH?
YOU KNOW! A SOLID YUSEI SLUGS HIM.
WE MADE SECT'S SENSE WINGS SOLID TO SET READERS UP FOR IT.
HIKOKUBO-SAN'S GONE ON A RAMPAGE! HELP, AIKAWA-SAN!
HEY, I LIKE IT!
DON'T JOIN HIM!!
NO... UH, GUYS? CROSS SENSE HAS ITS OWN BACK-GROUND SETTINGS TOO.
LET'S THINK ABOUT IT A LITTLE MORE, OKAY?
HUH? BUT IT'LL BE FUNNIER IF WE DEVIATE HERE.
NUH... NO, SEE...
...AND THAT'S WHY IT IS THE WAY IT IS NOW.
BUT, IN FUTURE DEVELOP-MENTS...
BAM
...SENSE IS GOING TO EVOLVE EVEN FURTHER!!

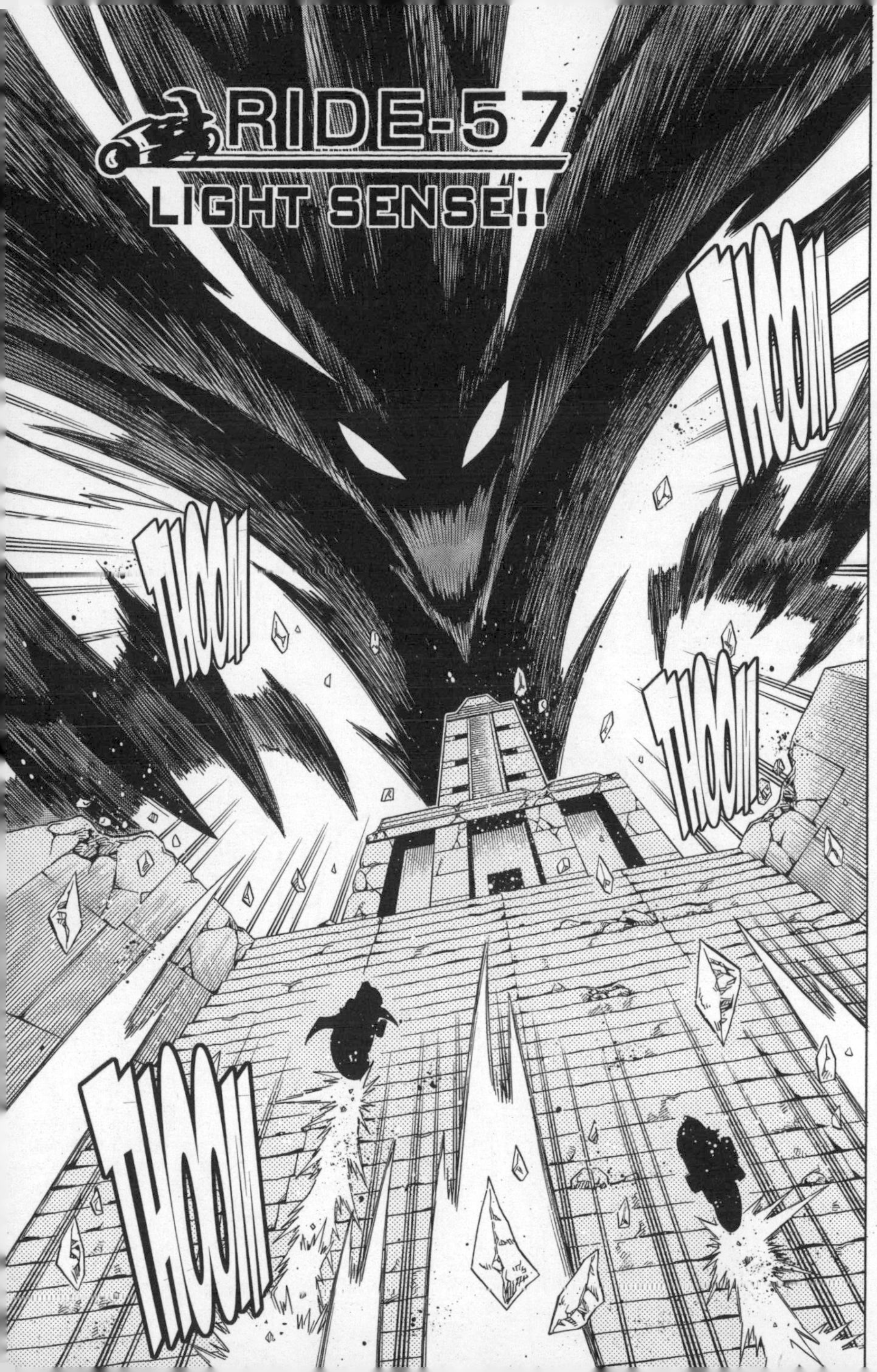
RIDE-57
LIGHT SENSE!!
THOOM
THOOM
THOOM
THOOM

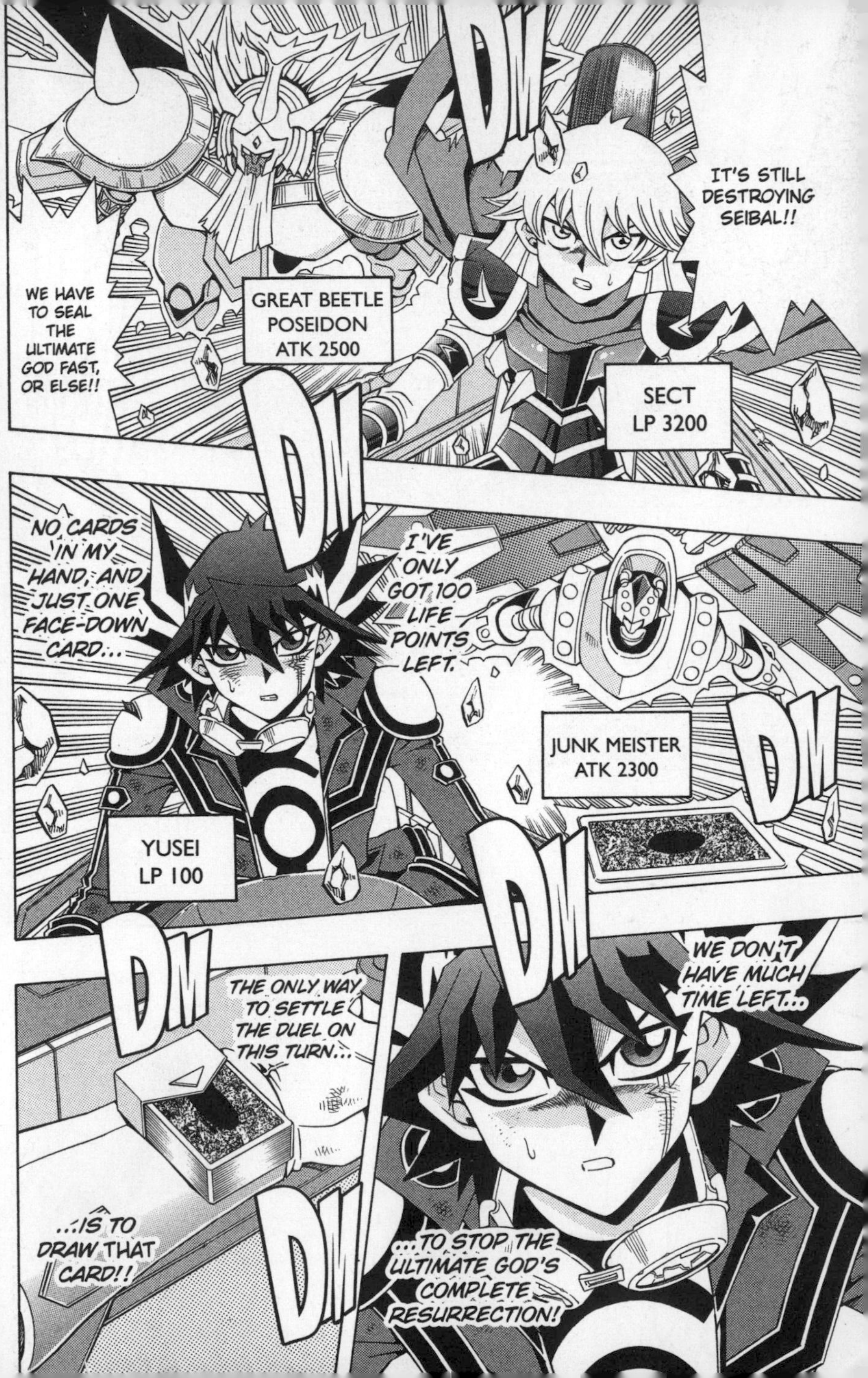
DM
IT'S STILL DESTROYING SEIBAL!!
SECT LP 3200
GREAT BEETLE POSEIDON ATK 2500
WE HAVE TO SEAL THE ULTIMATE GOD FAST, OR ELSE!!
DM
DM
I'VE ONLY GOT 100 LIFE POINTS LEFT.
JUNK MEISTER ATK 2300
NO CARDS IN MY HAND, AND JUST ONE FACE-DOWN CARD...
YUSEI LP 100
DM
DM
WE DON'T HAVE MUCH TIME LEFT...
...TO STOP THE ULTIMATE GOD'S COMPLETE RESURRECTION!
DM
DM
THE ONLY WAY TO SETTLE THE DUEL ON THIS TURN...
...IS TO DRAW THAT CARD!!

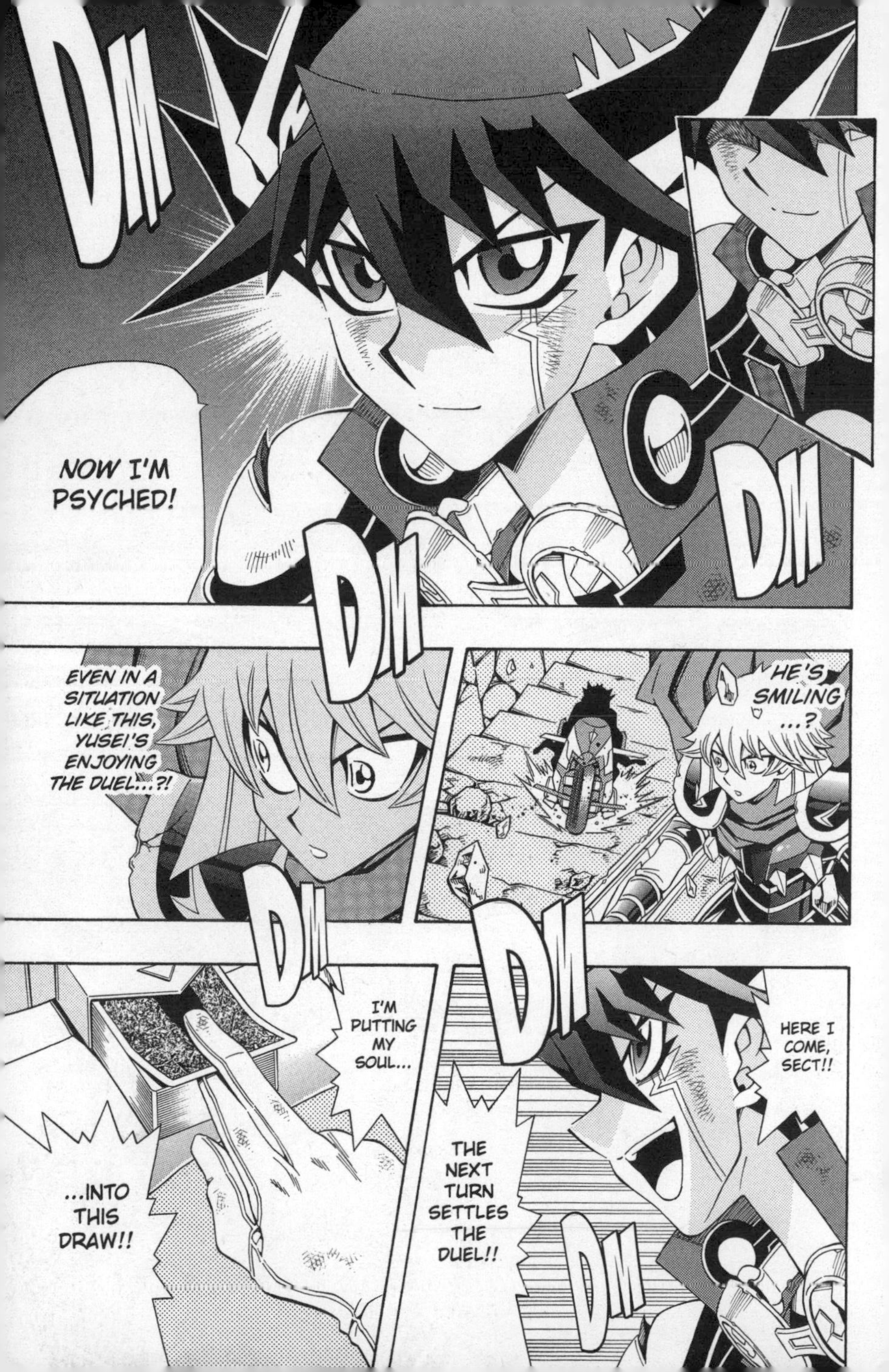
DM
DM
NOW I'M PSYCHED!
DM
HE'S SMILING ...?
EVEN IN A SITUATION LIKE THIS, YUSEI'S ENJOYING THE DUEL...?!
DM
DM
HERE I COME, SECT!!
THE NEXT TURN SETTLES THE DUEL!!
DM
I'M PUTTING MY SOUL...
...INTO THIS DRAW!!

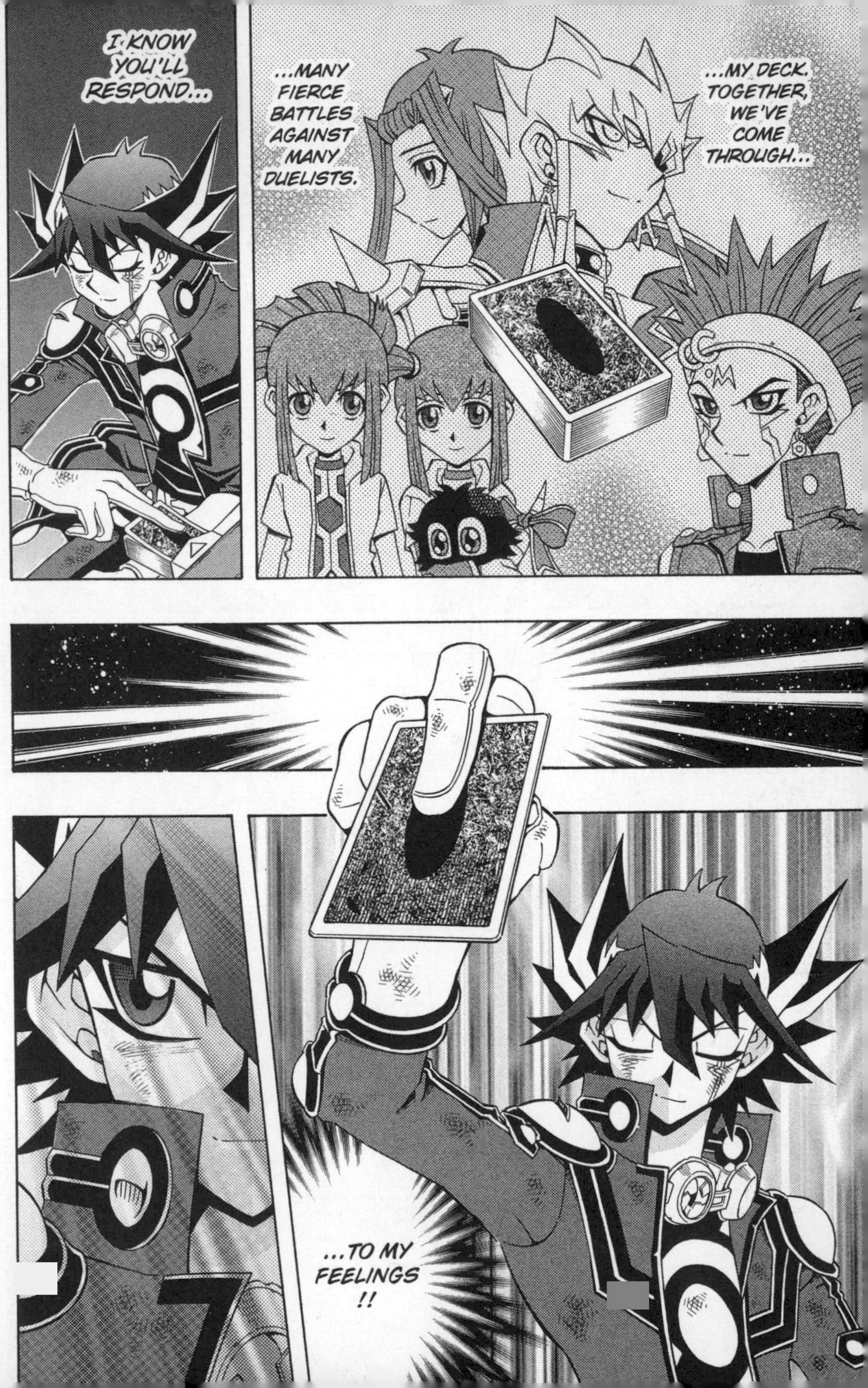
...MY DECK. TOGETHER, WE'VE COME THROUGH...
...MANY FIERCE BATTLES AGAINST MANY DUELISTS.
I KNOW YOU'LL RESPOND...
...TO MY FEELINGS!!

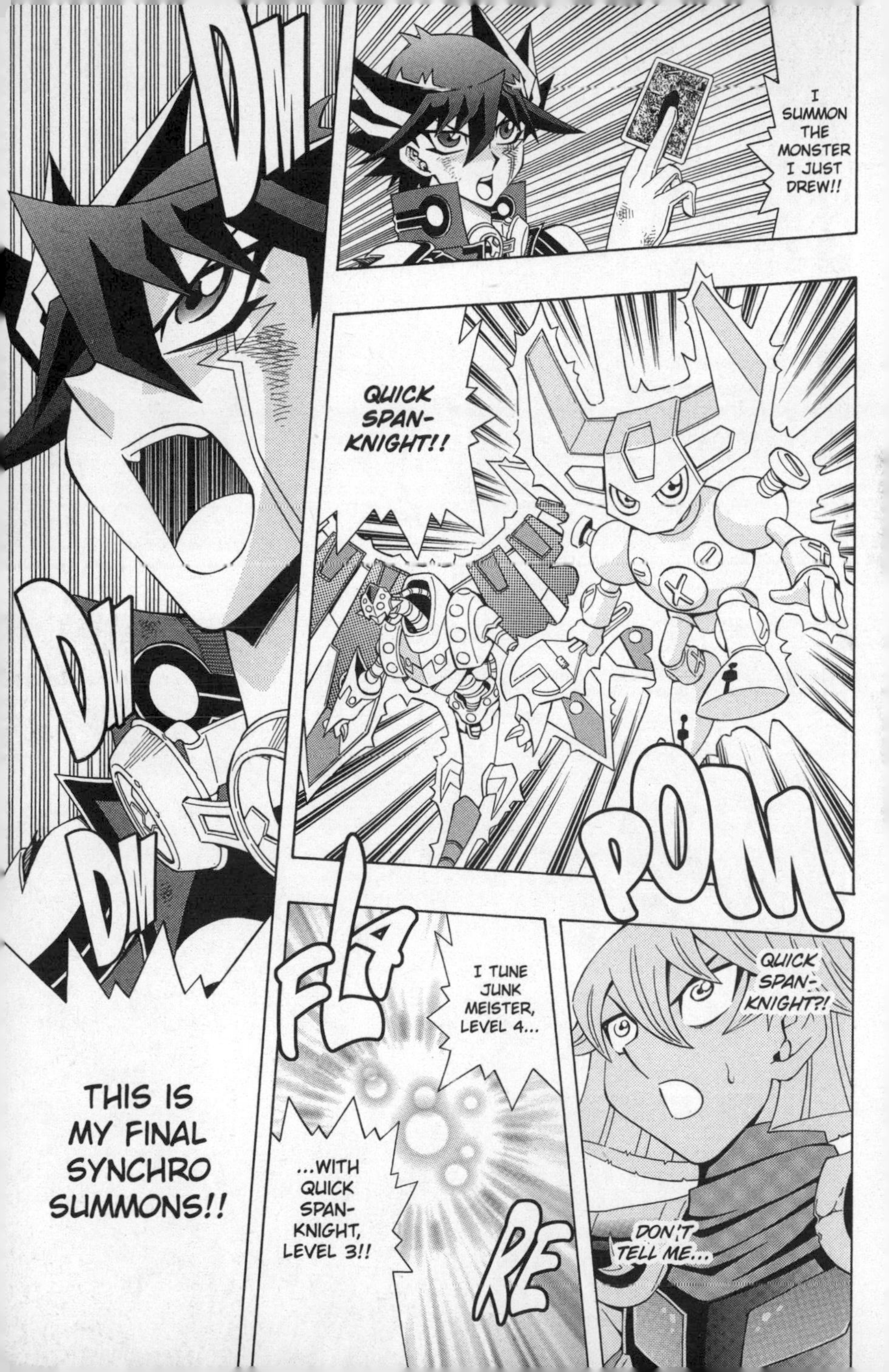
I SUMMON THE MONSTER I JUST DREW!!
QUICK SPAN-KNIGHT!!
POM
QUICK SPAN-KNIGHT?!
DON'T TELL ME...
I TUNE JUNK MEISTER, LEVEL 4...
FLA
...WITH QUICK SPAN-KNIGHT, LEVEL 3!!
RE
DM
DM
DM
THIS IS MY FINAL SYNCHRO SUMMONS!!

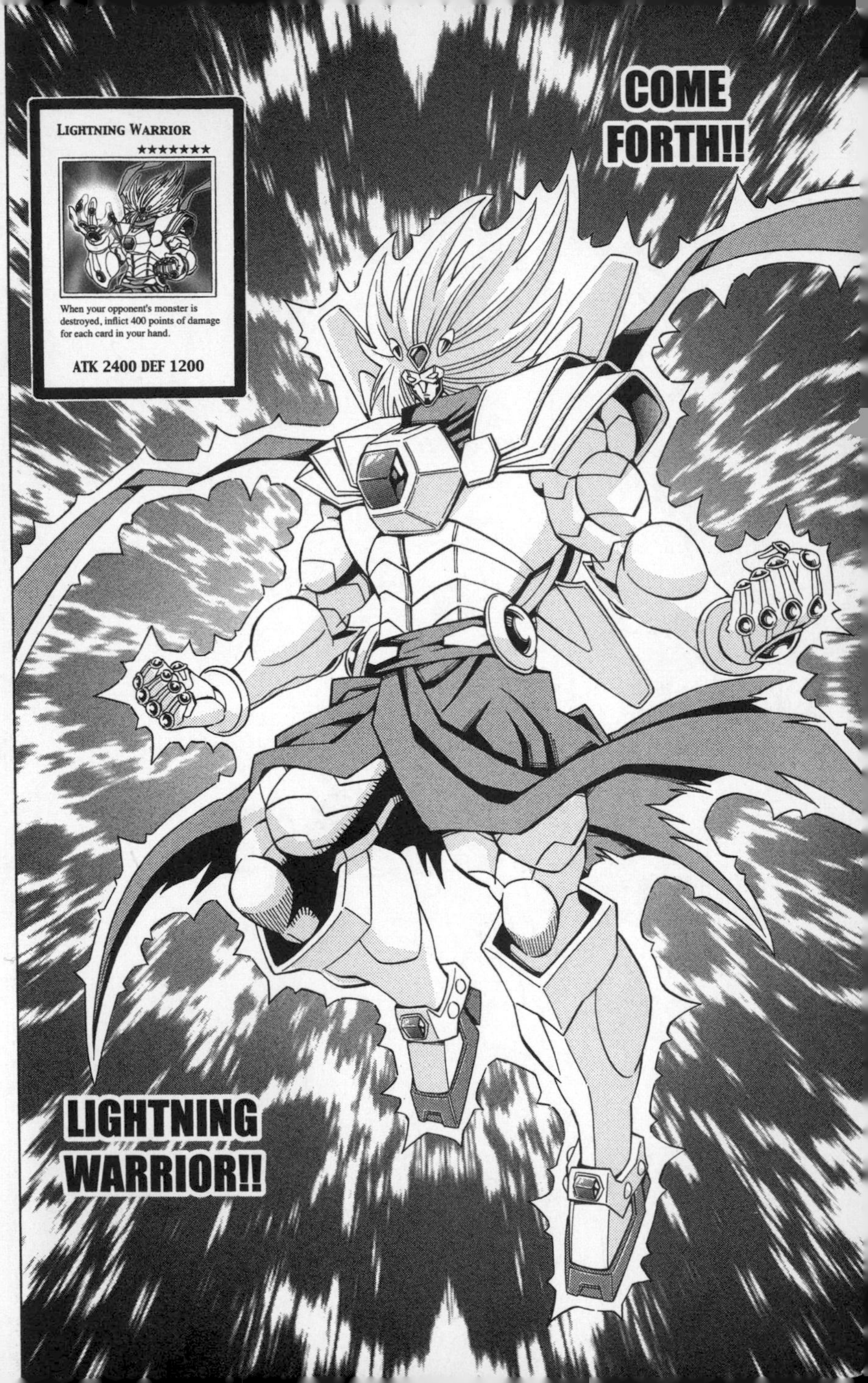
COME FORTH!!
LIGHTNING WARRIOR
★★★★★★★
When your opponent's monster is destroyed, inflict 400 points of damage for each card in your hand.
ATK 2400 DEF 1200
LIGHTNING WARRIOR!!

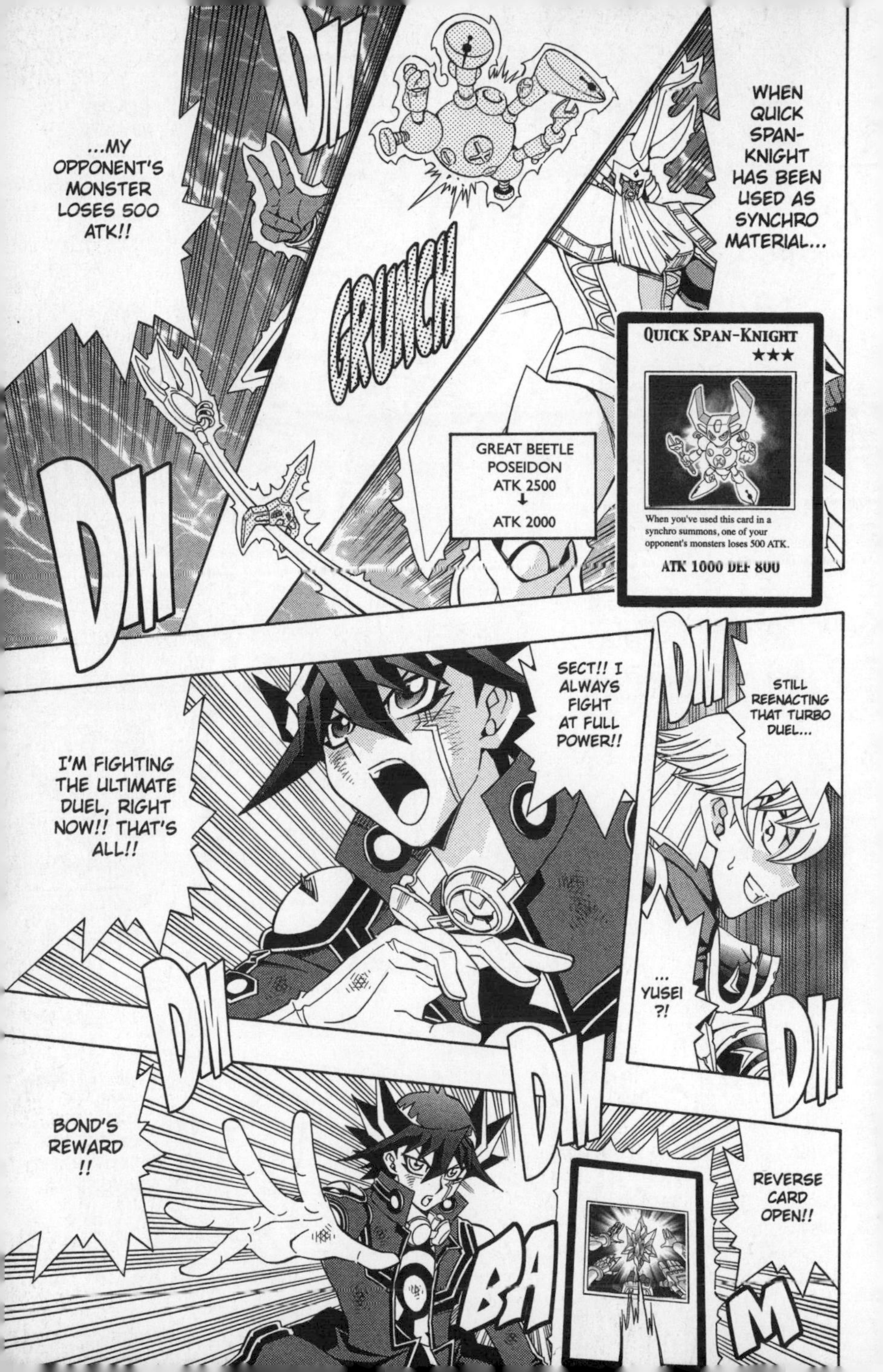
WHEN QUICK SPAN-KNIGHT HAS BEEN USED AS SYNCHRO MATERIAL...
QUICK SPAN-KNIGHT
★★★
When you've used this card in a synchro summons, one of your opponent's monsters loses 500 ATK.
ATK 1000 DEF 800
DM
...MY OPPONENT'S MONSTER LOSES 500 ATK!!
CRUNCH
GREAT BEETLE POSEIDON
ATK 2500
↓
ATK 2000
DM
DM
STILL REENACTING THAT TURBO DUEL...
... YUSEI ?!
DM
SECT!! I ALWAYS FIGHT AT FULL POWER!!
I'M FIGHTING THE ULTIMATE DUEL, RIGHT NOW!! THAT'S ALL!!
DM
DM
REVERSE CARD OPEN!!
BAM
BOND'S REWARD !!

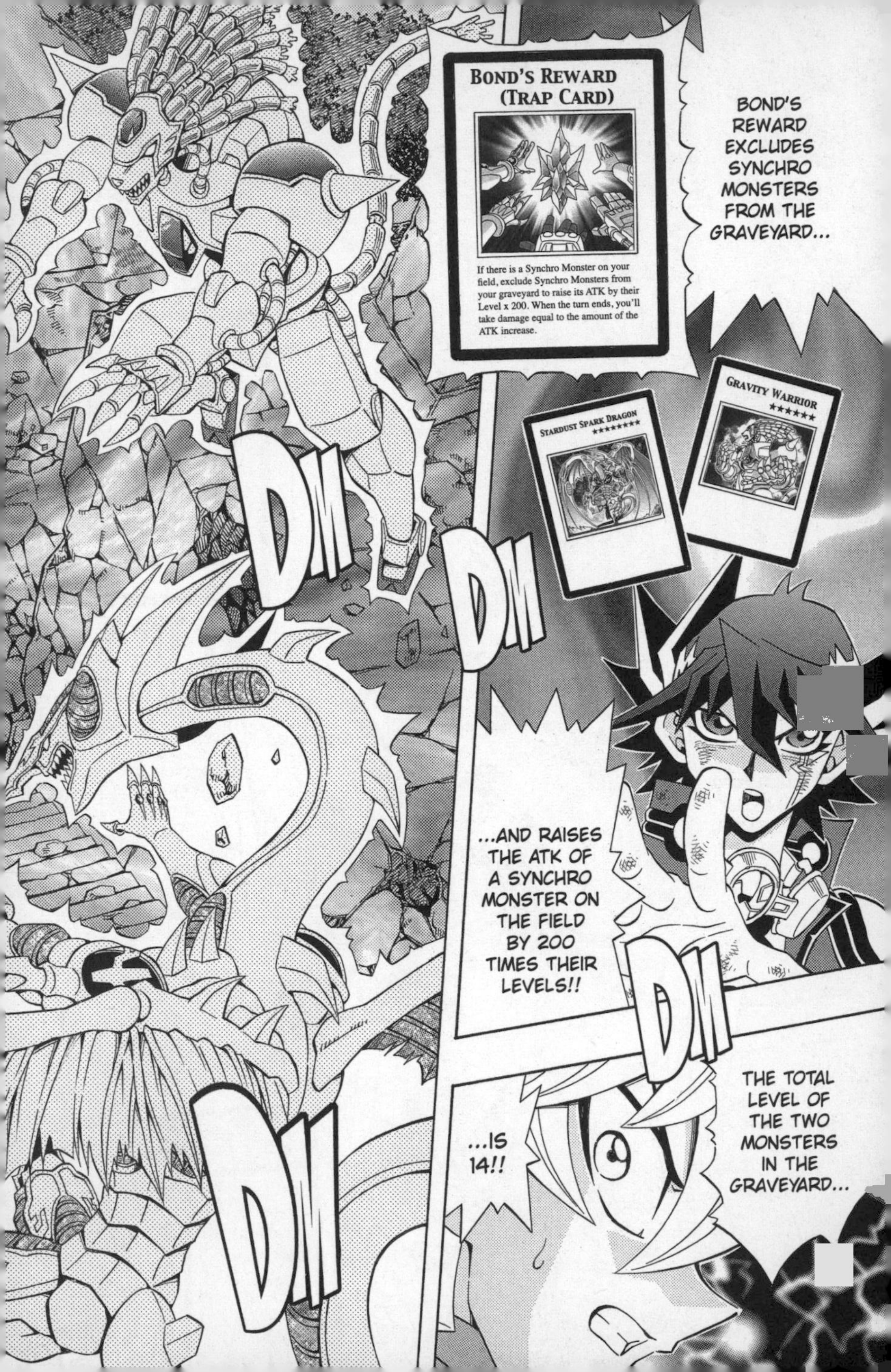
BOND'S REWARD EXCLUDES SYNCHRO MONSTERS FROM THE GRAVEYARD...
BOND'S REWARD (TRAP CARD)
If there is a Synchro Monster on your field, exclude Synchro Monsters from your graveyard to raise its ATK by their Level x 200. When the turn ends, you'll take damage equal to the amount of the ATK increase.
GRAVITY WARRIOR
STARDUST SPARK DRAGON
DM
...AND RAISES THE ATK OF A SYNCHRO MONSTER ON THE FIELD BY 200 TIMES THEIR LEVELS!!
DM
THE TOTAL LEVEL OF THE TWO MONSTERS IN THE GRAVEYARD...
...IS 14!!
DM
DM

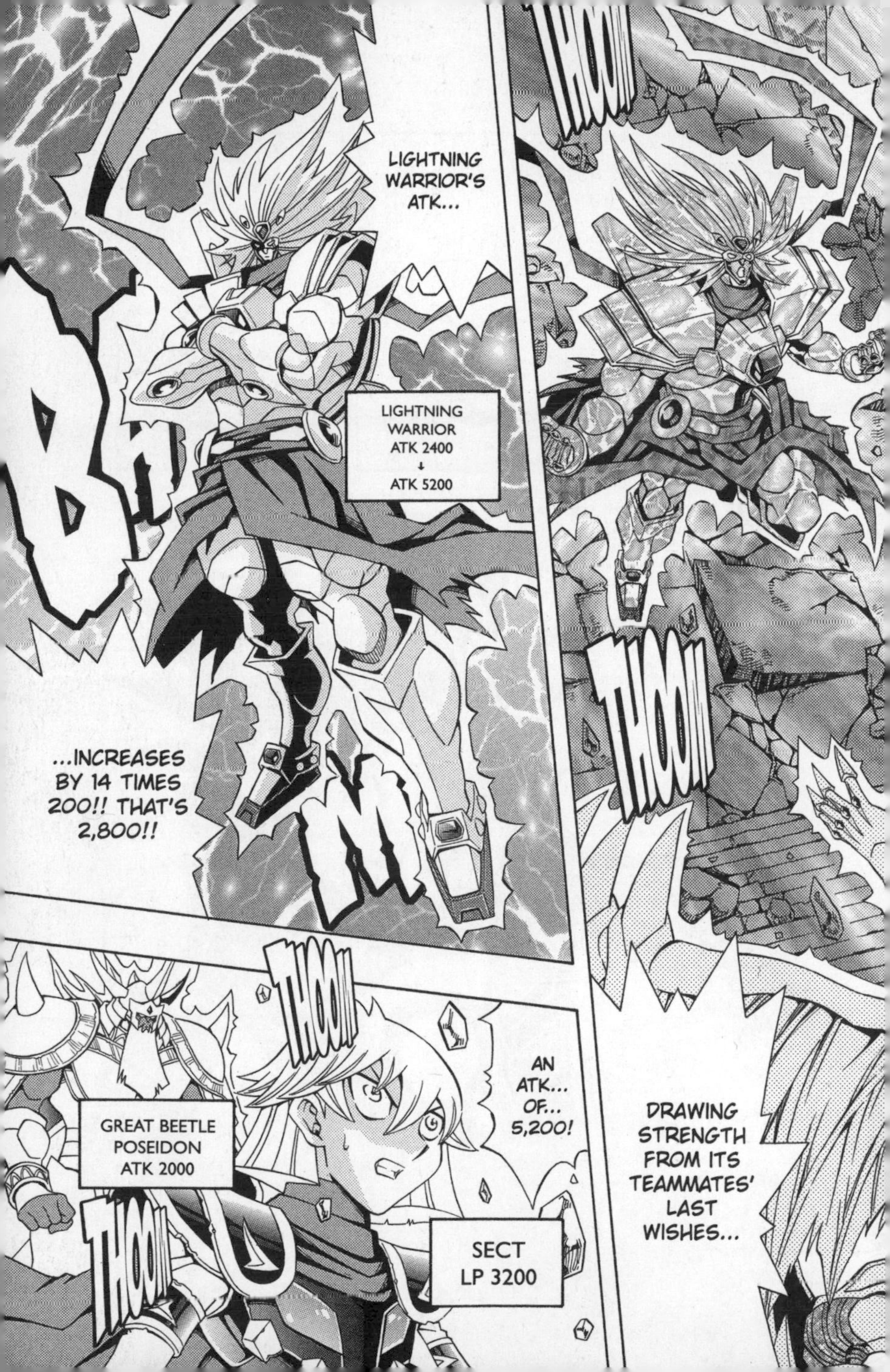
THOOM
THOOM
LIGHTNING WARRIOR'S ATK...
LIGHTNING WARRIOR
ATK 2400
↓
ATK 5200
BRM
...INCREASES BY 14 TIMES 200!! THAT'S 2,800!!
DRAWING STRENGTH FROM ITS TEAMMATES' LAST WISHES...
THOOM
AN ATK... OF... 5,200!
GREAT BEETLE POSEIDON ATK 2000
THOOM
SECT LP 3200

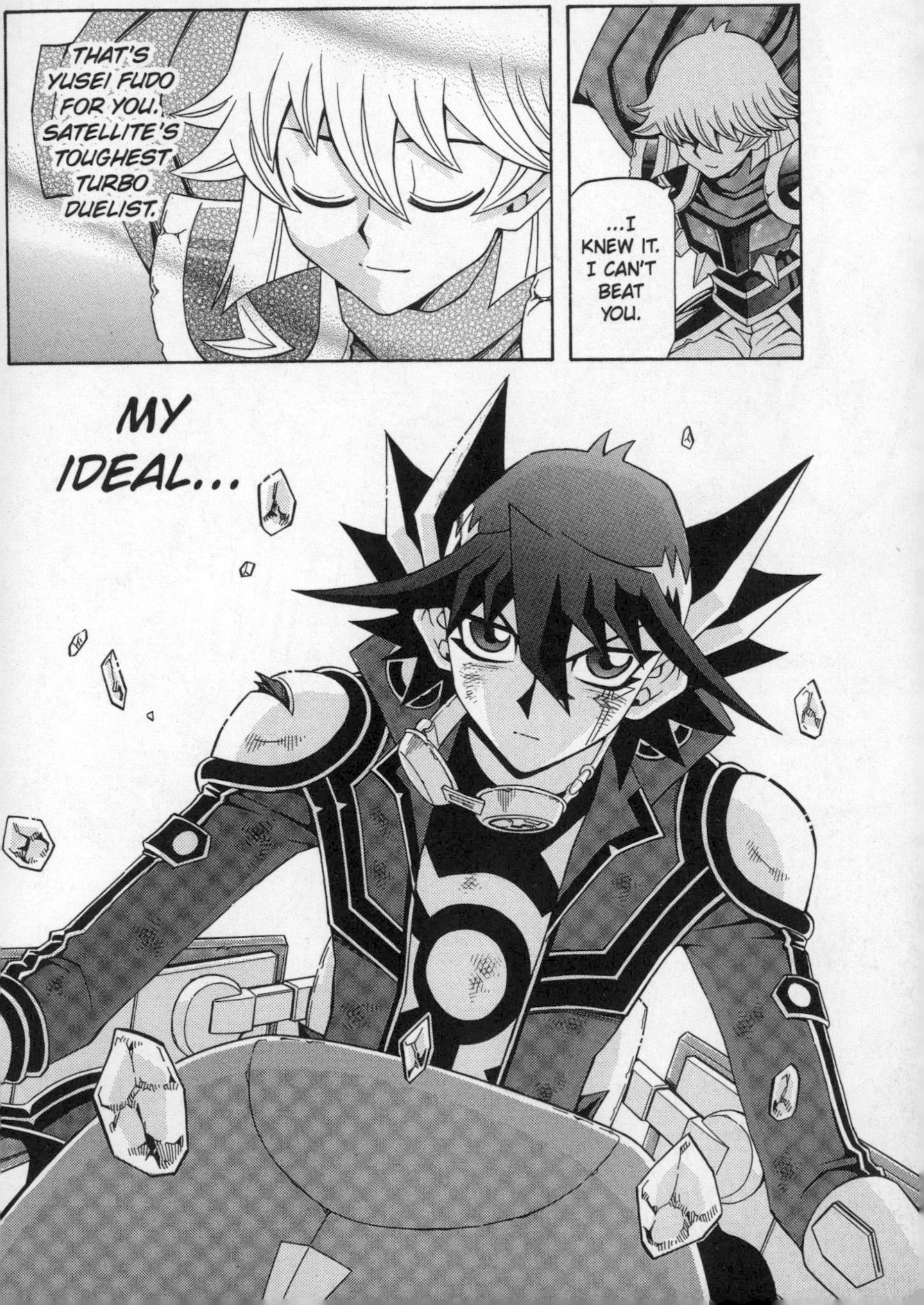
...I KNEW IT. I CAN'T BEAT YOU.
THAT'S YUSEI FUDO FOR YOU. SATELLITE'S TOUGHEST TURBO DUELIST.
MY IDEAL...

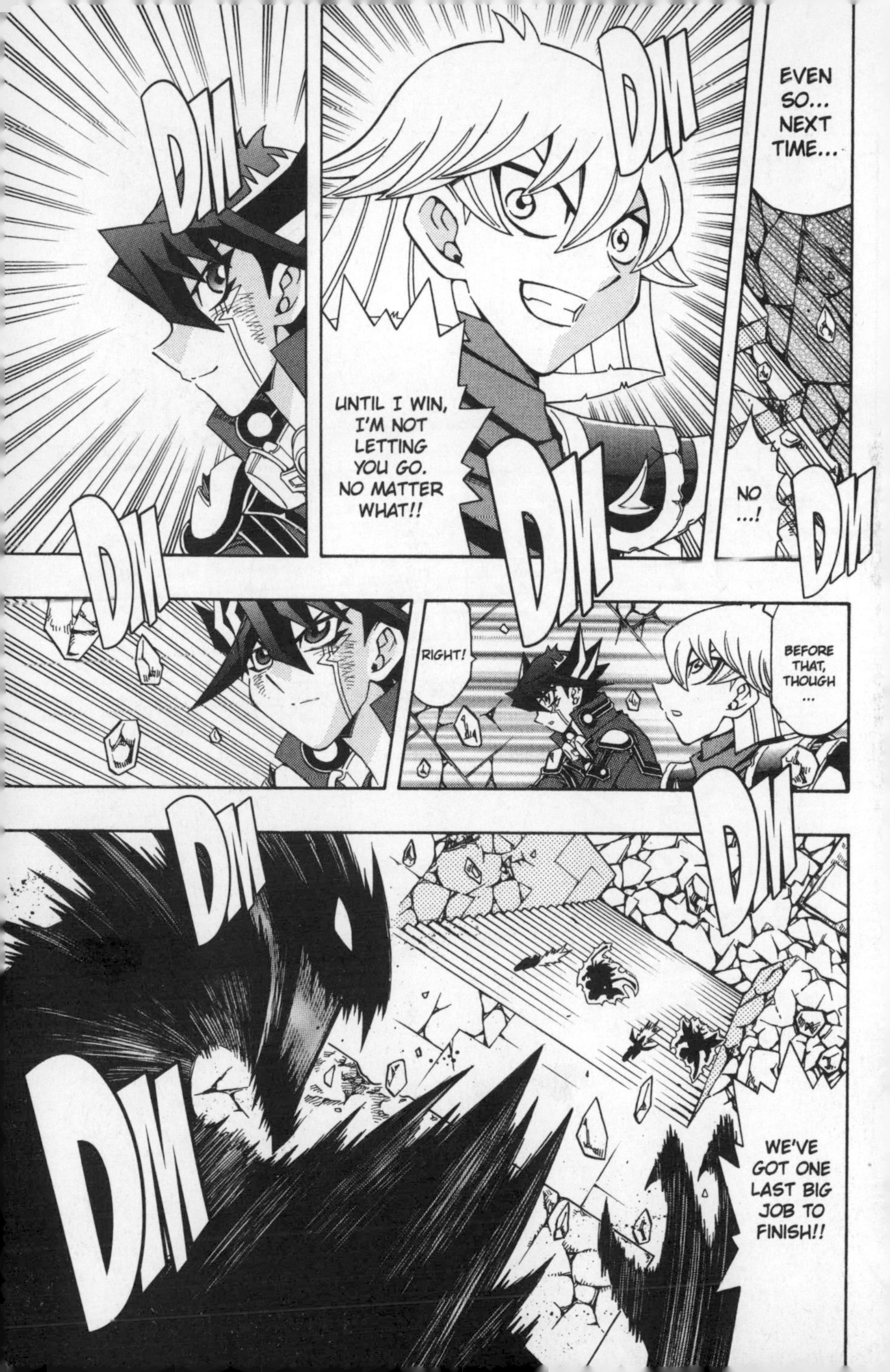
EVEN SO... NEXT TIME...
NO ...!
DM
DM
DM
UNTIL I WIN, I'M NOT LETTING YOU GO. NO MATTER WHAT!!
DM
DM
DM
DM
BEFORE THAT, THOUGH ...
RIGHT!
DM
DM
DM
WE'VE GOT ONE LAST BIG JOB TO FINISH!!

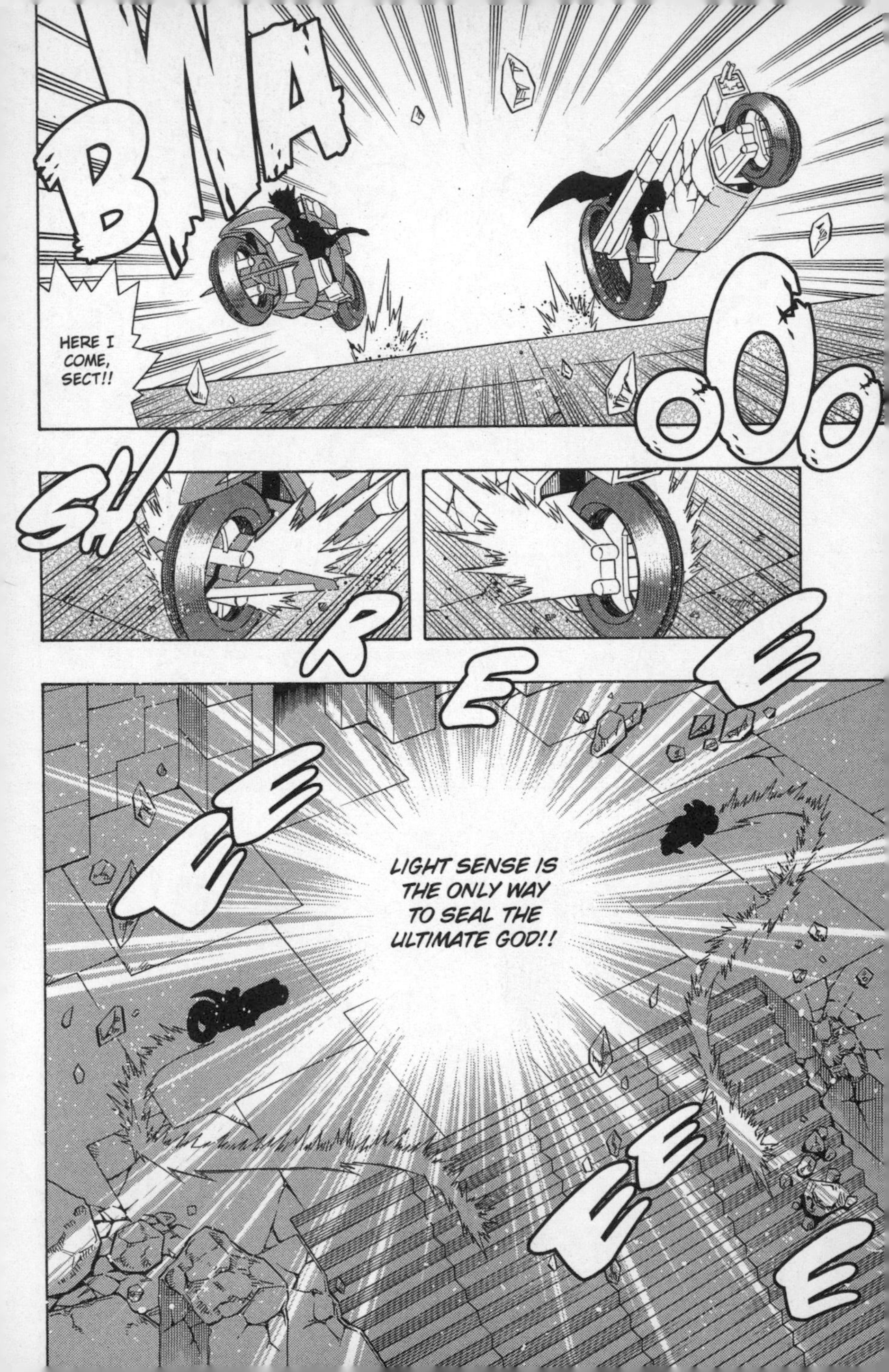
BWAOOO
HERE I COME, SECT!!
SHREEEEEEE
LIGHT SENSE IS THE ONLY WAY TO SEAL THE ULTIMATE GOD!!

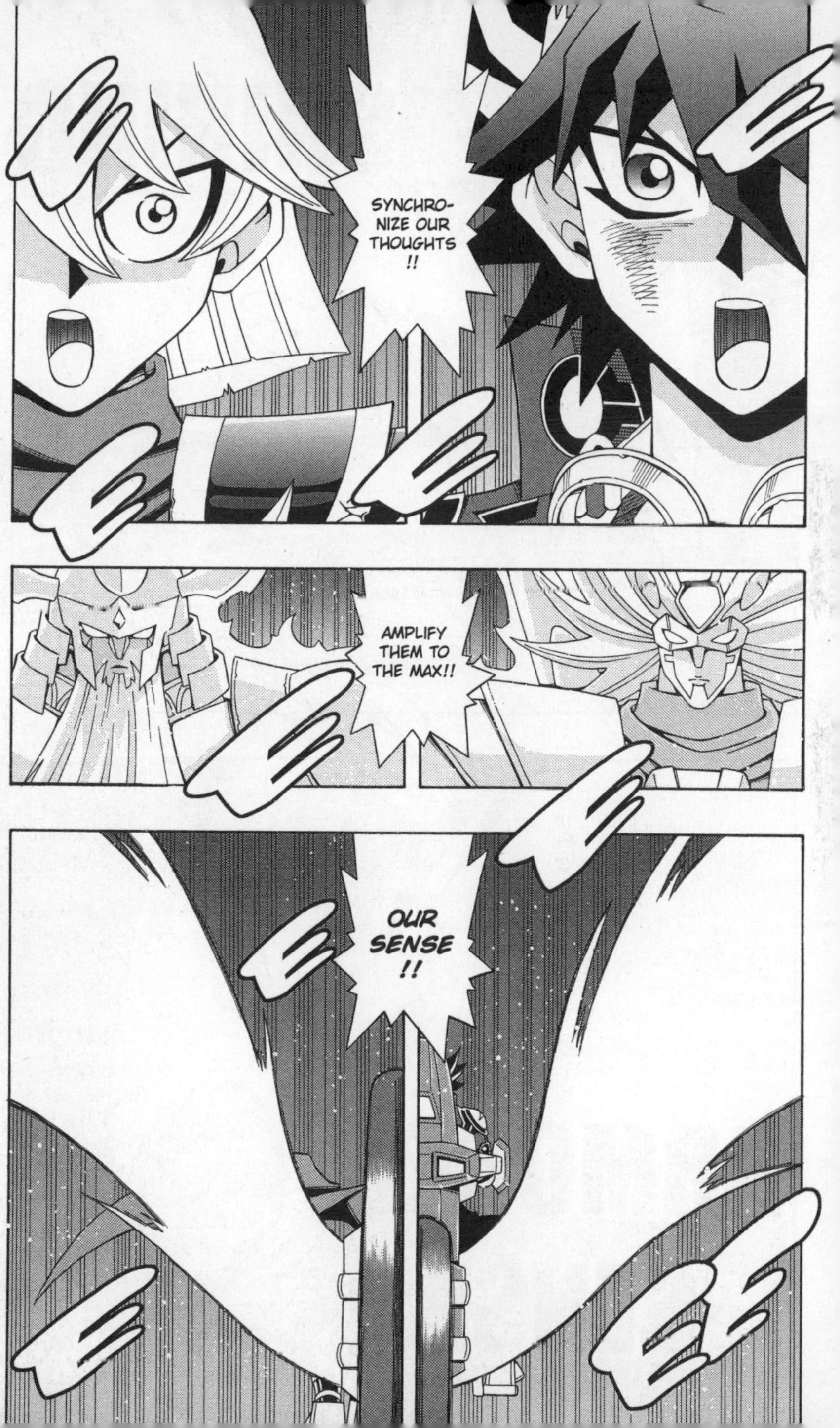
SYNCHRONIZE OUR THOUGHTS!!
AMPLIFY THEM TO THE MAX!!
OUR SENSE!!

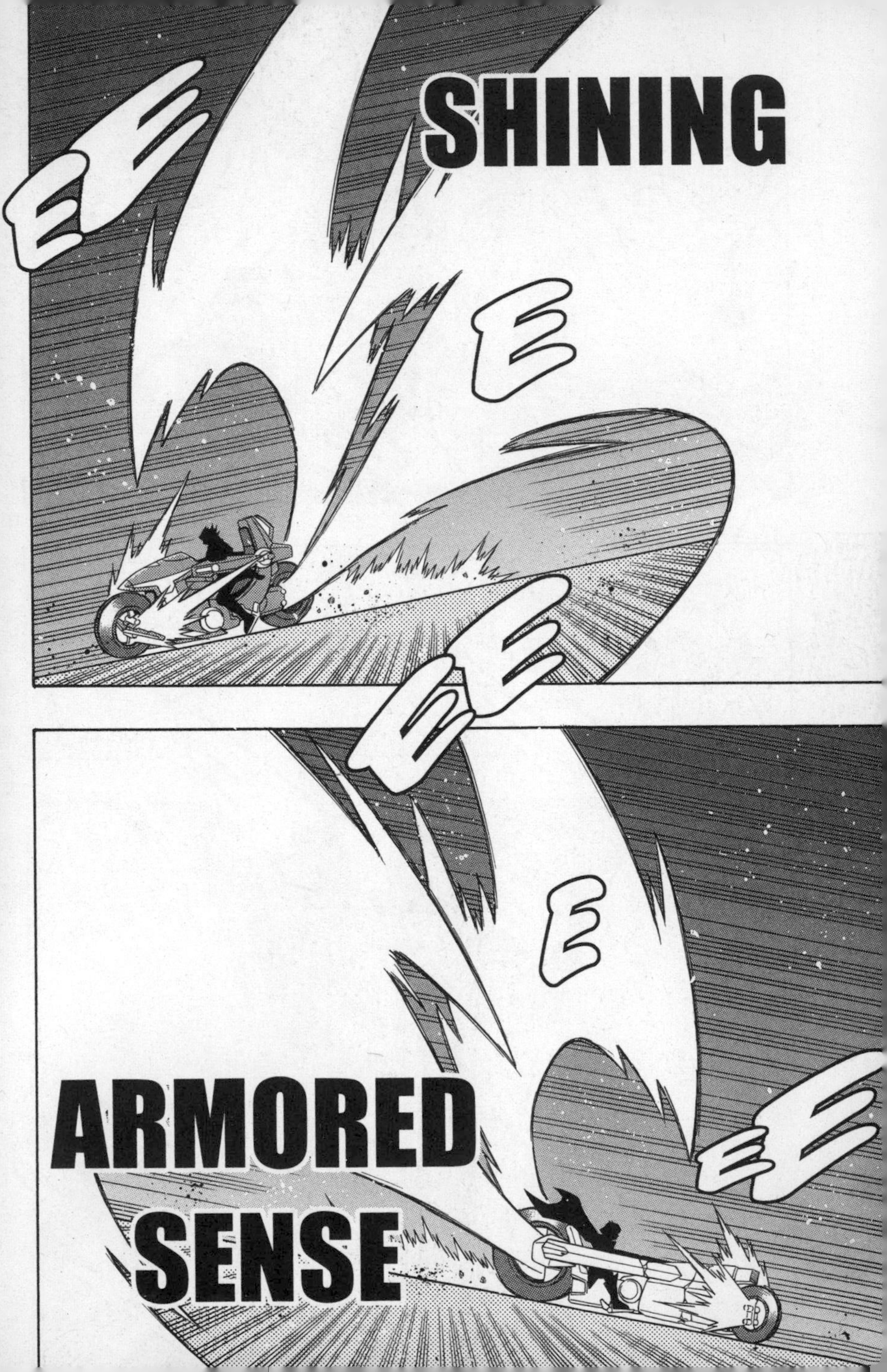
SHINING
ARMORED
SENSE

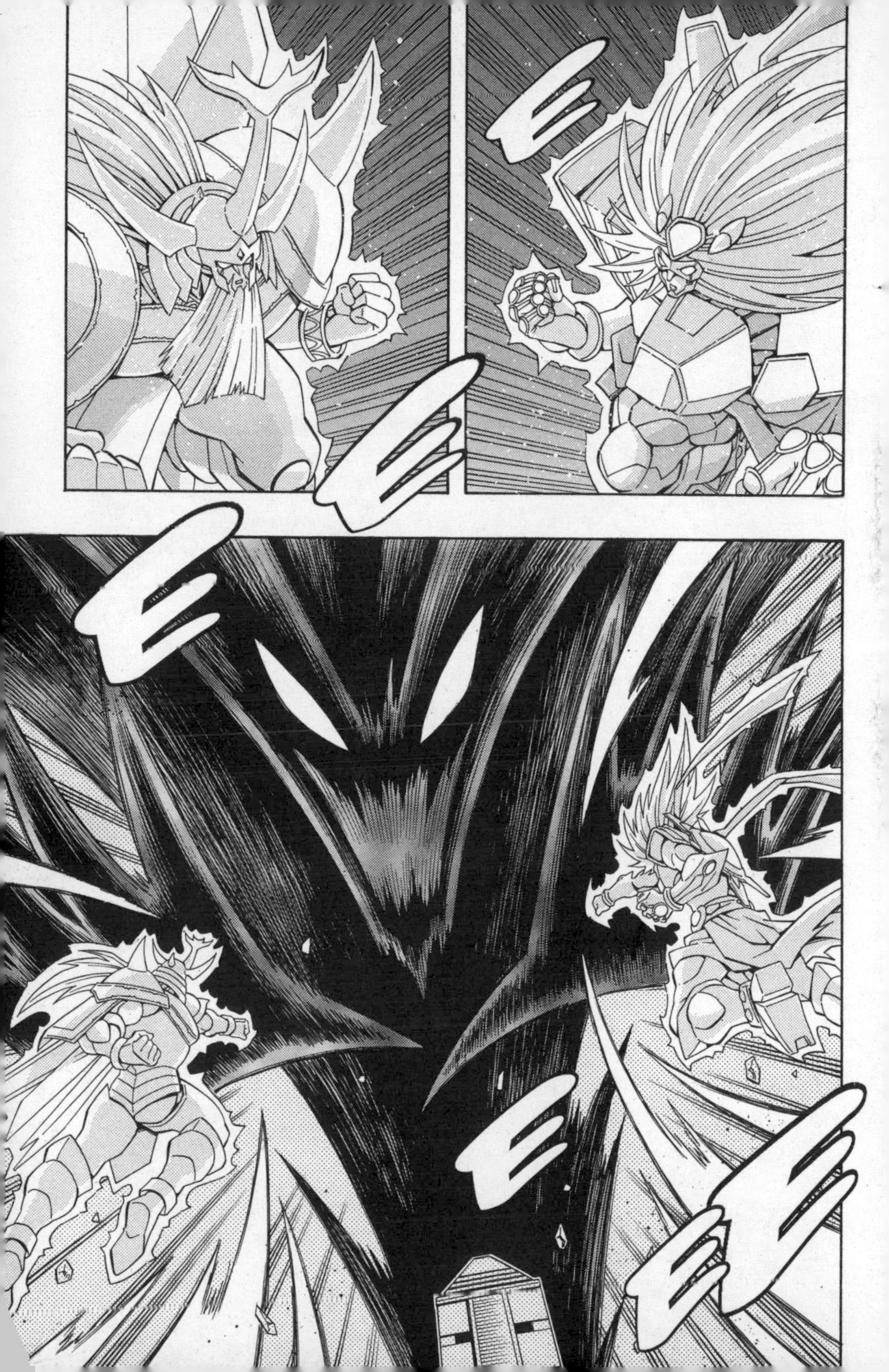

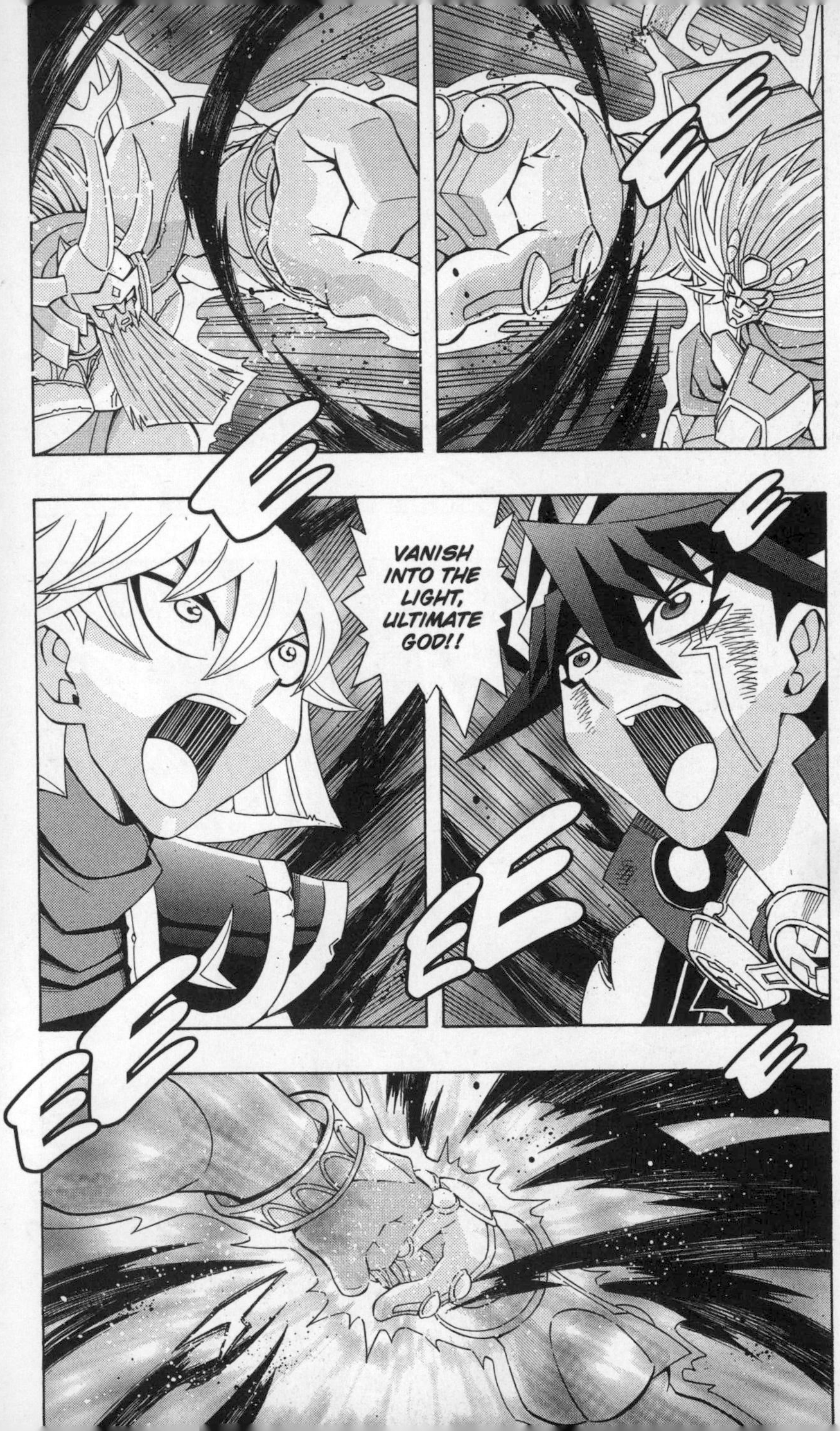
VANISH INTO THE LIGHT, ULTIMATE GOD!!

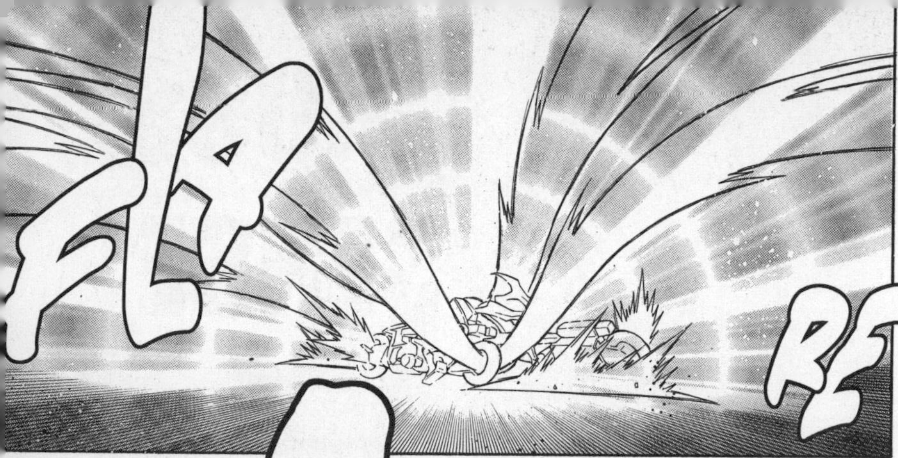
FLARE
KLAB
THIS IS OUR...
...LIGHT SENSE !!
OO

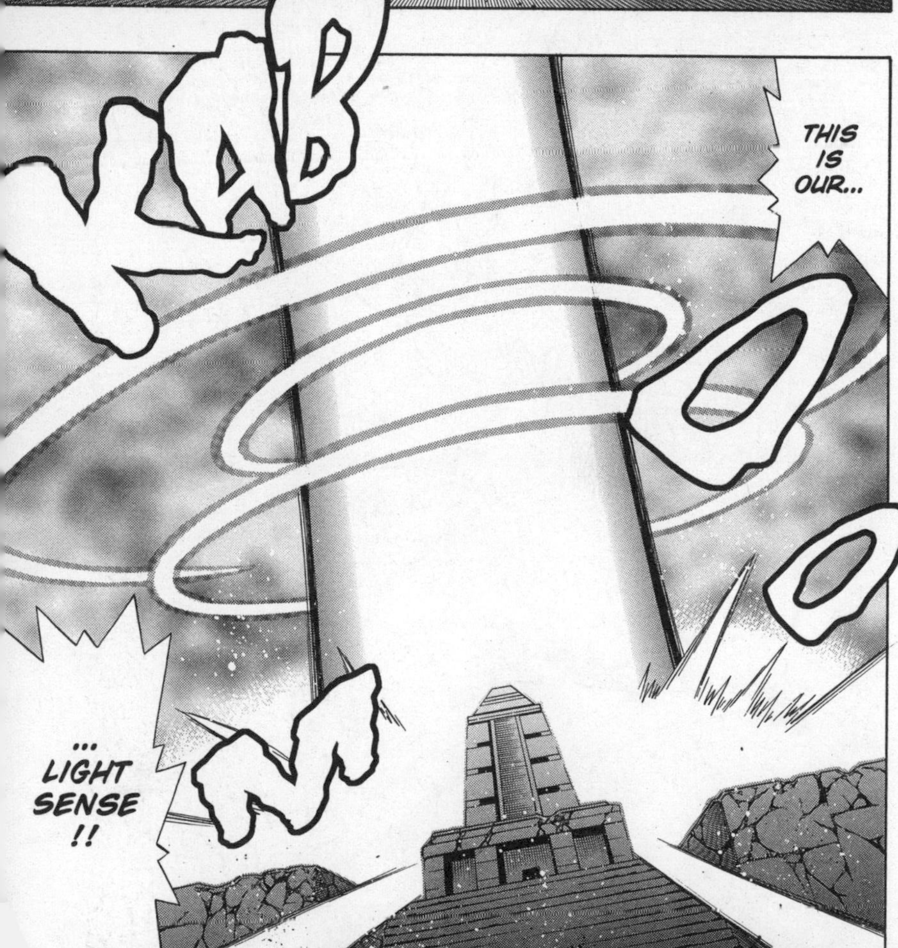

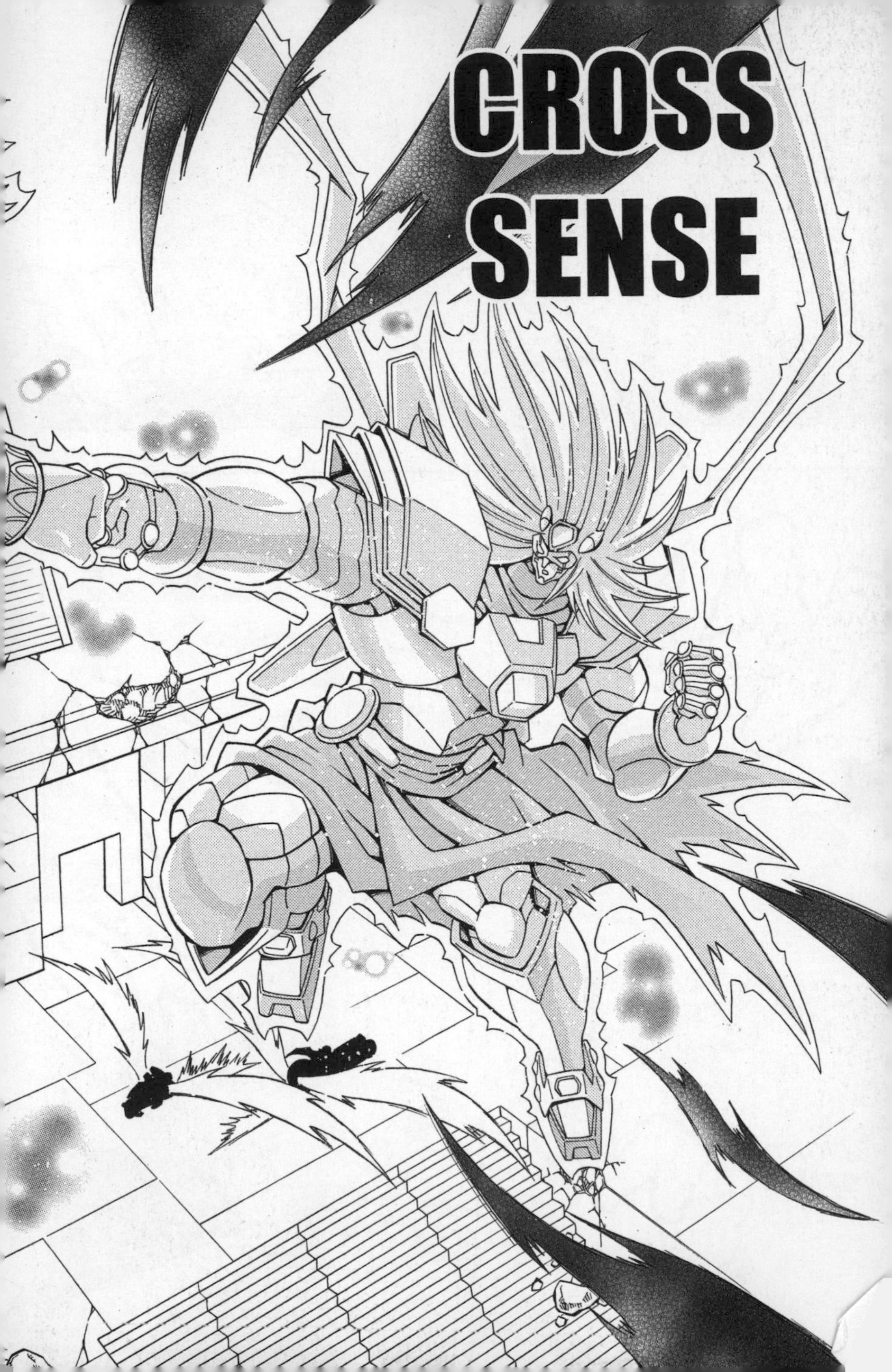
CROSS
SENSE

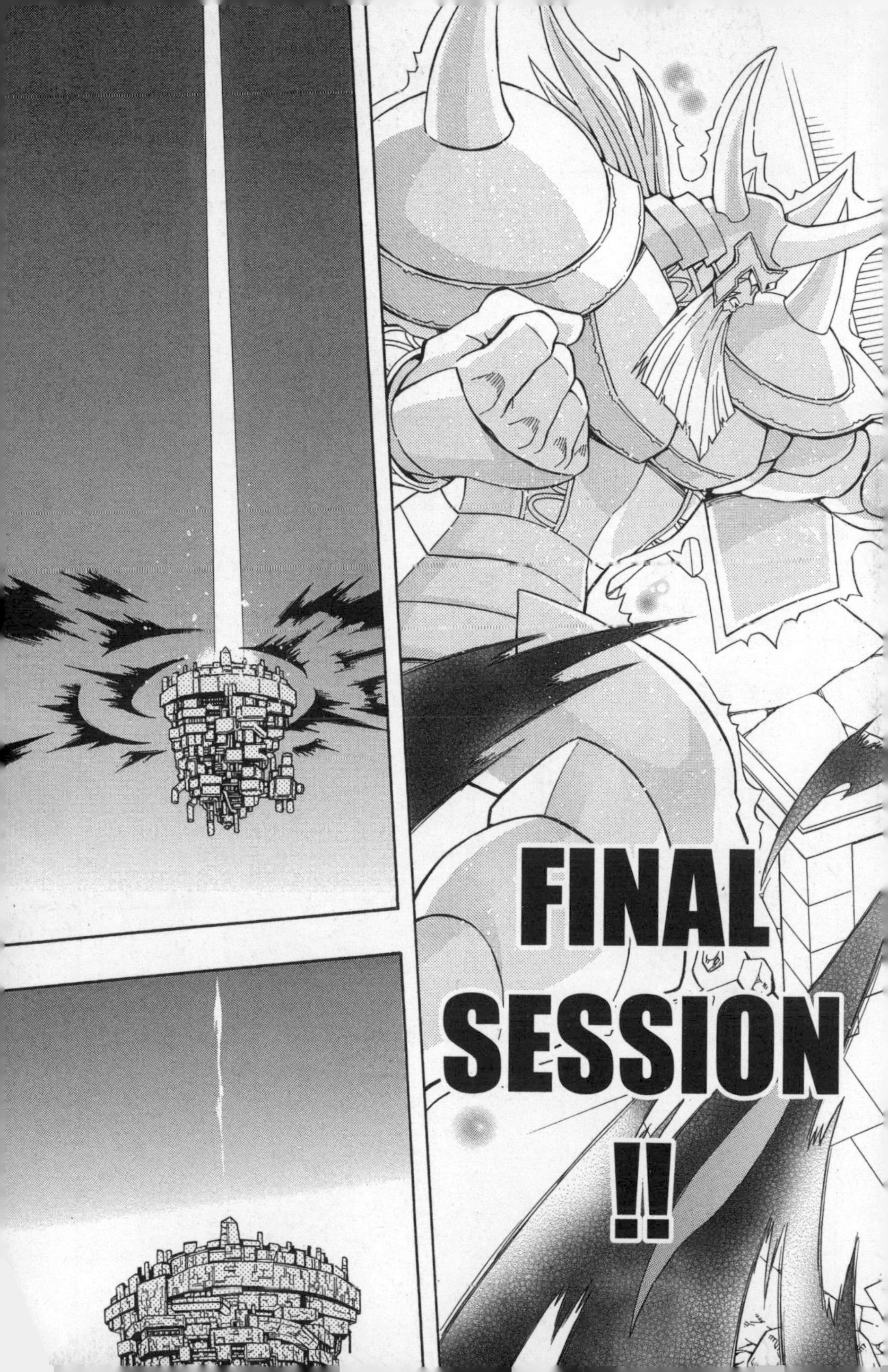
FINAL SESSION !!

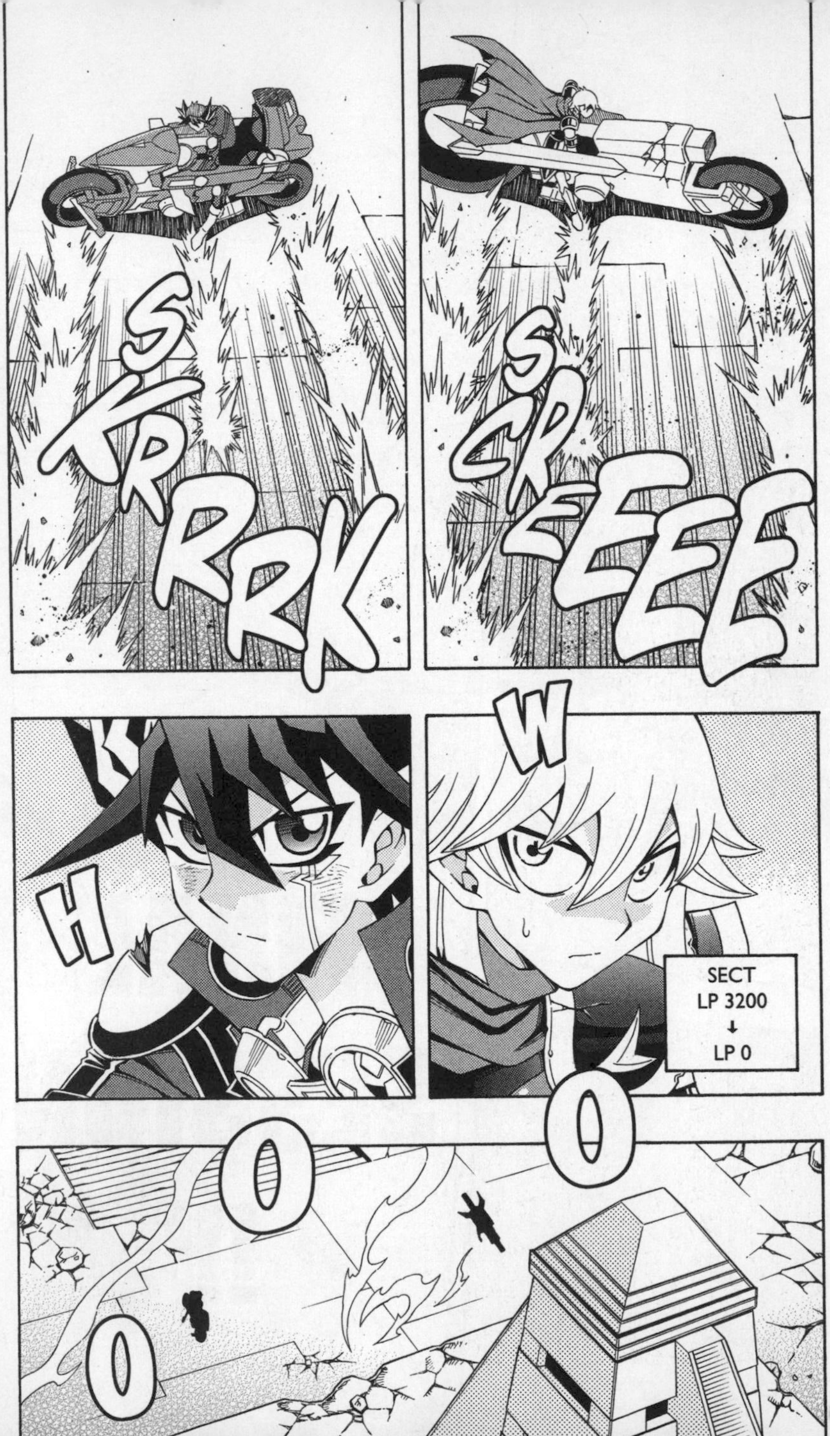
SCREEEE
SKRRRK
W
SECT
LP 3200
↓
LP 0
H
O
O
O
O

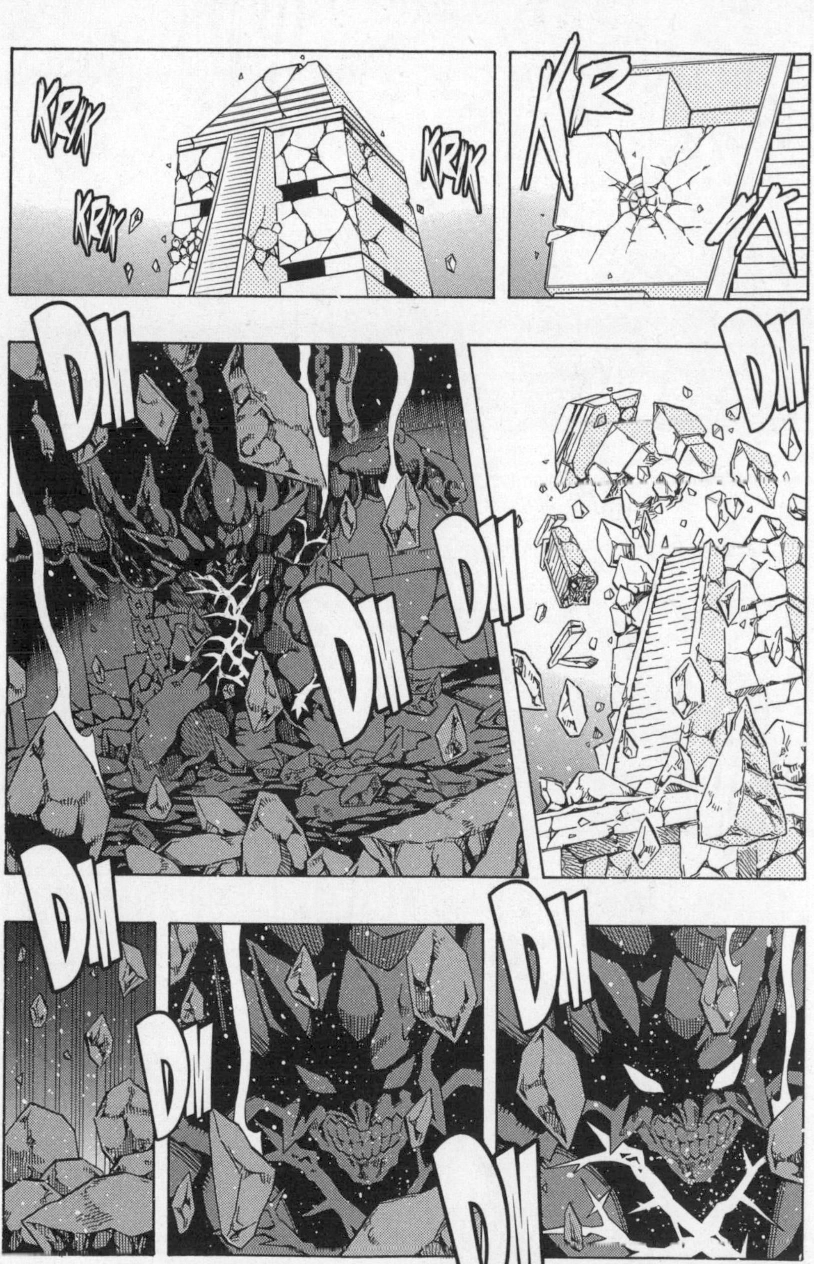
KR
KRIK
KRIK
KRIK
DM
DM
DM
DM
DM
DM
DM
DM

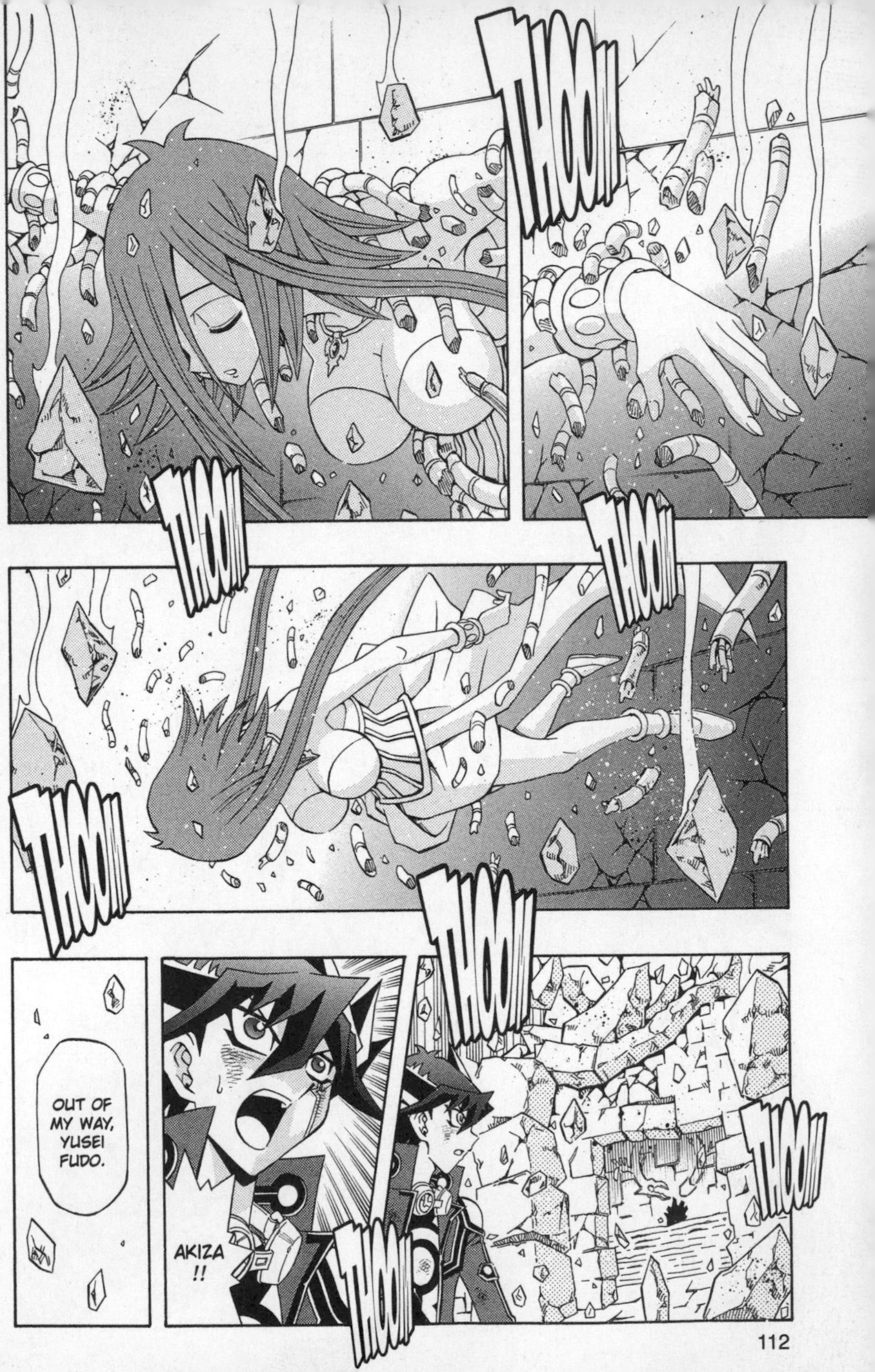
THOOM
THOOM
THOOM
THOOM
THOOM
THOOM
THOOM
AKIZA!!
THOOM
OUT OF MY WAY, YUSEI FUDO.

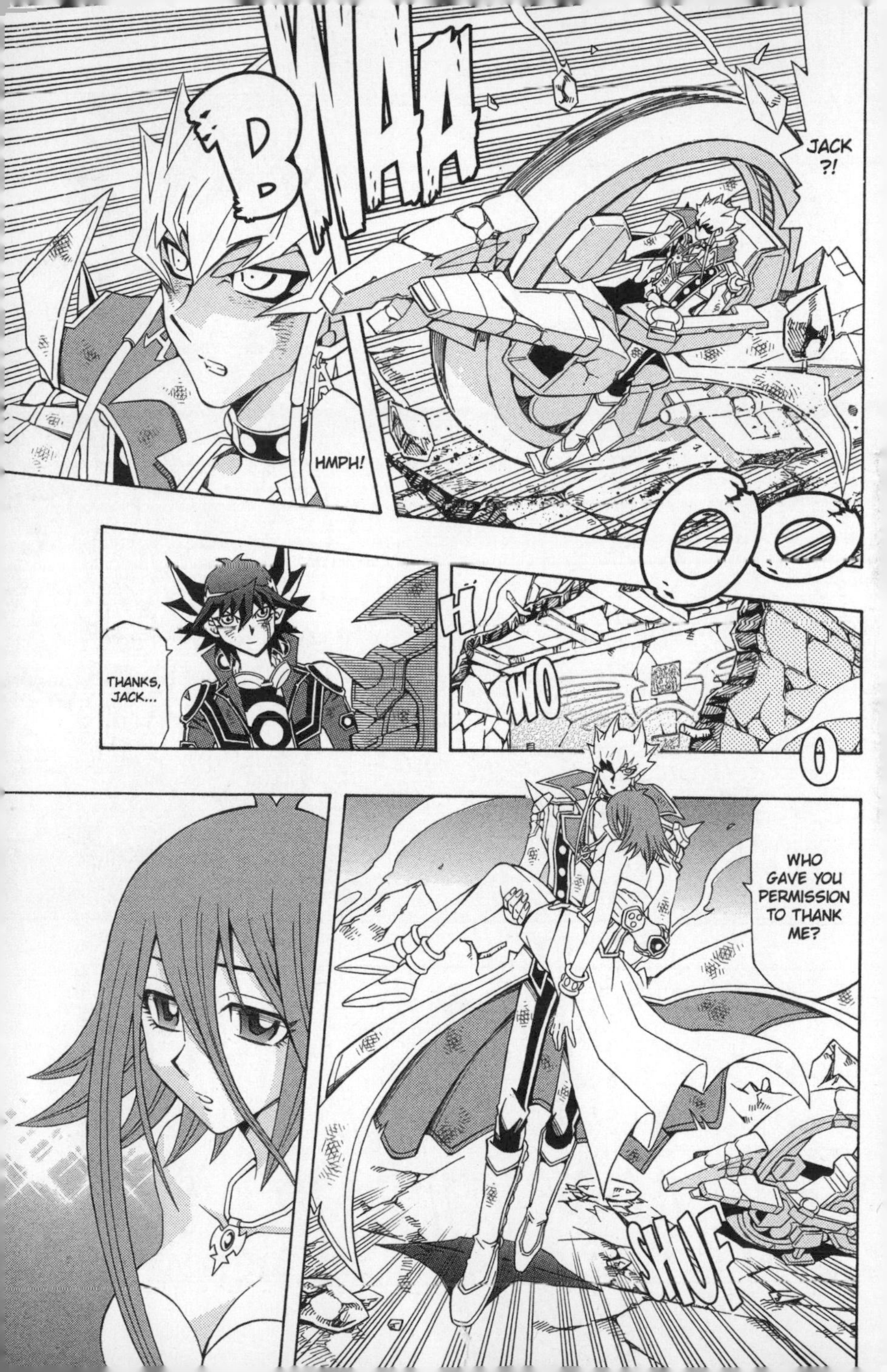
JACK ?!
BWAA
HMPH!
OO
HWOO
THANKS, JACK...
WHO GAVE YOU PERMISSION TO THANK ME?
SHUF

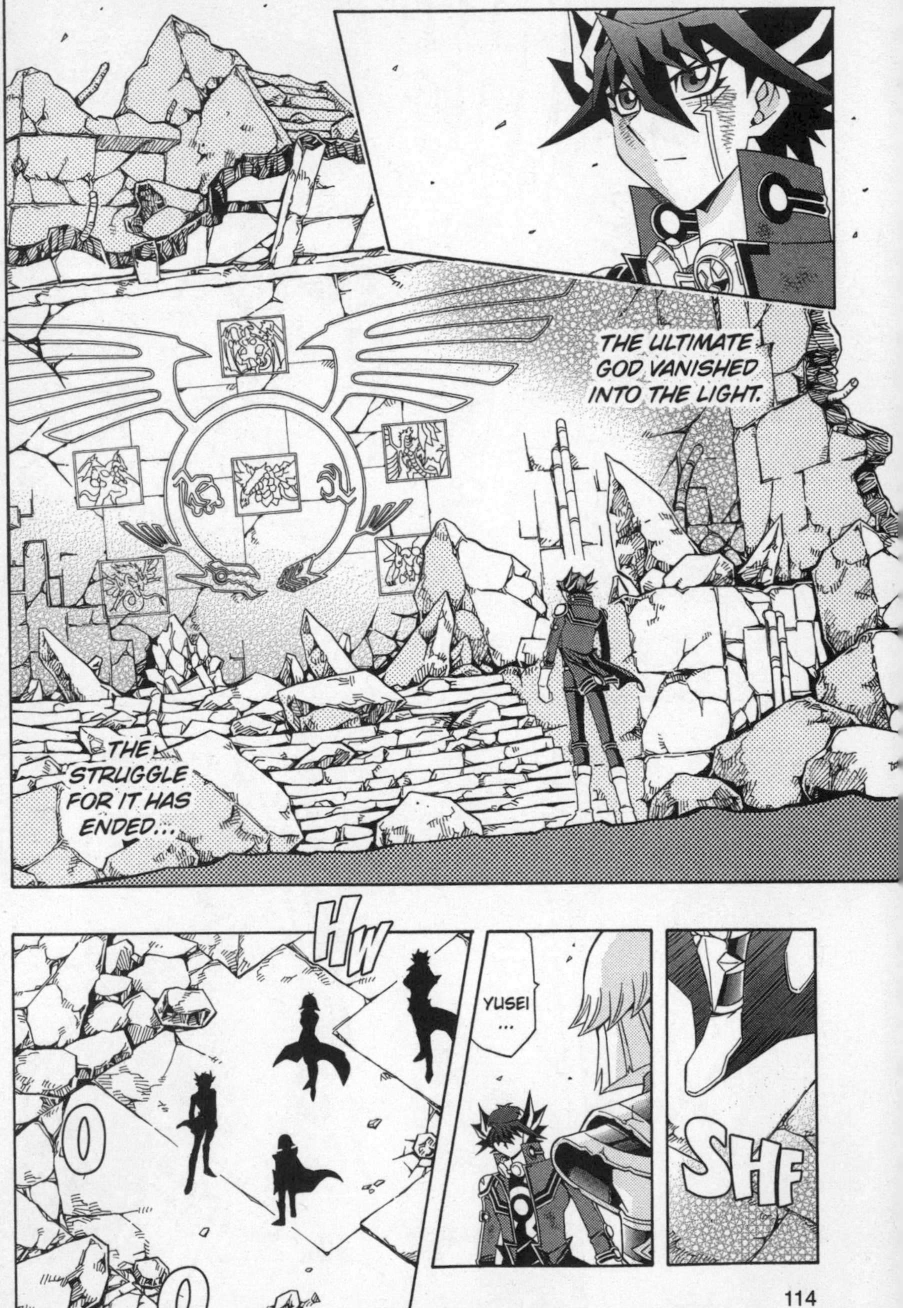
THE ULTIMATE GOD VANISHED INTO THE LIGHT.
THE STRUGGLE FOR IT HAS ENDED...
SHF
YUSEI ...
HW
O
O

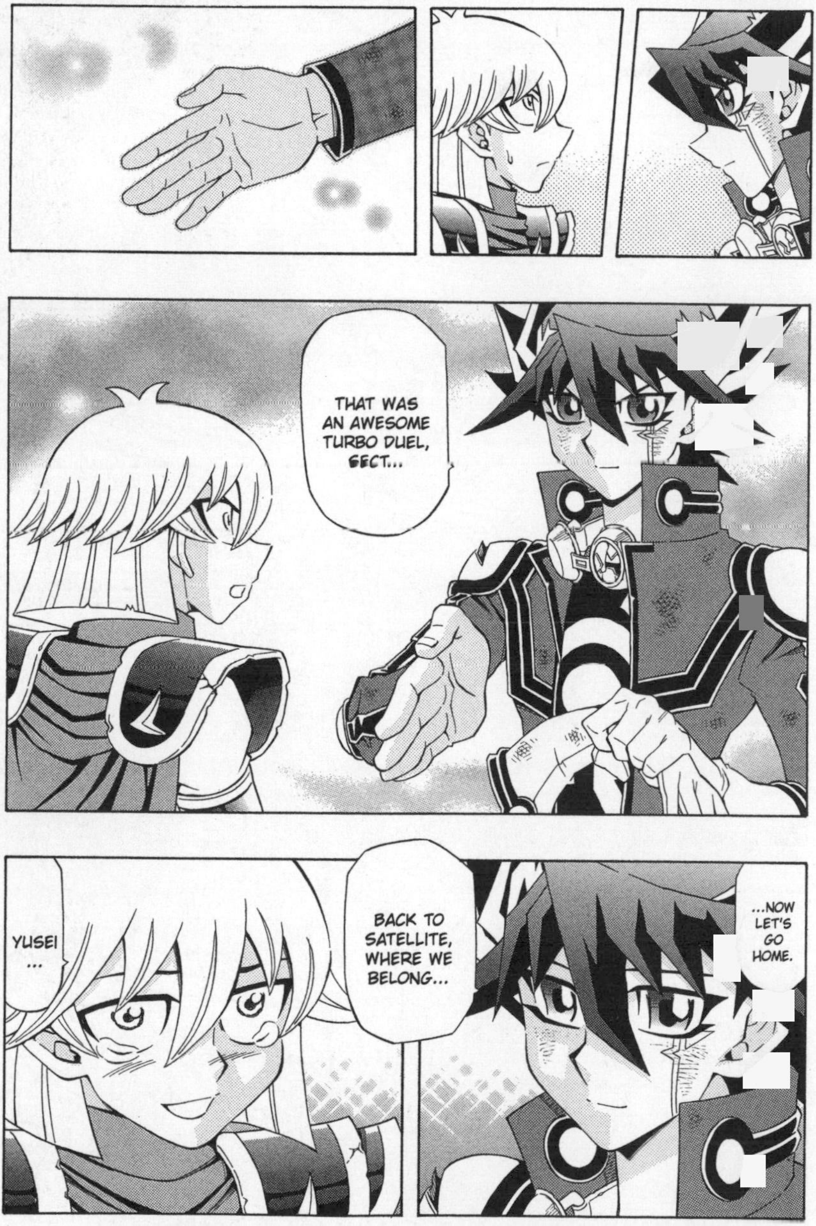

THAT WAS AN AWESOME TURBO DUEL, SECT...
...NOW LET'S GO HOME.
BACK TO SATELLITE, WHERE WE BELONG...
YUSEI ...

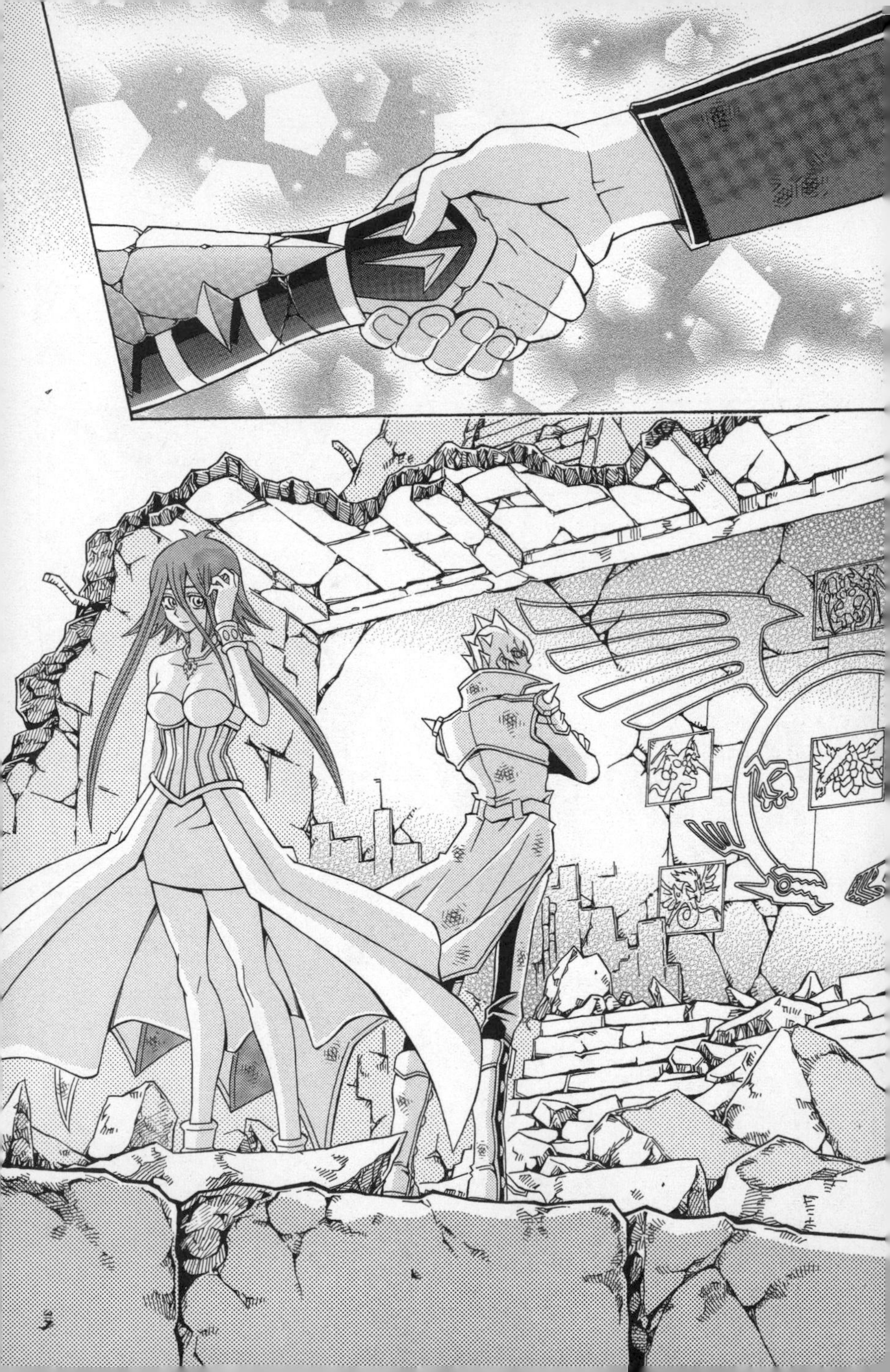

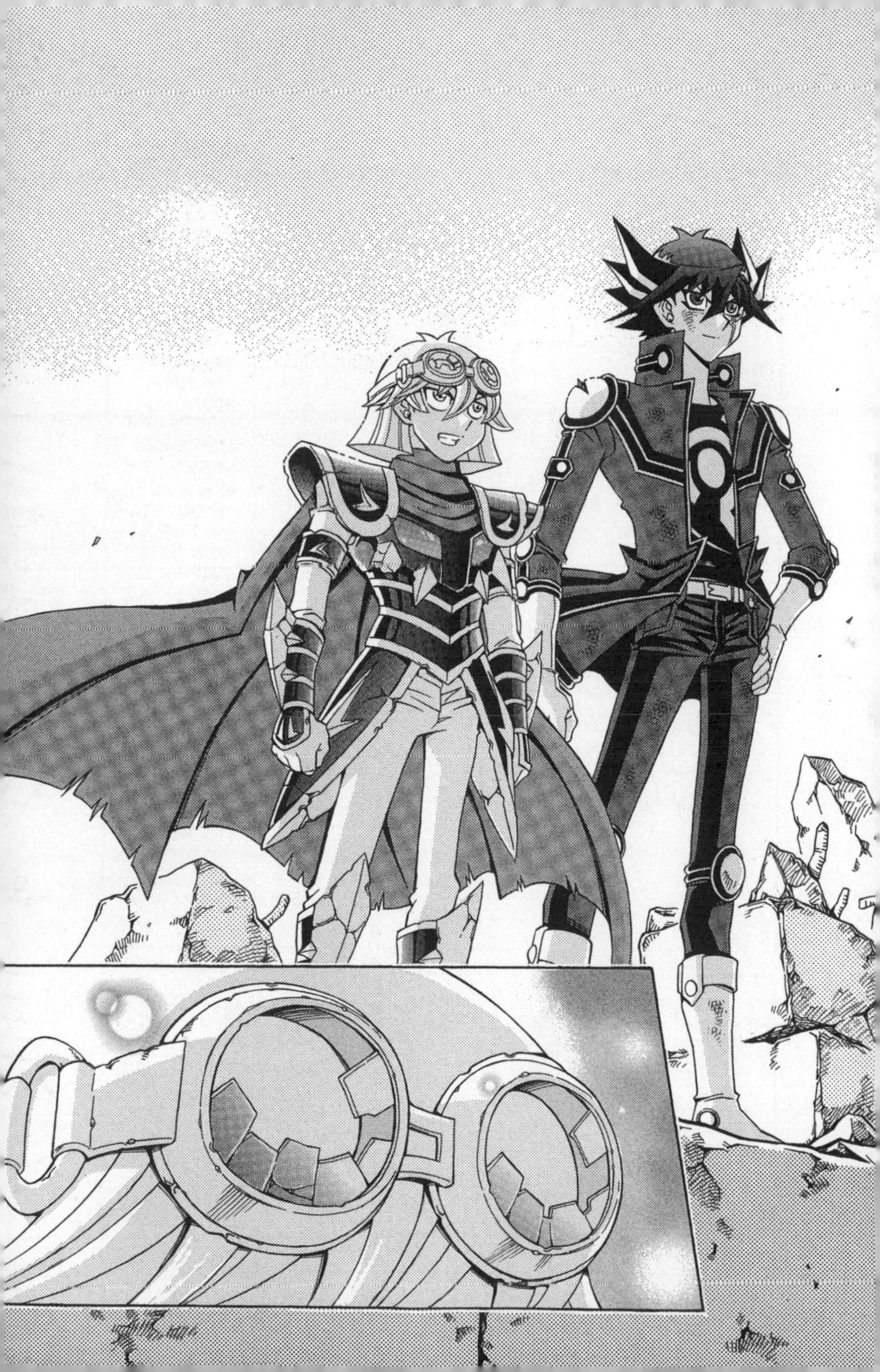

5D's TRACKS

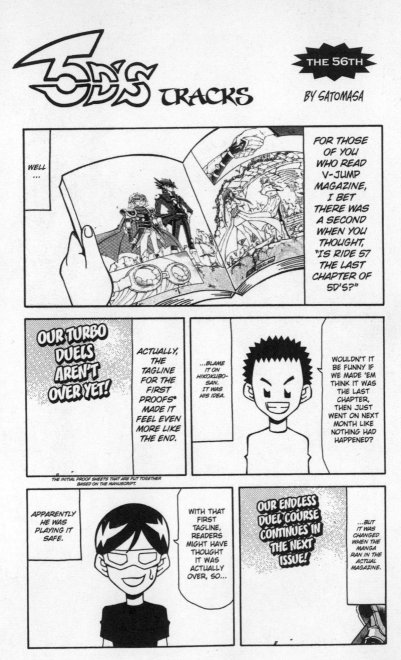

THE 56TH

BY SATOMASA

FOR THOSE OF YOU WHO READ V-JUMP MAGAZINE, I BET THERE WAS A SECOND WHEN YOU THOUGHT, "IS RIDE 57 THE LAST CHAPTER OF 5D'S?"
WELL...
WOULDN'T IT BE FUNNY IF WE MADE 'EM THINK IT WAS THE LAST CHAPTER, THEN JUST WENT ON NEXT MONTH LIKE NOTHING HAD HAPPENED?
...BLAME IT ON HIKOKUBO-SAN. IT WAS HIS IDEA.
ACTUALLY, THE TAGLINE FOR THE FIRST PROOFS* MADE IT FEEL EVEN MORE LIKE THE END.
OUR TURBO DUELS AREN'T OVER YET!
*THE INITIAL PROOF SHEETS THAT ARE PUT TOGETHER BASED ON THE MANUSCRIPT.
...BUT IT WAS CHANGED WHEN THE MANGA RAN IN THE ACTUAL MAGAZINE.
OUR ENDLESS DUEL COURSE CONTINUES IN THE NEXT ISSUE!
WITH THAT FIRST TAGLINE, READERS MIGHT HAVE THOUGHT IT WAS ACTUALLY OVER, SO...
APPARENTLY HE WAS PLAYING IT SAFE.

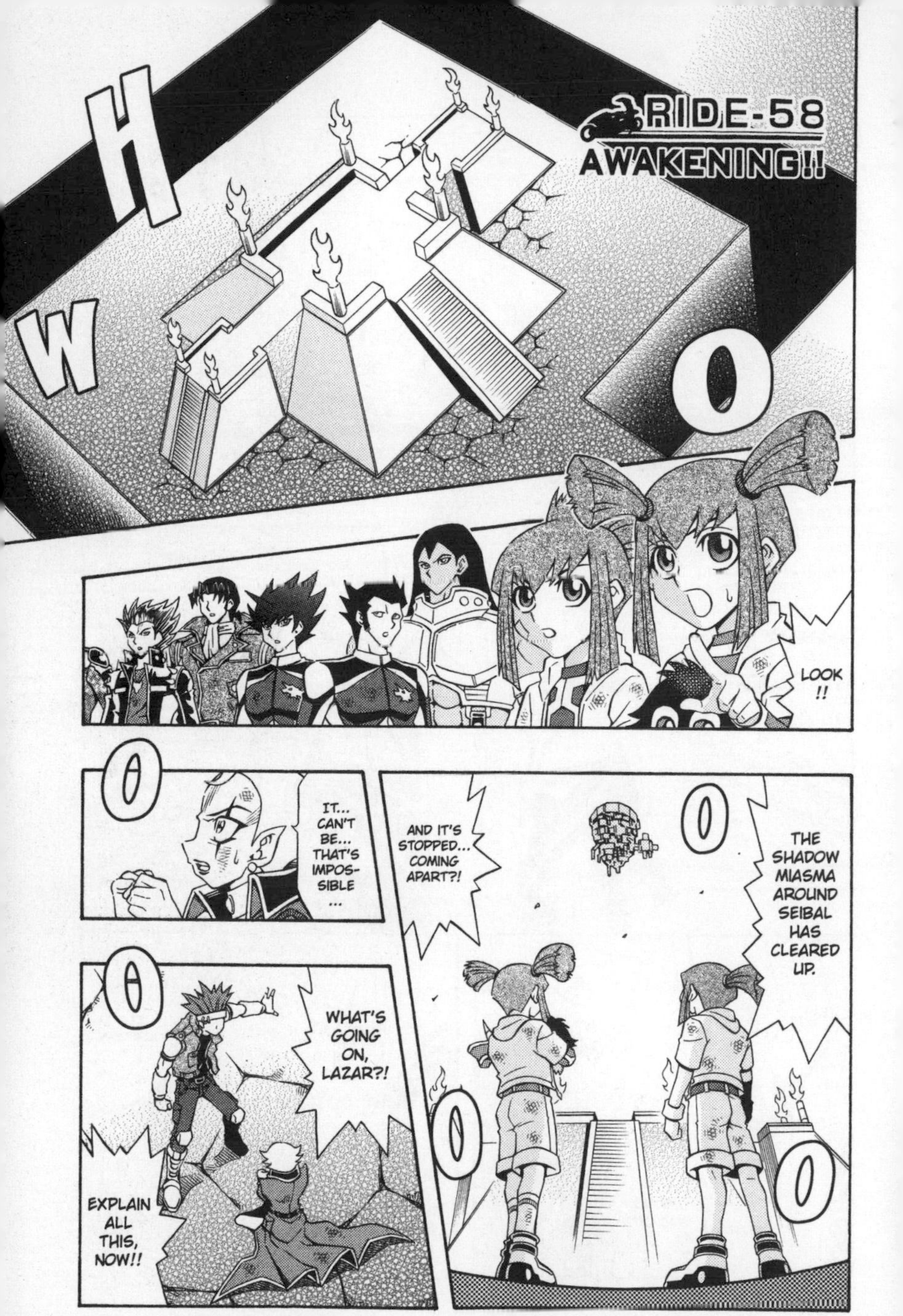
RIDE-58
AWAKENING!!
W
H
O
LOOK!!
O
THE SHADOW MIASMA AROUND SEIBAL HAS CLEARED UP.
O
AND IT'S STOPPED... COMING APART?!
O
O
IT... CAN'T BE... THAT'S IMPOSSIBLE...
O
WHAT'S GOING ON, LAZAR?!
EXPLAIN ALL THIS, NOW!!

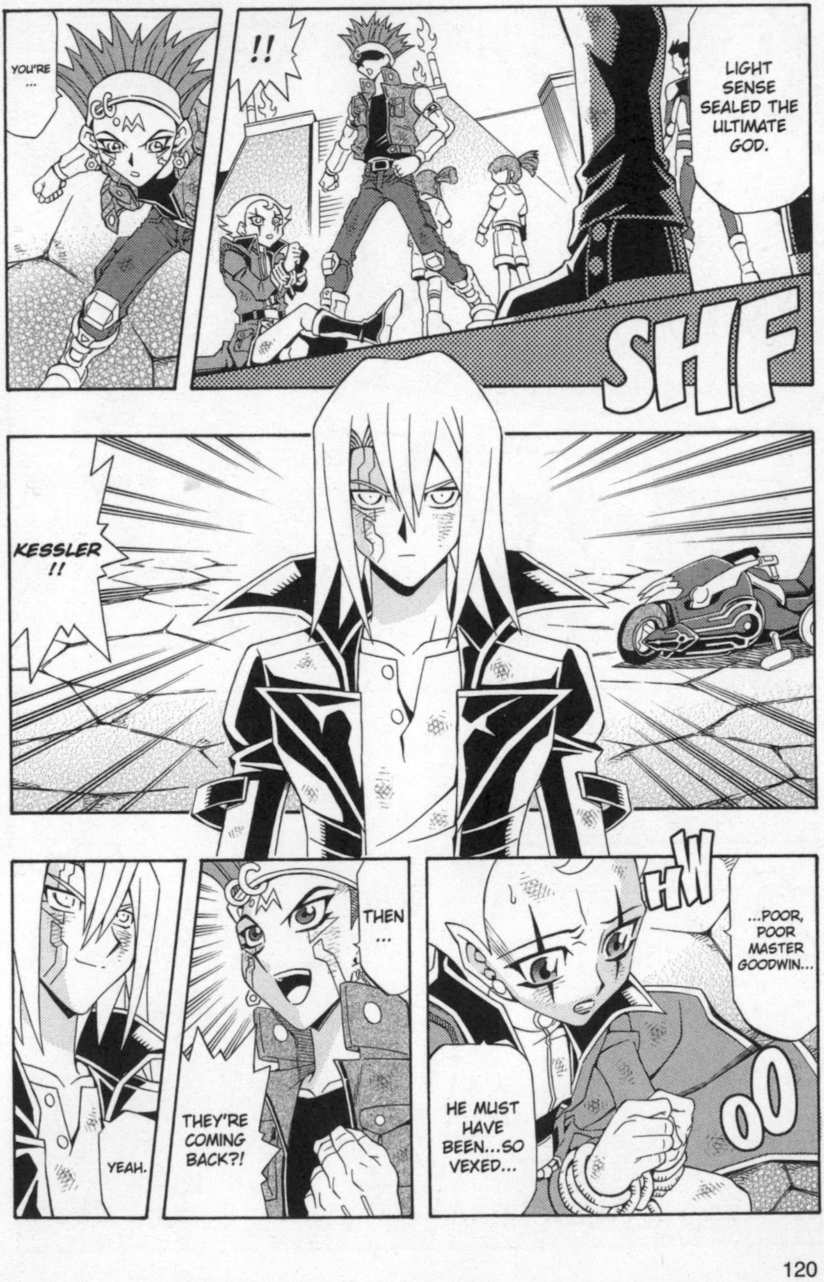
LIGHT SENSE SEALED THE ULTIMATE GOD.
!!
YOU'RE ...
SHF
KESSLER !!
HW
...POOR, POOR MASTER GOODWIN...
HE MUST HAVE BEEN...SO VEXED...
OO
THEN ...
THEY'RE COMING BACK?!
YEAH.

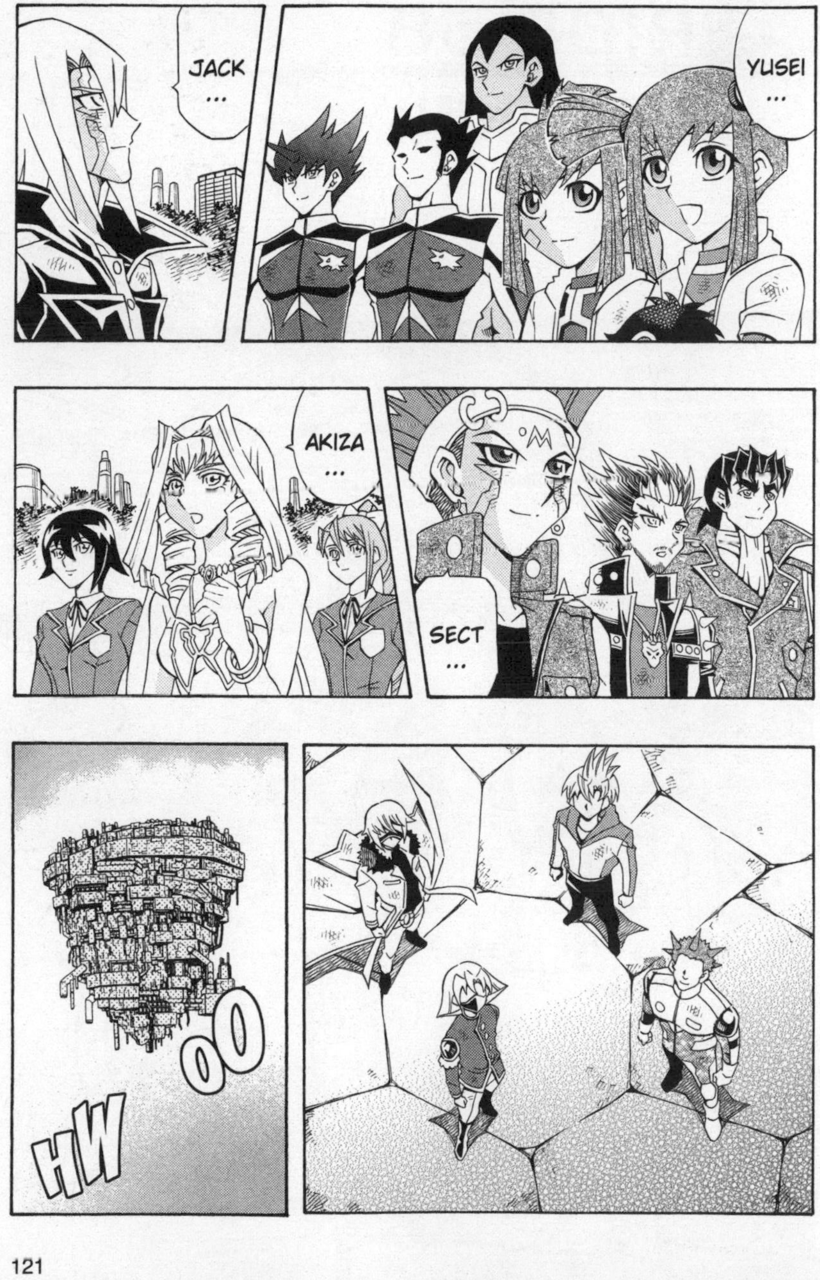
YUSEI ...
JACK ...
SECT ...
AKIZA ...
HWOO

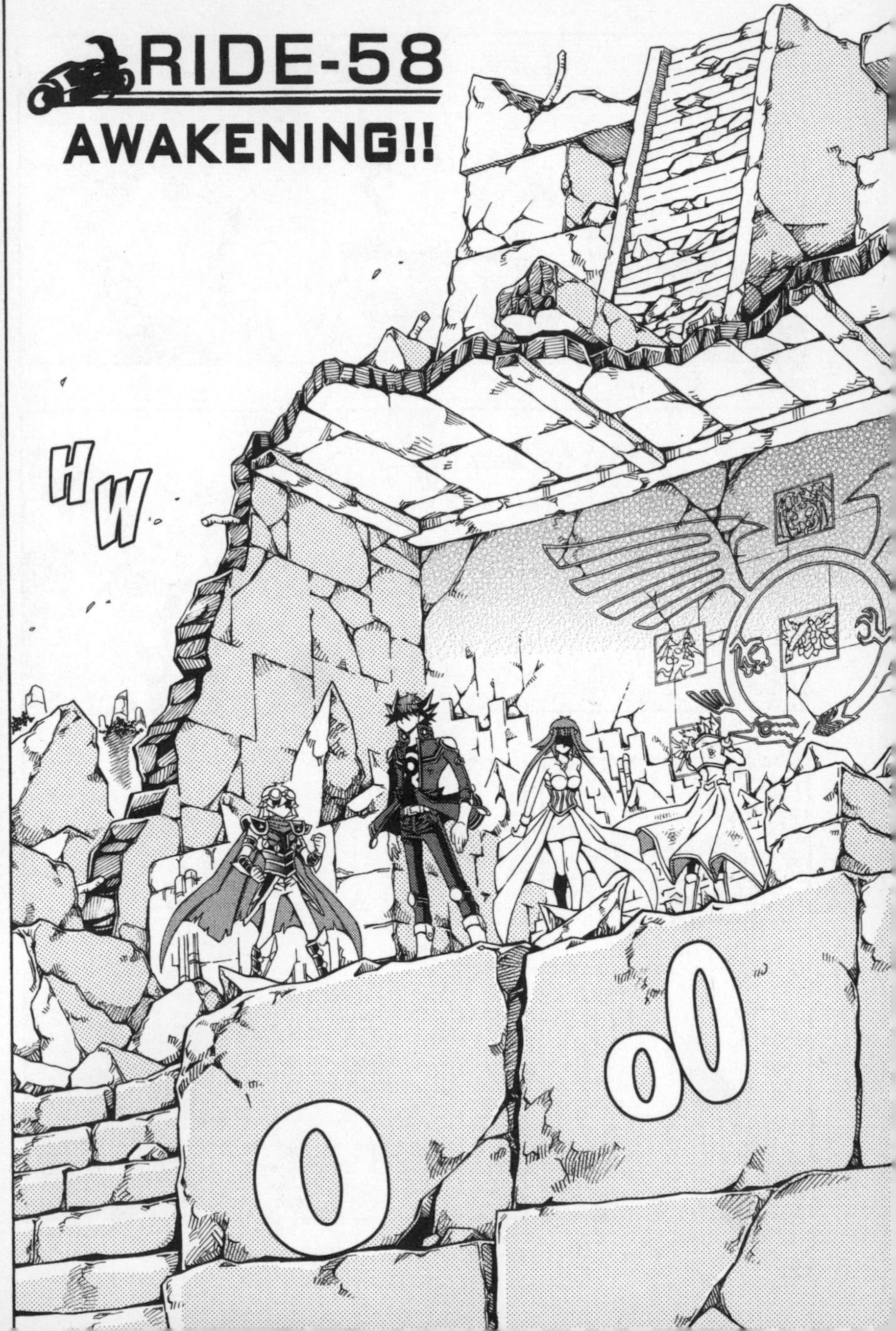
RIDE-58
AWAKENING!!
HW

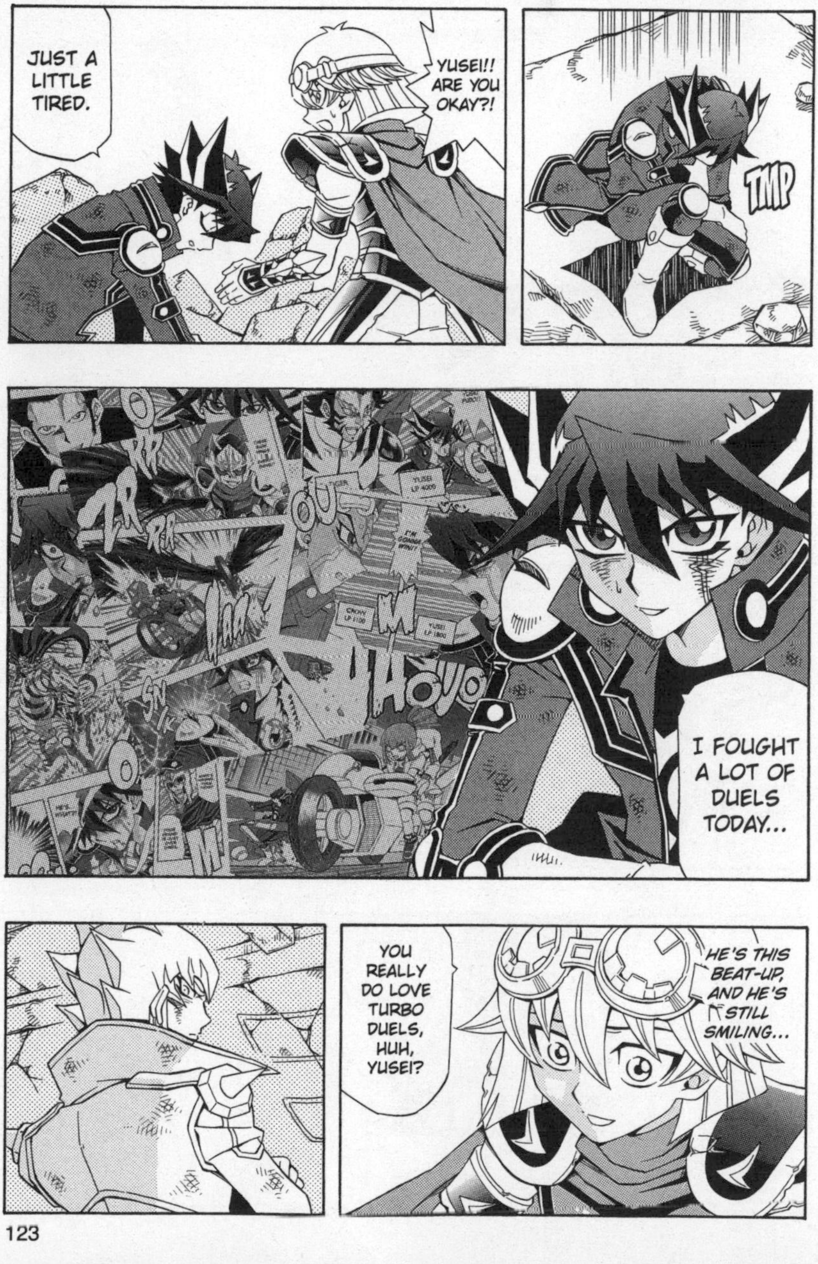
TMP
YUSEI!! ARE YOU OKAY?!
JUST A LITTLE TIRED.
I FOUGHT A LOT OF DUELS TODAY...
HE'S THIS BEAT-UP, AND HE'S STILL SMILING...
YOU REALLY DO LOVE TURBO DUELS, HUH, YUSEI?

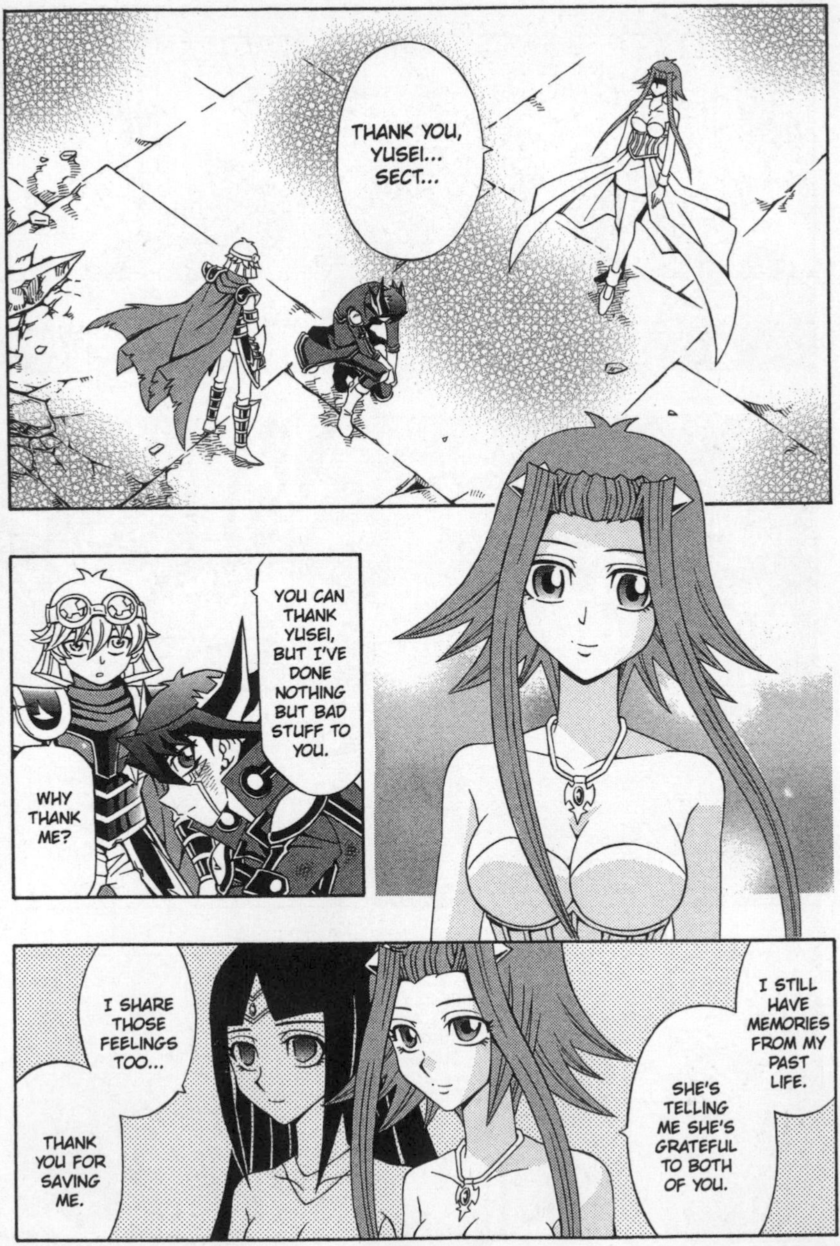
THANK YOU, YUSEI... SECT...
YOU CAN THANK YUSEI, BUT I'VE DONE NOTHING BUT BAD STUFF TO YOU.
WHY THANK ME?
I STILL HAVE MEMORIES FROM MY PAST LIFE.
SHE'S TELLING ME SHE'S GRATEFUL TO BOTH OF YOU.
I SHARE THOSE FEELINGS TOO...
THANK YOU FOR SAVING ME.

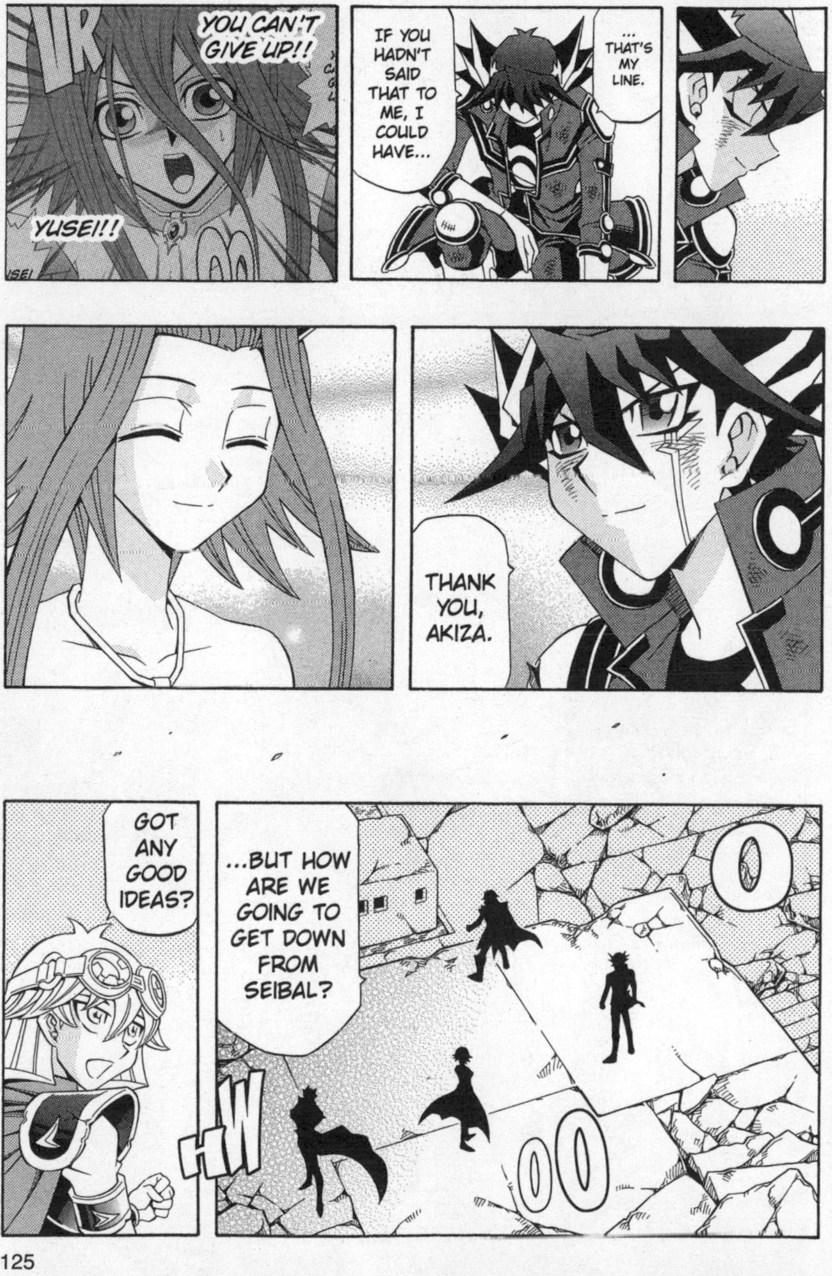
...THAT'S MY LINE.
IF YOU HADN'T SAID THAT TO ME, I COULD HAVE...
YOU CAN'T GIVE UP!!
YUSEI!!
THANK YOU, AKIZA.
...BUT HOW ARE WE GOING TO GET DOWN FROM SEIBAL?
GOT ANY GOOD IDEAS?

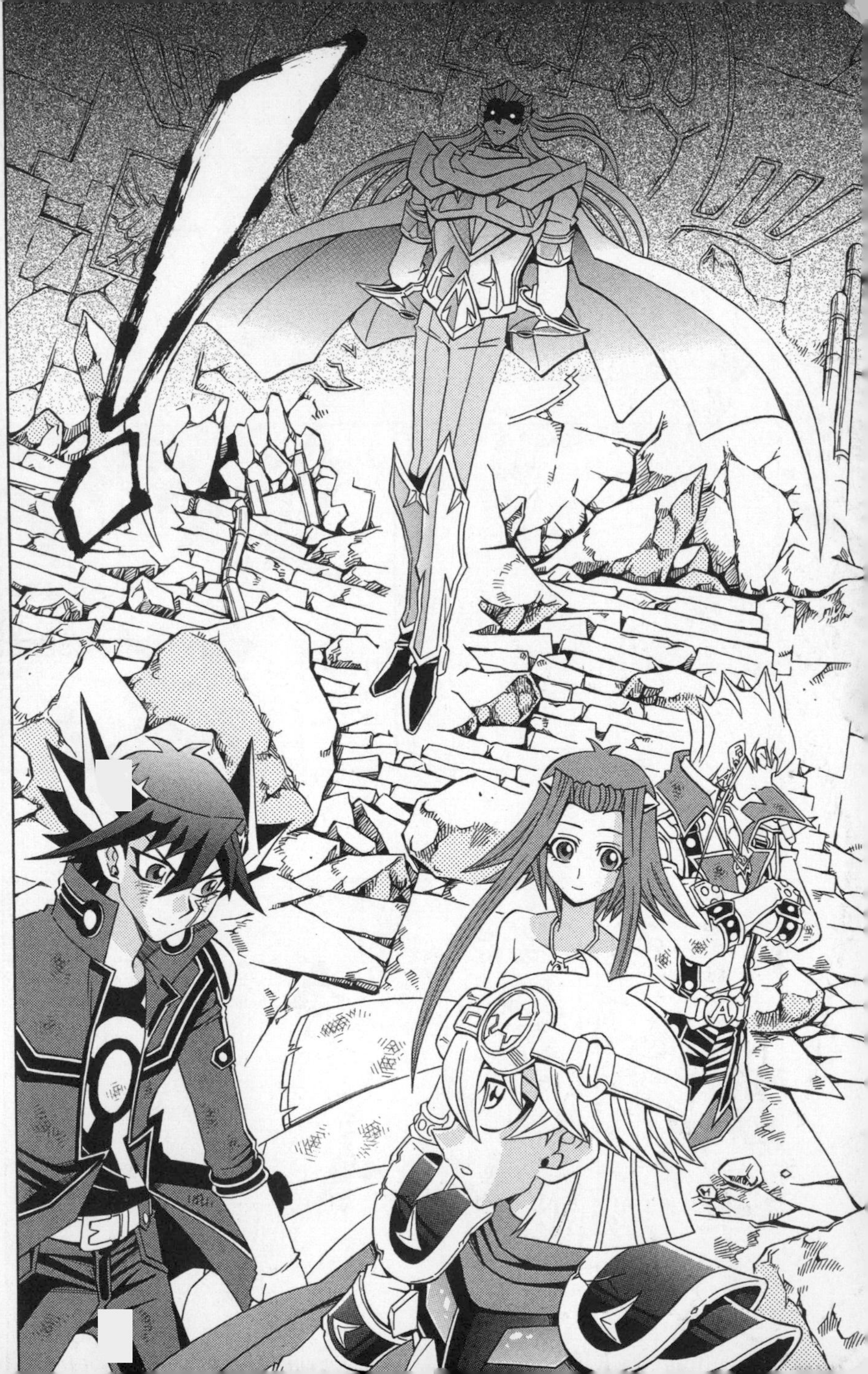

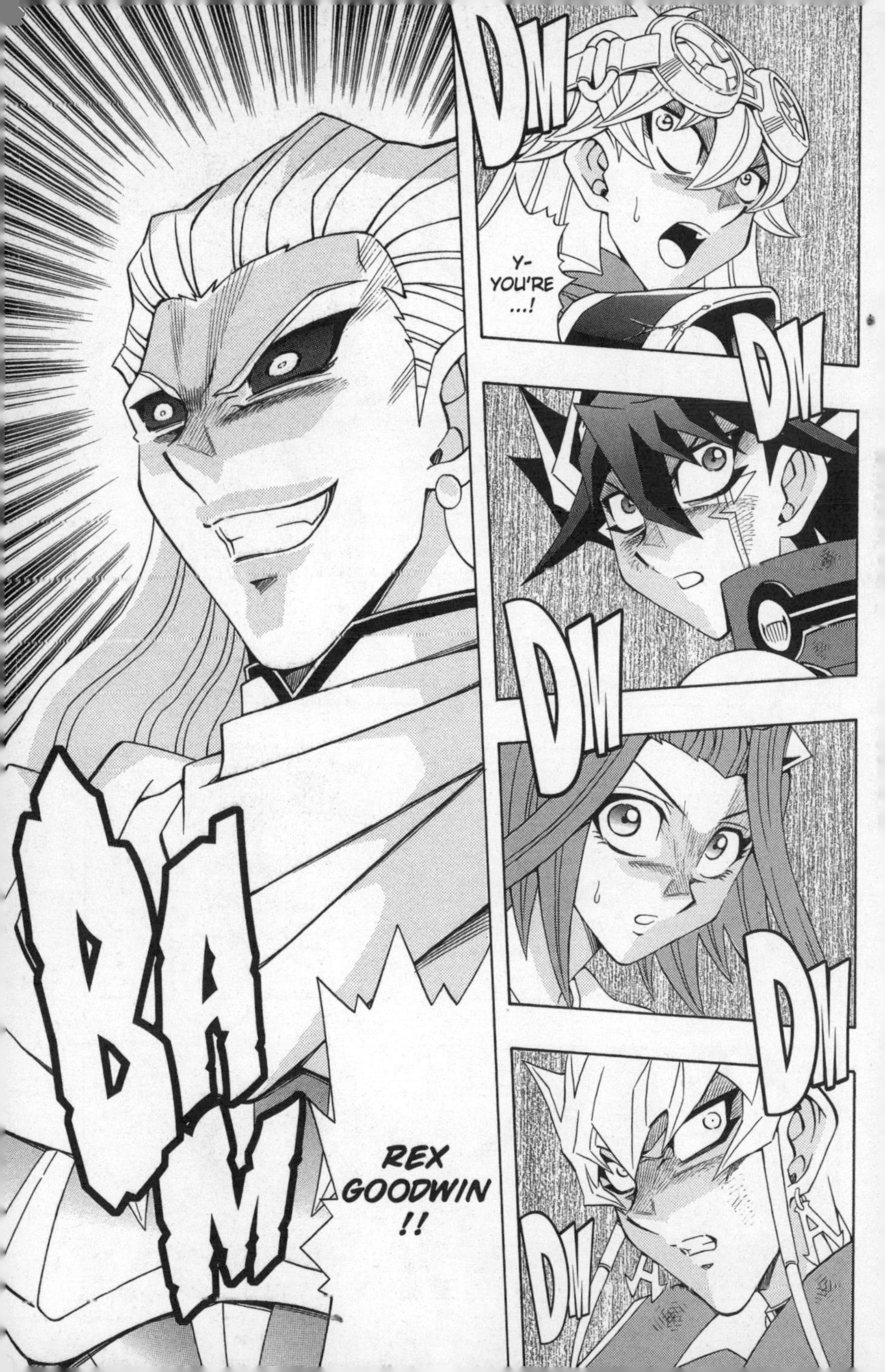
DM
Y- YOU'RE ...!
DM
DM
DM
DM
BAM
REX GOODWIN !!

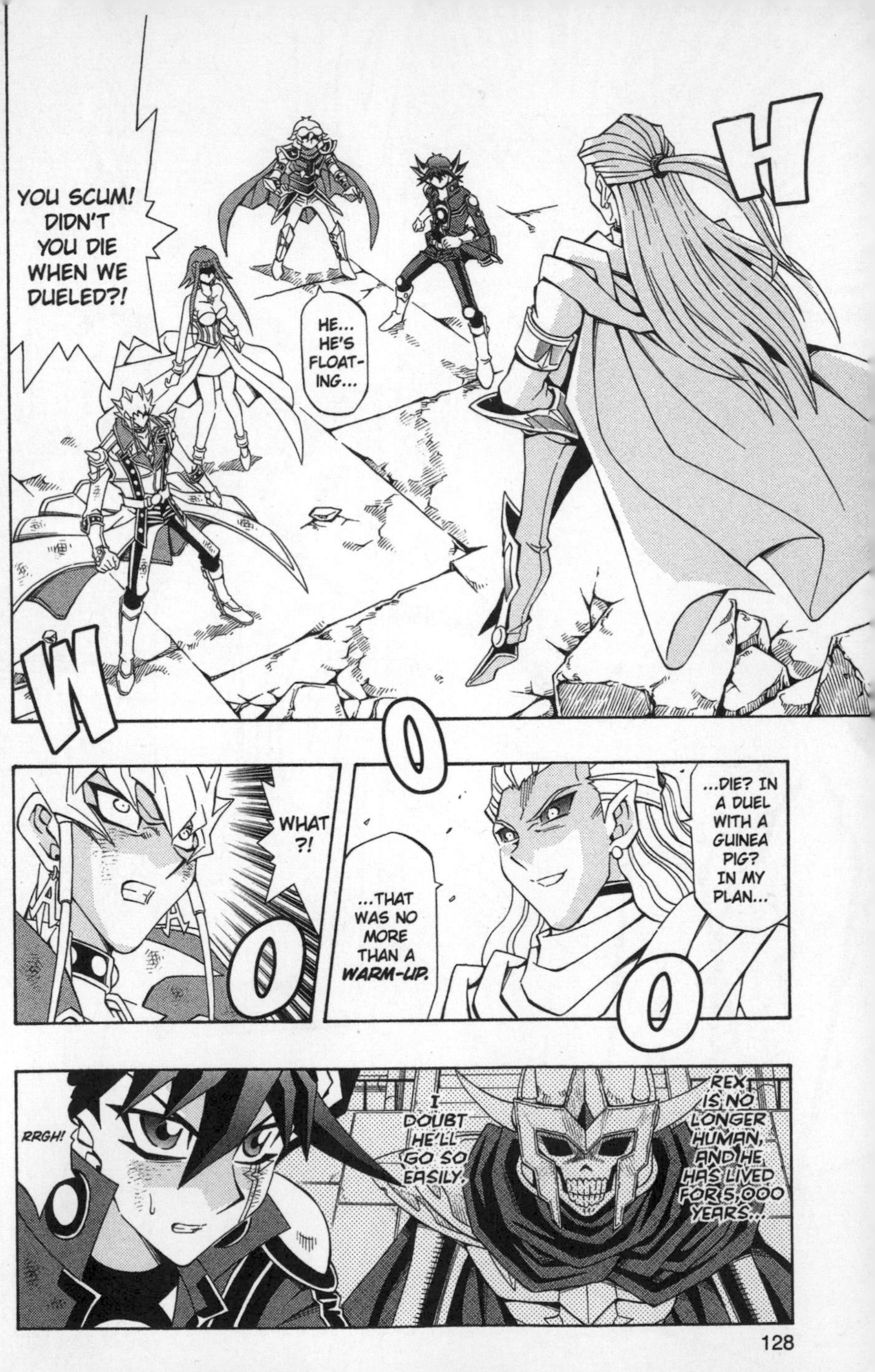
WHOOO
HE... HE'S FLOAT-ING...
YOU SCUM! DIDN'T YOU DIE WHEN WE DUELED?!
...DIE? IN A DUEL WITH A GUINEA PIG? IN MY PLAN...
...THAT WAS NO MORE THAN A *WARM-UP.*
WHAT?!
REX IS NO LONGER HUMAN, AND HE HAS LIVED FOR 5,000 YEARS...
I DOUBT HE'LL GO SO EASILY.
RRGH!

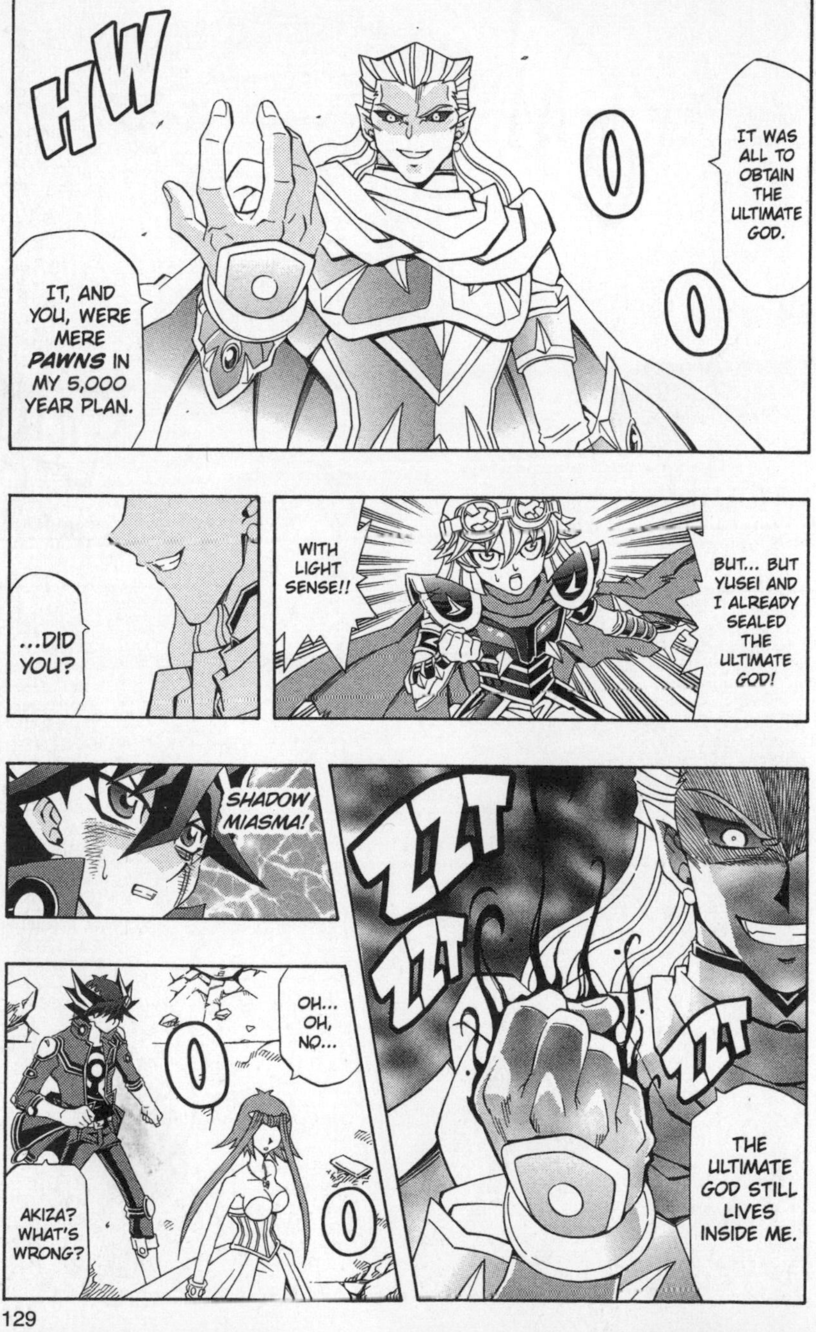
IT WAS ALL TO OBTAIN THE ULTIMATE GOD.
HW
IT, AND YOU, WERE MERE ***PAWNS*** IN MY 5,000 YEAR PLAN.
BUT... BUT YUSEI AND I ALREADY SEALED THE ULTIMATE GOD!
WITH LIGHT SENSE!!
...DID YOU?
ZZT
ZZT
ZZT
THE ULTIMATE GOD STILL LIVES INSIDE ME.
SHADOW MIASMA!
OH... OH, NO...
AKIZA? WHAT'S WRONG?

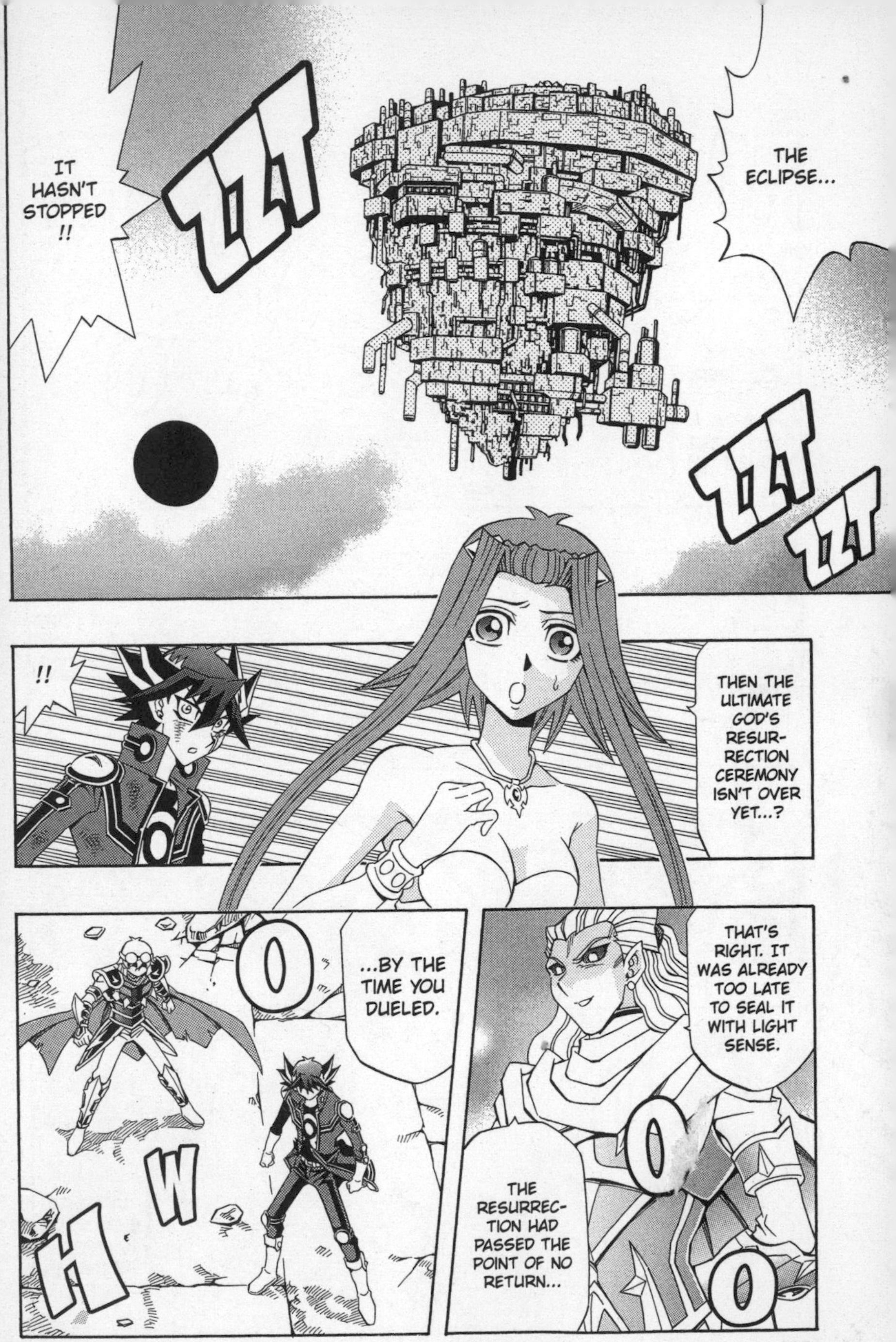
THE ECLIPSE...
IT HASN'T STOPPED !!
ZZT
ZZT
ZZT
THEN THE ULTIMATE GOD'S RESURRECTION CEREMONY ISN'T OVER YET...?
!!
THAT'S RIGHT. IT WAS ALREADY TOO LATE TO SEAL IT WITH LIGHT SENSE.
THE RESURRECTION HAD PASSED THE POINT OF NO RETURN...
O
O
...BY THE TIME YOU DUELED.
O
W
H

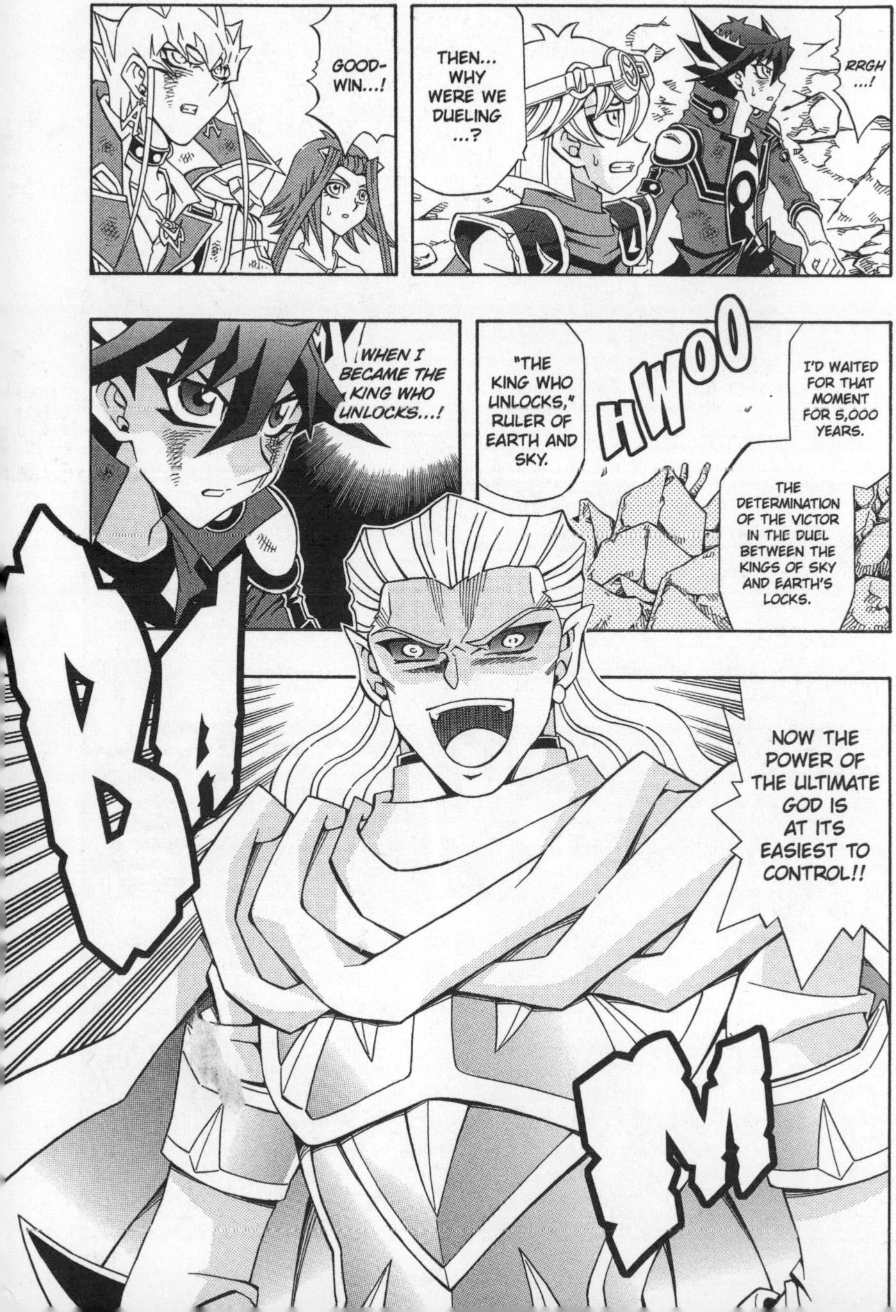
RRGH ...!
THEN... WHY WERE WE DUELING ...?
GOOD-WIN...!
I'D WAITED FOR THAT MOMENT FOR 5,000 YEARS.
HWOO
"THE KING WHO UNLOCKS," RULER OF EARTH AND SKY.
THE DETERMINATION OF THE VICTOR IN THE DUEL BETWEEN THE KINGS OF SKY AND EARTH'S LOCKS.
WHEN I BECAME THE KING WHO UNLOCKS...!
NOW THE POWER OF THE ULTIMATE GOD IS AT ITS EASIEST TO CONTROL!!
BA
M

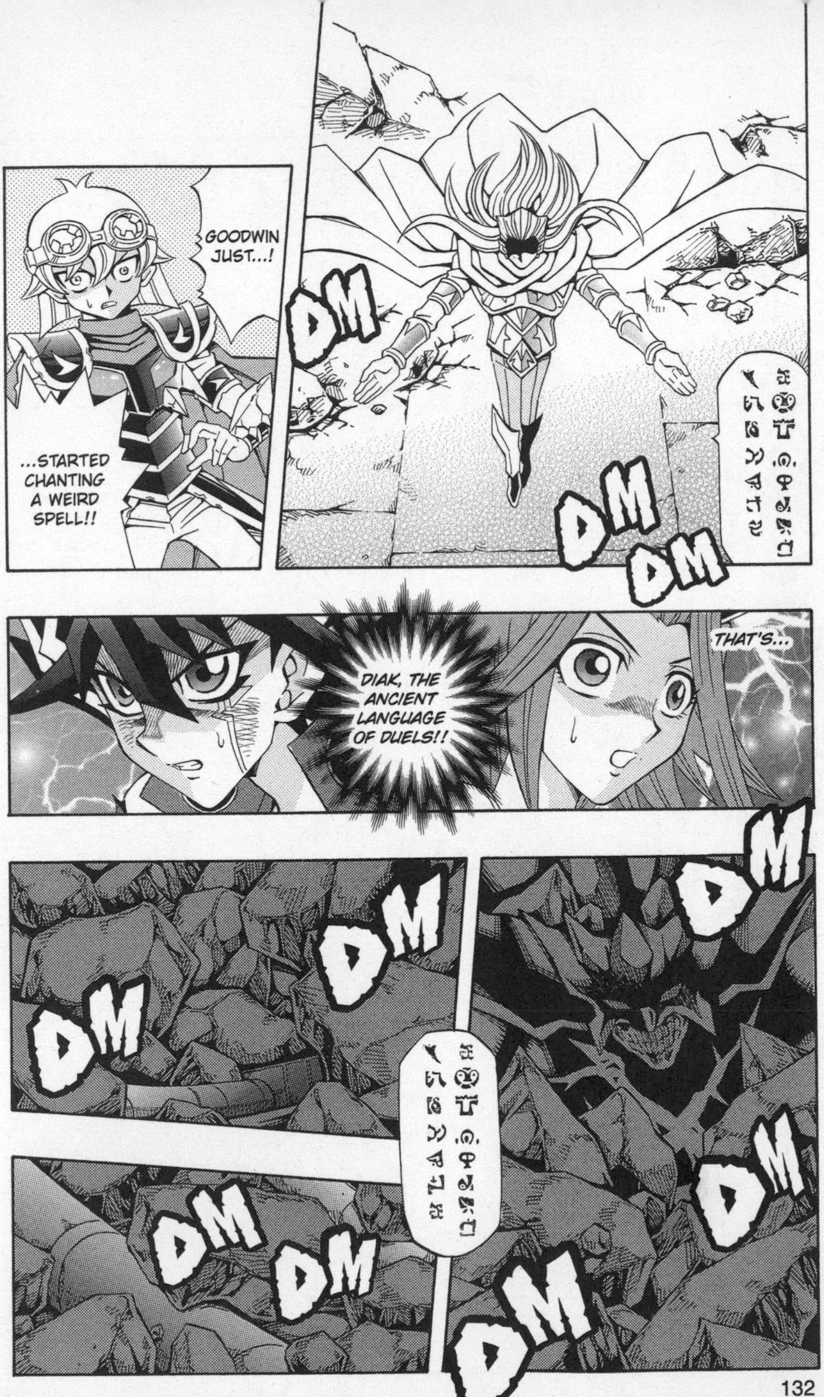
DM
DM
DM
GOODWIN JUST...!
...STARTED CHANTING A WEIRD SPELL!!
THAT'S...
DIAK, THE ANCIENT LANGUAGE OF DUELS!!
DM
DM
DM
DM
DM
DM
DM
DM

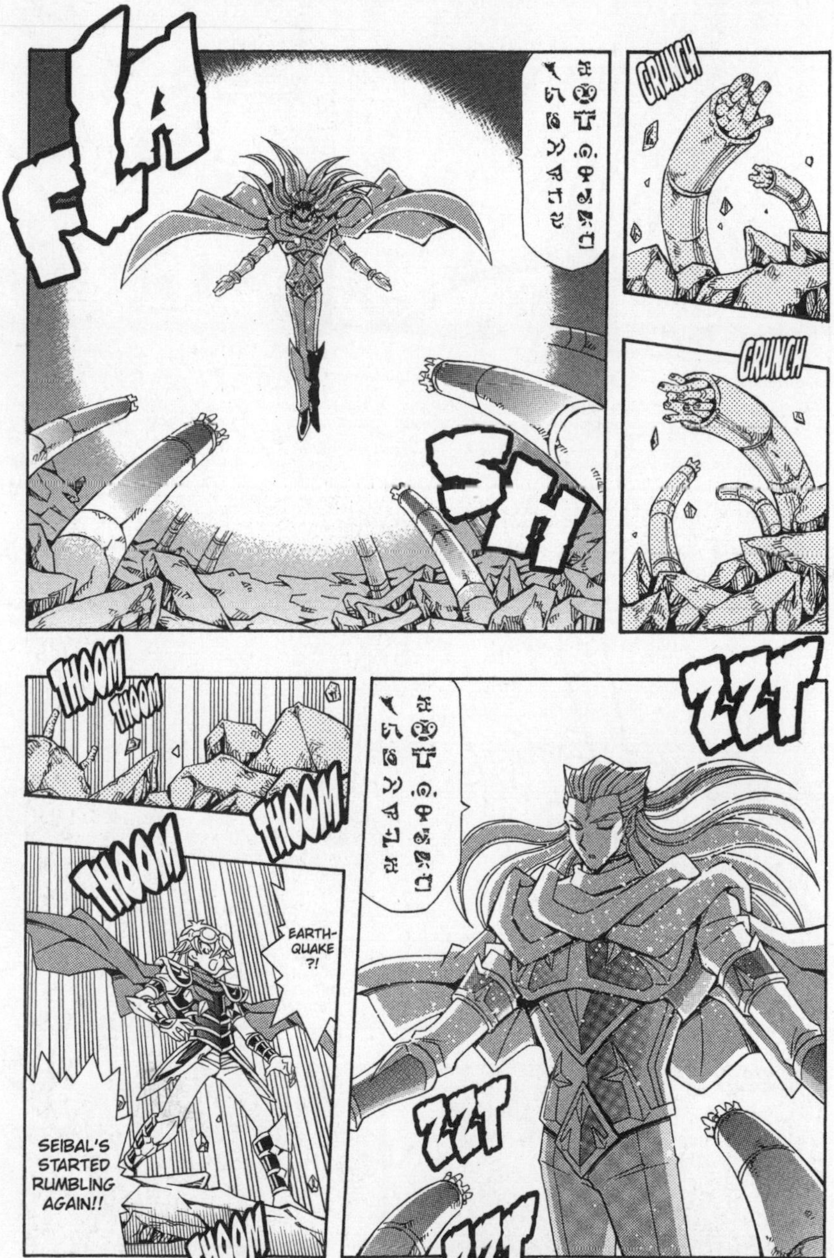

CRUNCH
CRUNCH
FLA
SH
ZZT
ZZT
ZZT
THOOM
THOOM
THOOM
THOOM
EARTHQUAKE?!
SEIBAL'S STARTED RUMBLING AGAIN!!
THOOM

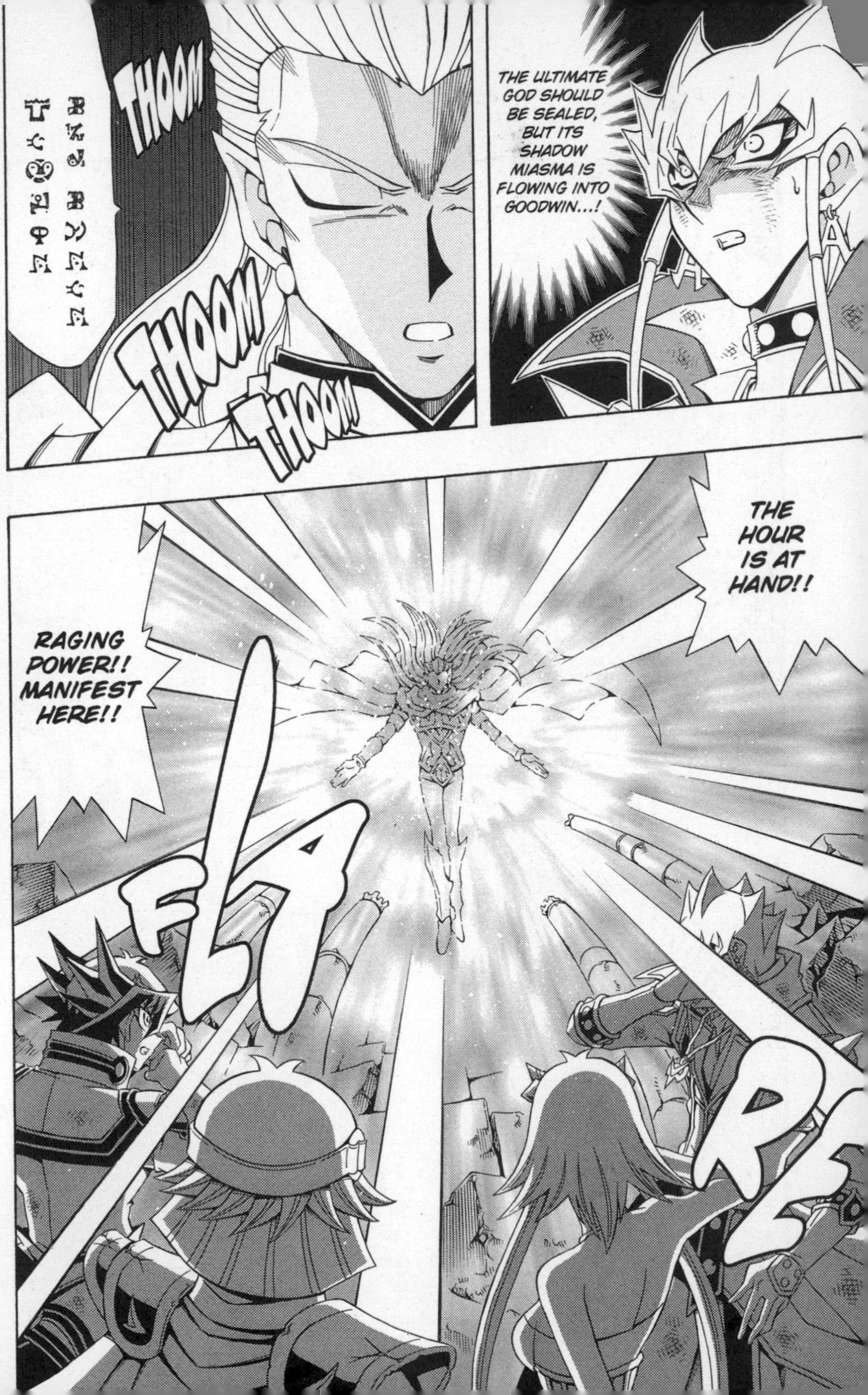

THE ULTIMATE GOD SHOULD BE SEALED, BUT ITS SHADOW MIASMA IS FLOWING INTO GOODWIN...!
THOOM
THOOM
THOOM
THE HOUR IS AT HAND!!
RAGING POWER!! MANIFEST HERE!!
FLA

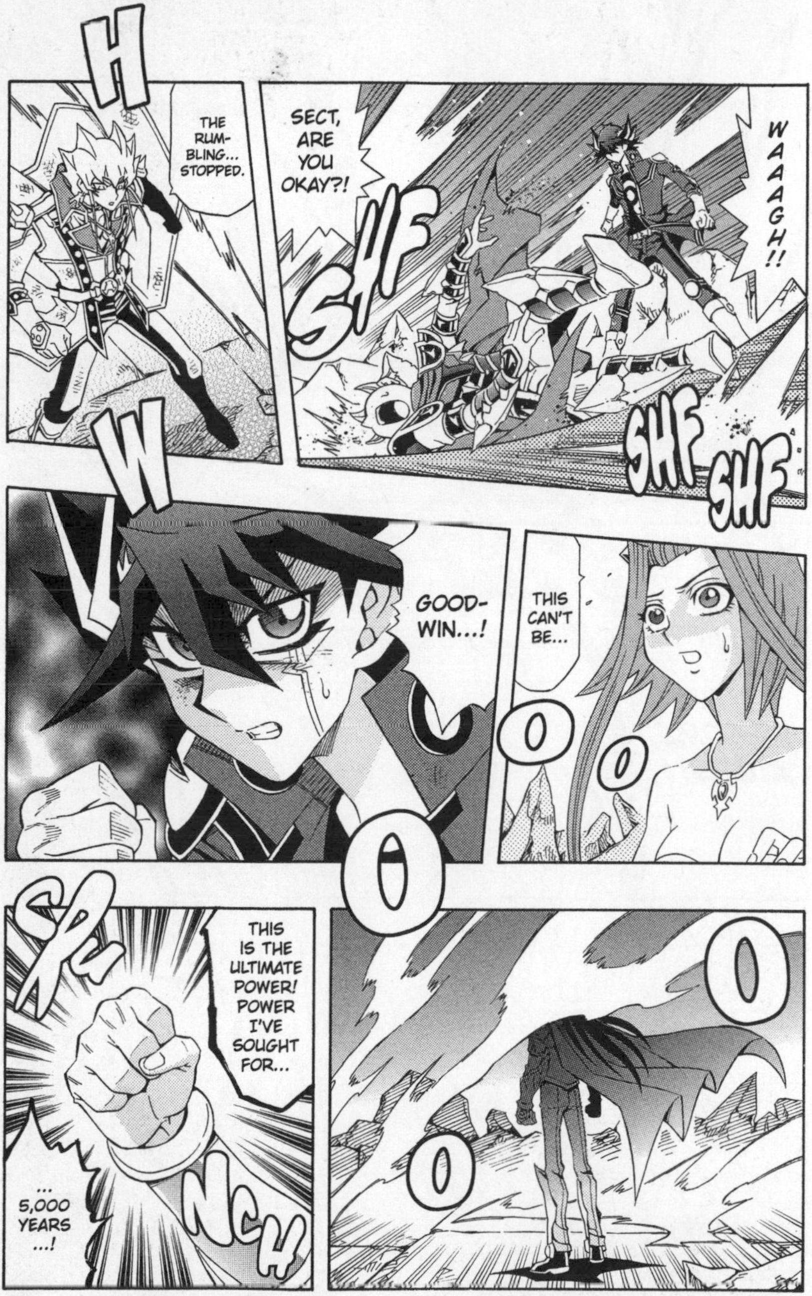

SECT, ARE YOU OKAY?!
WAAAAGH!!
SHF
SHF SHF SHF
H
THE RUM-BLING... STOPPED.
W
THIS CAN'T BE...
O O
GOOD-WIN...!
O
O O
THIS IS THE ULTIMATE POWER! POWER I'VE SOUGHT FOR...
... 5,000 YEARS ...!
SCRUNCH

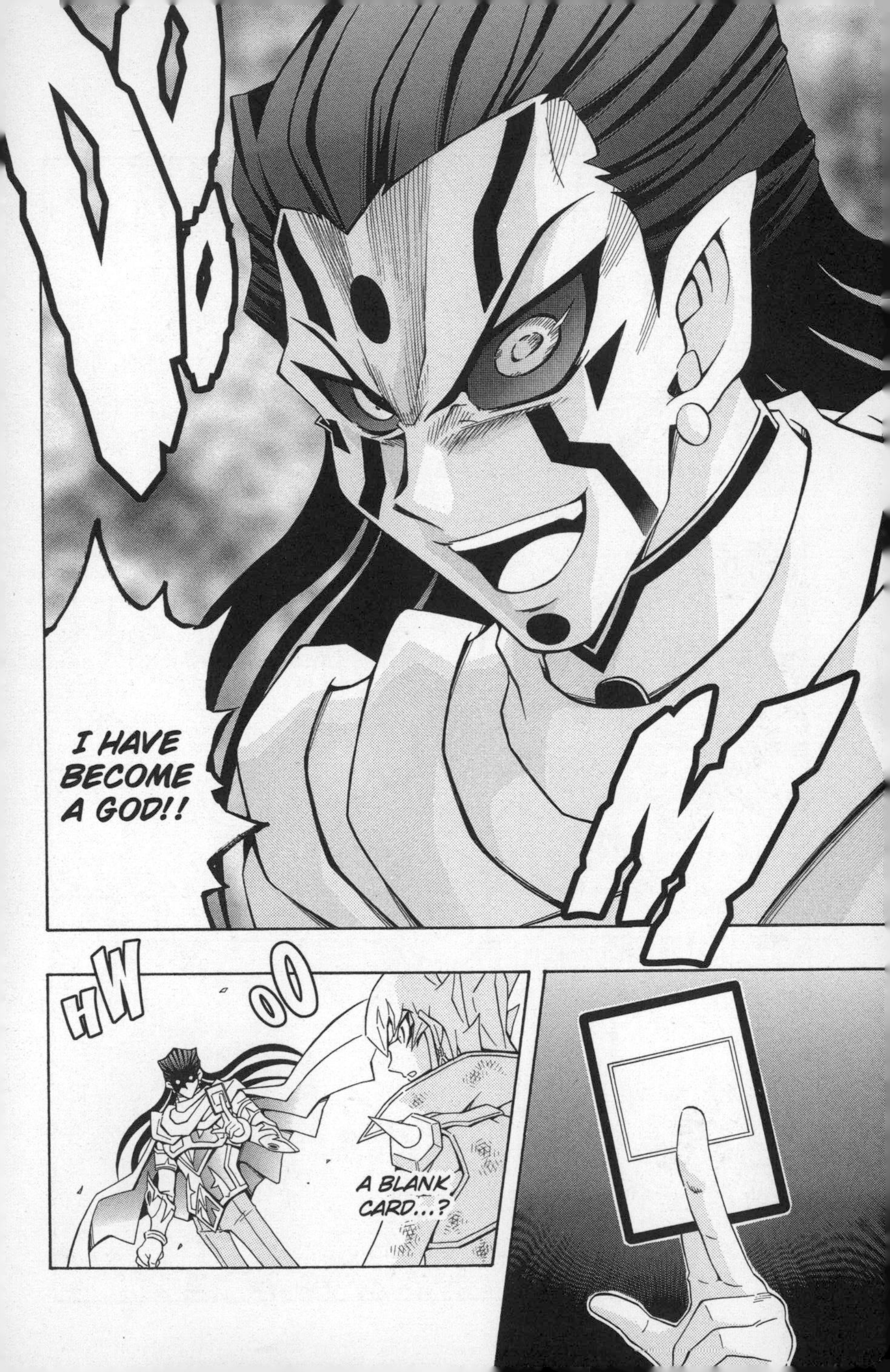
I HAVE BECOME A GOD!!
A BLANK CARD...?

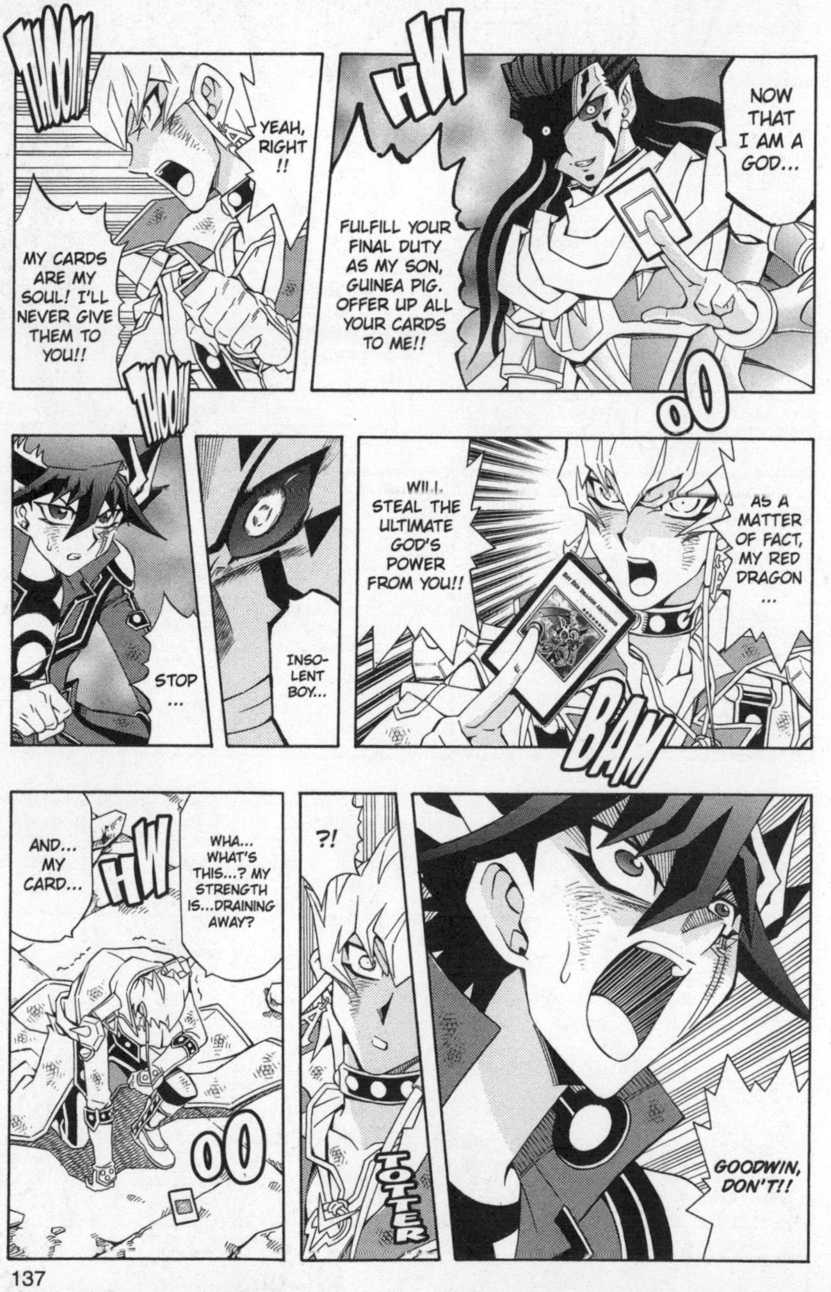

NOW THAT I AM A GOD...
HW
FULFILL YOUR FINAL DUTY AS MY SON, GUINEA PIG. OFFER UP ALL YOUR CARDS TO ME!!
OO
THOOM
YEAH, RIGHT!!
MY CARDS ARE MY SOUL! I'LL NEVER GIVE THEM TO YOU!!
THOOM
AS A MATTER OF FACT, MY RED DRAGON ...
WILL STEAL THE ULTIMATE GOD'S POWER FROM YOU!!
BAM
INSO-LENT BOY...
STOP ...
GOODWIN, DON'T!!
?!
TOTTER
WHA... WHAT'S THIS...? MY STRENGTH IS...DRAINING AWAY?
AND... MY CARD...
HW
OO

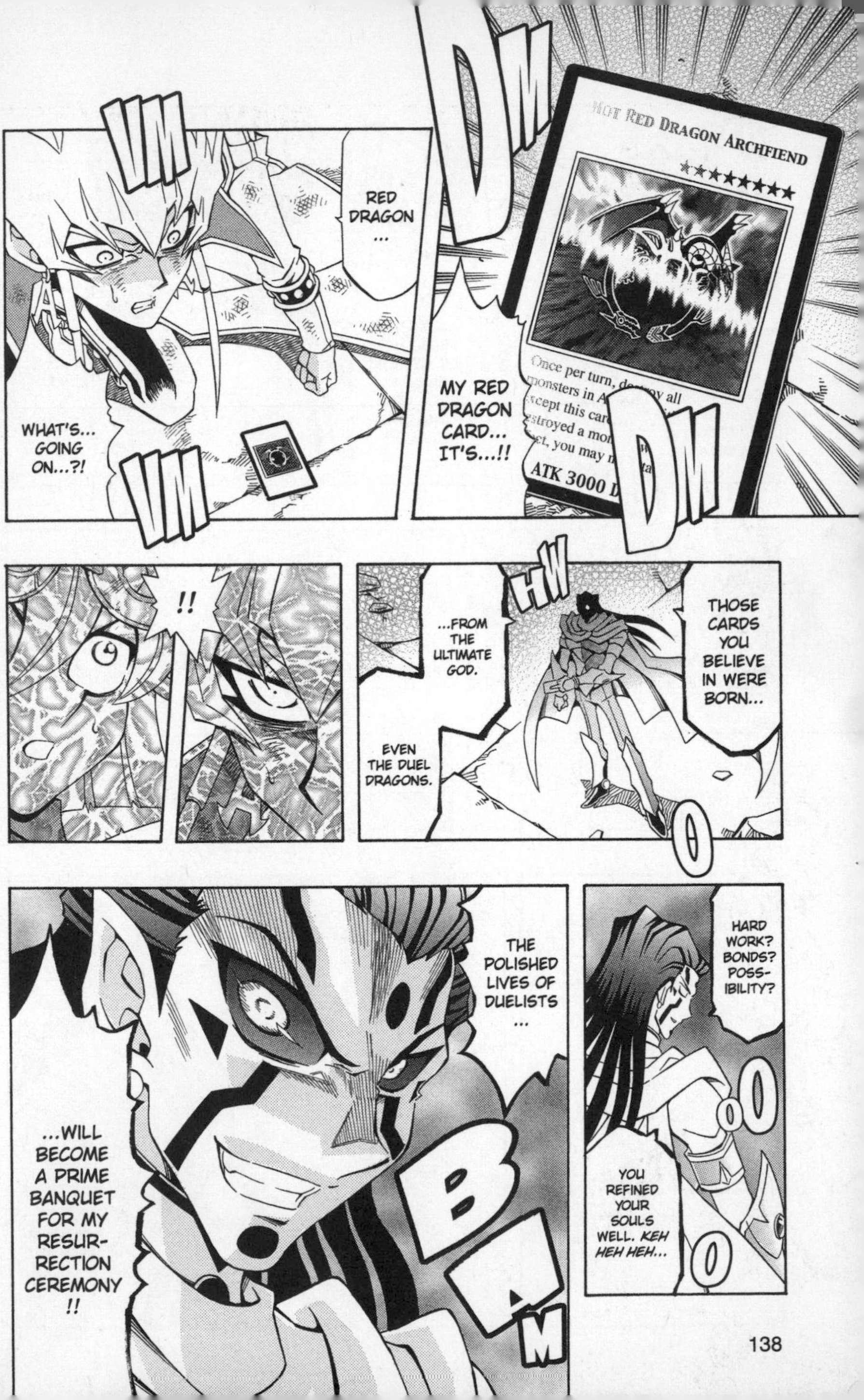
DM
HOT RED DRAGON ARCHFIEND
ATK 3000
MY RED DRAGON CARD... IT'S...!!
DM
VM
RED DRAGON...
WHAT'S... GOING ON...?!
VM
HW
THOSE CARDS YOU BELIEVE IN WERE BORN...
...FROM THE ULTIMATE GOD.
EVEN THE DUEL DRAGONS.
O
!!
HARD WORK? BONDS? POSSIBILITY?
OO
YOU REFINED YOUR SOULS WELL. KEH HEH HEH...
O
THE POLISHED LIVES OF DUELISTS...
...WILL BECOME A PRIME BANQUET FOR MY RESURRECTION CEREMONY!!
BAM

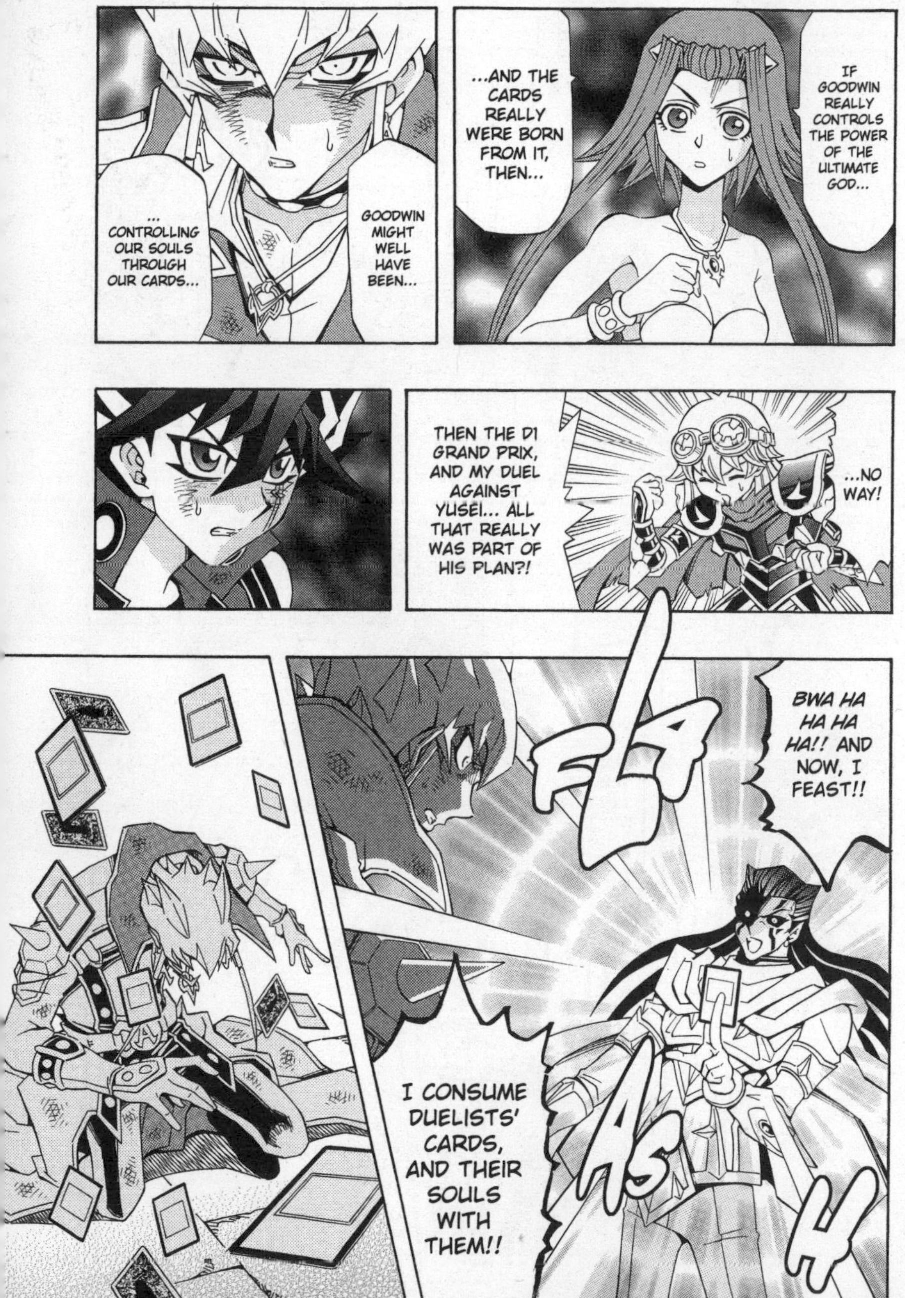
IF GOODWIN REALLY CONTROLS THE POWER OF THE ULTIMATE GOD...
...AND THE CARDS REALLY WERE BORN FROM IT, THEN...
GOODWIN MIGHT WELL HAVE BEEN...
... CONTROLLING OUR SOULS THROUGH OUR CARDS...
...NO WAY!
THEN THE D1 GRAND PRIX, AND MY DUEL AGAINST YUSEI... ALL THAT REALLY WAS PART OF HIS PLAN?!
BWA HA HA HA HA!! AND NOW, I FEAST!!
FLASH
I CONSUME DUELISTS' CARDS, AND THEIR SOULS WITH THEM!!

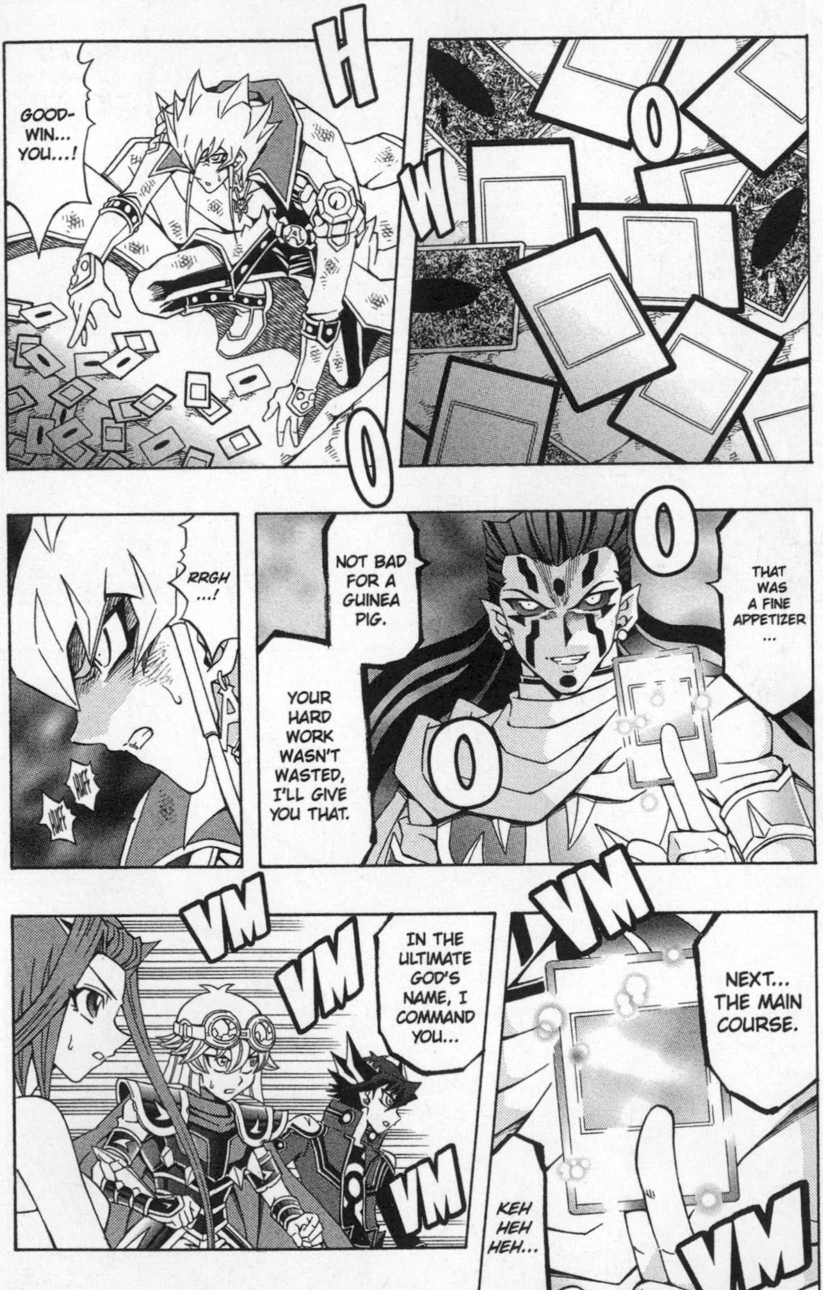
H
O
W
O
GOOD-WIN... YOU...!
O
THAT WAS A FINE APPETIZER ...
NOT BAD FOR A GUINEA PIG.
O
YOUR HARD WORK WASN'T WASTED, I'LL GIVE YOU THAT.
RRGH ...!
HUFF
HUFF
VM
NEXT... THE MAIN COURSE.
KEH HEH HEH...
VM
VM
VM
IN THE ULTIMATE GOD'S NAME, I COMMAND YOU...
VM

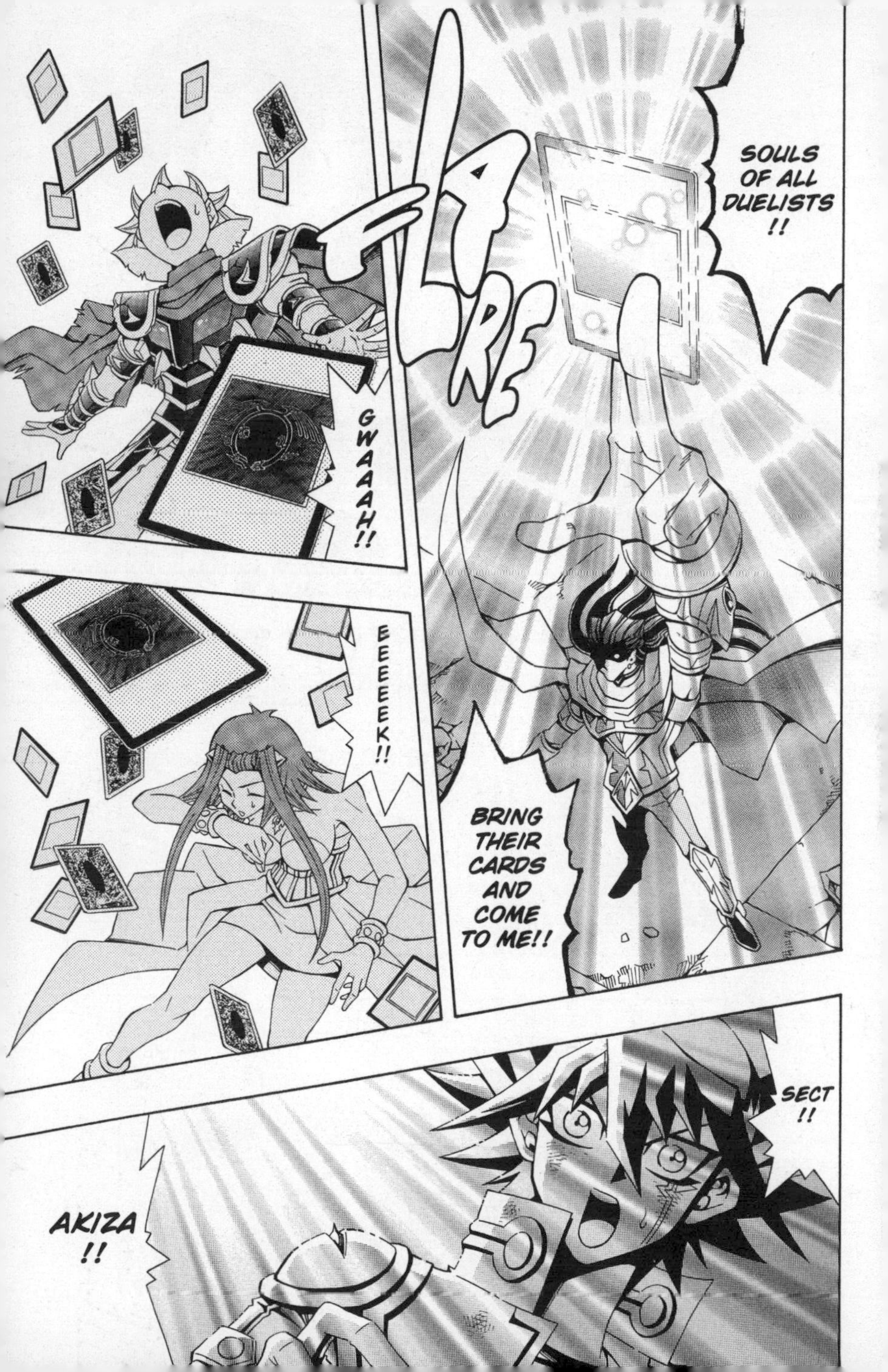
SOULS OF ALL DUELISTS!!
FLARE
BRING THEIR CARDS AND COME TO ME!!
GWAAAAH!!
EEEEEEK!!
SECT!!
AKIZA!!

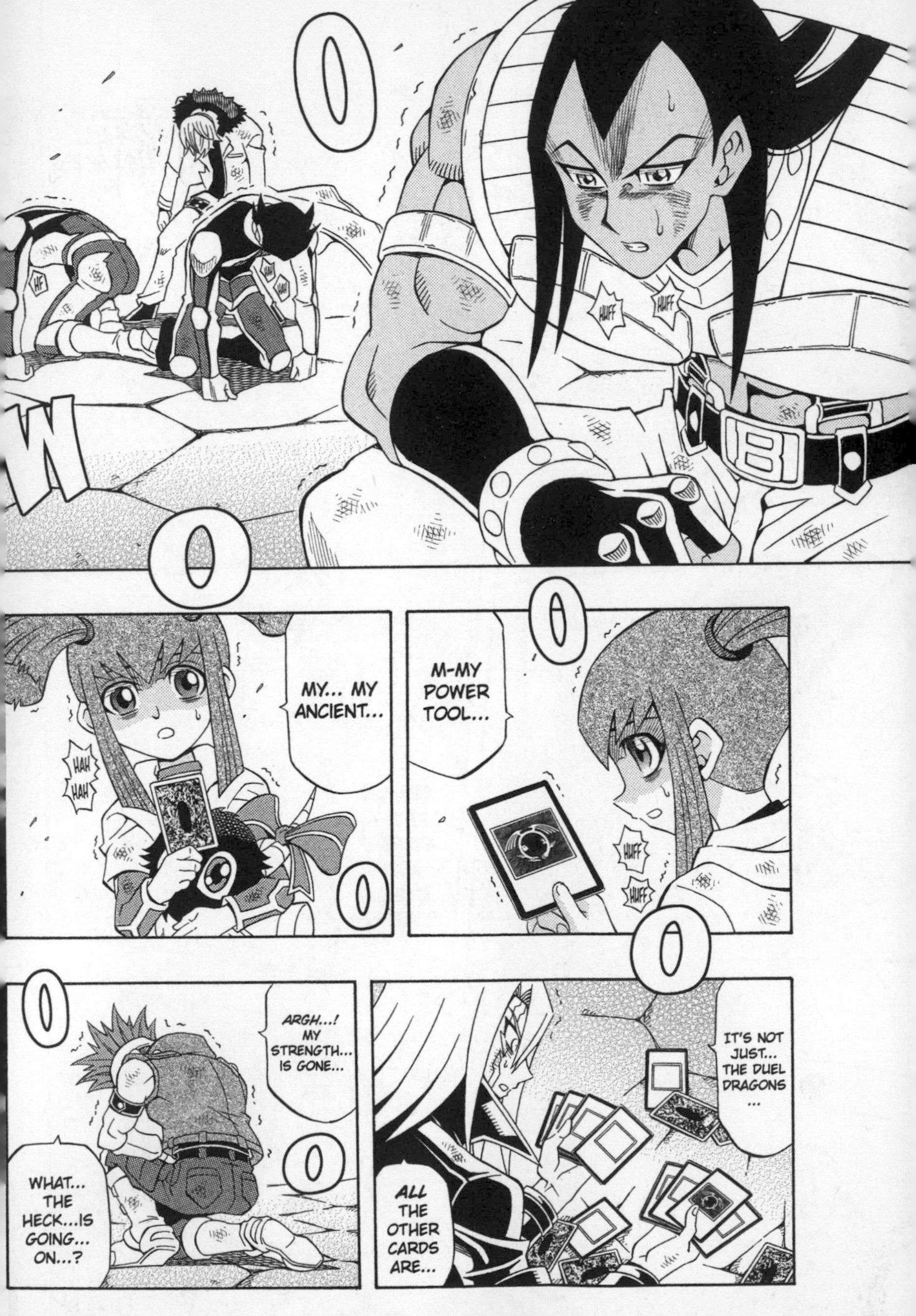
WOOOOOOO
HUFF
HUFF
HF
HAH
HAH
M-MY POWER TOOL...
HUFF
HUFF
MY... MY ANCIENT...
HAH
HAH
IT'S NOT JUST... THE DUEL DRAGONS ...
ALL THE OTHER CARDS ARE...
ARGH...! MY STRENGTH... IS GONE...
WHAT... THE HECK...IS GOING... ON...?

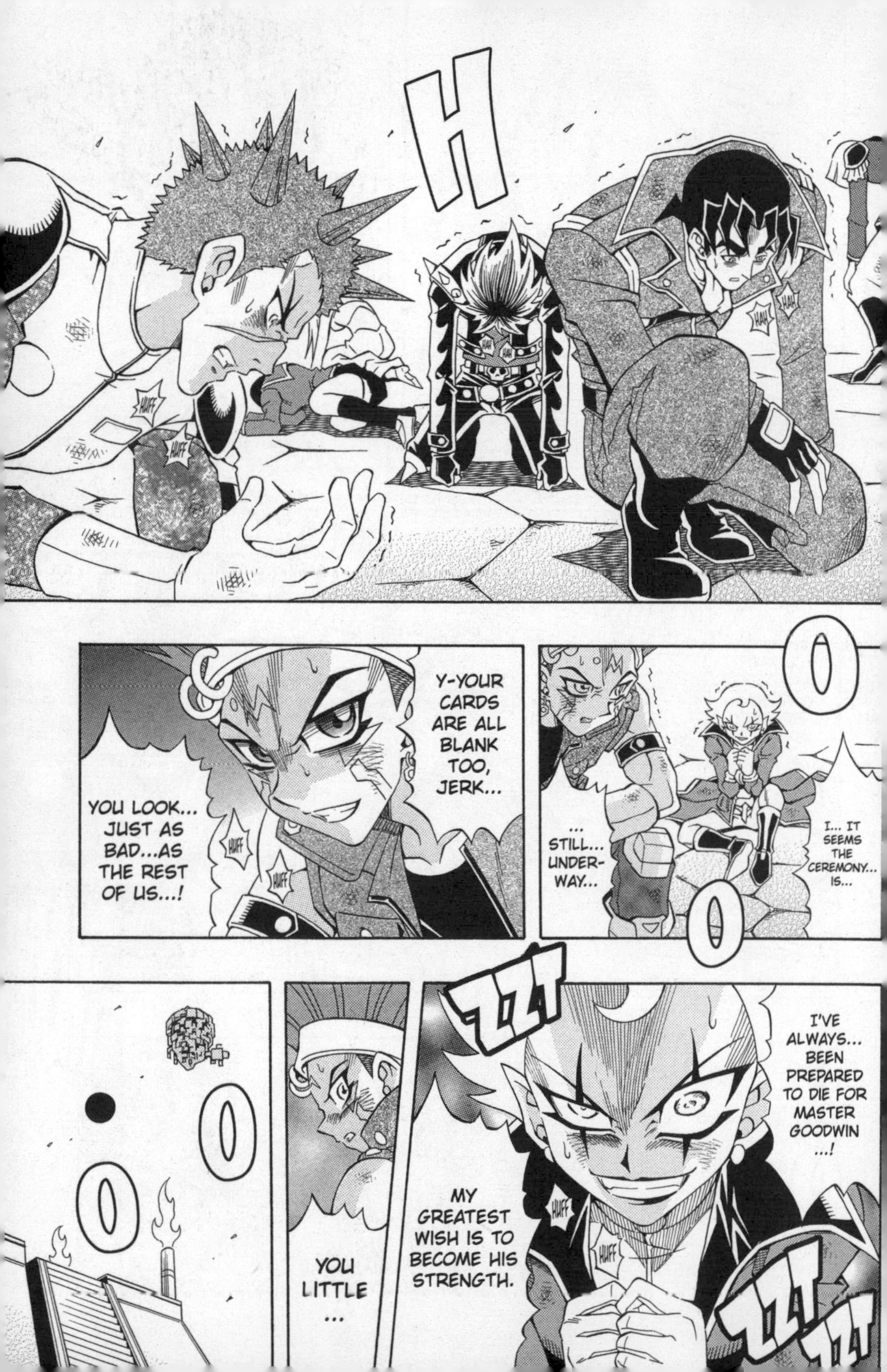
H
HAH
HAH
HAH
HAH
HUFF
HUFF
O
I... IT SEEMS THE CEREMONY... IS...
... STILL... UNDER-WAY...
O
Y-YOUR CARDS ARE ALL BLANK TOO, JERK...
YOU LOOK... JUST AS BAD...AS THE REST OF US...!
HUFF
HUFF
ZZZT
I'VE ALWAYS... BEEN PREPARED TO DIE FOR MASTER GOODWIN ...!
MY GREATEST WISH IS TO BECOME HIS STRENGTH.
HUFF
HUFF
ZZZT
ZZZT
YOU LITTLE ...
O
O

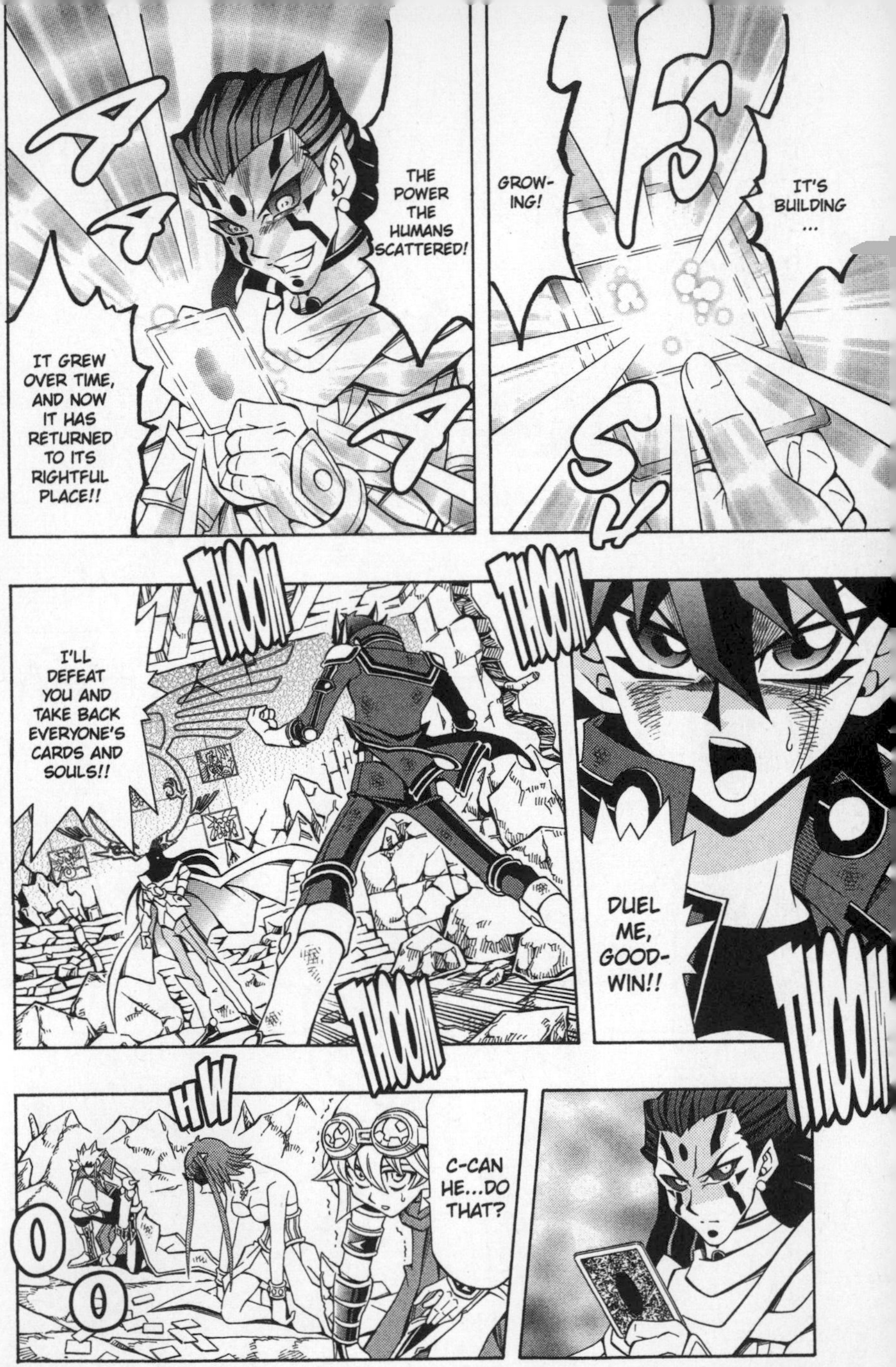
IT'S BUILDING ...
GROWING!
THE POWER THE HUMANS SCATTERED!
IT GREW OVER TIME, AND NOW IT HAS RETURNED TO ITS RIGHTFUL PLACE!!
THOOM
DUEL ME, GOOD-WIN!!
THOOM
THOOM
I'LL DEFEAT YOU AND TAKE BACK EVERYONE'S CARDS AND SOULS!!
THOOM
C-CAN HE...DO THAT?

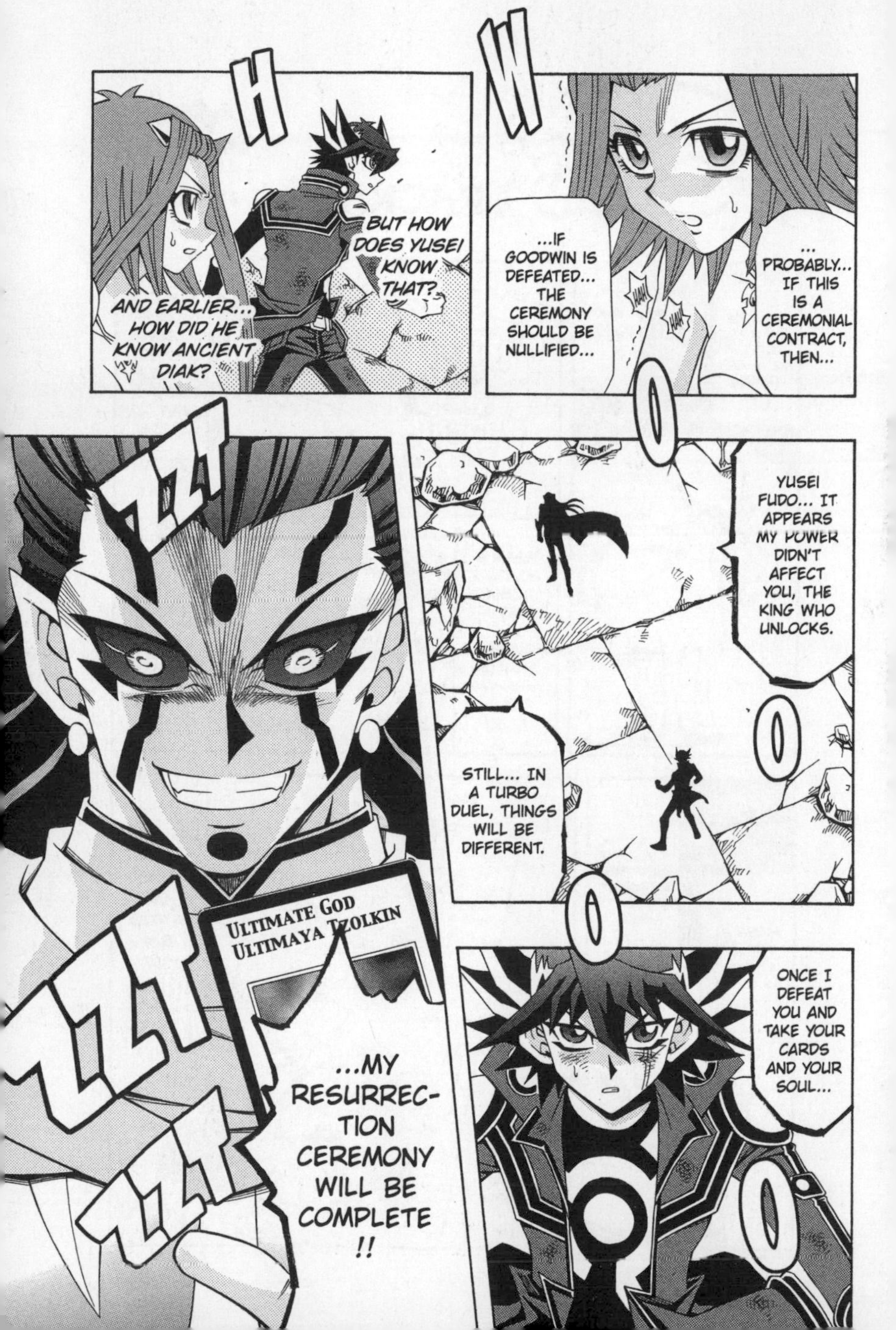

W
H
...PROBABLY... IF THIS IS A CEREMONIAL CONTRACT, THEN...
HAH
HAH
...IF GOODWIN IS DEFEATED... THE CEREMONY SHOULD BE NULLIFIED...
BUT HOW DOES YUSEI KNOW THAT?
AND EARLIER... HOW DID HE KNOW ANCIENT DIAK?
O
YUSEI FUDO... IT APPEARS MY POWER DIDN'T AFFECT YOU, THE KING WHO UNLOCKS.
O
STILL... IN A TURBO DUEL, THINGS WILL BE DIFFERENT.
O
O
ONCE I DEFEAT YOU AND TAKE YOUR CARDS AND YOUR SOUL...
O
ZZZT
ULTIMATE GOD ULTIMAYA TZOLKIN
ZZZT
ZZZT
...MY RESURRECTION CEREMONY WILL BE COMPLETE!!

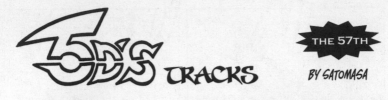

5D's TRACKS

THE 57TH

BY SATOMASA

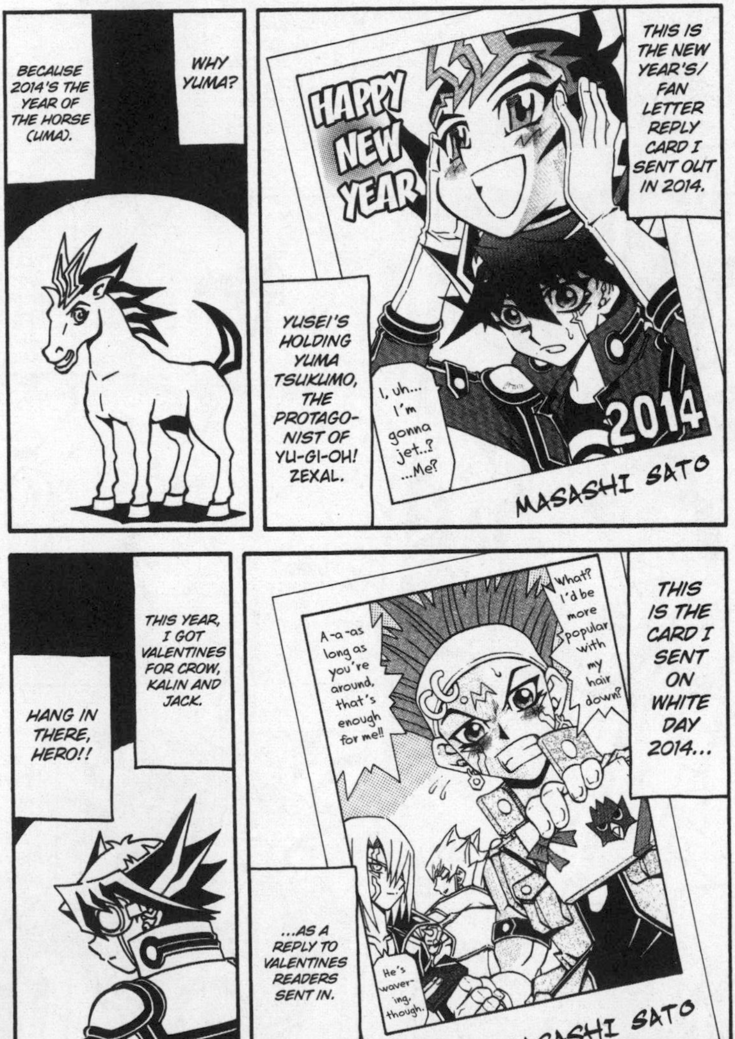
THIS IS THE NEW YEAR'S/ FAN LETTER REPLY CARD I SENT OUT IN 2014.
HAPPY NEW YEAR
YUSEI'S HOLDING YUMA TSUKUMO, THE PROTAGONIST OF YU-GI-OH! ZEXAL.
I, uh... I'm gonna jet..? ...Me?
2014
MASASHI SATO
WHY YUMA?
BECAUSE 2014'S THE YEAR OF THE HORSE (UMA).
THIS IS THE CARD I SENT ON WHITE DAY 2014...
What? I'd be more popular with my hair down?
A-a-as long as you're around, that's enough for me!!
...AS A REPLY TO VALENTINES READERS SENT IN.
He's wavering, though.
ASASHI SATO
THIS YEAR, I GOT VALENTINES FOR CROW, KALIN AND JACK.
HANG IN THERE, HERO!!

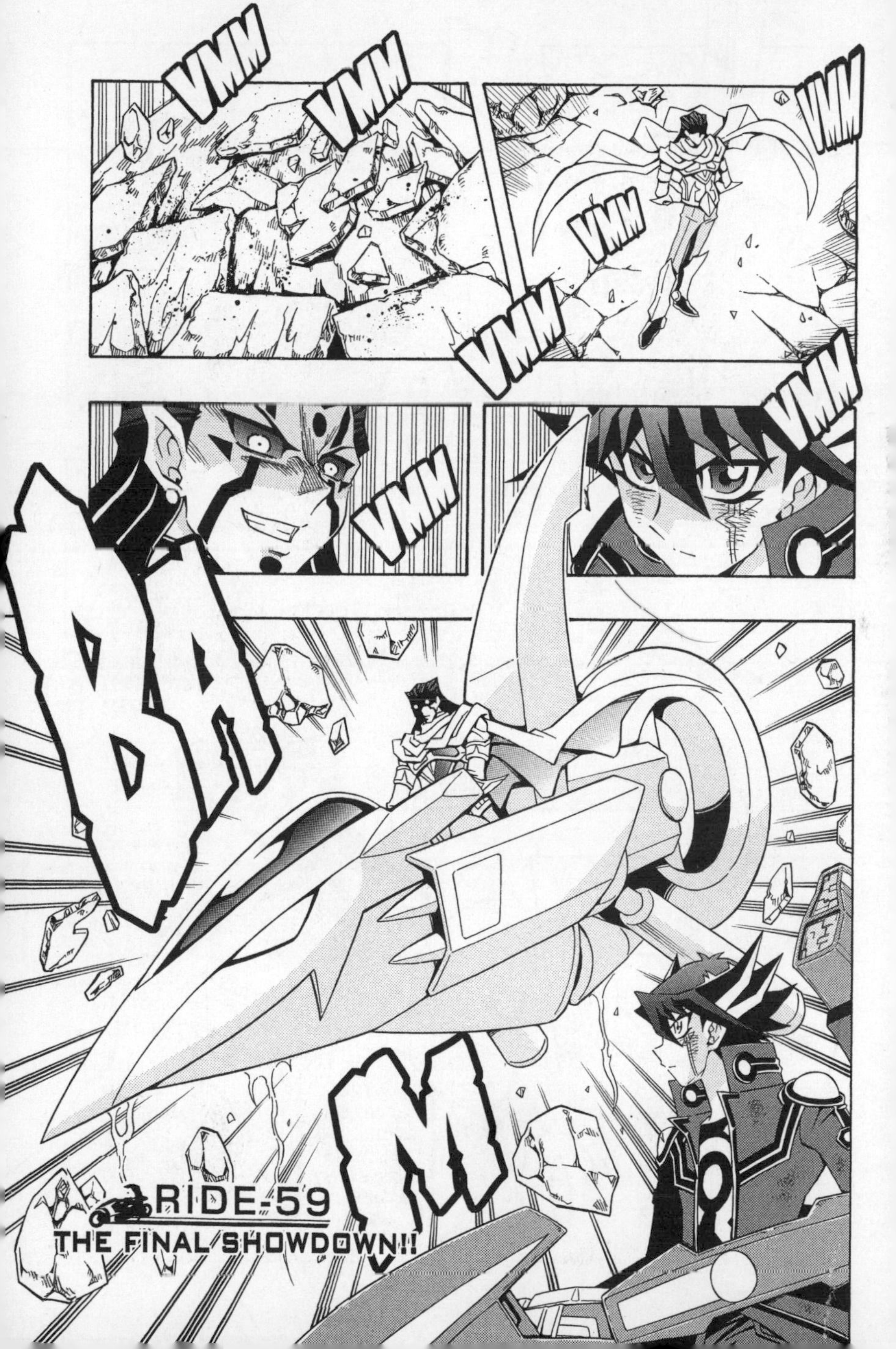
VMM
VMM
VMM
VMM
VMM
VMM
VMM
BAM
RIDE-59
THE FINAL SHOWDOWN!!

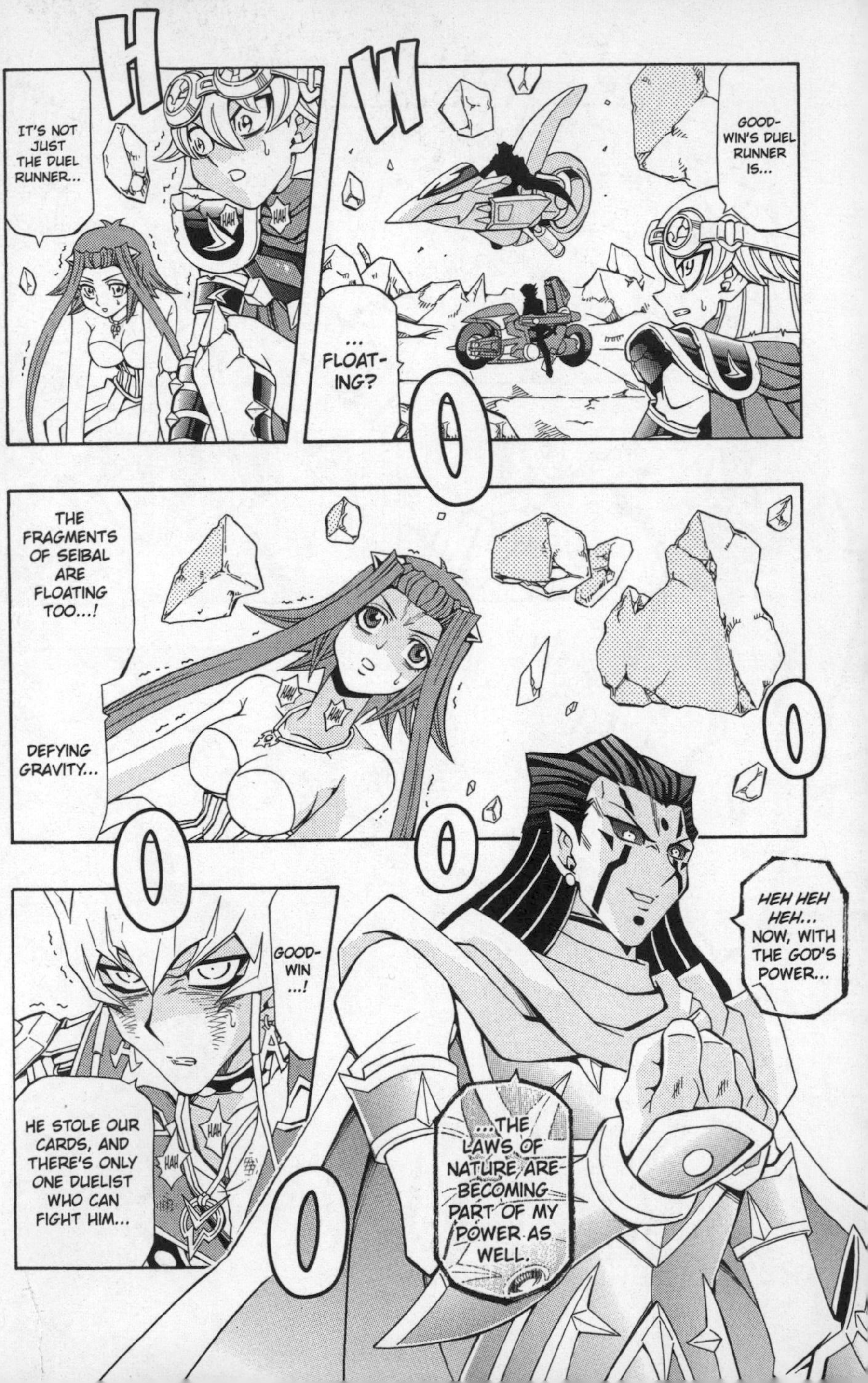
GOOD-WIN'S DUEL RUNNER IS...
... FLOATING?
IT'S NOT JUST THE DUEL RUNNER...
HAH
HAH
THE FRAGMENTS OF SEIBAL ARE FLOATING TOO...!
DEFYING GRAVITY...
HAH
HAH
HEH HEH HEH... NOW, WITH THE GOD'S POWER...
...THE LAWS OF NATURE ARE BECOMING PART OF MY POWER AS WELL.
GOOD-WIN ...!
HE STOLE OUR CARDS, AND THERE'S ONLY ONE DUELIST WHO CAN FIGHT HIM...
HAH
HAH

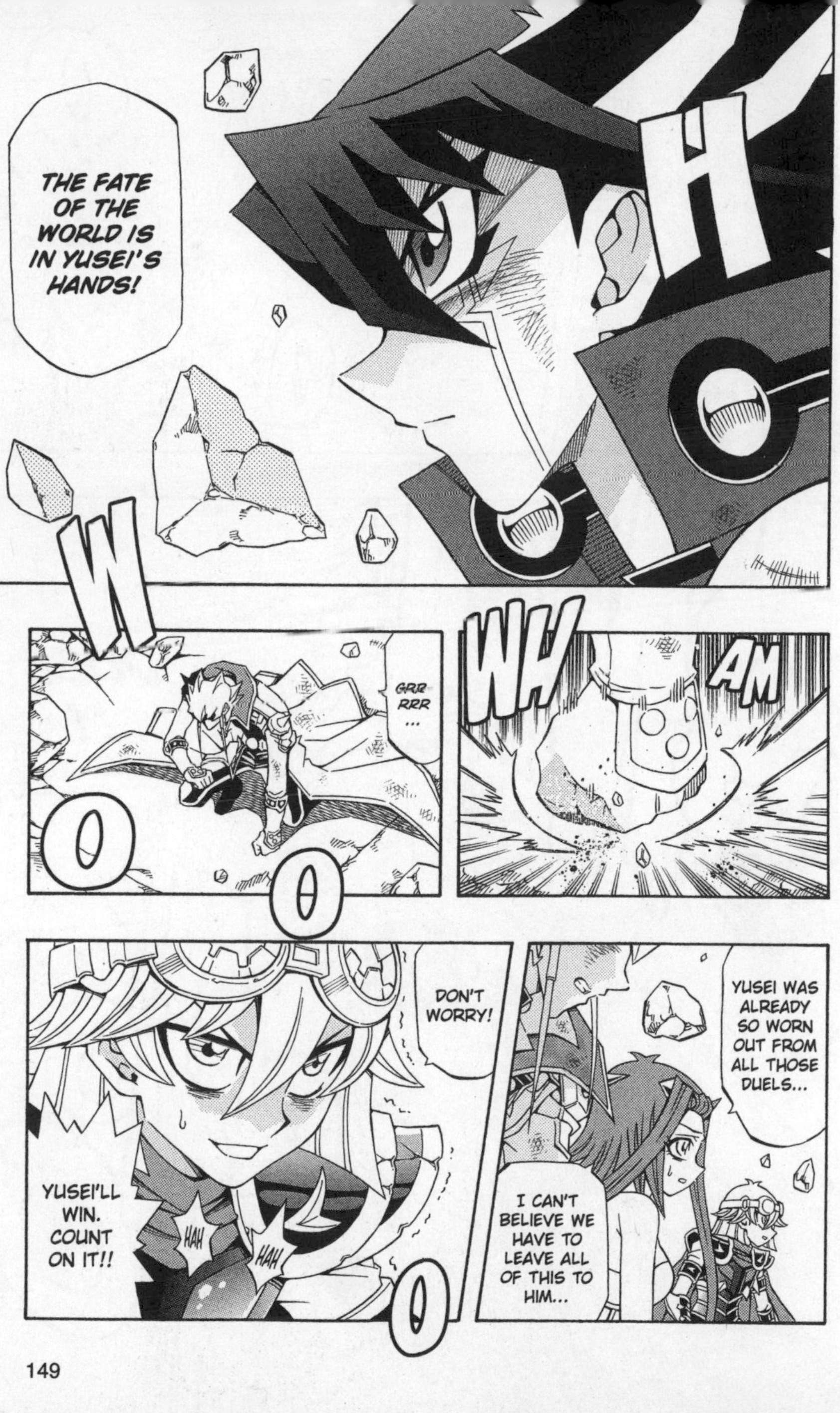
THE FATE OF THE WORLD IS IN YUSEI'S HANDS!
WHOOO
WHAM
GRRRRR...
YUSEI WAS ALREADY SO WORN OUT FROM ALL THOSE DUELS...
I CAN'T BELIEVE WE HAVE TO LEAVE ALL OF THIS TO HIM...
DON'T WORRY!
YUSEI'LL WIN. COUNT ON IT!!
HAH
HAH

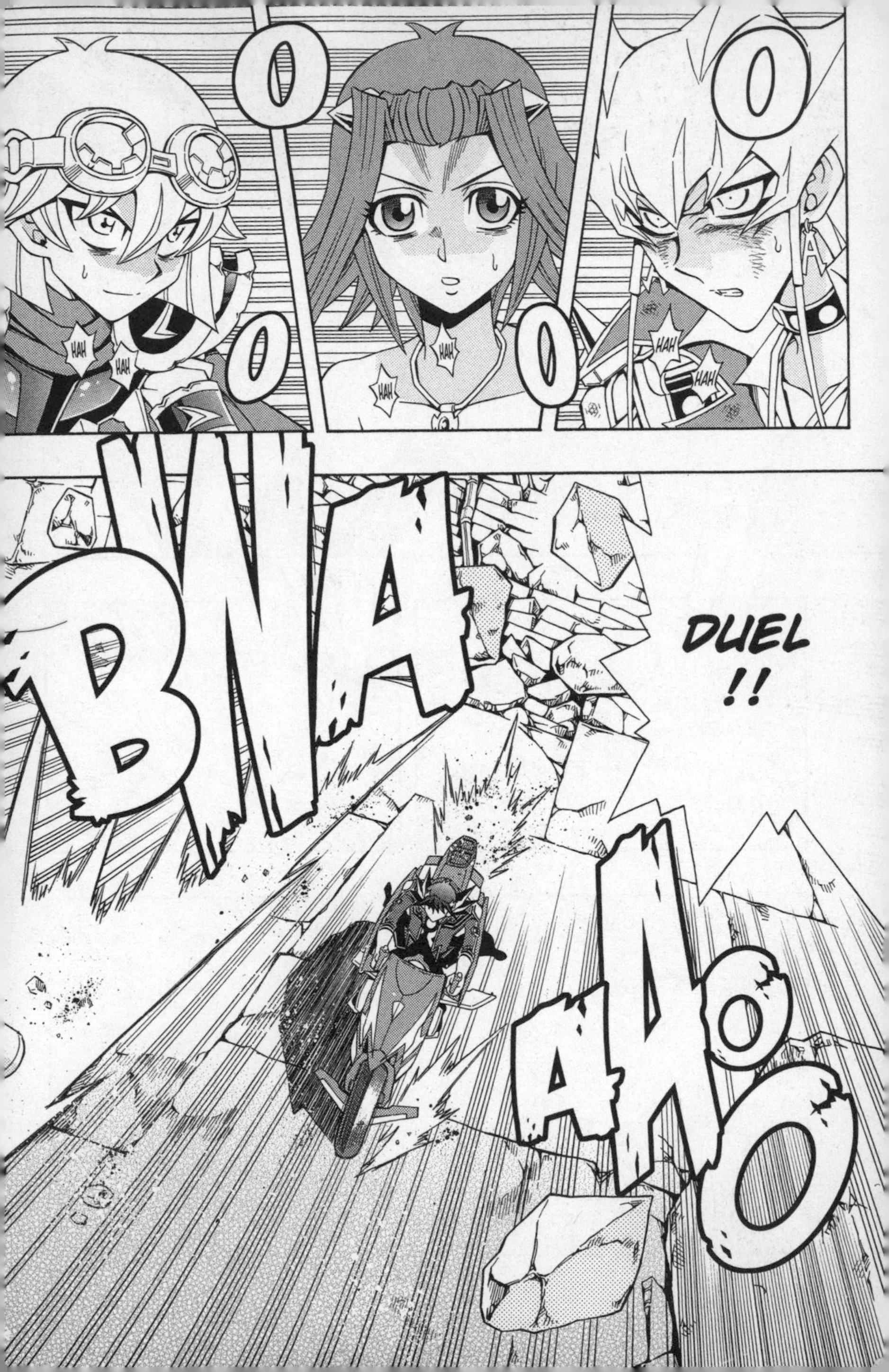
O
O
HAH
HAH
O
O
HAH
HAH
O
O
HAH
HAH
DUEL !!
BWAAAO

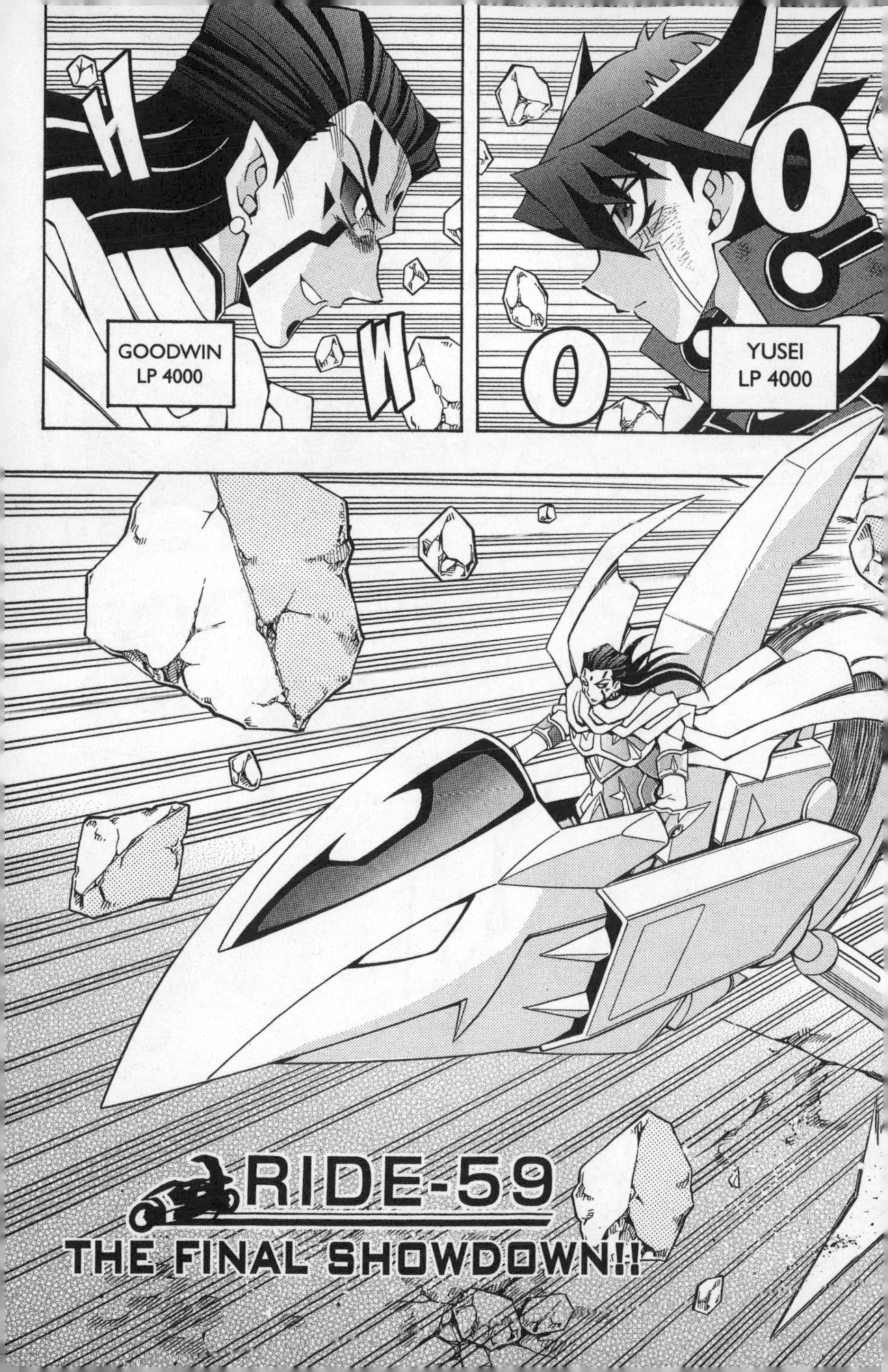
YUSEI
LP 4000
GOODWIN
LP 4000
RIDE-59
THE FINAL SHOWDOWN!!

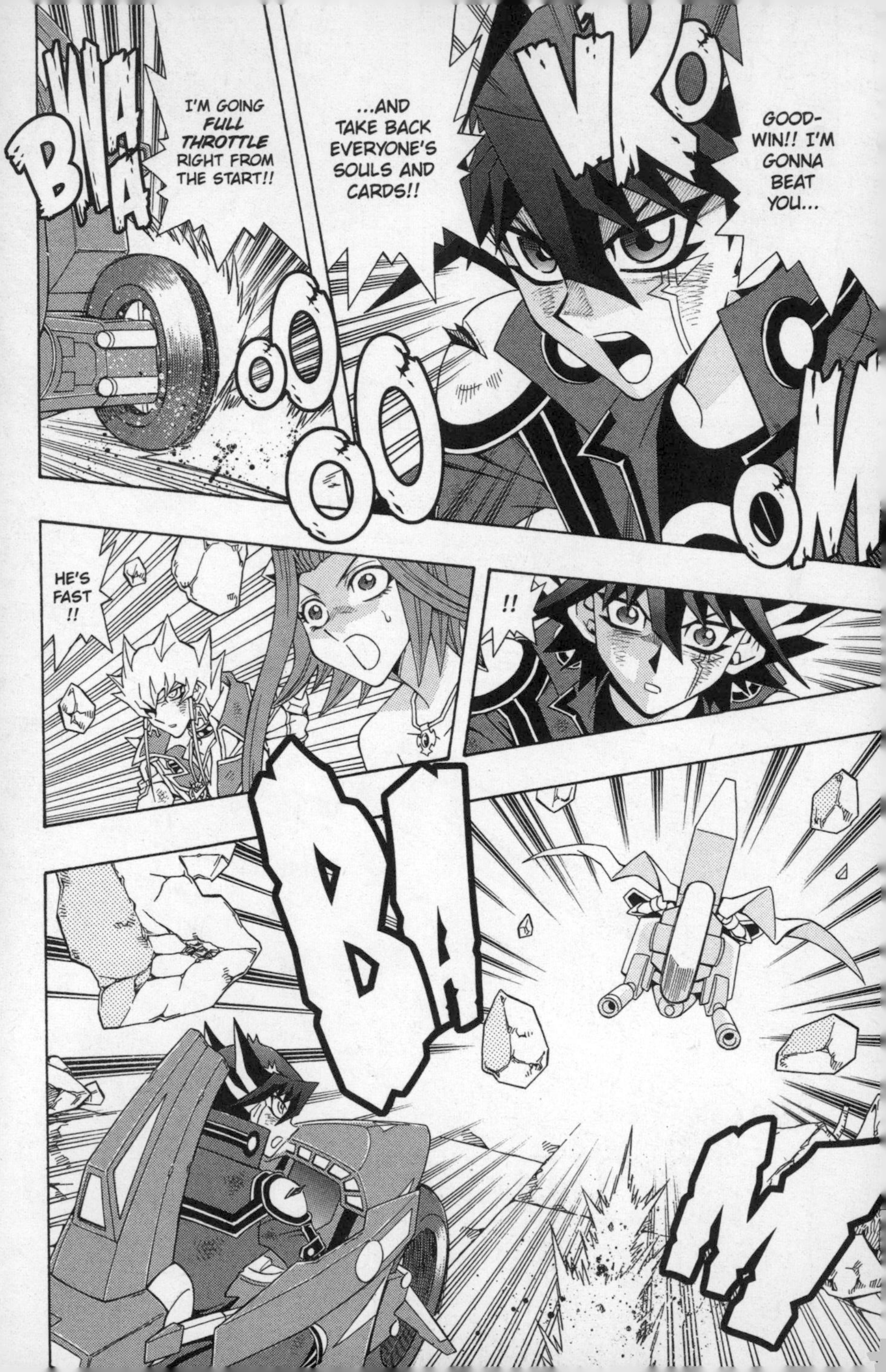
GOOD-WIN!! I'M GONNA BEAT YOU...
...AND TAKE BACK EVERYONE'S SOULS AND CARDS!!
I'M GOING *FULL THROTTLE* RIGHT FROM THE START!!
!!
HE'S FAST !!
BA

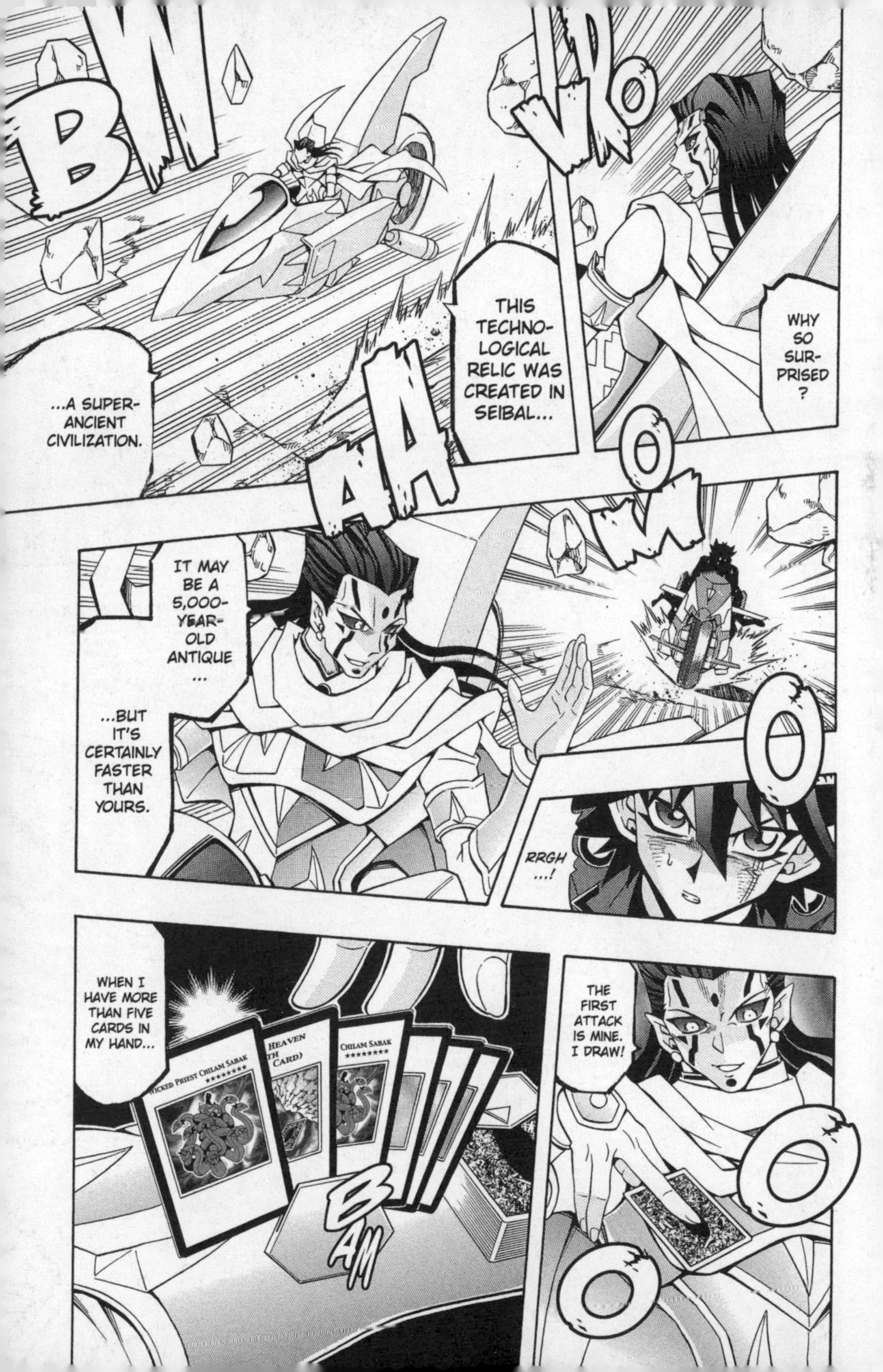
WHY SO SUR-PRISED?
THIS TECHNO-LOGICAL RELIC WAS CREATED IN SEIBAL...
...A SUPER-ANCIENT CIVILIZATION.
RRGH...!
IT MAY BE A 5,000-YEAR-OLD ANTIQUE...
...BUT IT'S CERTAINLY FASTER THAN YOURS.
THE FIRST ATTACK IS MINE. I DRAW!
WHEN I HAVE MORE THAN FIVE CARDS IN MY HAND...
CHILAM SABAK
BAM

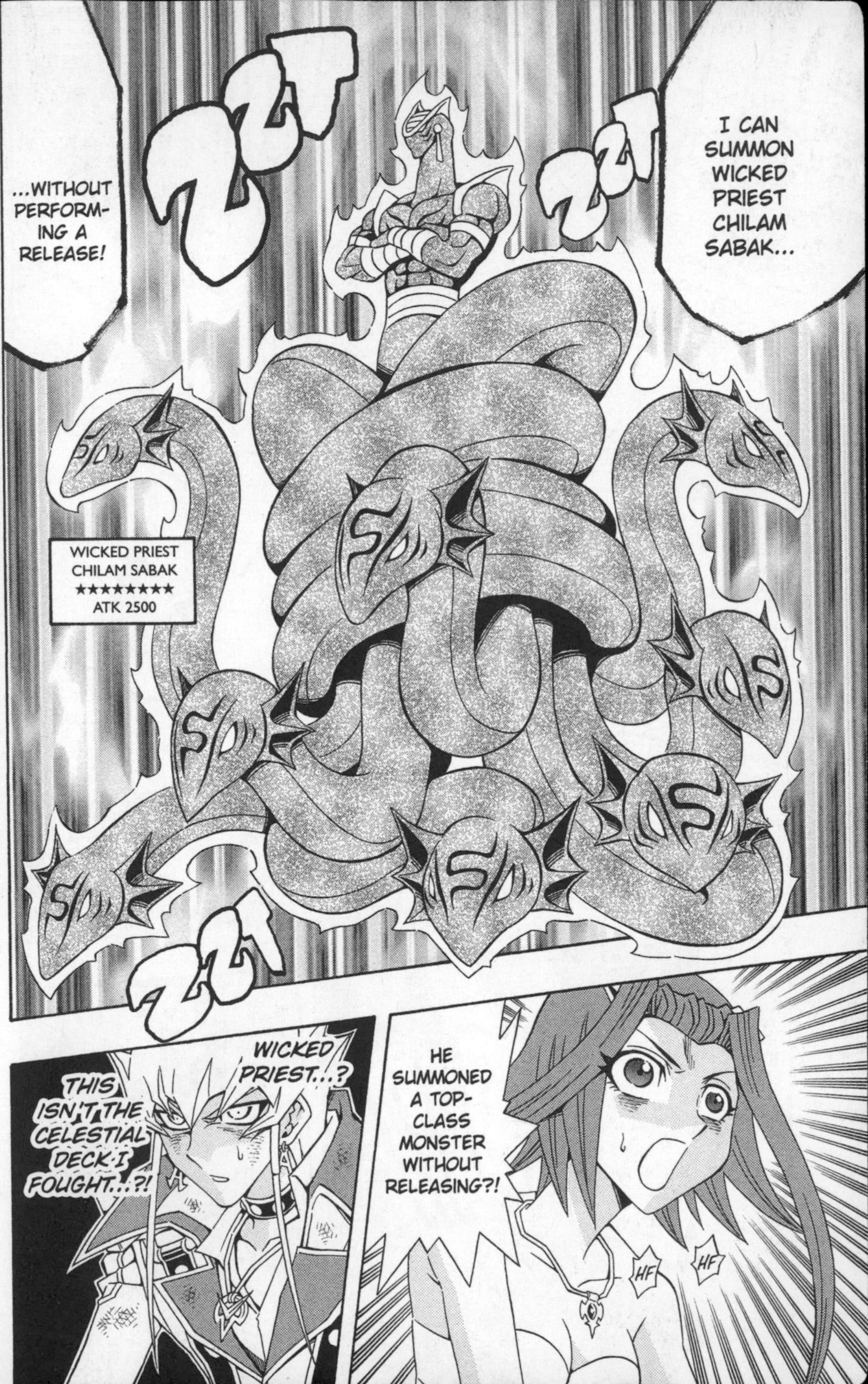
I CAN SUMMON WICKED PRIEST CHILAM SABAK...
ZZT
ZZT
...WITHOUT PERFORMING A RELEASE!
WICKED PRIEST CHILAM SABAK ★★★★★★★★ ATK 2500
ZZT
HE SUMMONED A TOP-CLASS MONSTER WITHOUT RELEASING?!
HF
HF
WICKED PRIEST...?
THIS ISN'T THE CELESTIAL DECK I FOUGHT...?!

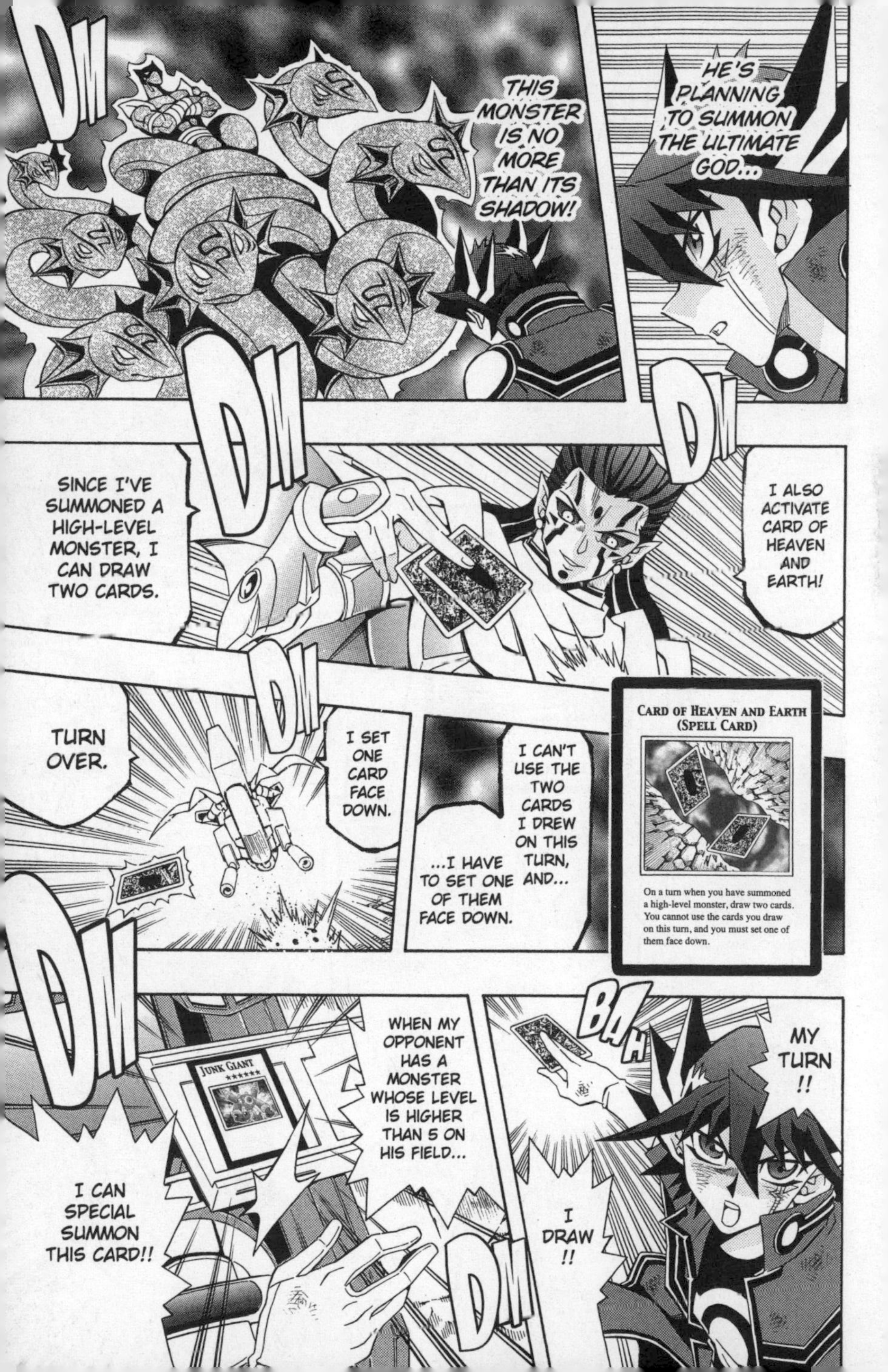
HE'S PLANNING TO SUMMON THE ULTIMATE GOD...
DM
THIS MONSTER IS NO MORE THAN ITS SHADOW!
DM
DM
I ALSO ACTIVATE CARD OF HEAVEN AND EARTH!
DM
SINCE I'VE SUMMONED A HIGH-LEVEL MONSTER, I CAN DRAW TWO CARDS.
CARD OF HEAVEN AND EARTH (SPELL CARD)
On a turn when you have summoned a high-level monster, draw two cards. You cannot use the cards you draw on this turn, and you must set one of them face down.
I CAN'T USE THE TWO CARDS I DREW ON THIS TURN, AND...
...I HAVE TO SET ONE OF THEM FACE DOWN.
DM
I SET ONE CARD FACE DOWN.
TURN OVER.
MY TURN!!
BAH
I DRAW!!
WHEN MY OPPONENT HAS A MONSTER WHOSE LEVEL IS HIGHER THAN 5 ON HIS FIELD...
JUNK GIANT
DM
DM
I CAN SPECIAL SUMMON THIS CARD!!

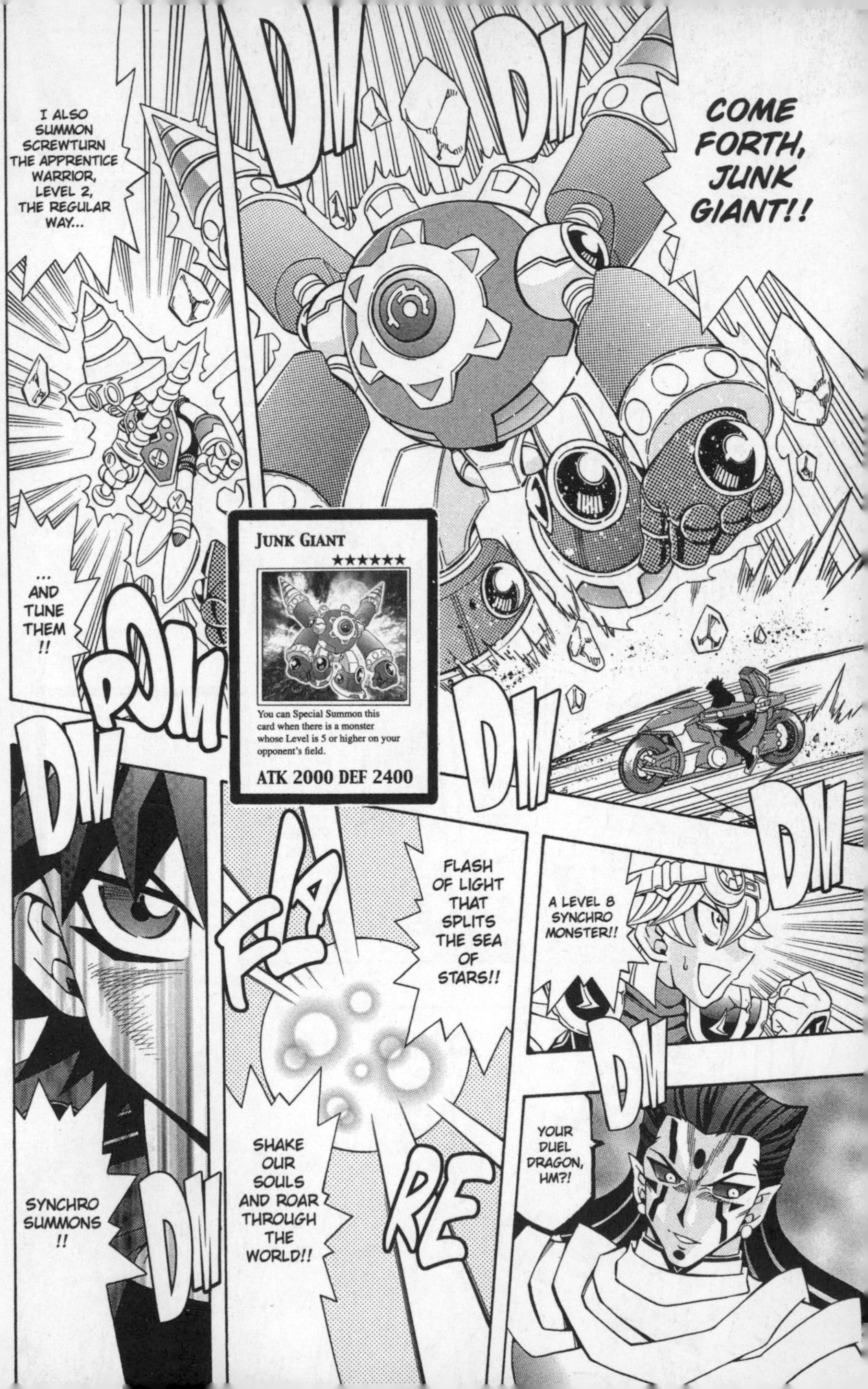

DM DM
COME FORTH, JUNK GIANT!!
I ALSO SUMMON SCREWTURN THE APPRENTICE WARRIOR, LEVEL 2, THE REGULAR WAY...
... AND TUNE THEM !!
POM
JUNK GIANT
★★★★★★
You can Special Summon this card when there is a monster whose Level is 5 or higher on your opponent's field.
ATK 2000 DEF 2400
DM
DM
DM
A LEVEL 8 SYNCHRO MONSTER!!
DM
YOUR DUEL DRAGON, HM?!
FLASH OF LIGHT THAT SPLITS THE SEA OF STARS!!
FLA
SHAKE OUR SOULS AND ROAR THROUGH THE WORLD!!
RE
DM
SYNCHRO SUMMONS !!
DM

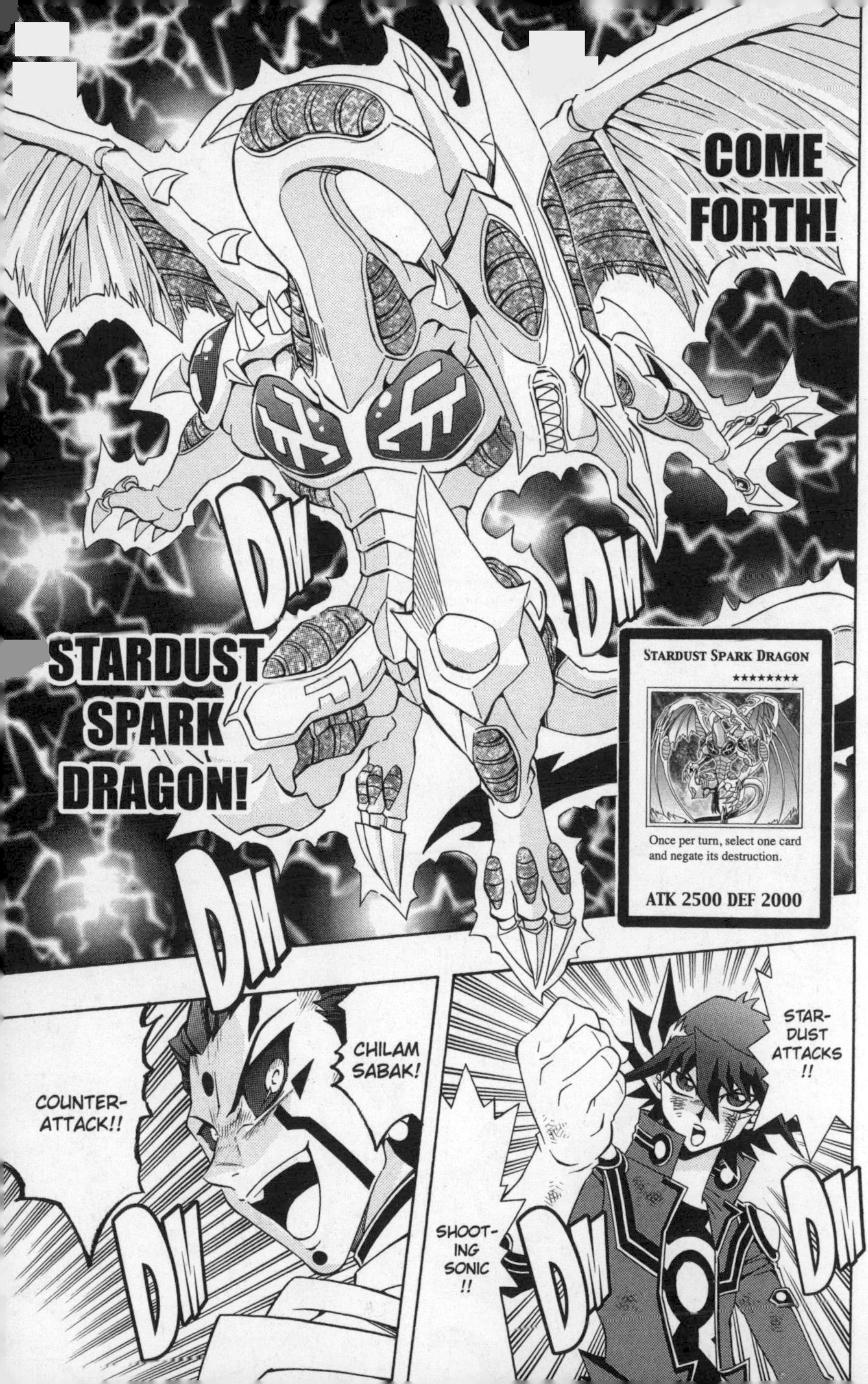
COME FORTH!
DM
DM
STARDUST SPARK DRAGON!
STARDUST SPARK DRAGON
****
Once per turn, select one card and negate its destruction.
ATK 2500 DEF 2000
DM
STARDUST ATTACKS!!
DM
DM
SHOOTING SONIC!!
CHILAM SABAK!
COUNTER-ATTACK!!
DM

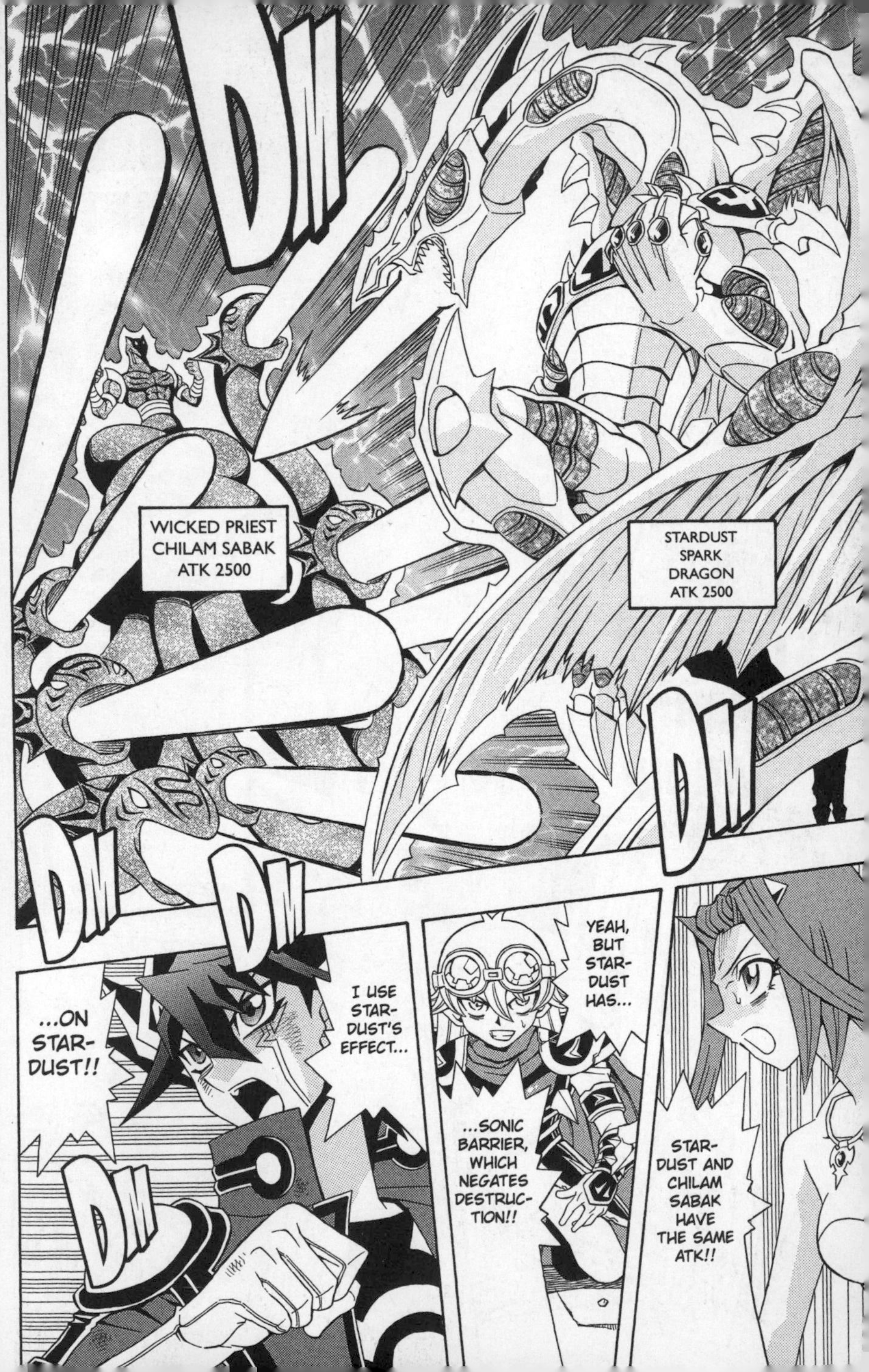
DM
STARDUST SPARK DRAGON ATK 2500
WICKED PRIEST CHILAM SABAK ATK 2500
DM
DM
DM
STAR-DUST AND CHILAM SABAK HAVE THE SAME ATK!!
YEAH, BUT STAR-DUST HAS...
...SONIC BARRIER, WHICH NEGATES DESTRUC-TION!!
I USE STAR-DUST'S EFFECT...
...ON STAR-DUST!!
DM

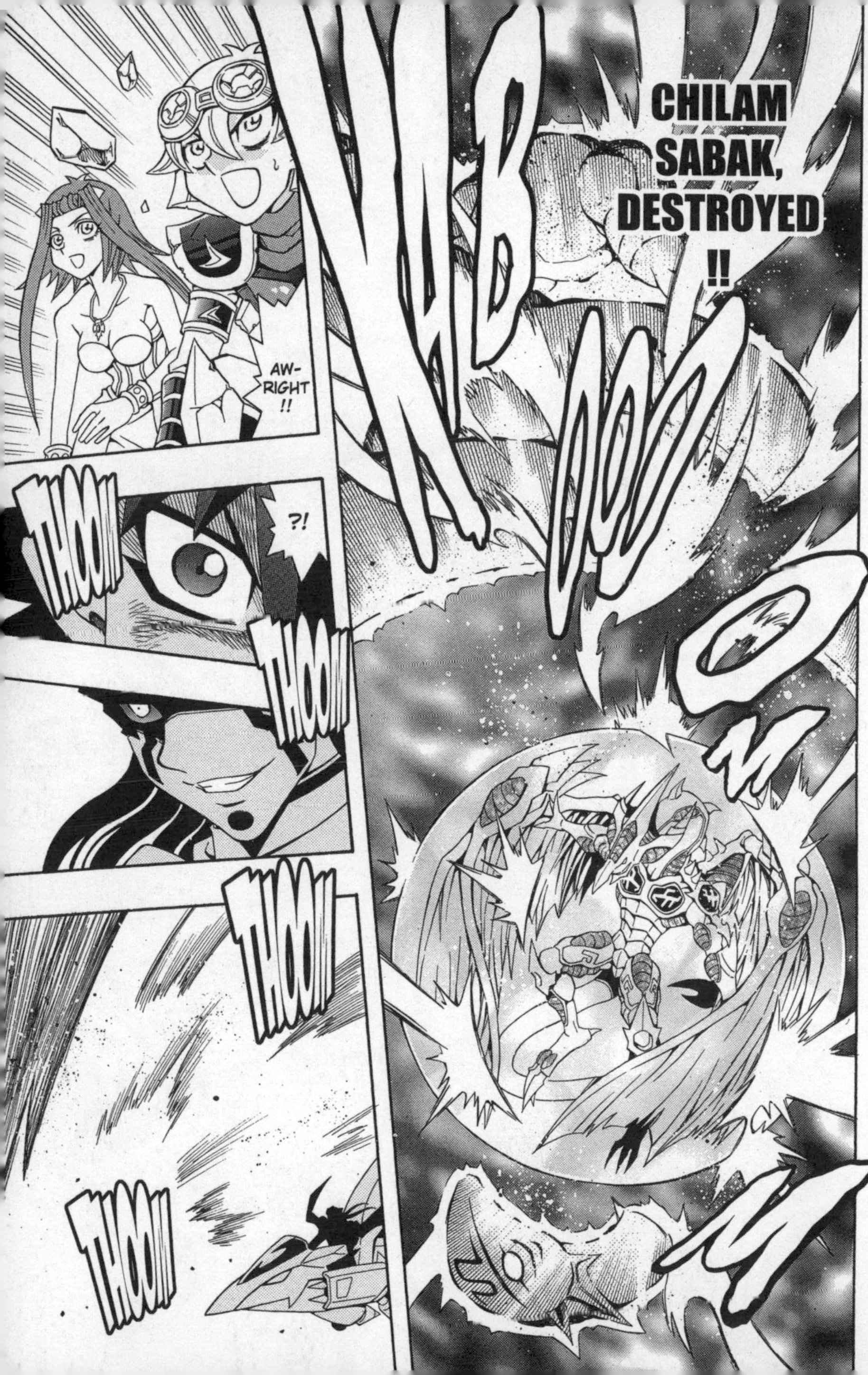
CHILAM SABAK, DESTROYED !!
AW-RIGHT !!
THOOM
?!
THOOM
THOOM
THOOM

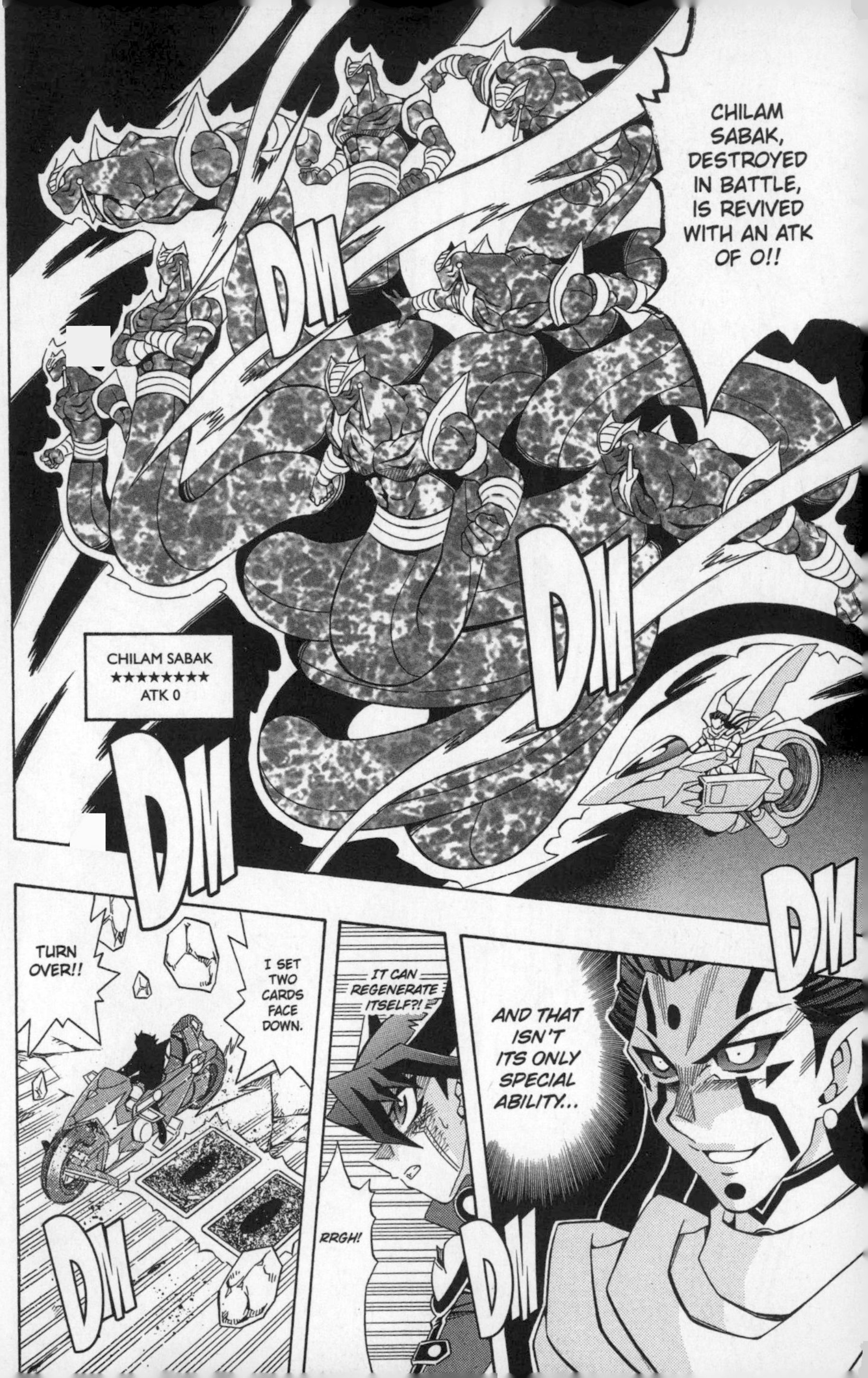
CHILAM SABAK, DESTROYED IN BATTLE, IS REVIVED WITH AN ATK OF 0!!
DM
DM
CHILAM SABAK ★★★★★★★★ ATK 0
DM
DM
AND THAT ISN'T ITS ONLY SPECIAL ABILITY...
DM
IT CAN REGENERATE ITSELF?!
RRGH!
I SET TWO CARDS FACE DOWN.
TURN OVER!!
DM

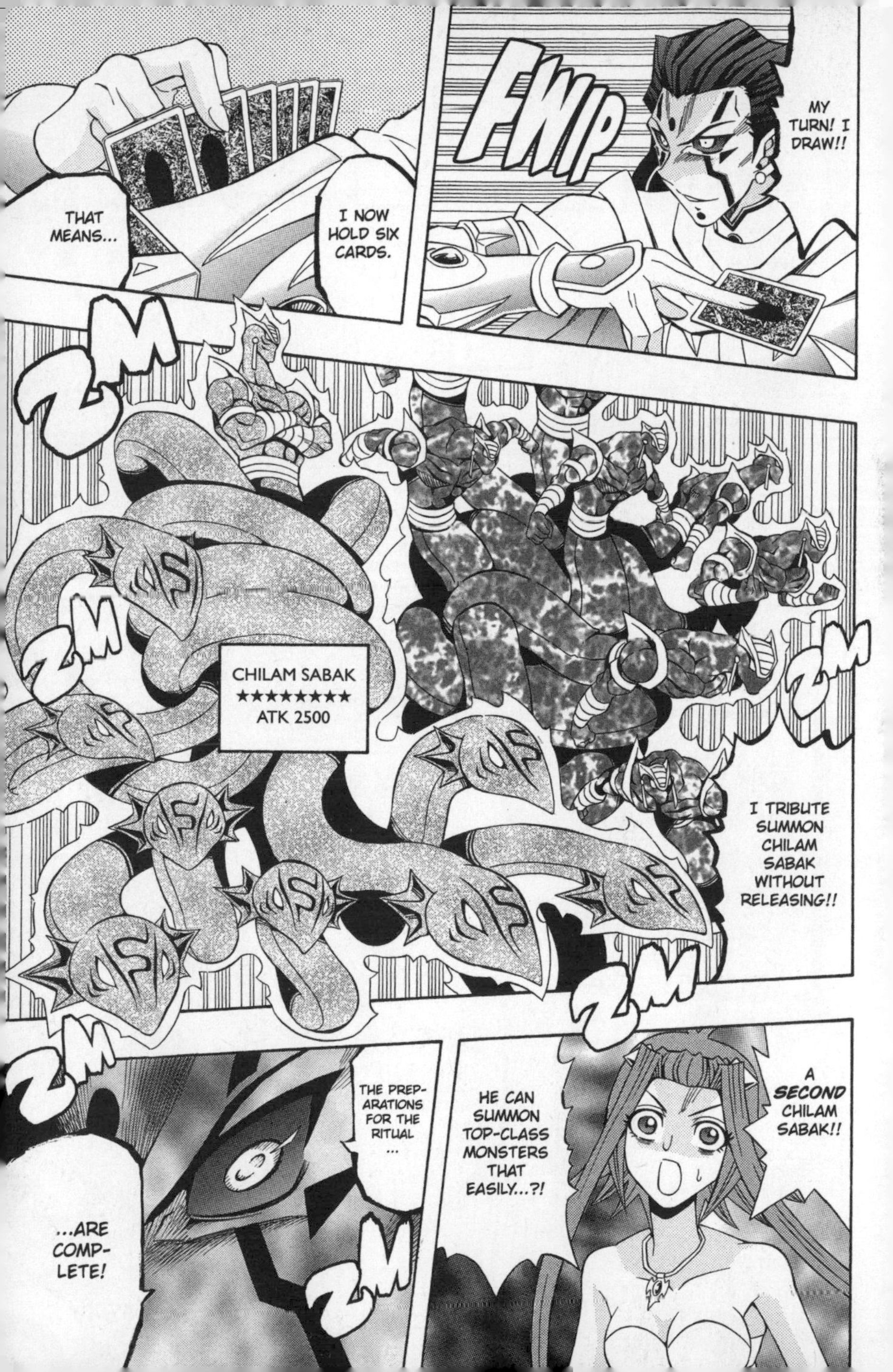
FWIP
MY TURN! I DRAW!!
I NOW HOLD SIX CARDS.
THAT MEANS...
ZM
ZM
I TRIBUTE SUMMON CHILAM SABAK WITHOUT RELEASING!!
ZM
CHILAM SABAK
★★★★★★★★
ATK 2500
ZM
ZM
A *SECOND* CHILAM SABAK!!
HE CAN SUMMON TOP-CLASS MONSTERS THAT EASILY...?!
THE PREP-ARATIONS FOR THE RITUAL ...
...ARE COMP-LETE!
ZM

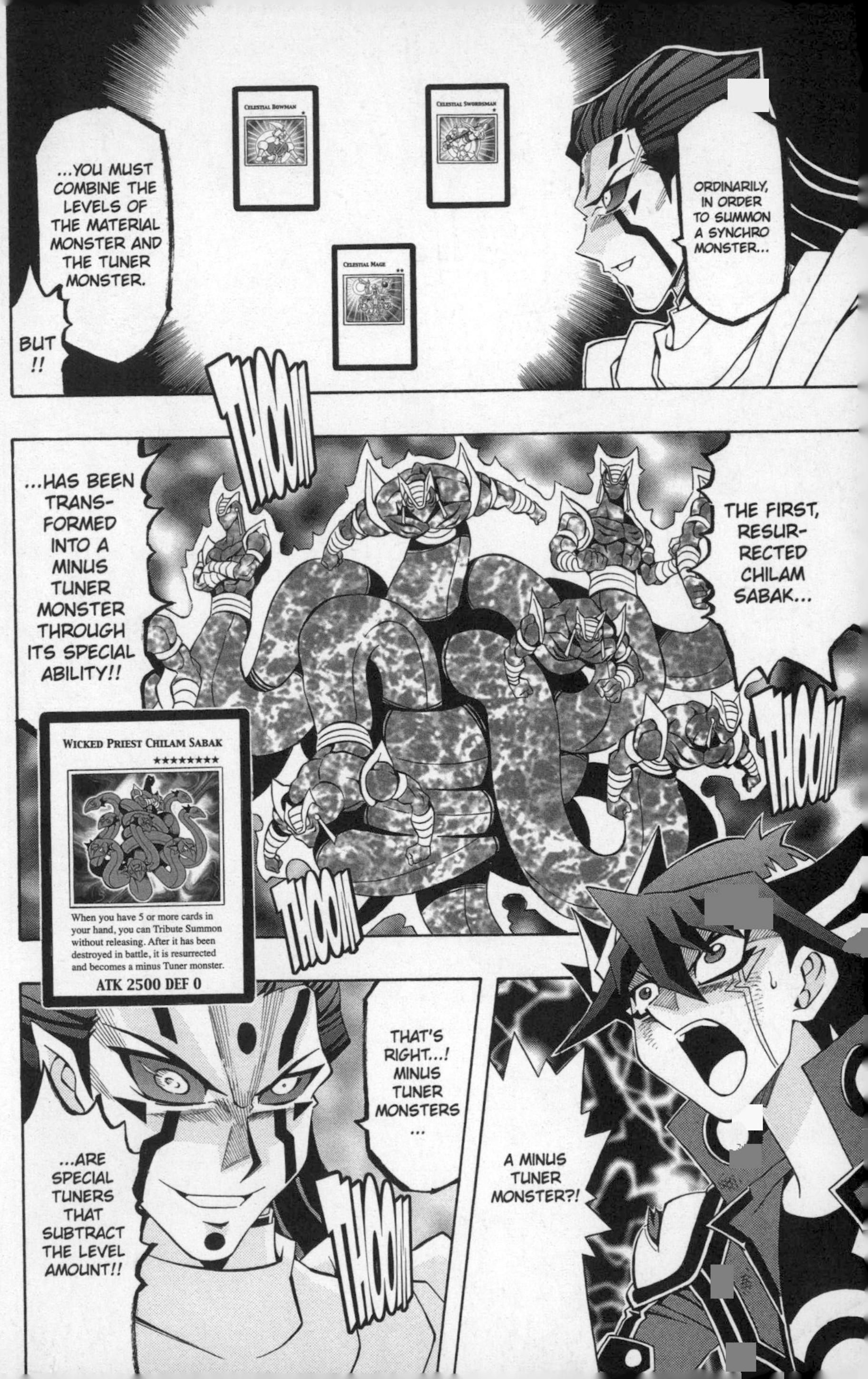
ORDINARILY, IN ORDER TO SUMMON A SYNCHRO MONSTER...
Celestial Swordsman
Celestial Bowman
Celestial Mage
...YOU MUST COMBINE THE LEVELS OF THE MATERIAL MONSTER AND THE TUNER MONSTER.
BUT !!
THOOM
THE FIRST, RESURRECTED CHILAM SABAK...
...HAS BEEN TRANS-FORMED INTO A MINUS TUNER MONSTER THROUGH ITS SPECIAL ABILITY!!
THOOM
THOOM
Wicked Priest Chilam Sabak
When you have 5 or more cards in your hand, you can Tribute Summon without releasing. After it has been destroyed in battle, it is resurrected and becomes a minus Tuner monster.
ATK 2500 DEF 0
A MINUS TUNER MONSTER?!
THAT'S RIGHT...! MINUS TUNER MONSTERS...
...ARE SPECIAL TUNERS THAT SUBTRACT THE LEVEL AMOUNT!!
THOOM

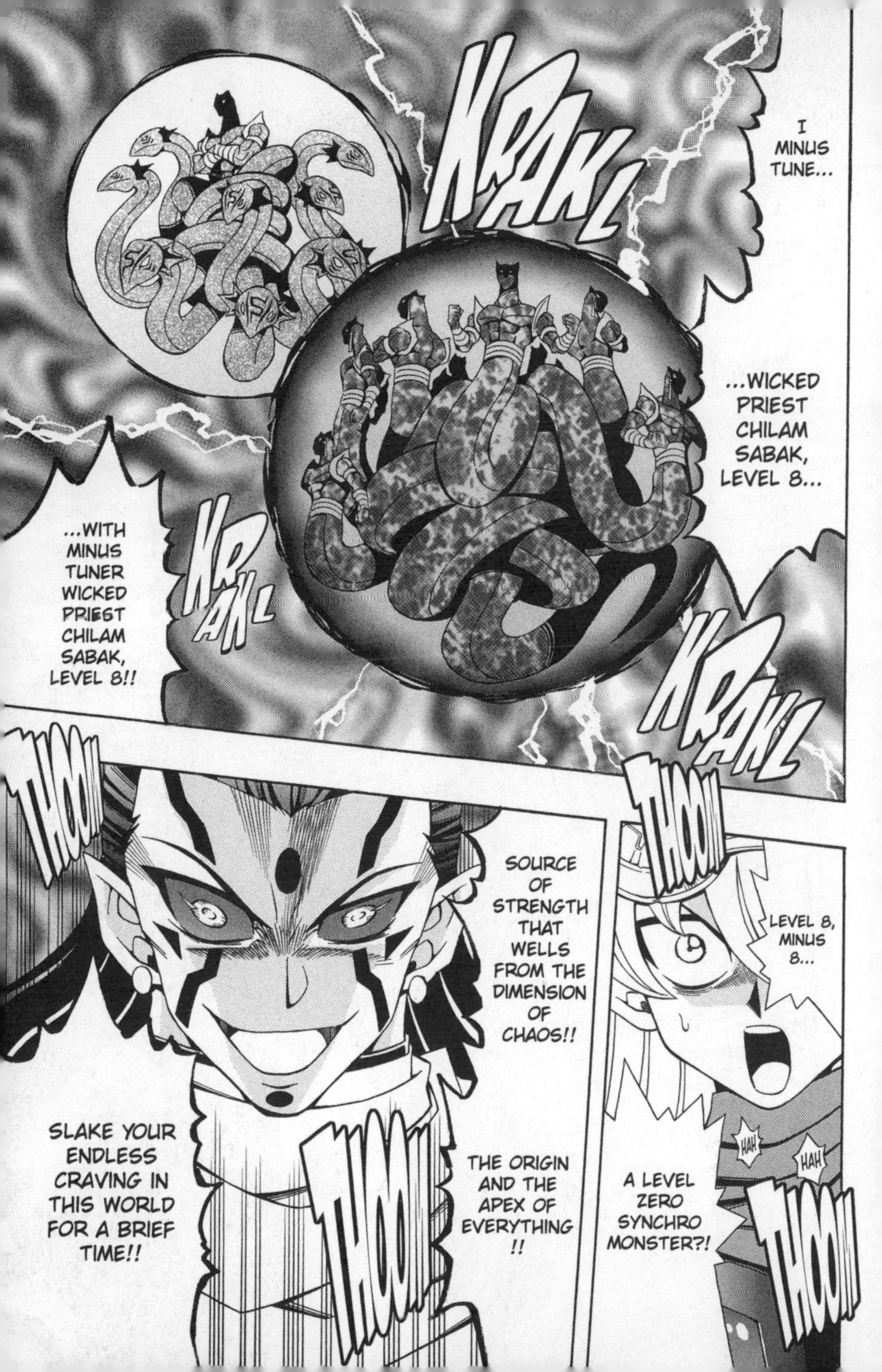
I MINUS TUNE...
KRAKL
...WICKED PRIEST CHILAM SABAK, LEVEL 8...
KRAKL
...WITH MINUS TUNER WICKED PRIEST CHILAM SABAK, LEVEL 8!!
KRAKL
THOOM
LEVEL 8, MINUS 8...
HAH HAH
A LEVEL ZERO SYNCHRO MONSTER?!
THOOM
THOOM
SOURCE OF STRENGTH THAT WELLS FROM THE DIMENSION OF CHAOS!!
THE ORIGIN AND THE APEX OF EVERYTHING!!
SLAKE YOUR ENDLESS CRAVING IN THIS WORLD FOR A BRIEF TIME!!
THOOM

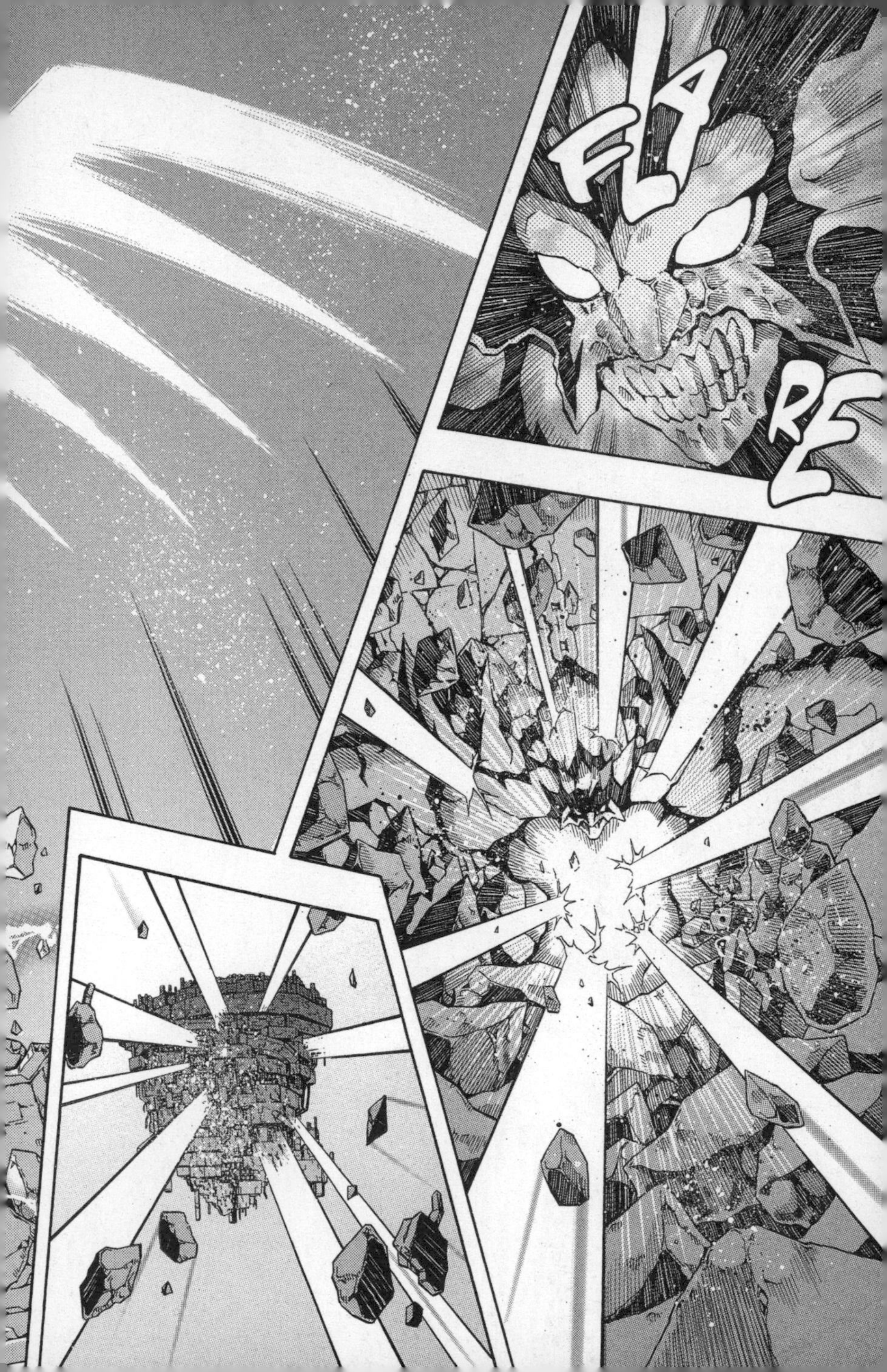
FLARE

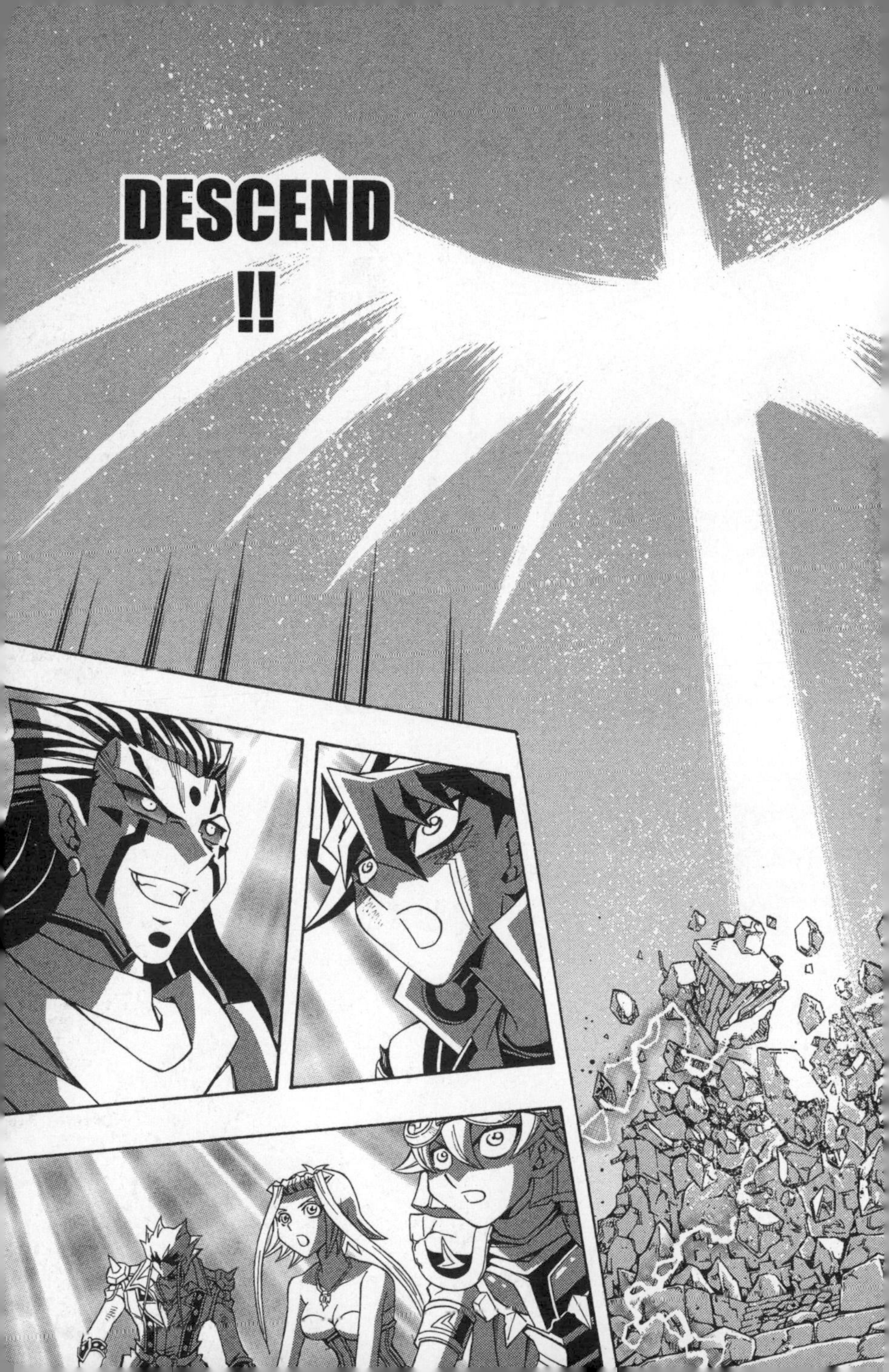
DESCEND
!!

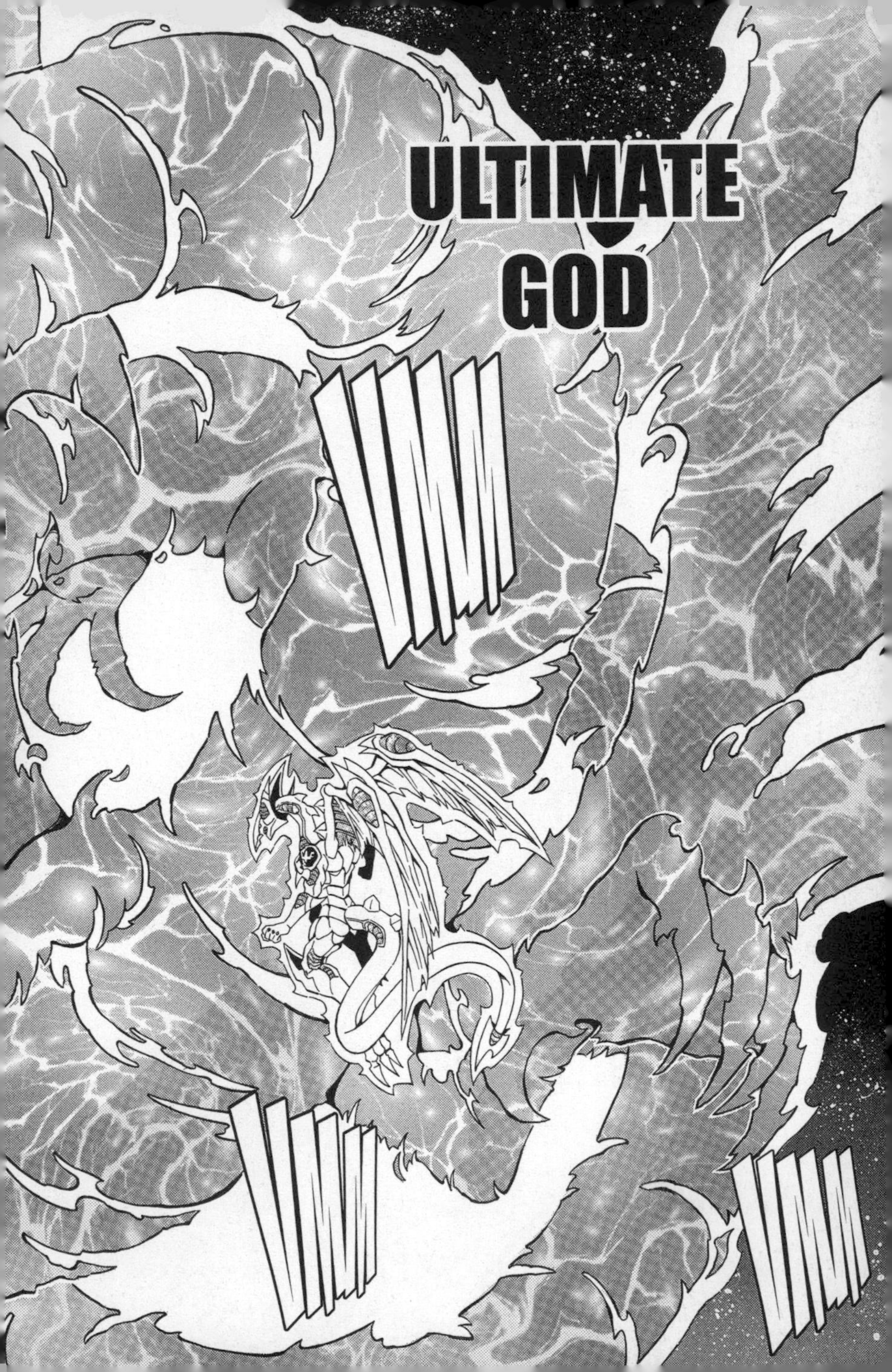
ULTIMATE GOD

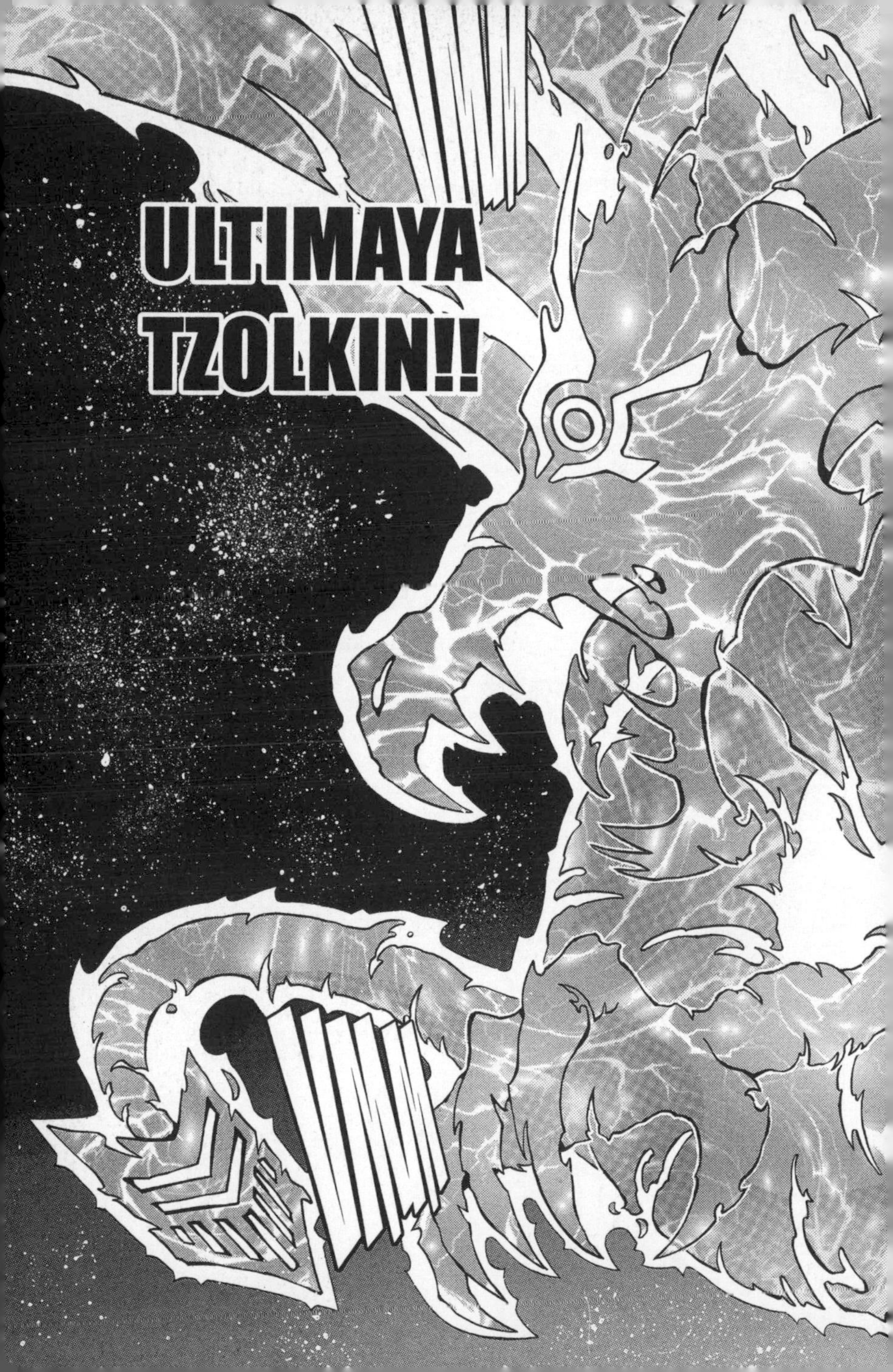
ULTIMAYA TZOLKIN!!

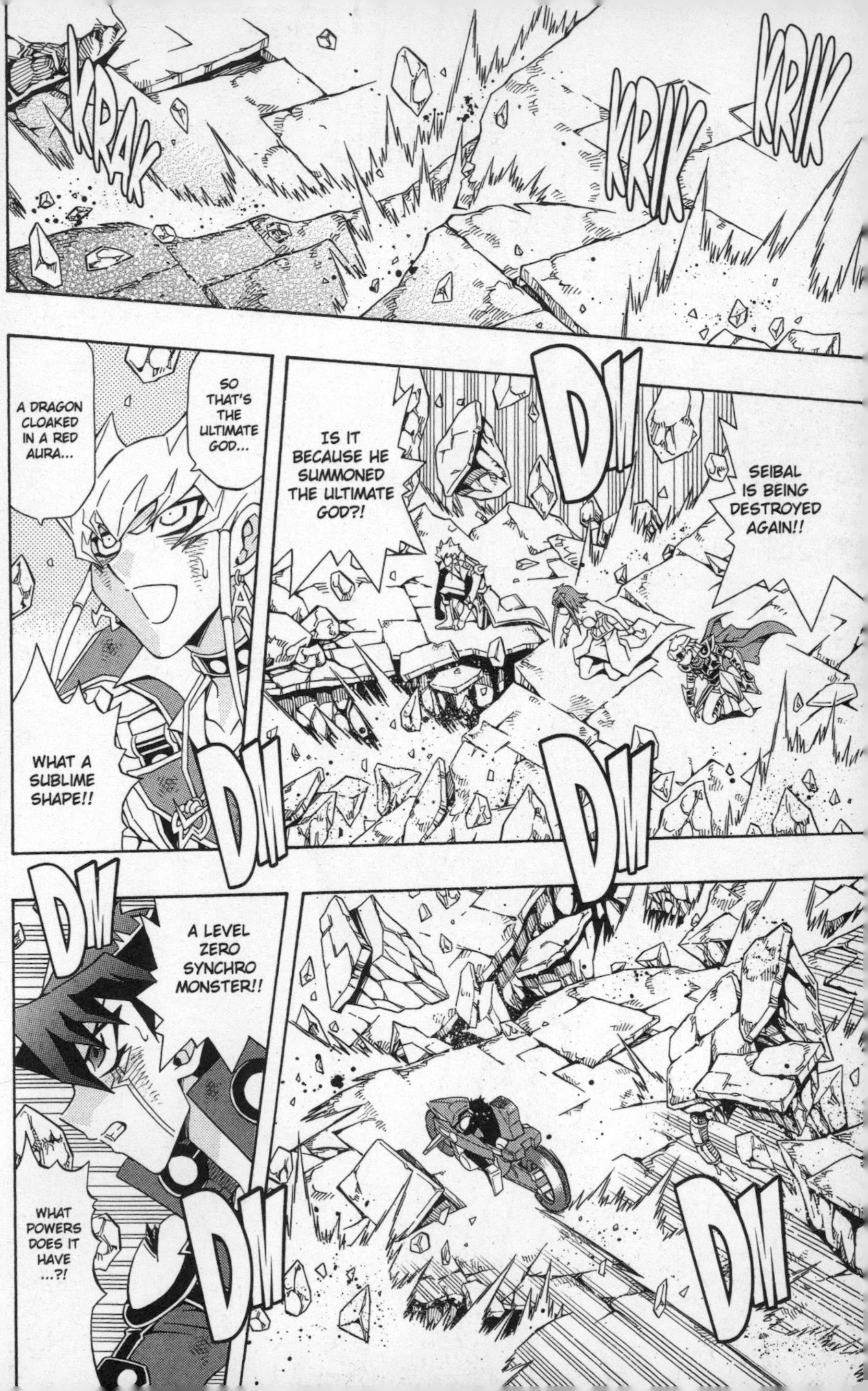
KRIK
KRIK
KRAK
DM
SEIBAL IS BEING DESTROYED AGAIN!!
IS IT BECAUSE HE SUMMONED THE ULTIMATE GOD?!
DM
SO THAT'S THE ULTIMATE GOD...
A DRAGON CLOAKED IN A RED AURA...
WHAT A SUBLIME SHAPE!!
DM
DM
DM
A LEVEL ZERO SYNCHRO MONSTER!!
WHAT POWERS DOES IT HAVE ...?!
DM

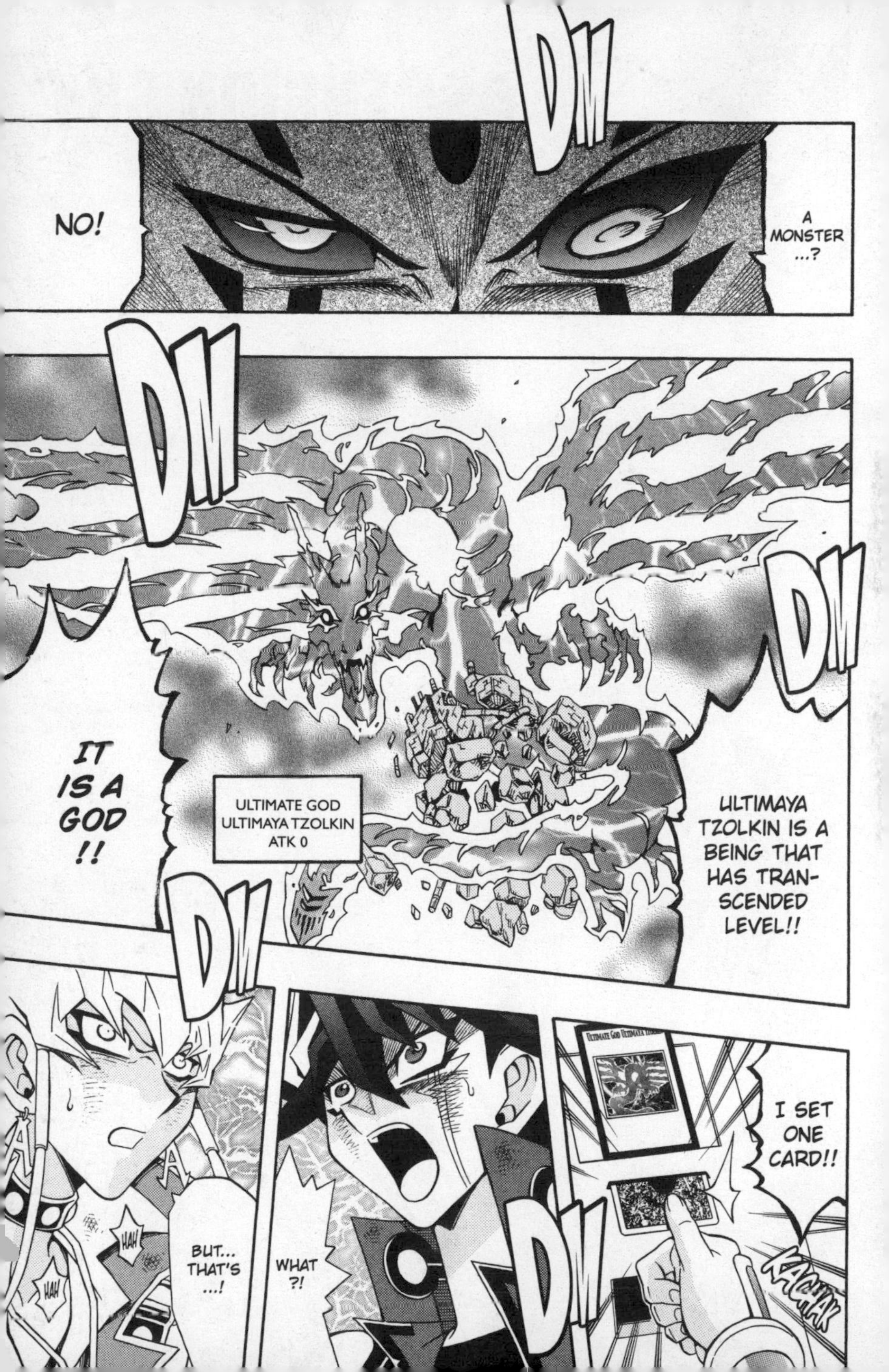

DM
A MONSTER ...?
NO!
DM
DM
ULTIMAYA TZOLKIN IS A BEING THAT HAS TRAN-SCENDED LEVEL!!
ULTIMATE GOD ULTIMAYA TZOLKIN ATK 0
IT IS A GOD!!
I SET ONE CARD!!
KACHAK
DM
DM
WHAT ?!
BUT... THAT'S ...!
HAH
HAH

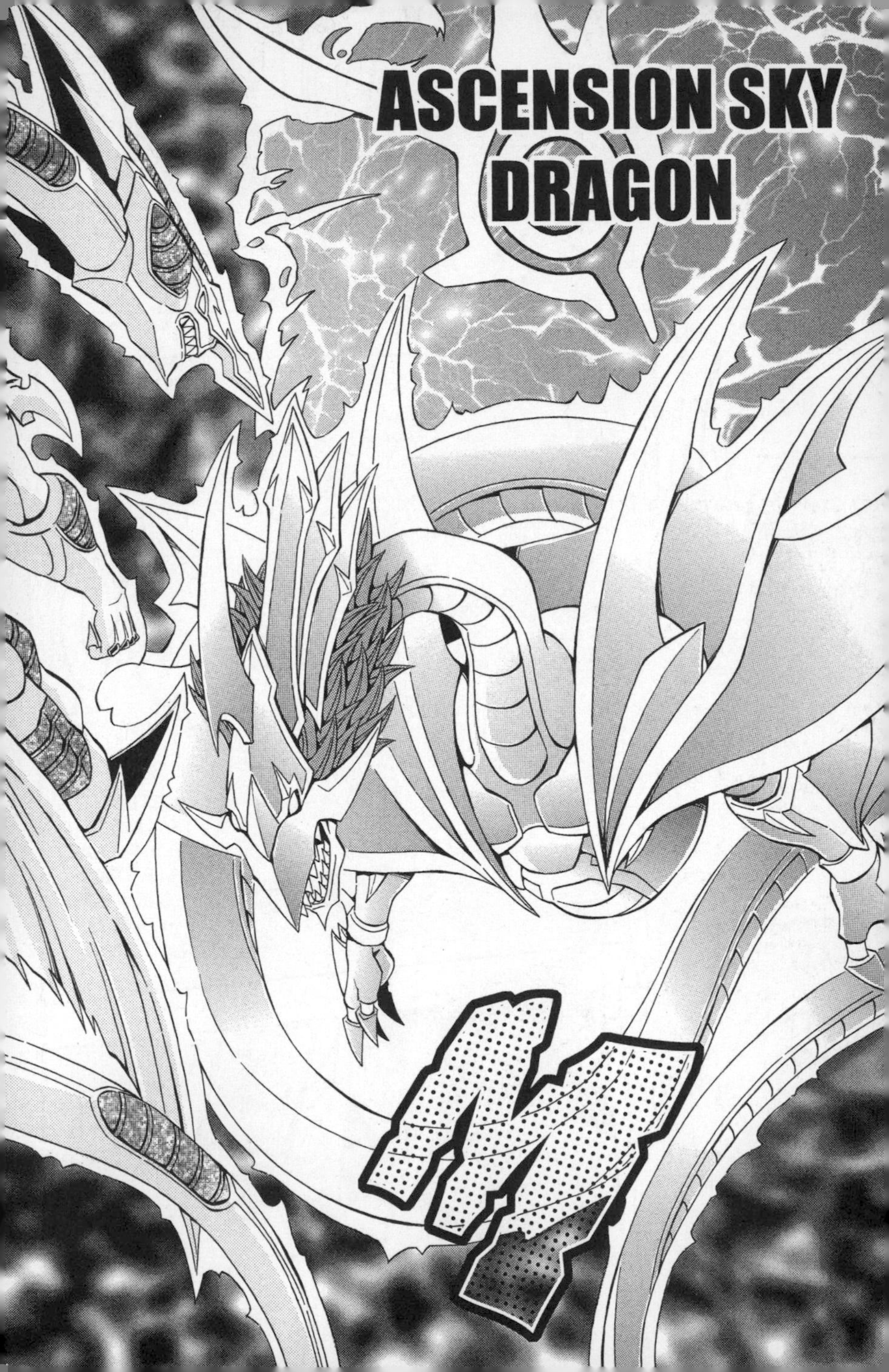
ASCENSION SKY DRAGON
11

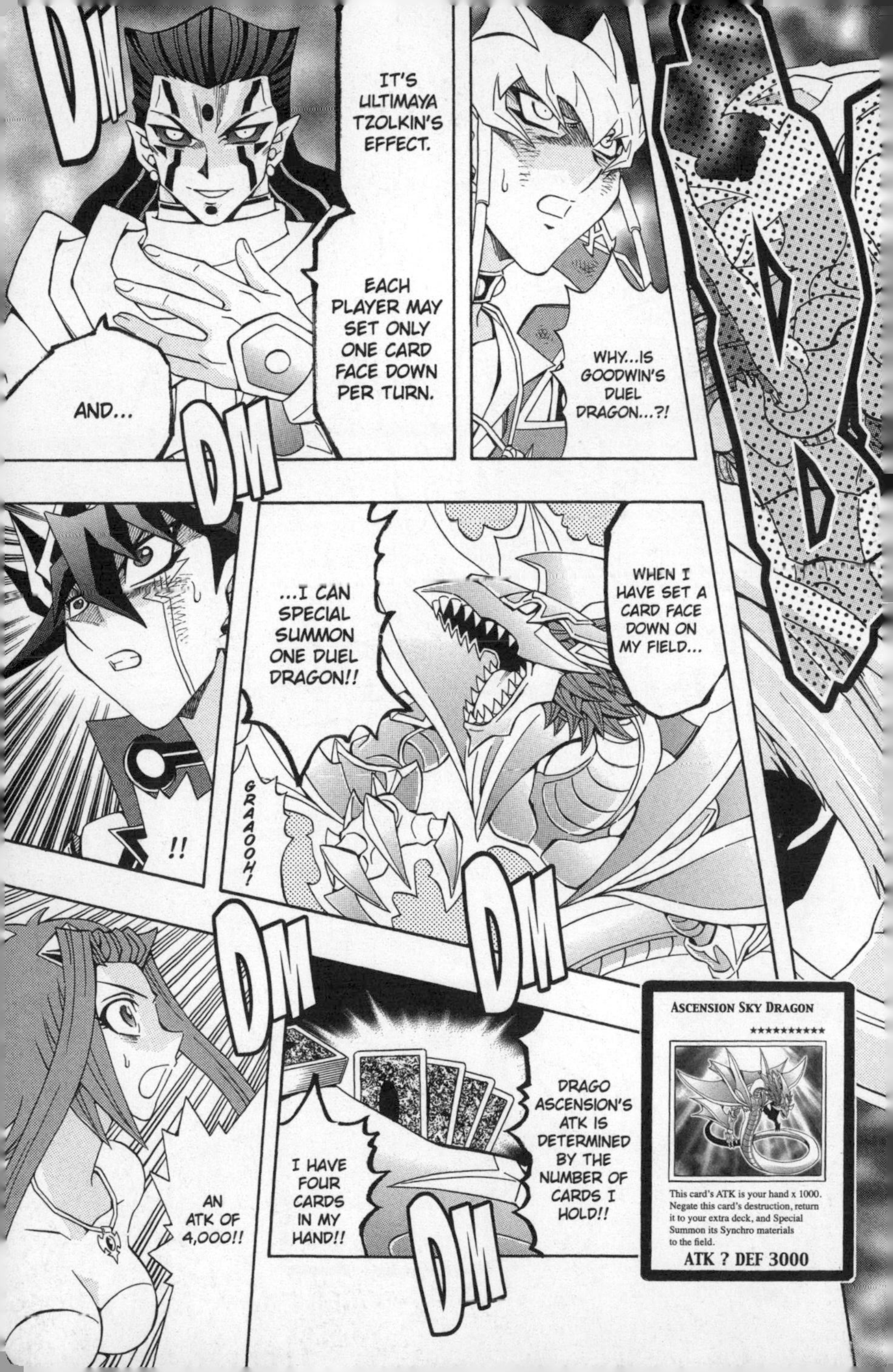
DM
WHY...IS GOODWIN'S DUEL DRAGON...?!
IT'S ULTIMAYA TZOLKIN'S EFFECT.
EACH PLAYER MAY SET ONLY ONE CARD FACE DOWN PER TURN.
DM
AND...
DM
WHEN I HAVE SET A CARD FACE DOWN ON MY FIELD...
...I CAN SPECIAL SUMMON ONE DUEL DRAGON!!
GRAAAOOH!
!!
DM
DM
ASCENSION SKY DRAGON
★★★★★★★★★★★
This card's ATK is your hand x 1000. Negate this card's destruction, return it to your extra deck, and Special Summon its Synchro materials to the field.
ATK ? DEF 3000
DRAGO ASCENSION'S ATK IS DETERMINED BY THE NUMBER OF CARDS I HOLD!!
I HAVE FOUR CARDS IN MY HAND!!
DM
AN ATK OF 4,000!!

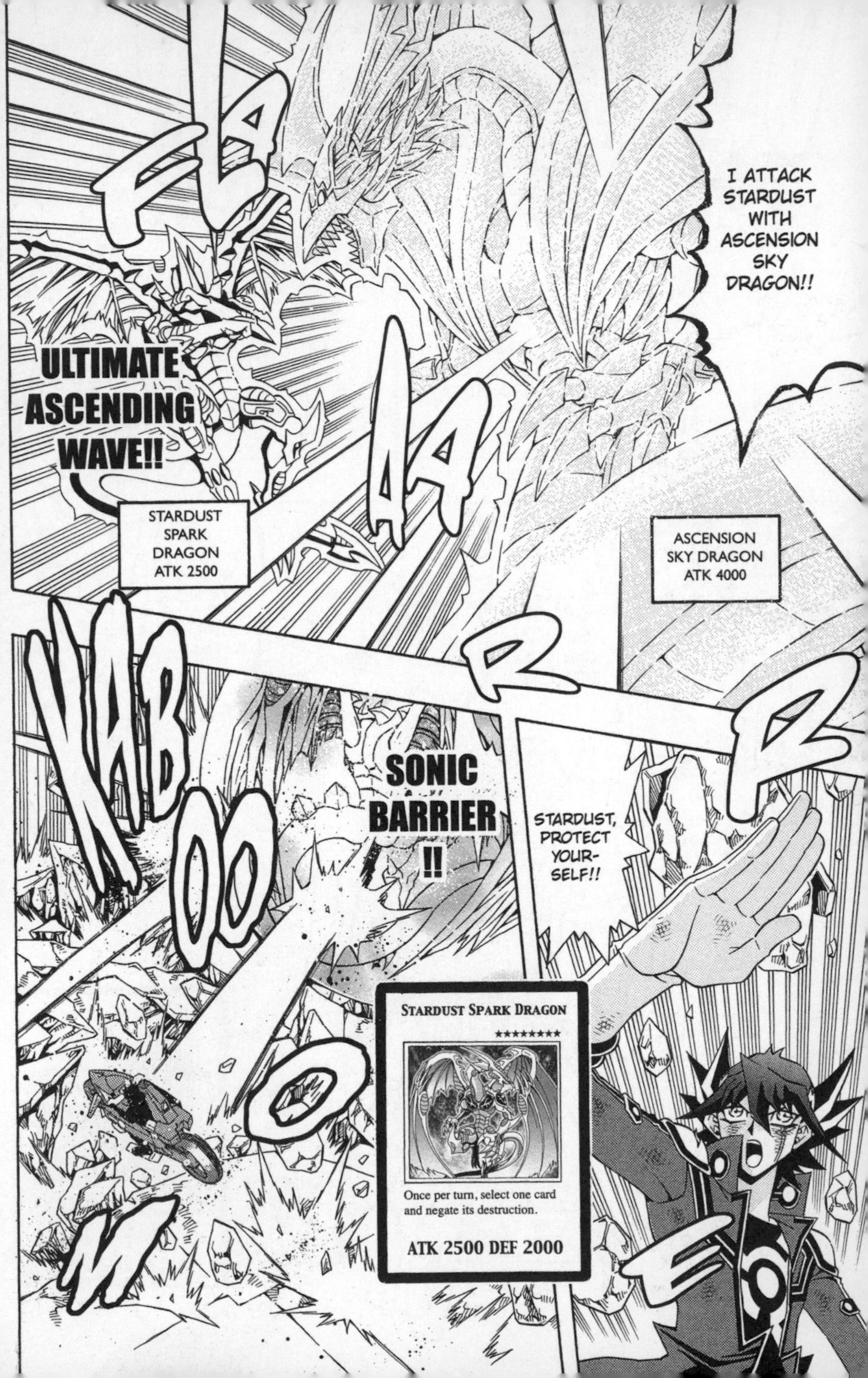

I ATTACK STARDUST WITH ASCENSION SKY DRAGON!!
ASCENSION SKY DRAGON ATK 4000
FLAAARRR
ULTIMATE ASCENDING WAVE!!
STARDUST SPARK DRAGON ATK 2500
STARDUST, PROTECT YOURSELF!!
SONIC BARRIER!!
STARDUST SPARK DRAGON
Once per turn, select one card and negate its destruction.
ATK 2500 DEF 2000
VABOOOM

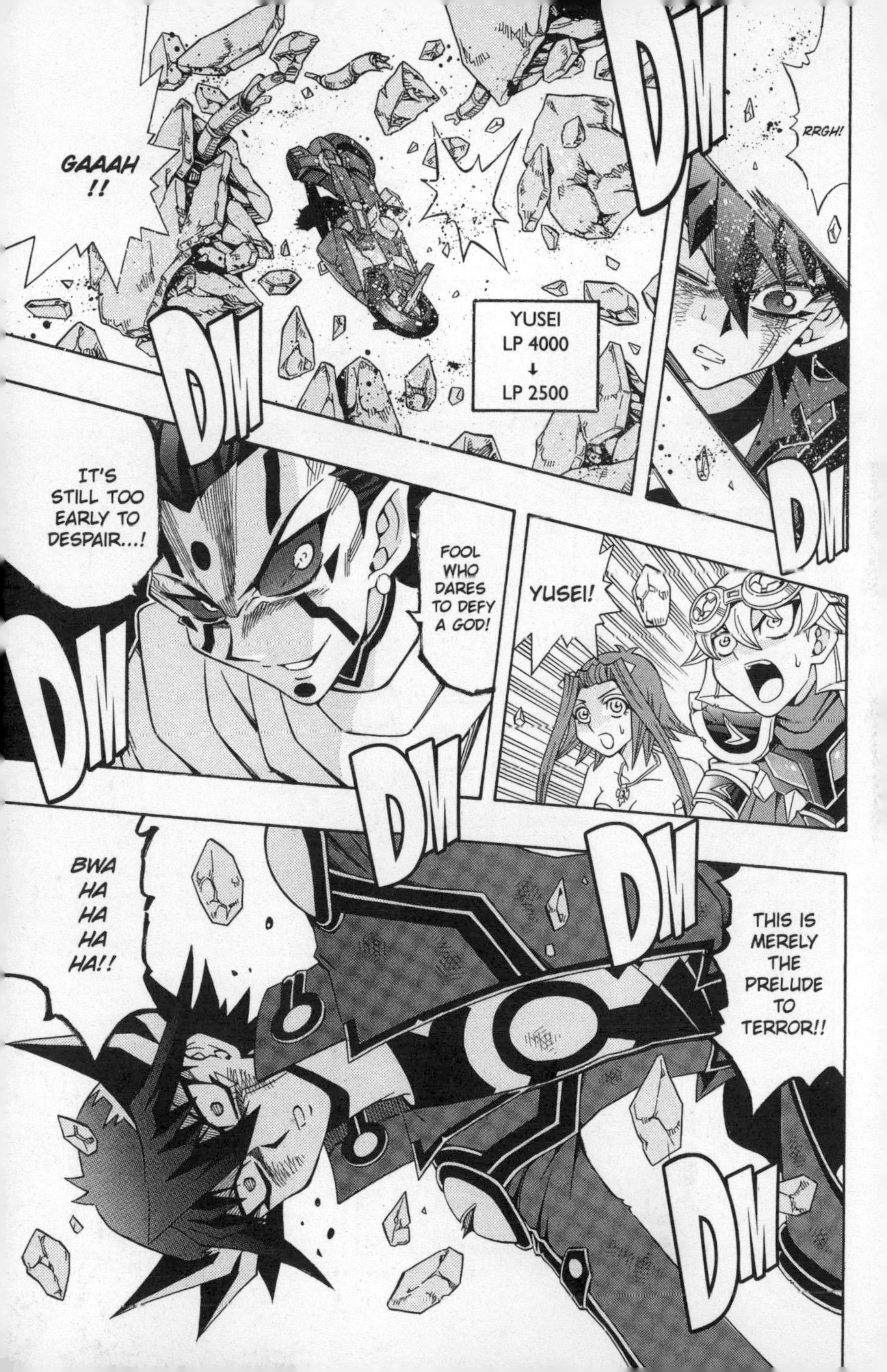
DM
RRGH!
DM
GAAAH!!
YUSEI
LP 4000
↓
LP 2500
DM
YUSEI!
IT'S STILL TOO EARLY TO DESPAIR...!
FOOL WHO DARES TO DEFY A GOD!
DM
DM
DM
THIS IS MERELY THE PRELUDE TO TERROR!!
DM
BWA HA HA HA HA!!
DM

5D's Tracks

THE 58TH

BY SATOMASA

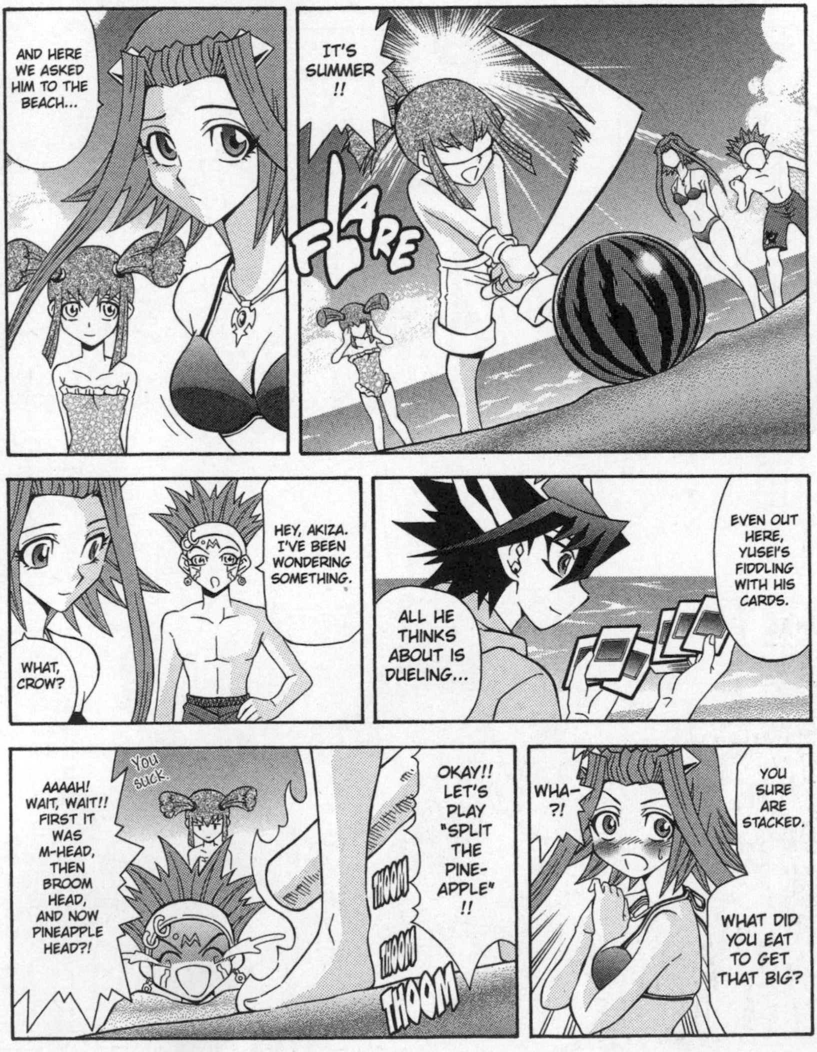
IT'S SUMMER!!
FLARE
AND HERE WE ASKED HIM TO THE BEACH...
EVEN OUT HERE, YUSEI'S FIDDLING WITH HIS CARDS.
ALL HE THINKS ABOUT IS DUELING...
HEY, AKIZA. I'VE BEEN WONDERING SOMETHING.
WHAT, CROW?
YOU SURE ARE STACKED.
WHA-?!
WHAT DID YOU EAT TO GET THAT BIG?
OKAY!! LET'S PLAY "SPLIT THE PINE-APPLE"!!
THOOM
THOOM
THOOM
You suck.
AAAAH! WAIT, WAIT!! FIRST IT WAS M-HEAD, THEN BROOM HEAD, AND NOW PINEAPPLE HEAD?!

RIDE-60
DECK OF A GOD!!

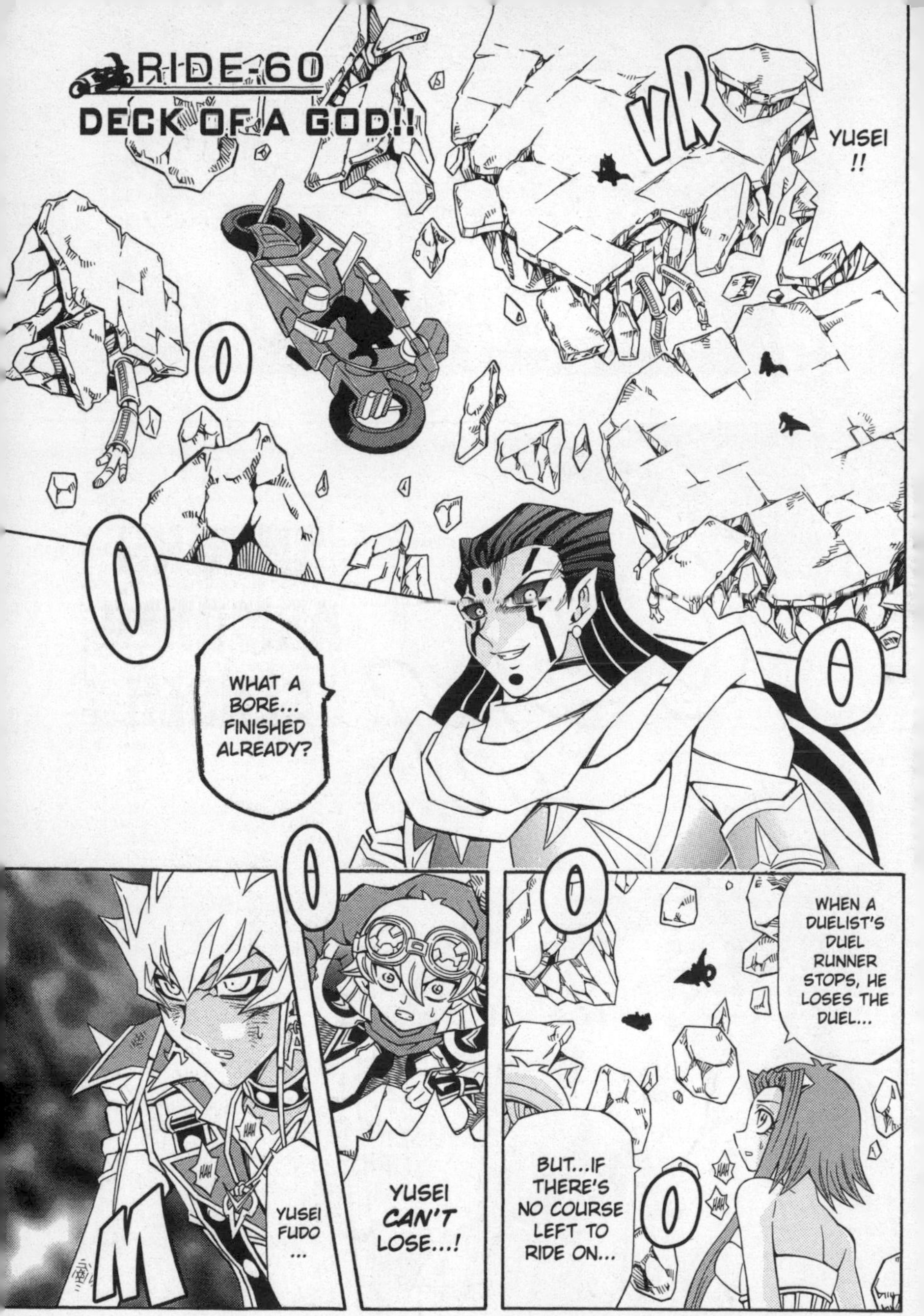

VR
YUSEI!!
O
O
O
WHAT A BORE... FINISHED ALREADY?
O
O
WHEN A DUELIST'S DUEL RUNNER STOPS, HE LOSES THE DUEL...
BUT...IF THERE'S NO COURSE LEFT TO RIDE ON...
O
YUSEI *CAN'T* LOSE...!
YUSEI FUDO...
M

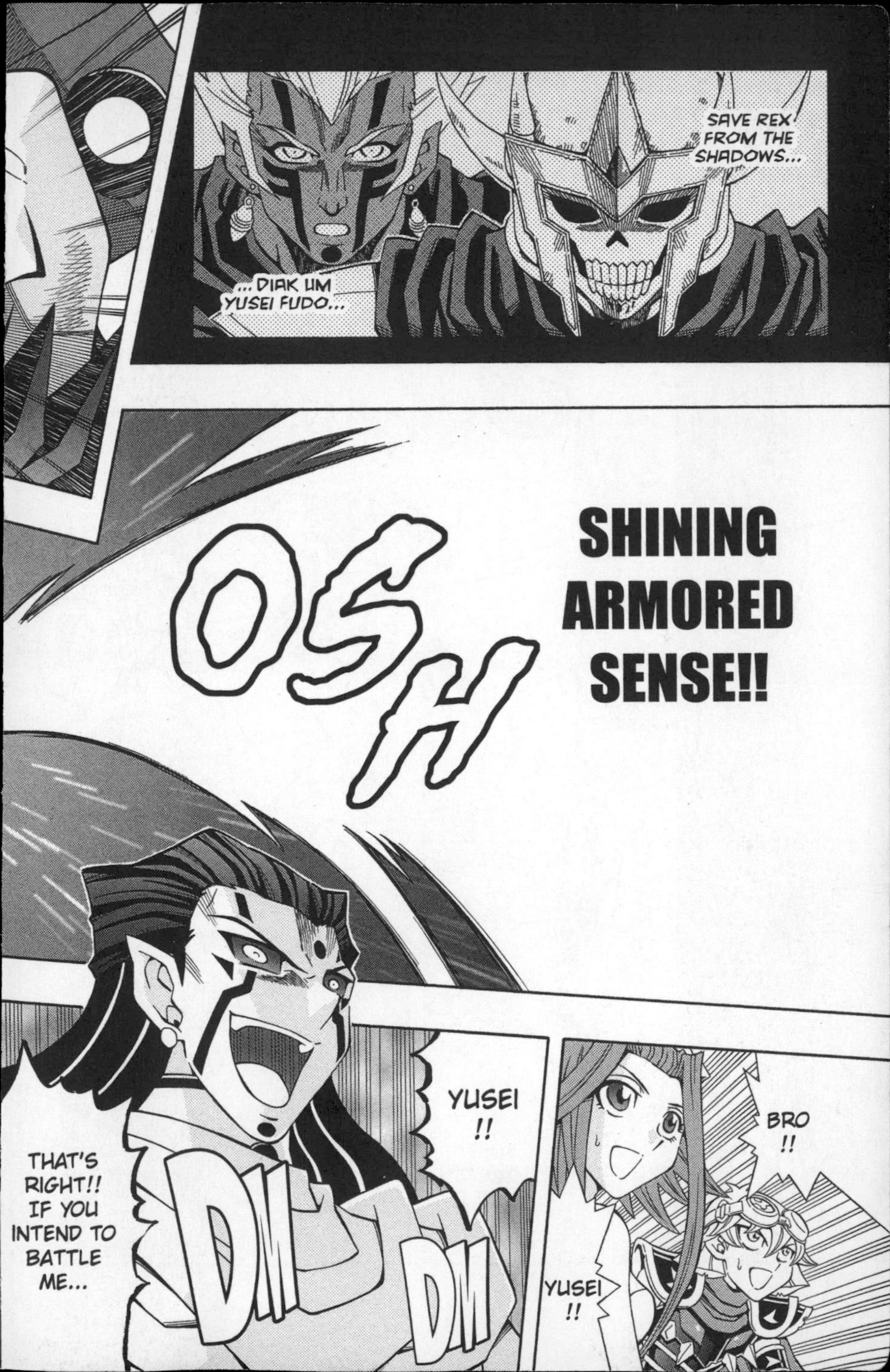
SAVE REX FROM THE SHADOWS...
...DIAK UM YUSEI FUDO...
SHINING ARMORED SENSE!!
OSH
BRO!!
YUSEI!!
YUSEI!!
THAT'S RIGHT!! IF YOU INTEND TO BATTLE ME...
DM
DM

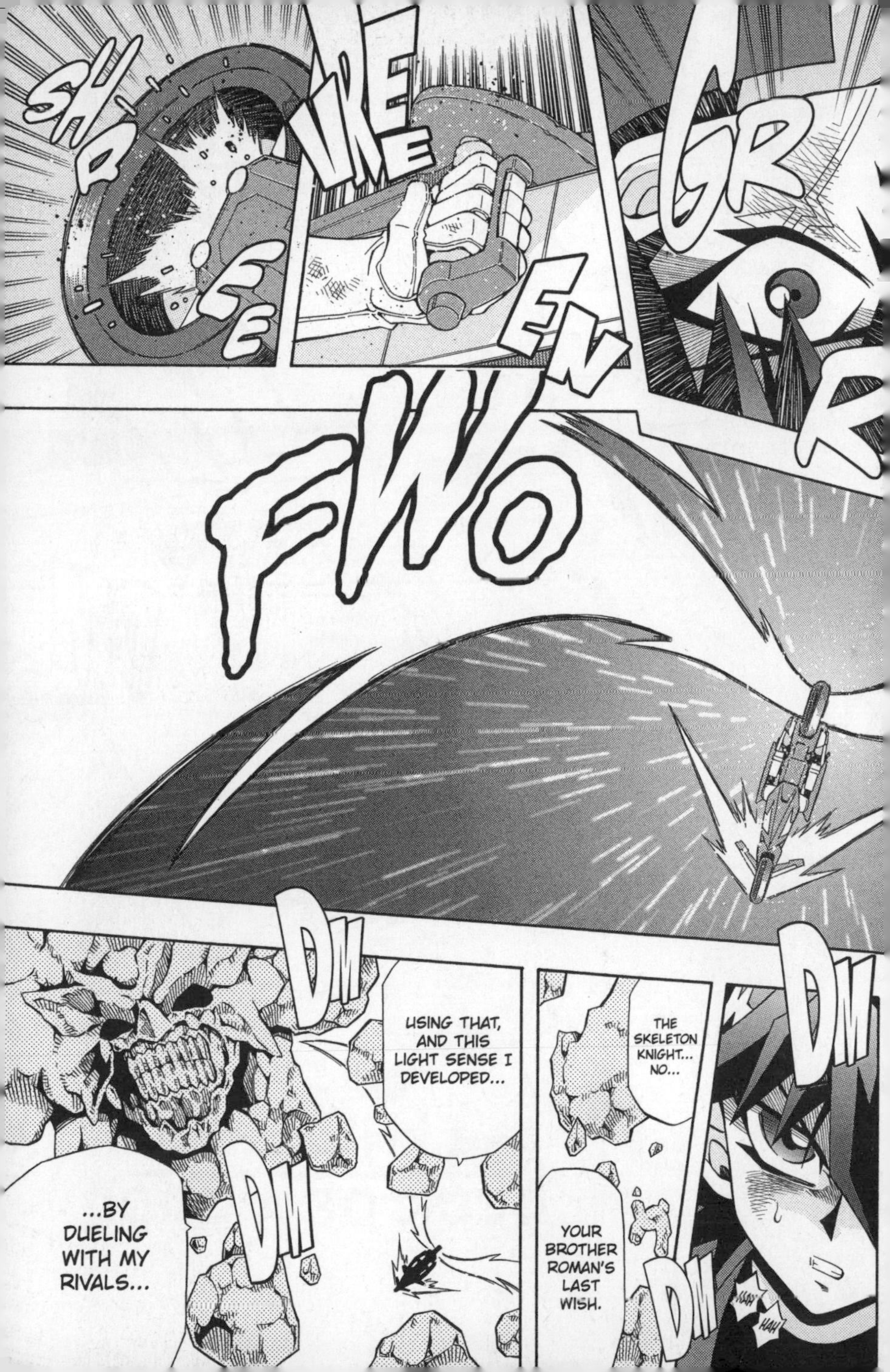
FWO
DM
THE SKELETON KNIGHT... NO...
YOUR BROTHER ROMAN'S LAST WISH.
DM
HAH
HAH
DM
USING THAT, AND THIS LIGHT SENSE I DEVELOPED...
DM
...BY DUELING WITH MY RIVALS...
DM

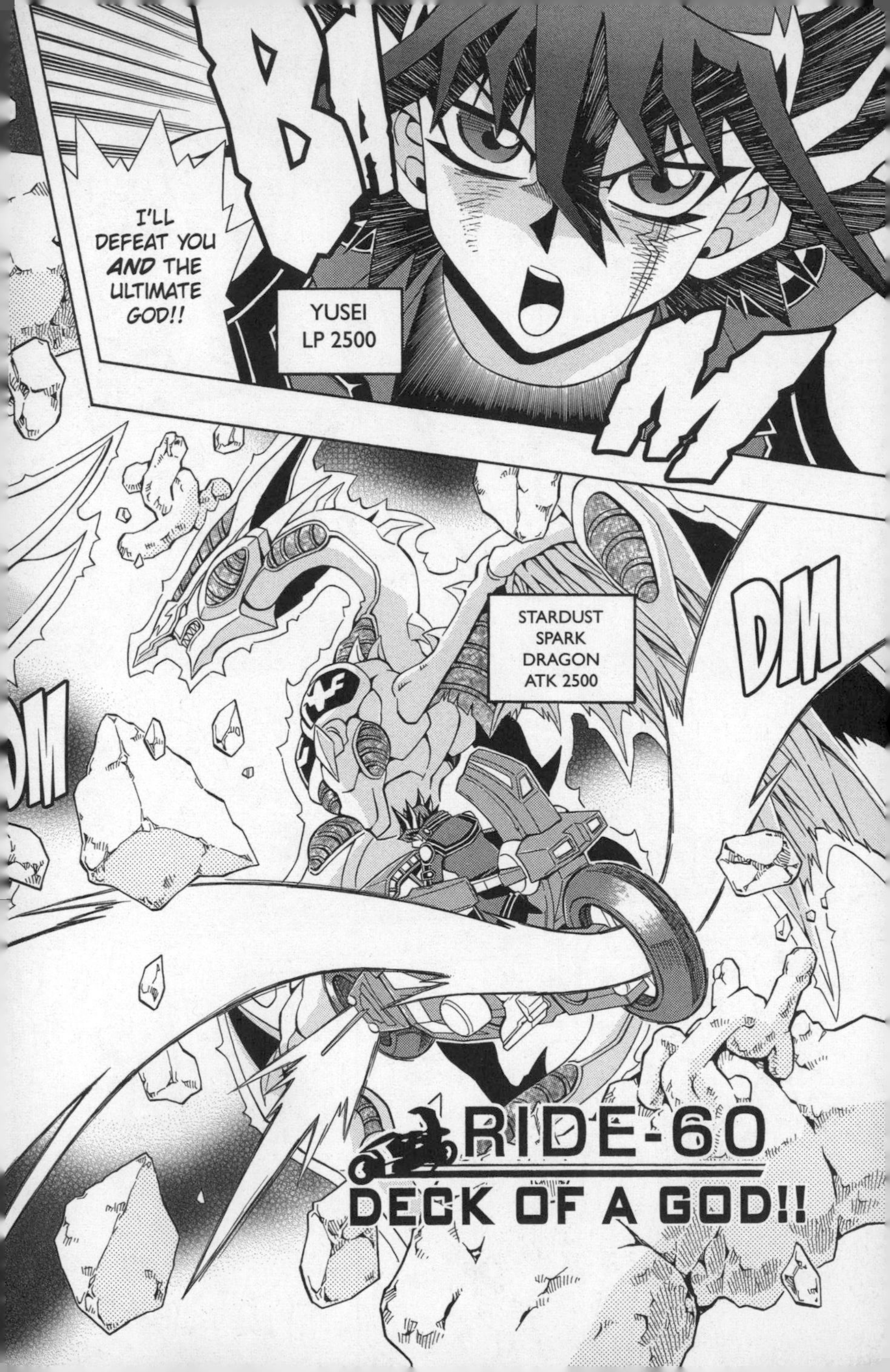
BAM
I'LL DEFEAT YOU *AND* THE ULTIMATE GOD!!
YUSEI LP 2500
DM
STARDUST SPARK DRAGON ATK 2500
RIDE-60
DECK OF A GOD!!

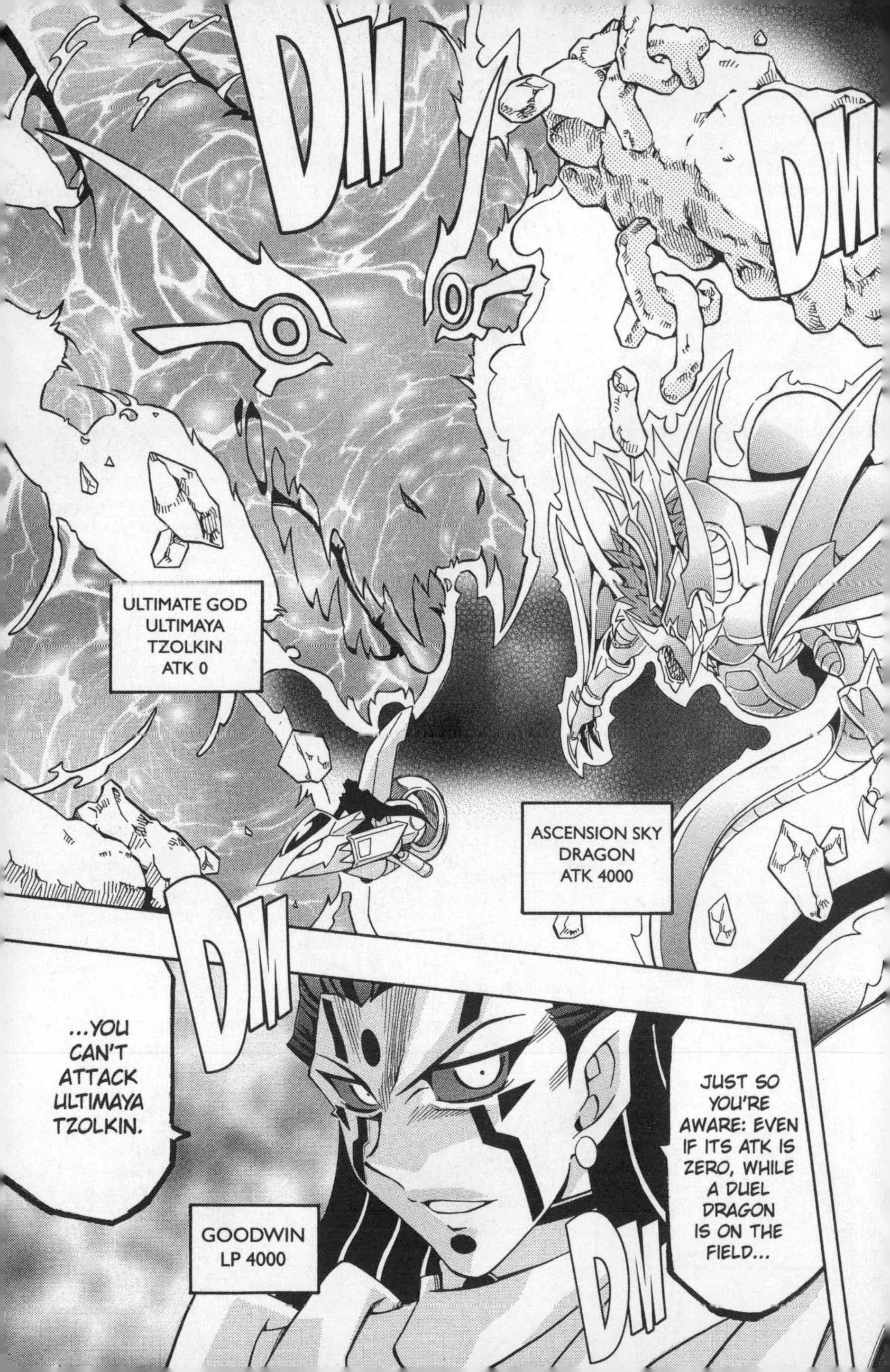
DM
DM
ULTIMATE GOD ULTIMAYA TZOLKIN ATK 0
ASCENSION SKY DRAGON ATK 4000
DM
JUST SO YOU'RE AWARE: EVEN IF ITS ATK IS ZERO, WHILE A DUEL DRAGON IS ON THE FIELD...
...YOU CAN'T ATTACK ULTIMAYA TZOLKIN.
GOODWIN LP 4000
DM

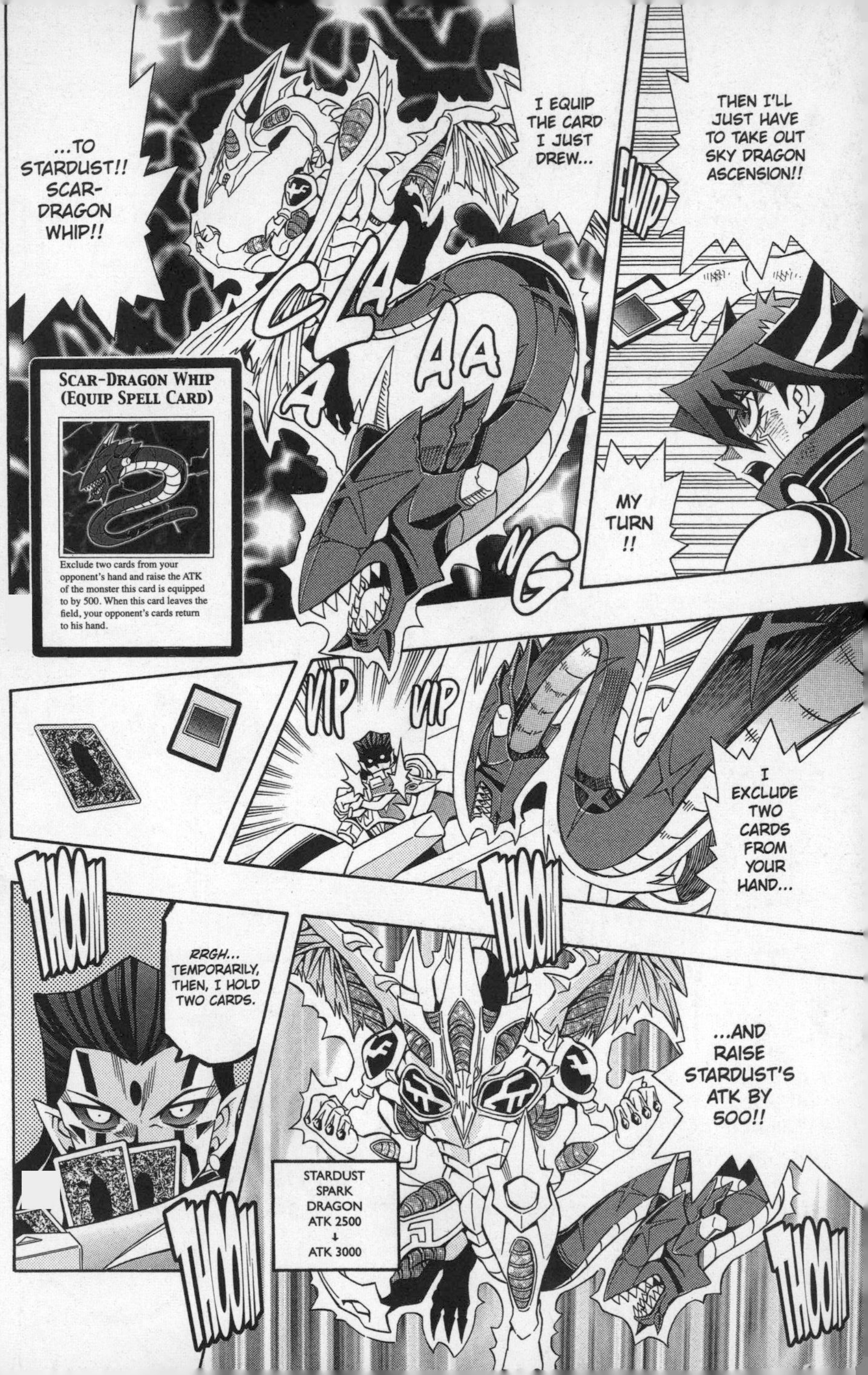
THEN I'LL JUST HAVE TO TAKE OUT SKY DRAGON ASCENSION!!
FWIP
MY TURN!!
I EQUIP THE CARD I JUST DREW...
...TO STARDUST!! SCAR-DRAGON WHIP!!
CLAAAANG
SCAR-DRAGON WHIP (EQUIP SPELL CARD)
Exclude two cards from your opponent's hand and raise the ATK of the monster this card is equipped to by 500. When this card leaves the field, your opponent's cards return to his hand.
I EXCLUDE TWO CARDS FROM YOUR HAND...
VIP
VIP
THOOM
...AND RAISE STARDUST'S ATK BY 500!!
STARDUST SPARK DRAGON ATK 2500 ↓ ATK 3000
THOOM
THOOM
RRGH... TEMPORARILY, THEN, I HOLD TWO CARDS.
THOOM

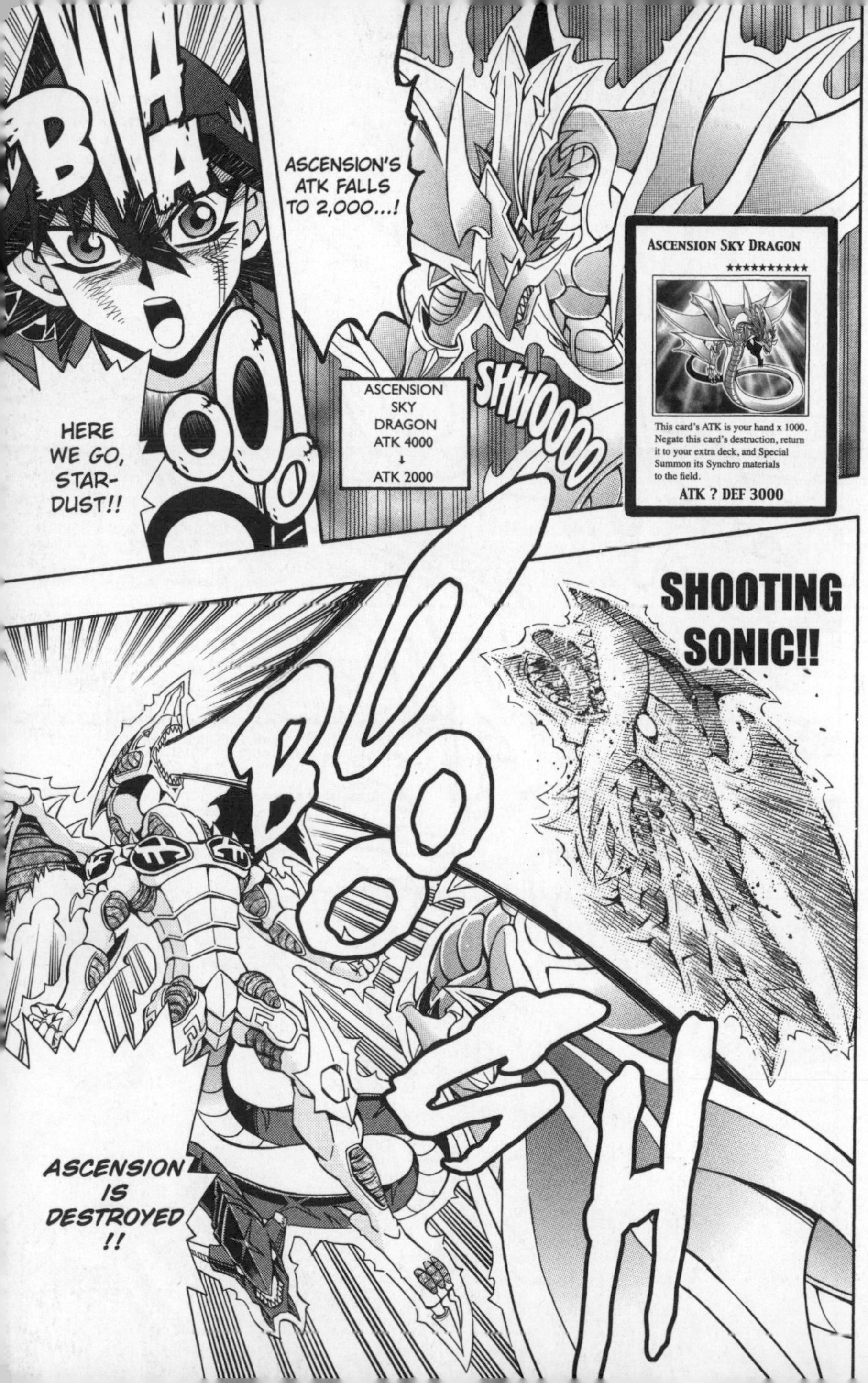
ASCENSION'S ATK FALLS TO 2,000...!
ASCENSION SKY DRAGON ATK 4000 ↓ ATK 2000
SHWOOOO
ASCENSION SKY DRAGON
★★★★★★★★★★★
This card's ATK is your hand x 1000. Negate this card's destruction, return it to your extra deck, and Special Summon its Synchro materials to the field.
ATK ? DEF 3000
BWAA
HERE WE GO, STAR-DUST!!
SHOOTING SONIC!!
BOOOSH
ASCENSION IS DESTROYED!!

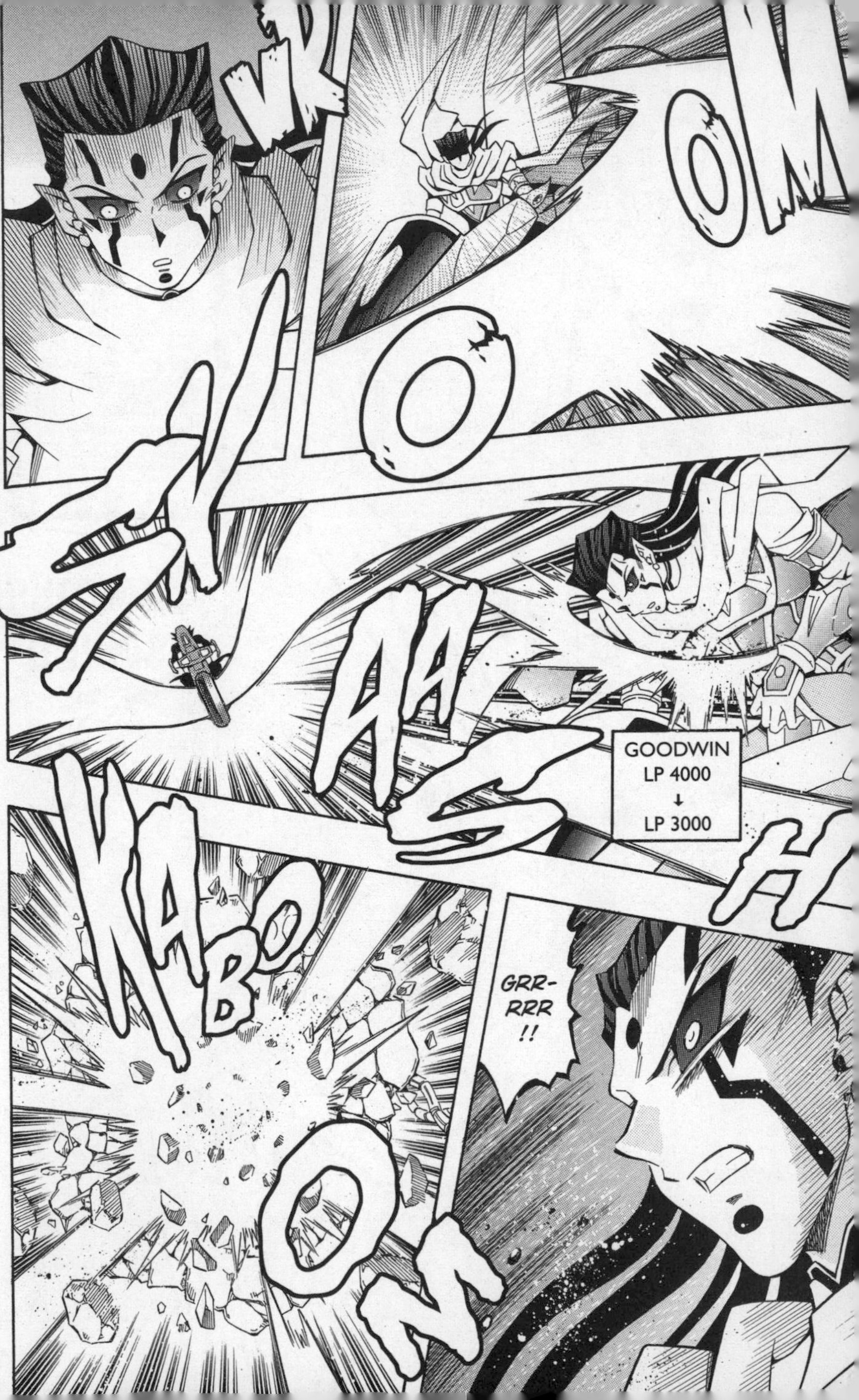
GOODWIN
LP 4000
↓
LP 3000
GRR-RRR!!
KABOOM

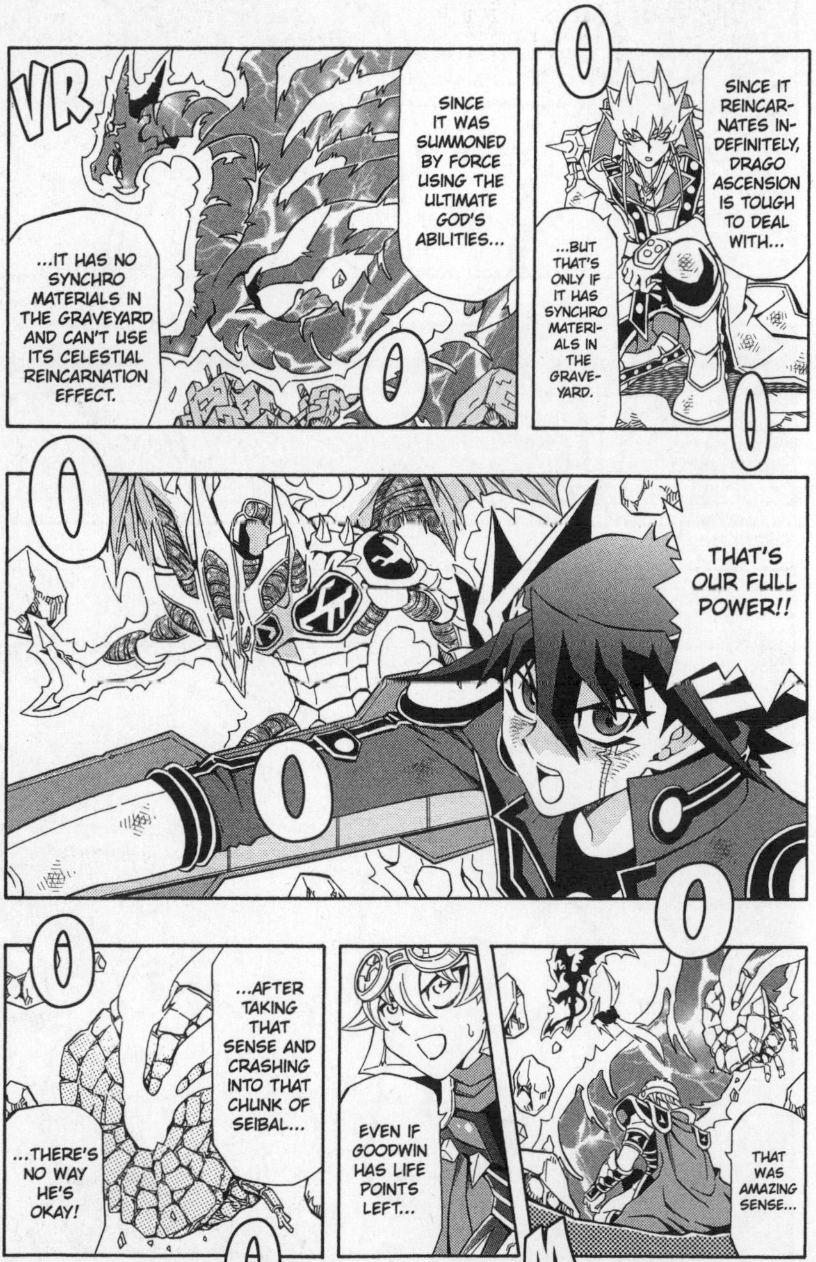
SINCE IT REINCARNATES INDEFINITELY, DRAGO ASCENSION IS TOUGH TO DEAL WITH...
...BUT THAT'S ONLY IF IT HAS SYNCHRO MATERIALS IN THE GRAVEYARD.
SINCE IT WAS SUMMONED BY FORCE USING THE ULTIMATE GOD'S ABILITIES...
...IT HAS NO SYNCHRO MATERIALS IN THE GRAVEYARD AND CAN'T USE ITS CELESTIAL REINCARNATION EFFECT.
VROOOOOOOOM
THAT'S OUR FULL POWER!!
THAT WAS AMAZING SENSE...
EVEN IF GOODWIN HAS LIFE POINTS LEFT...
...AFTER TAKING THAT SENSE AND CRASHING INTO THAT CHUNK OF SEIBAL...
...THERE'S NO WAY HE'S OKAY!

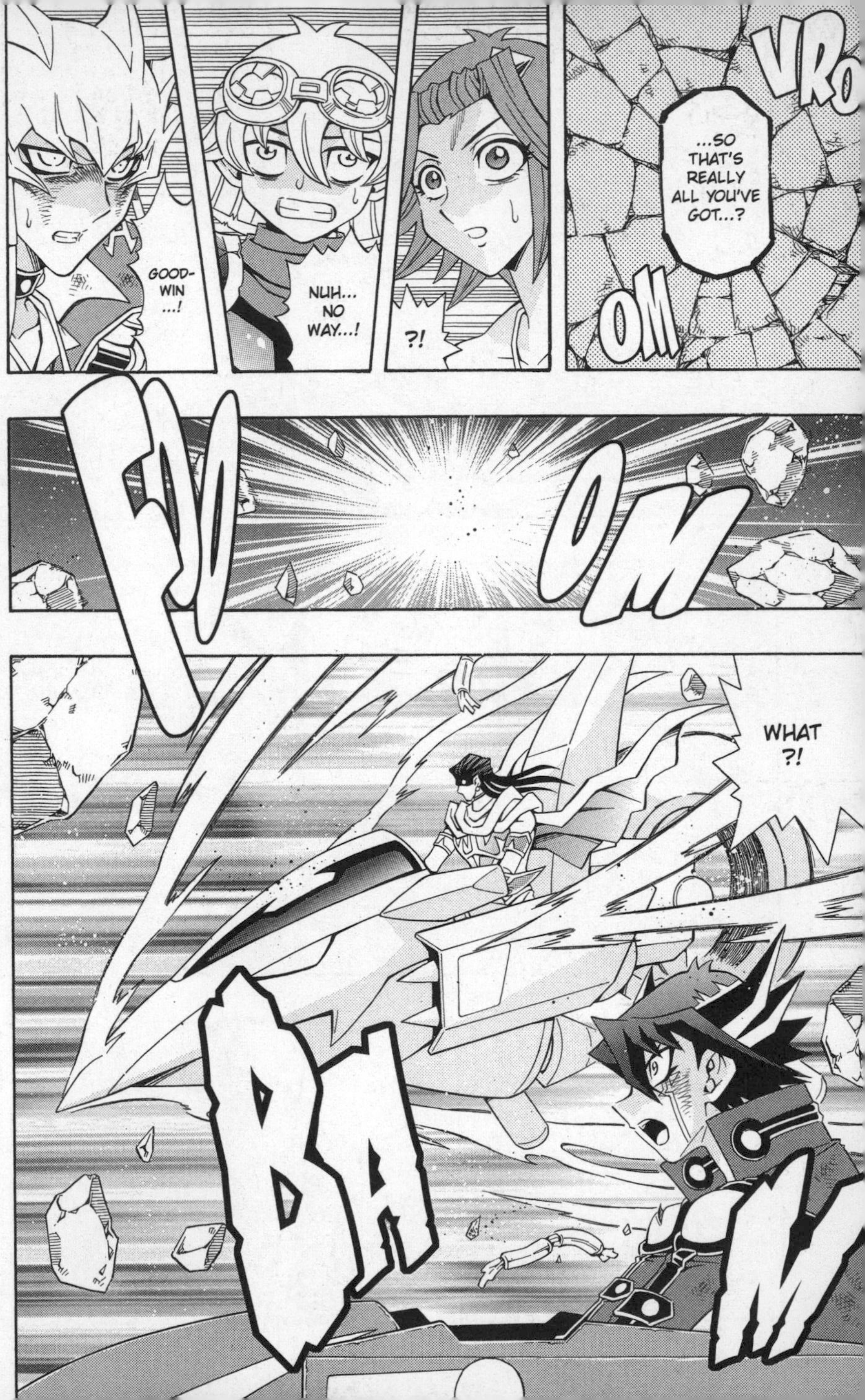
VROOM
...SO THAT'S REALLY ALL YOU'VE GOT...?
?!
NUH... NO WAY...!
GOOD-WIN ...!
FOOM
WHAT ?!
BAM

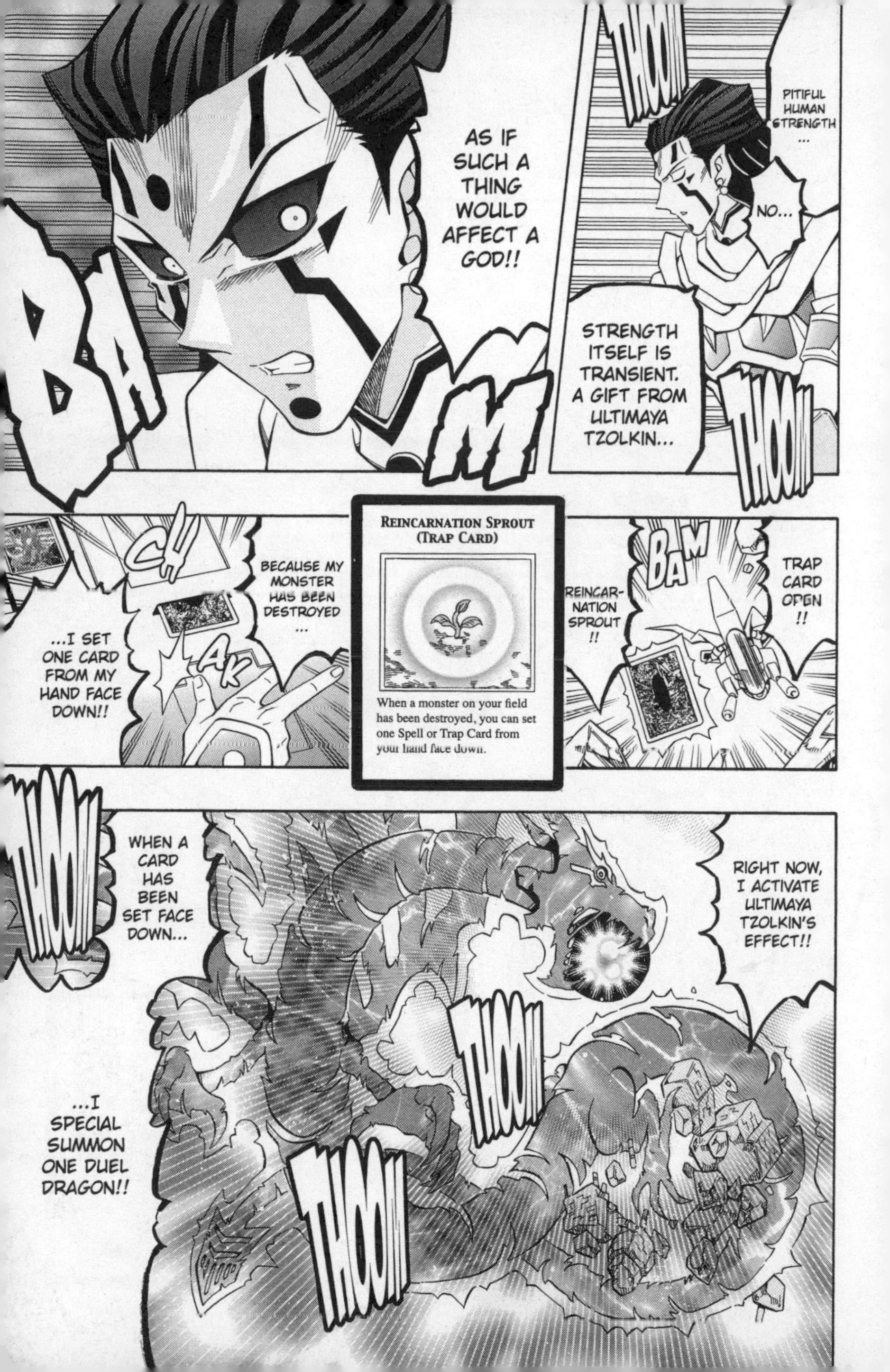
THOOM
PITIFUL HUMAN STRENGTH...
NO...
STRENGTH ITSELF IS TRANSIENT. A GIFT FROM ULTIMAYA TZOLKIN...
THOOM
BAM
AS IF SUCH A THING WOULD AFFECT A GOD!!
BAM
TRAP CARD OPEN!!
REINCARNATION SPROUT!!
REINCARNATION SPROUT
(TRAP CARD)
When a monster on your field has been destroyed, you can set one Spell or Trap Card from your hand face down.
CH
AK
BECAUSE MY MONSTER HAS BEEN DESTROYED...
...I SET ONE CARD FROM MY HAND FACE DOWN!!
RIGHT NOW, I ACTIVATE ULTIMAYA TZOLKIN'S EFFECT!!
WHEN A CARD HAS BEEN SET FACE DOWN...
THOOM
THOOM
...I SPECIAL SUMMON ONE DUEL DRAGON!!
THOOM

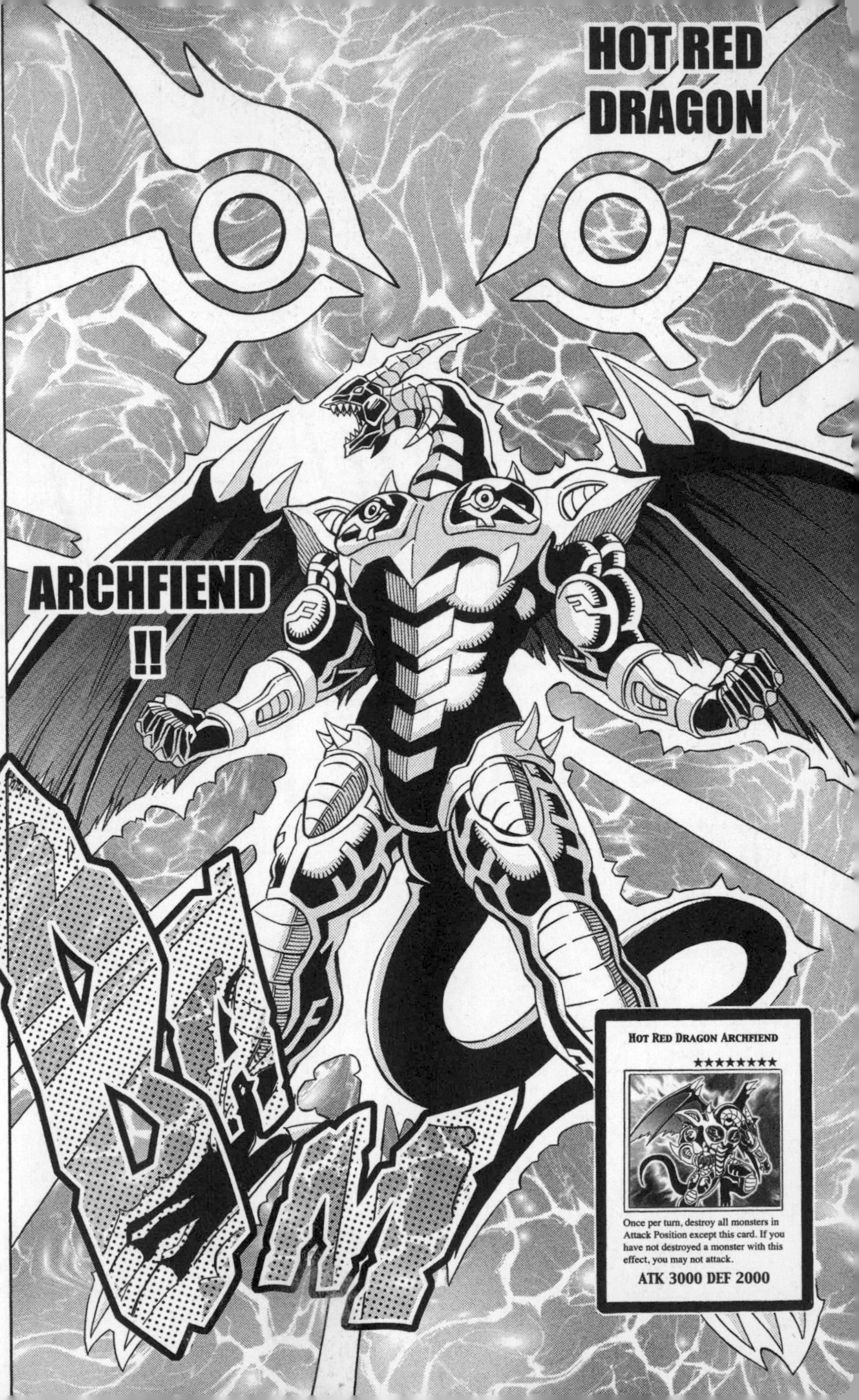
HOT RED DRAGON
ARCHFIEND !!
HOT RED DRAGON ARCHFIEND
★★★★★★★★
Once per turn, destroy all monsters in Attack Position except this card. If you have not destroyed a monster with this effect, you may not attack.
ATK 3000 DEF 2000

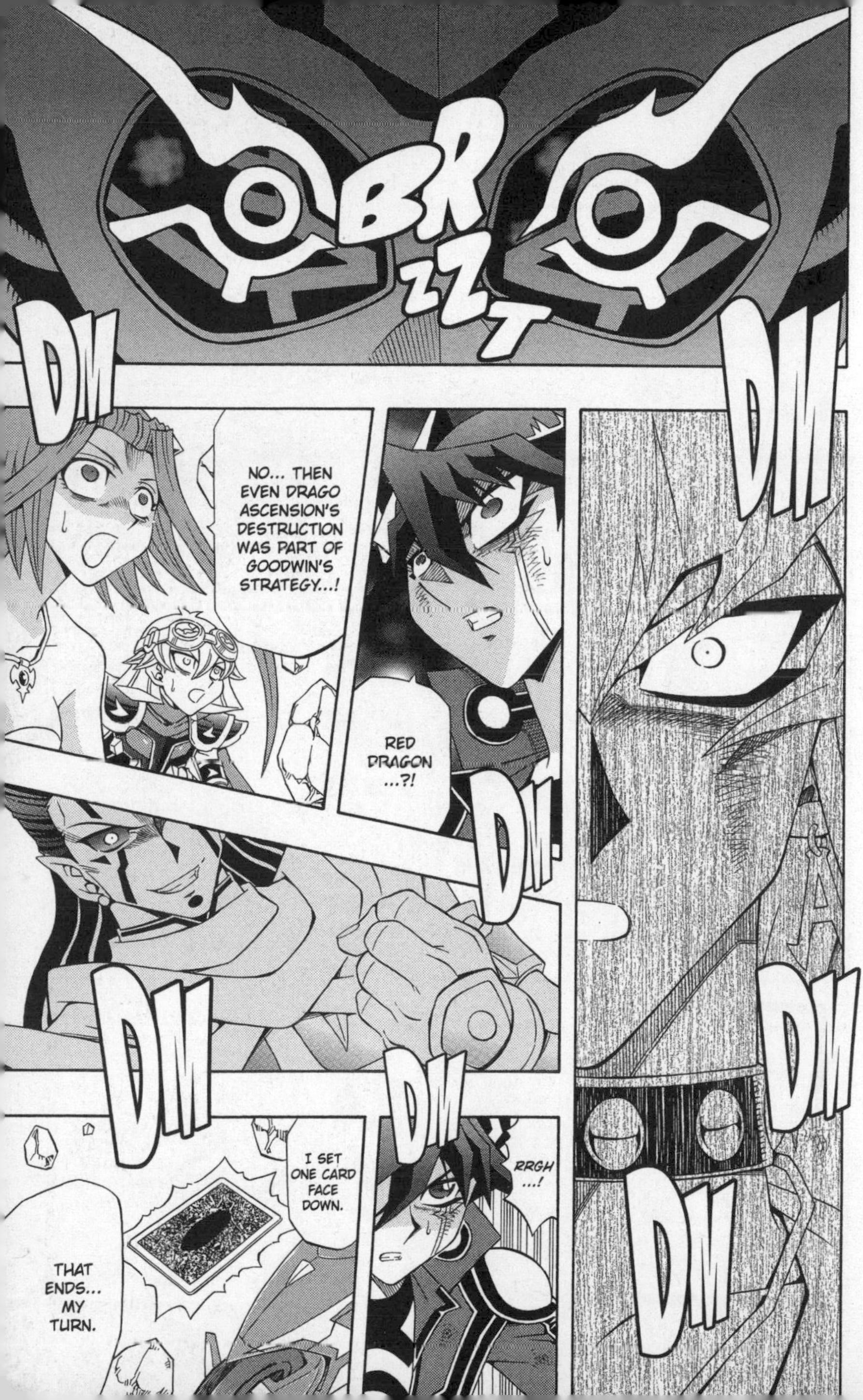
BRZZZT
DM
DM
DM
DM
RED DRAGON ...?!
NO... THEN EVEN DRAGO ASCENSION'S DESTRUCTION WAS PART OF GOODWIN'S STRATEGY...!
DM
DM
DM
DM
RRGH ...!
I SET ONE CARD FACE DOWN.
THAT ENDS... MY TURN.

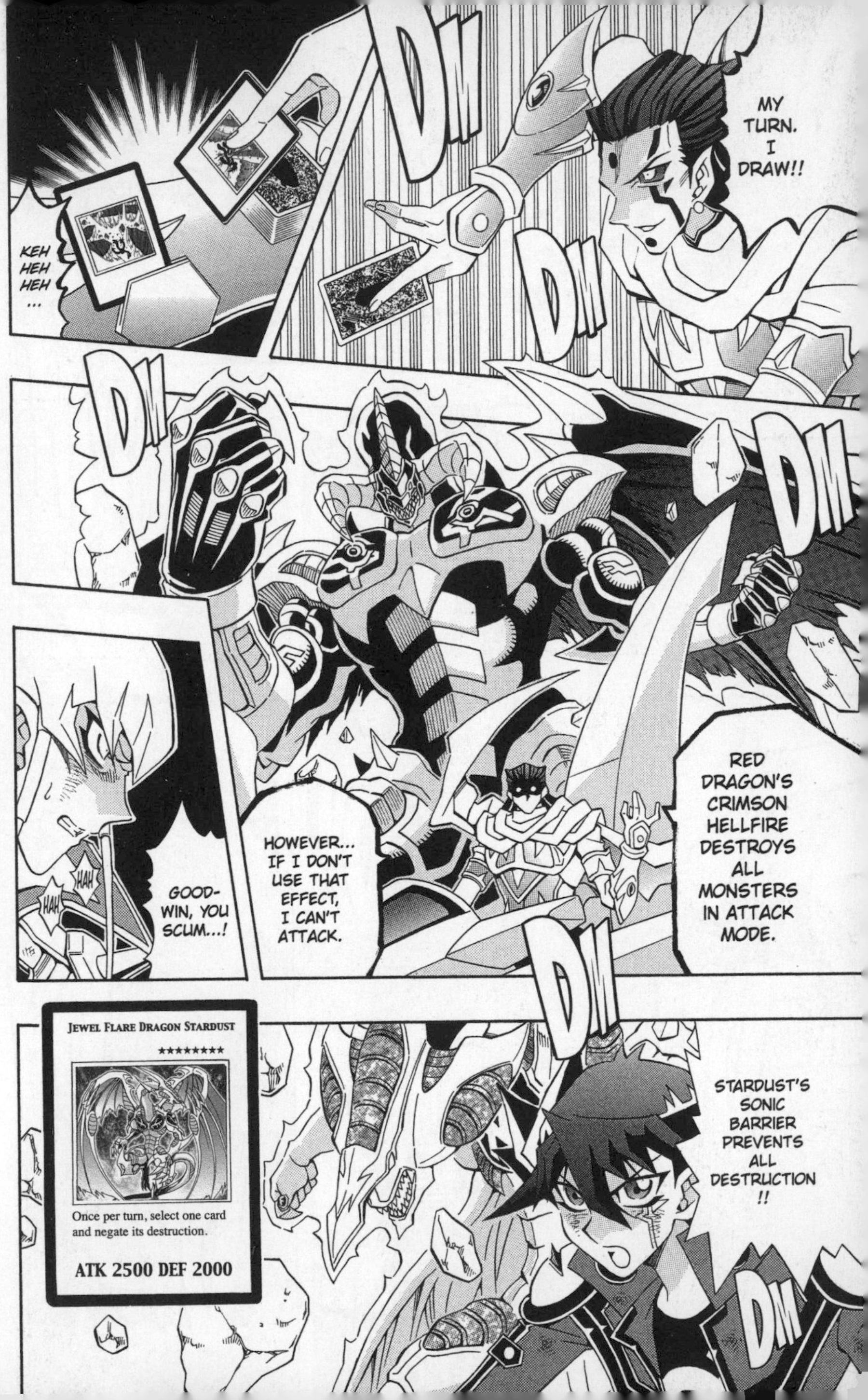
DM
MY TURN. I DRAW!!
DM
KEH HEH HEH ...
DM
DM
RED DRAGON'S CRIMSON HELLFIRE DESTROYS ALL MONSTERS IN ATTACK MODE.
HOWEVER... IF I DON'T USE THAT EFFECT, I CAN'T ATTACK.
GOOD-WIN, YOU SCUM...!
HAH
HAH
DM
STARDUST'S SONIC BARRIER PREVENTS ALL DESTRUCTION !!
DM
JEWEL FLARE DRAGON STARDUST
★★★★★★★★
Once per turn, select one card and negate its destruction.
ATK 2500 DEF 2000

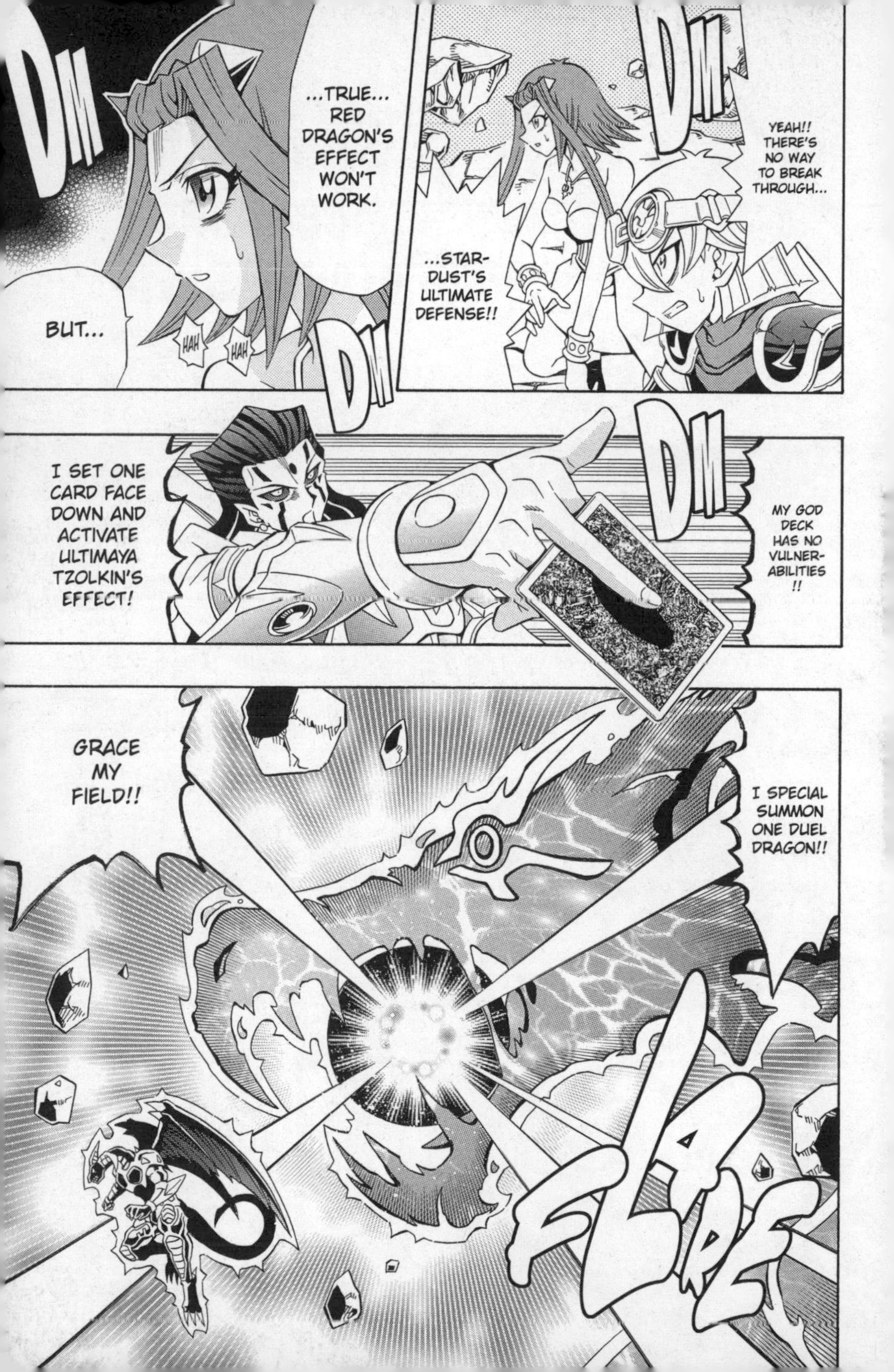
DM
YEAH!! THERE'S NO WAY TO BREAK THROUGH...
...STAR-DUST'S ULTIMATE DEFENSE!!
DM
...TRUE... RED DRAGON'S EFFECT WON'T WORK.
BUT...
HAH
HAH
DM
DM
MY GOD DECK HAS NO VULNER-ABILITIES!!
I SET ONE CARD FACE DOWN AND ACTIVATE ULTIMAYA TZOLKIN'S EFFECT!
I SPECIAL SUMMON ONE DUEL DRAGON!!
GRACE MY FIELD!!
FLARE

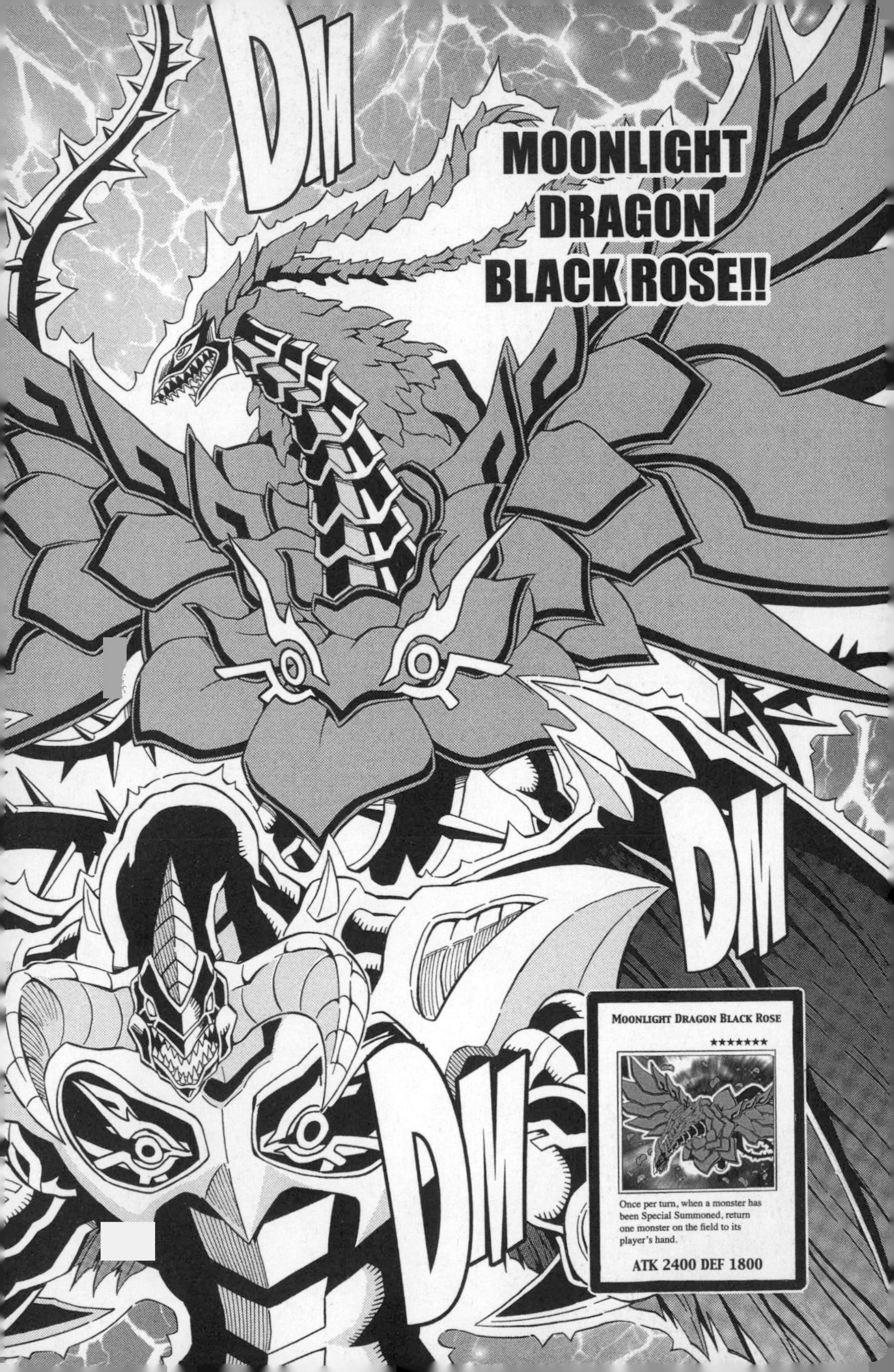
MOONLIGHT DRAGON BLACK ROSE!!
DM
DM
MOONLIGHT DRAGON BLACK ROSE
★★★★★★★
Once per turn, when a monster has been Special Summoned, return one monster on the field to its player's hand.
ATK 2400 DEF 1800
DM

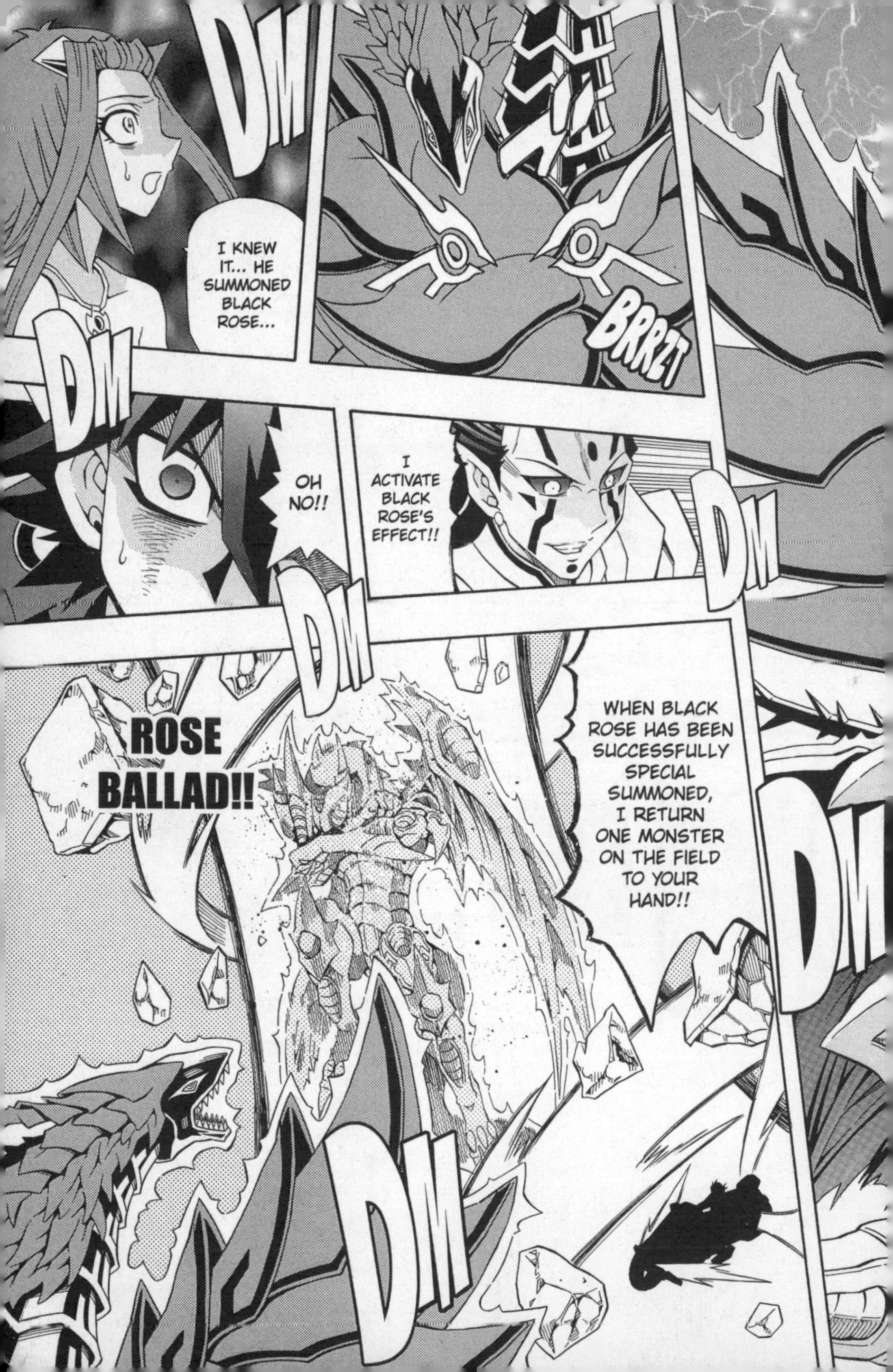

BRRZT
DM
I KNEW IT... HE SUMMONED BLACK ROSE...
DM
DM
I ACTIVATE BLACK ROSE'S EFFECT!!
OH NO!!
DM
DM
WHEN BLACK ROSE HAS BEEN SUCCESSFULLY SPECIAL SUMMONED, I RETURN ONE MONSTER ON THE FIELD TO YOUR HAND!!
ROSE BALLAD!!
DM
DM

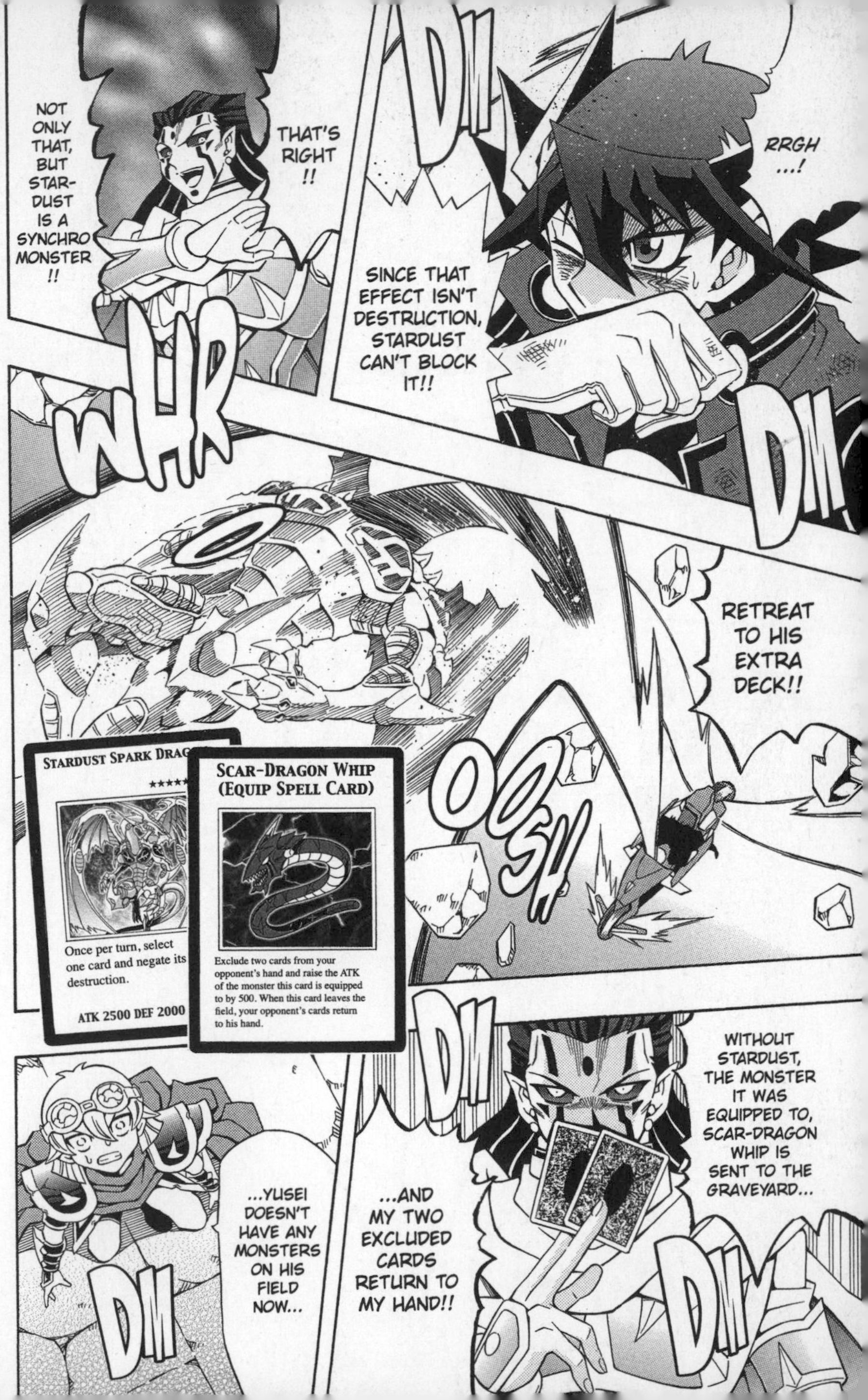
DM
RRGH ...!
SINCE THAT EFFECT ISN'T DESTRUCTION, STARDUST CAN'T BLOCK IT!!
DM
THAT'S RIGHT!!
NOT ONLY THAT, BUT STARDUST IS A SYNCHRO MONSTER!!
WHR
RETREAT TO HIS EXTRA DECK!!
OOSH
STARDUST SPARK DRAG
Once per turn, select one card and negate its destruction.
ATK 2500 DEF 2000
SCAR-DRAGON WHIP (EQUIP SPELL CARD)
Exclude two cards from your opponent's hand and raise the ATK of the monster this card is equipped to by 500. When this card leaves the field, your opponent's cards return to his hand.
DM
WITHOUT STARDUST, THE MONSTER IT WAS EQUIPPED TO, SCAR-DRAGON WHIP IS SENT TO THE GRAVEYARD...
...AND MY TWO EXCLUDED CARDS RETURN TO MY HAND!!
DM
...YUSEI DOESN'T HAVE ANY MONSTERS ON HIS FIELD NOW...
DM

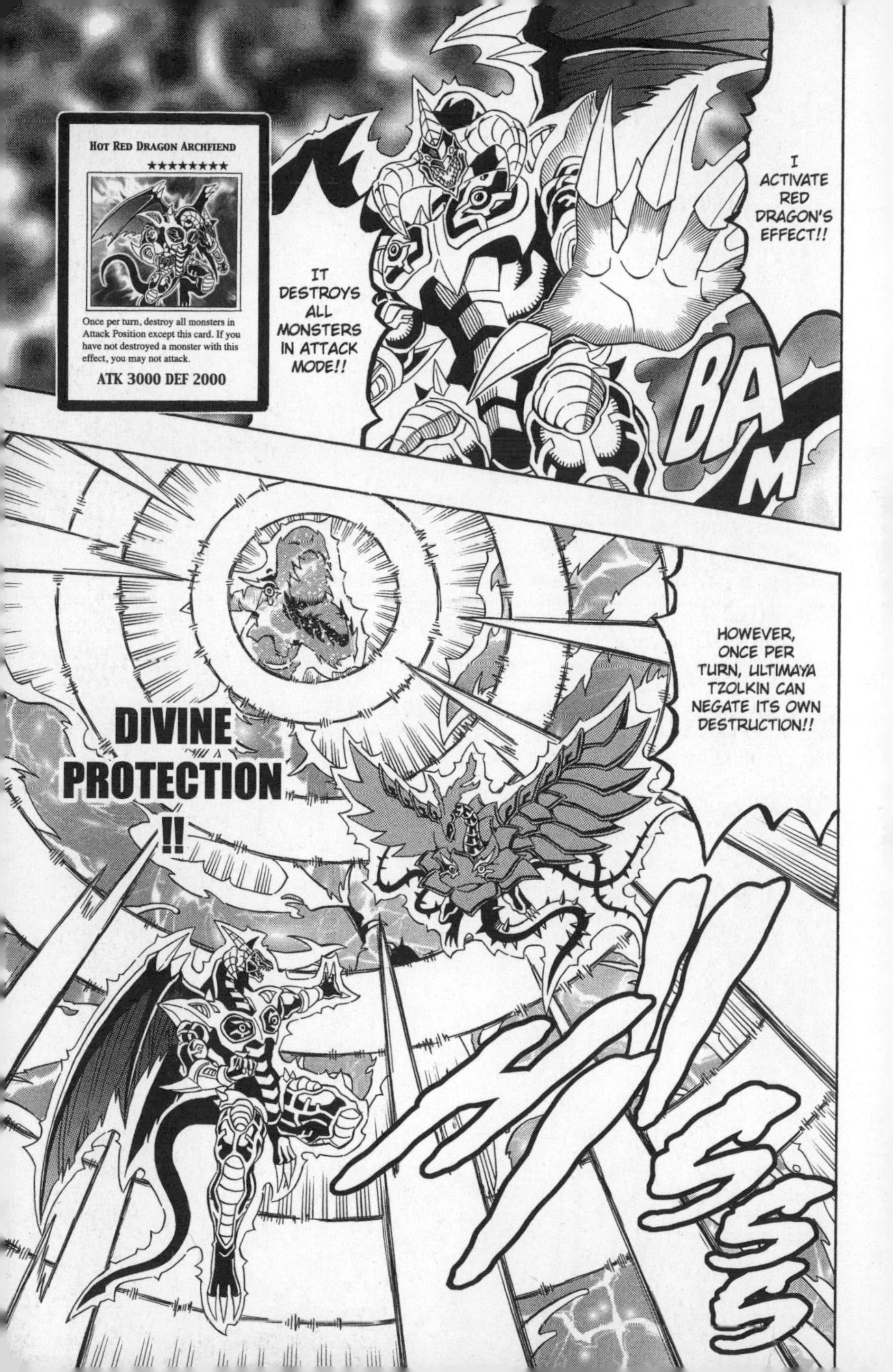
I ACTIVATE RED DRAGON'S EFFECT!!
IT DESTROYS ALL MONSTERS IN ATTACK MODE!!
HOT RED DRAGON ARCHFIEND
★★★★★★★★
Once per turn, destroy all monsters in Attack Position except this card. If you have not destroyed a monster with this effect, you may not attack.
ATK 3000 DEF 2000
BAM
HOWEVER, ONCE PER TURN, ULTIMAYA TZOLKIN CAN NEGATE ITS OWN DESTRUCTION!!
DIVINE PROTECTION!!

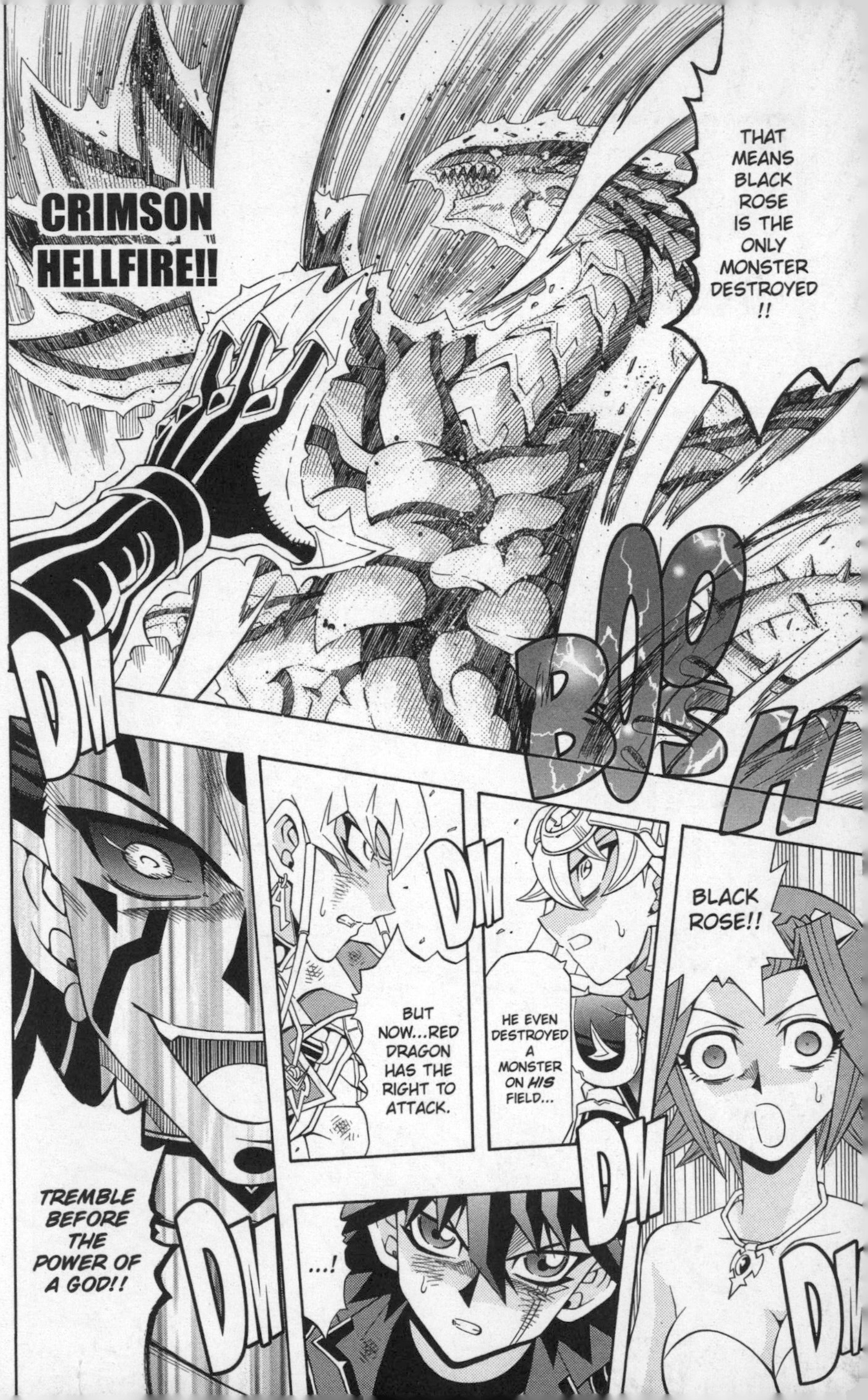
THAT MEANS BLACK ROSE IS THE ONLY MONSTER DESTROYED!!
CRIMSON HELLFIRE!!
BOOSH
DM
BLACK ROSE!!
DM
HE EVEN DESTROYED A MONSTER ON *HIS* FIELD...
DM
BUT NOW...RED DRAGON HAS THE RIGHT TO ATTACK.
DM
...!
DM
TREMBLE BEFORE THE POWER OF A GOD!!
DM

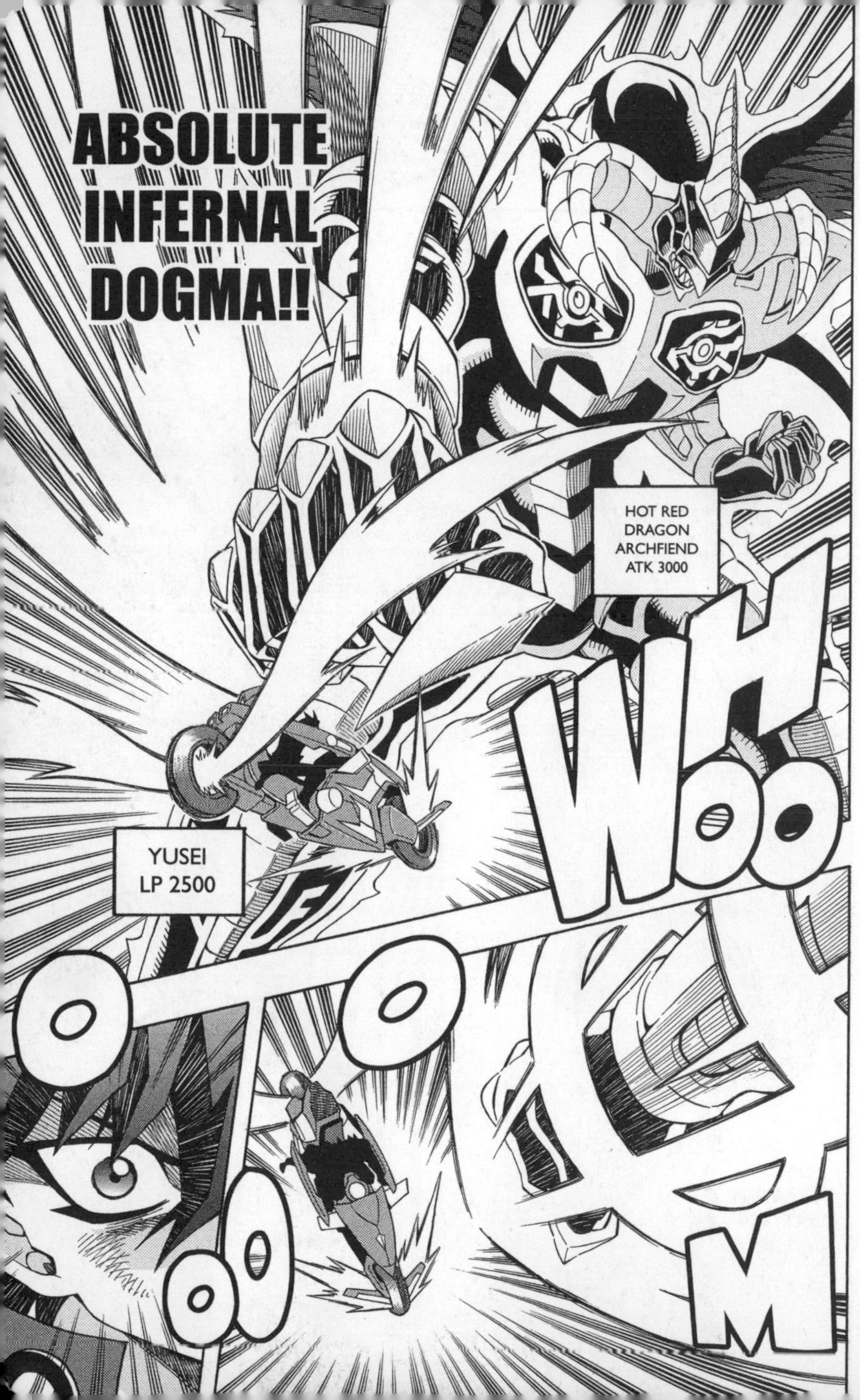
ABSOLUTE INFERNAL DOGMA!!
HOT RED DRAGON ARCHFIEND ATK 3000
WHOOOOOOM
YUSEI LP 2500

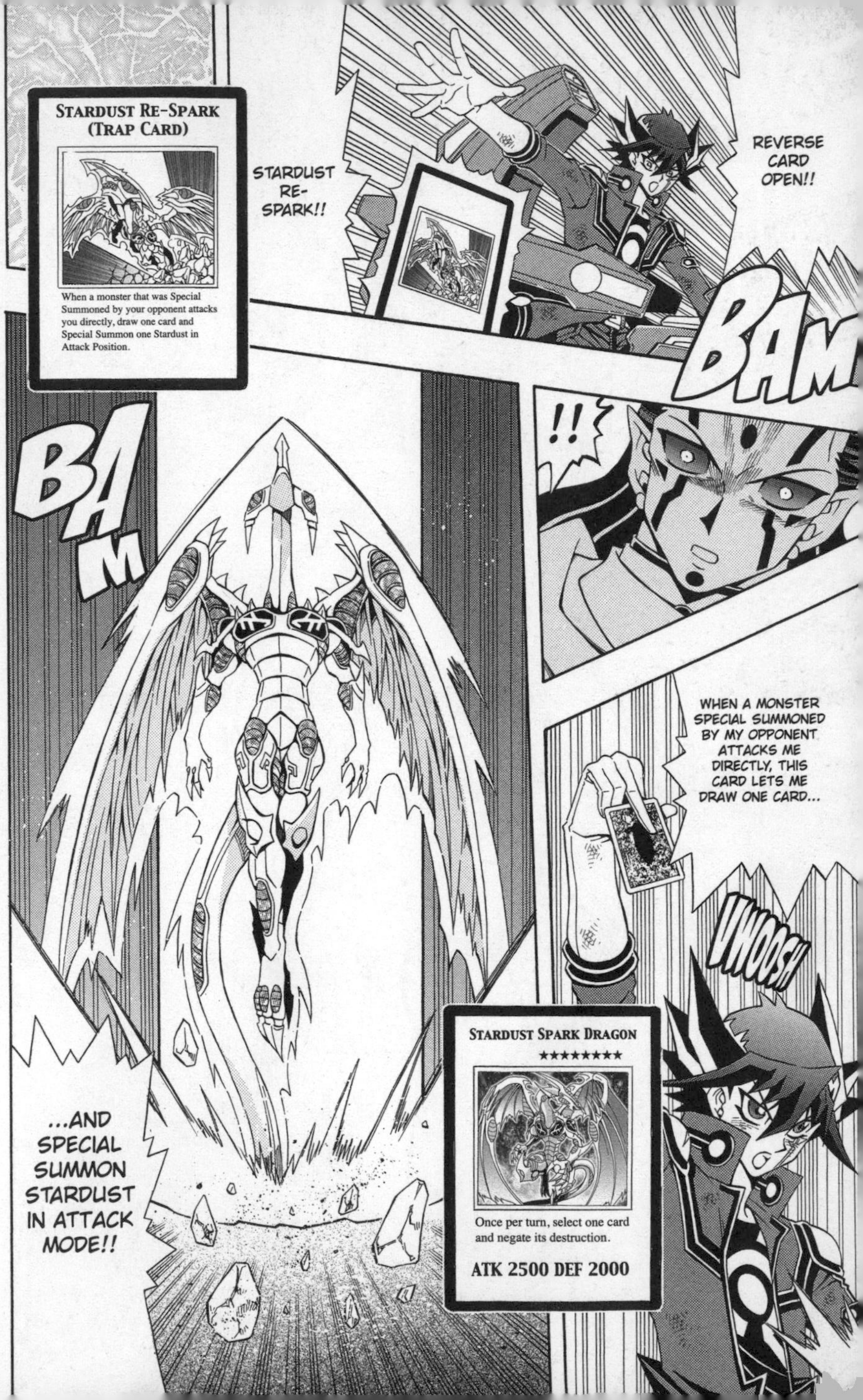
REVERSE CARD OPEN!!
STARDUST RE-SPARK!!
BAM
STARDUST RE-SPARK (TRAP CARD)
When a monster that was Special Summoned by your opponent attacks you directly, draw one card and Special Summon one Stardust in Attack Position.
!!
WHEN A MONSTER SPECIAL SUMMONED BY MY OPPONENT ATTACKS ME DIRECTLY, THIS CARD LETS ME DRAW ONE CARD...
VWOOSH
STARDUST SPARK DRAGON
★★★★★★★★
Once per turn, select one card and negate its destruction.
ATK 2500 DEF 2000
BAM
...AND SPECIAL SUMMON STARDUST IN ATTACK MODE!!

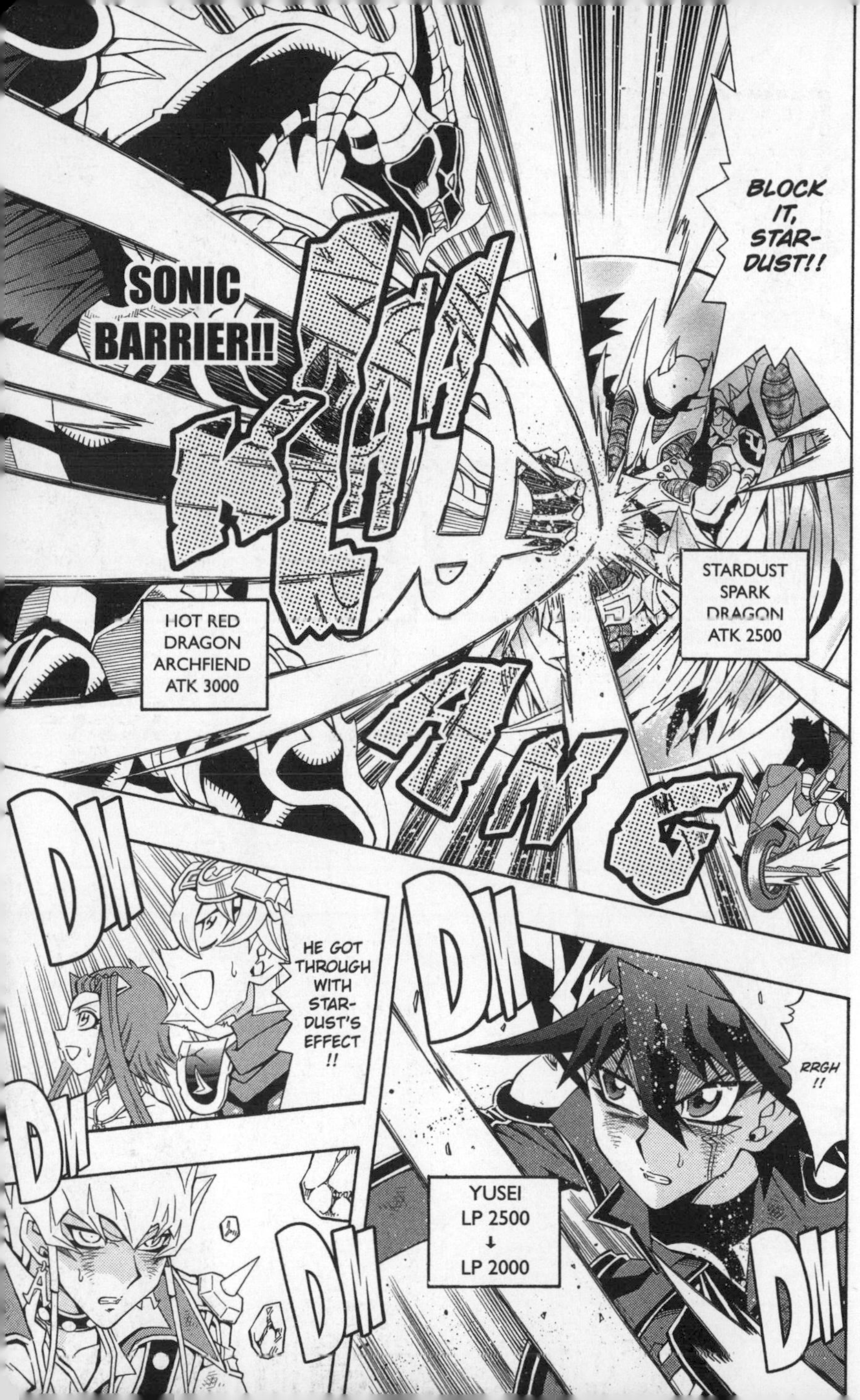

BLOCK IT, STAR-DUST!!
STARDUST SPARK DRAGON ATK 2500
SONIC BARRIER!!
HOT RED DRAGON ARCHFIEND ATK 3000
RRGH!!
YUSEI LP 2500 ↓ LP 2000
DM
DM
HE GOT THROUGH WITH STAR-DUST'S EFFECT!!
DM
DM
DM

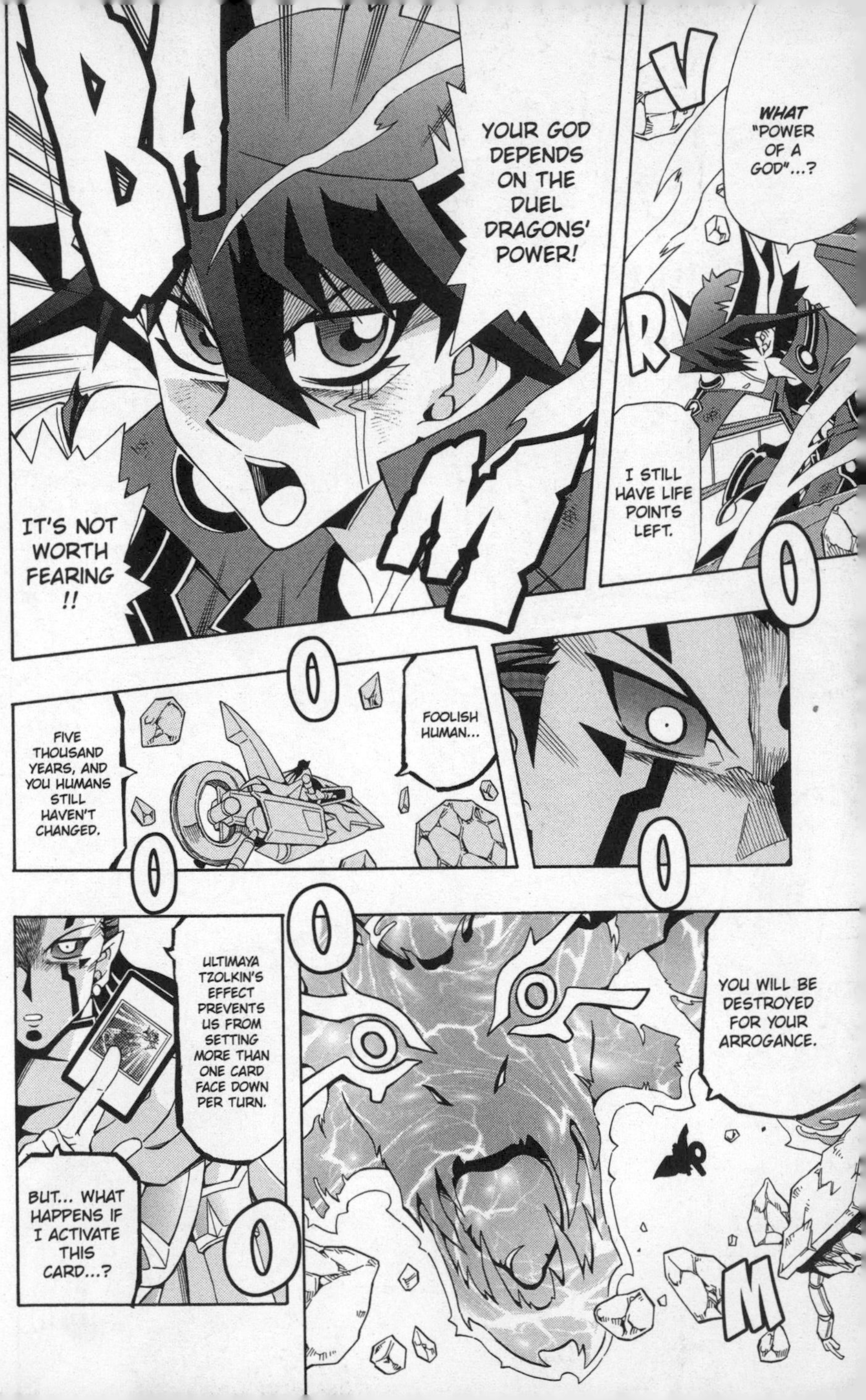
WHAT "POWER OF A GOD"...?
I STILL HAVE LIFE POINTS LEFT.
YOUR GOD DEPENDS ON THE DUEL DRAGONS' POWER!
BAM
IT'S NOT WORTH FEARING!!
VROOOOOOM
FOOLISH HUMAN...
FIVE THOUSAND YEARS, AND YOU HUMANS STILL HAVEN'T CHANGED.
YOU WILL BE DESTROYED FOR YOUR ARROGANCE.
ULTIMAYA TZOLKIN'S EFFECT PREVENTS US FROM SETTING MORE THAN ONE CARD FACE DOWN PER TURN.
BUT... WHAT HAPPENS IF I ACTIVATE THIS CARD...?

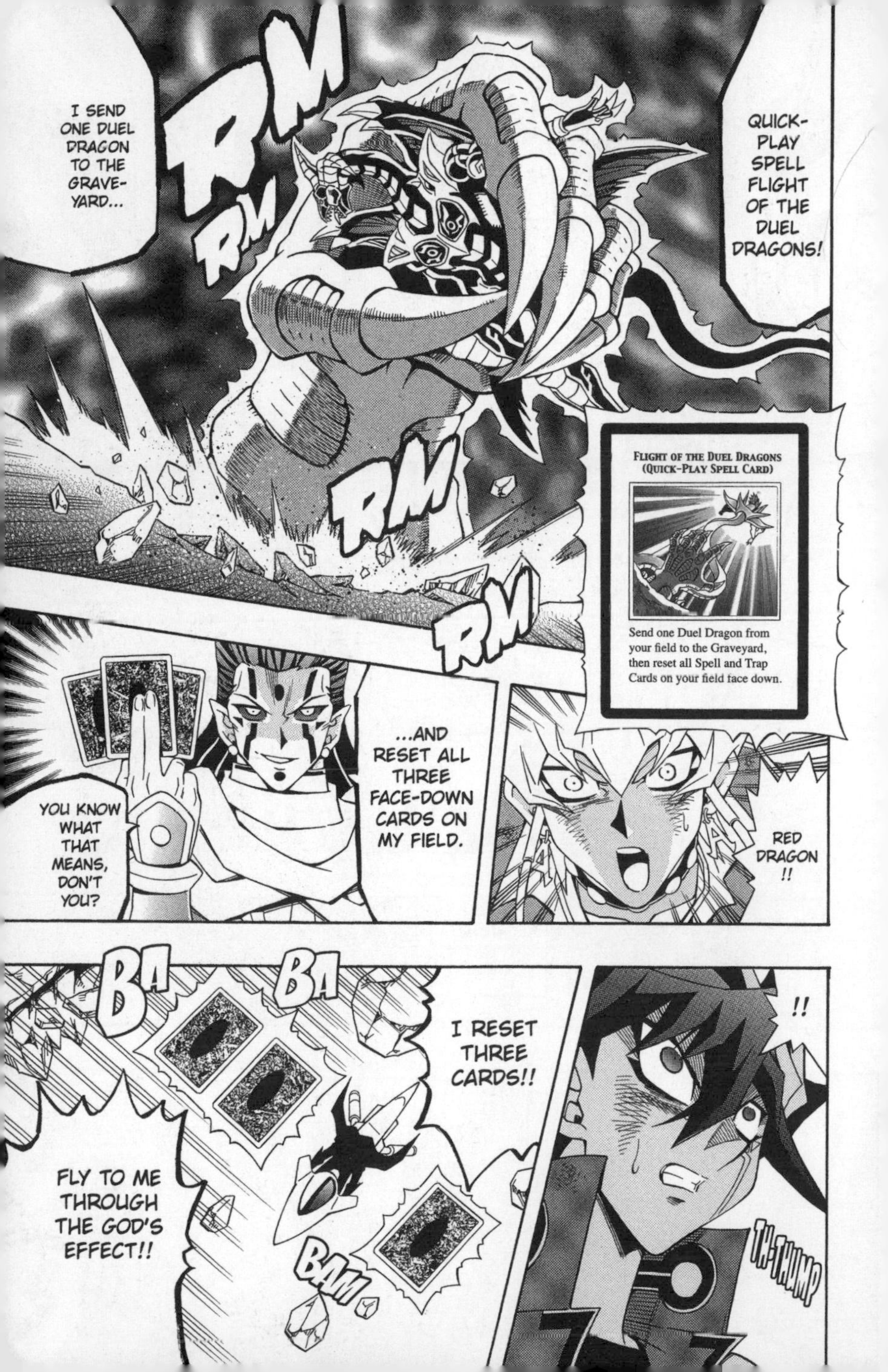
QUICK-PLAY SPELL FLIGHT OF THE DUEL DRAGONS!
I SEND ONE DUEL DRAGON TO THE GRAVEYARD...
RM
RM
RM
RM
FLIGHT OF THE DUEL DRAGONS
(QUICK-PLAY SPELL CARD)
Send one Duel Dragon from your field to the Graveyard, then reset all Spell and Trap Cards on your field face down.
RED DRAGON !!
...AND RESET ALL THREE FACE-DOWN CARDS ON MY FIELD.
YOU KNOW WHAT THAT MEANS, DON'T YOU?
!!
TH-THUMP
I RESET THREE CARDS!!
BA
BA
FLY TO ME THROUGH THE GOD'S EFFECT!!
BAM

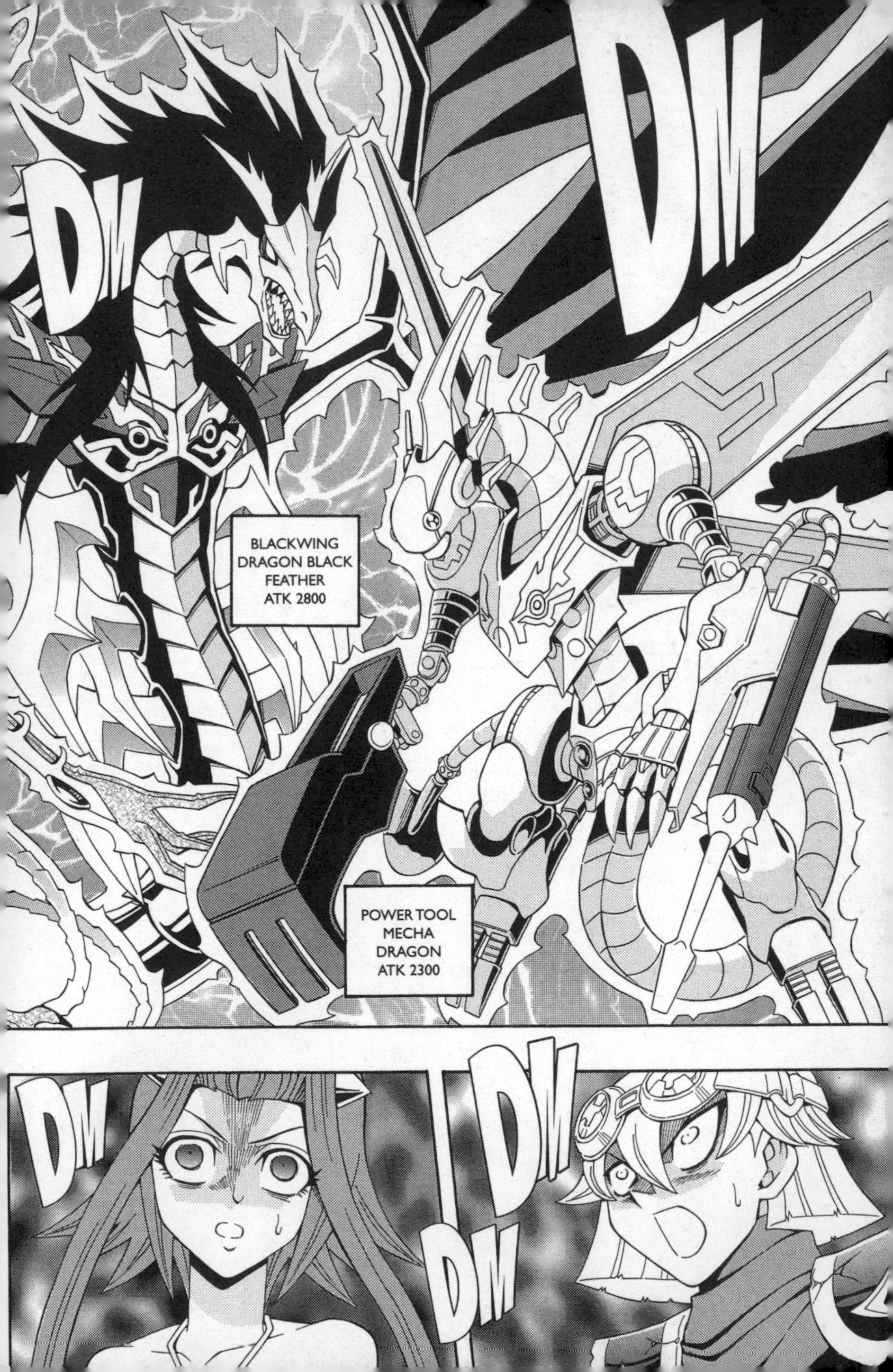
DM
DM
BLACKWING DRAGON BLACK FEATHER ATK 2800
POWER TOOL MECHA DRAGON ATK 2300
DM
DM
DM

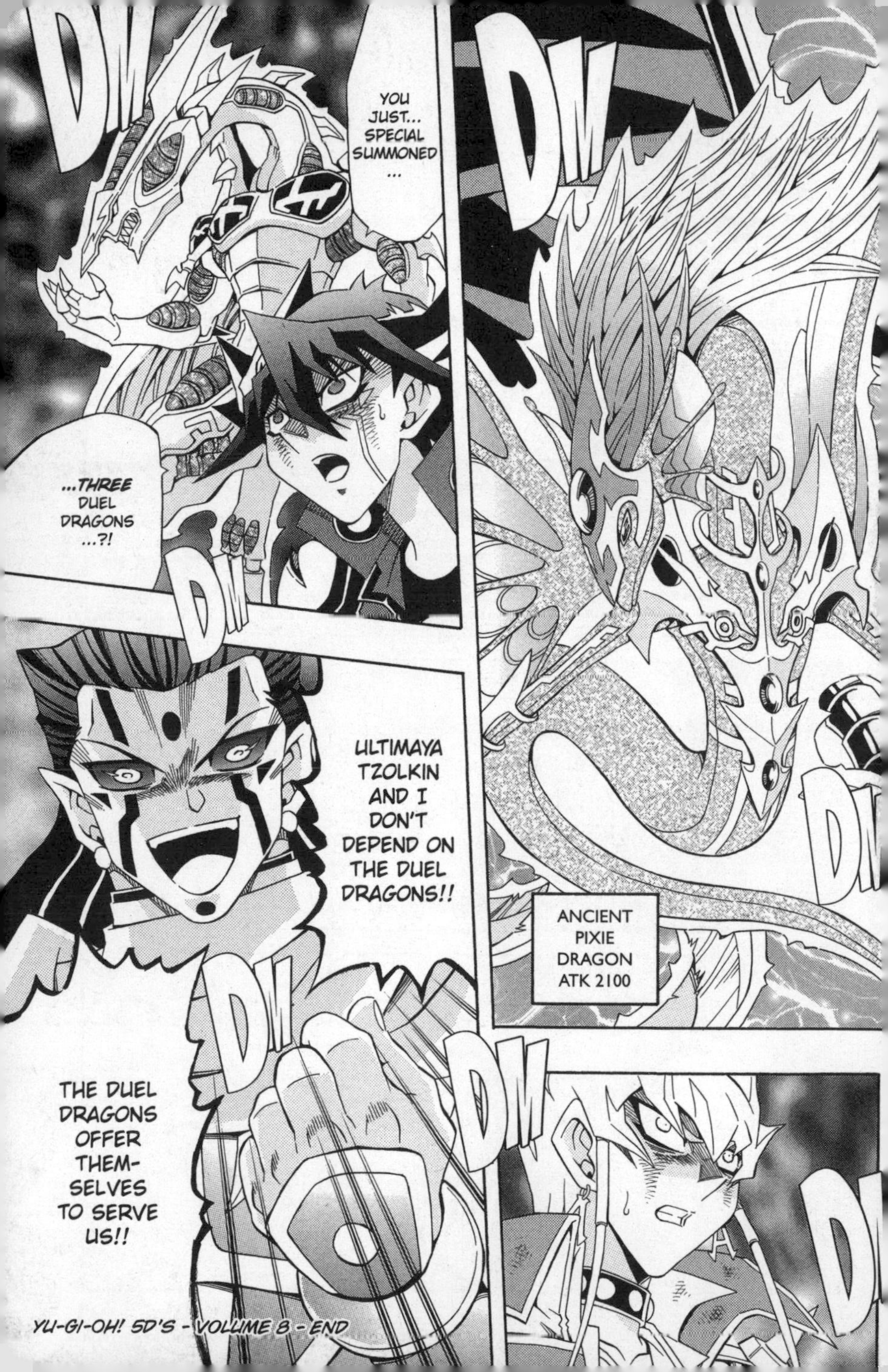
DM
ANCIENT PIXIE DRAGON ATK 2100
DM
YOU JUST... SPECIAL SUMMONED ...
...THREE DUEL DRAGONS ...?!
DM
ULTIMAYA TZOLKIN AND I DON'T DEPEND ON THE DUEL DRAGONS!!
DM
DM
THE DUEL DRAGONS OFFER THEM-SELVES TO SERVE US!!
YU-GI-OH! 5D'S - VOLUME 8 - END

5D's TRACKS

THE 59TH

BY SATOMASA

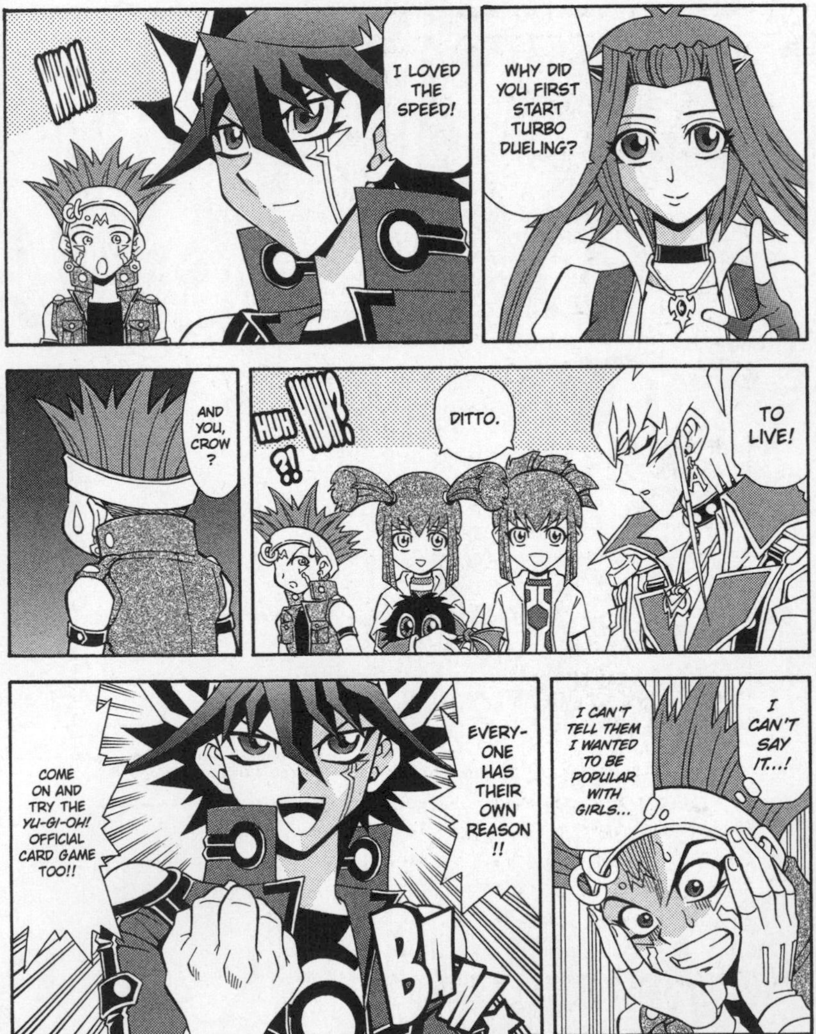

WHY DID YOU FIRST START TURBO DUELING?
I LOVED THE SPEED!
WHOA!
TO LIVE!
DITTO.
HUH HUH?
?!
AND YOU, CROW?
I CAN'T SAY IT...!
I CAN'T TELL THEM I WANTED TO BE POPULAR WITH GIRLS...
EVERY-ONE HAS THEIR OWN REASON!!
COME ON AND TRY THE YU-GI-OH! OFFICIAL CARD GAME TOO!!
BAM

IN THE NEXT VOLUME...

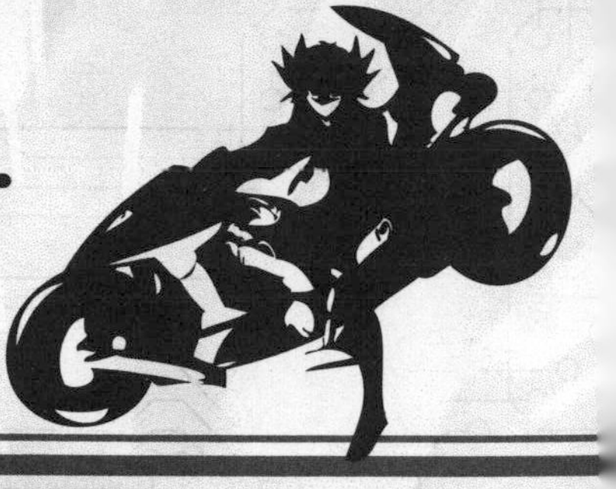

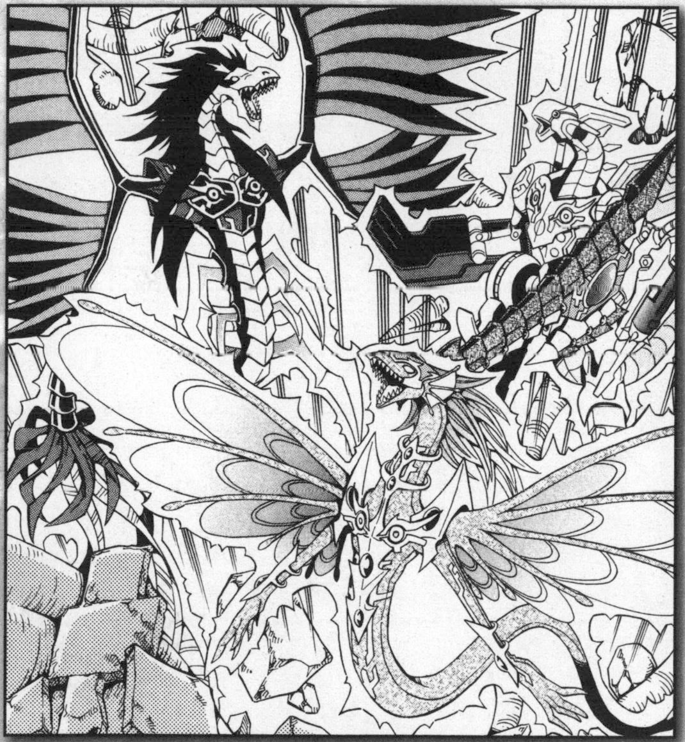

Yusei and Goodwin are locked in their final Duel. Having now harnessed the power of the Ultimate God, Goodwin can turn Yusei's Duel Dragons against him. The assault may be more than Yusei can bear, and he will need his friends' help to have any chance of winning, but will it be enough?

COMING APRIL 2016!!

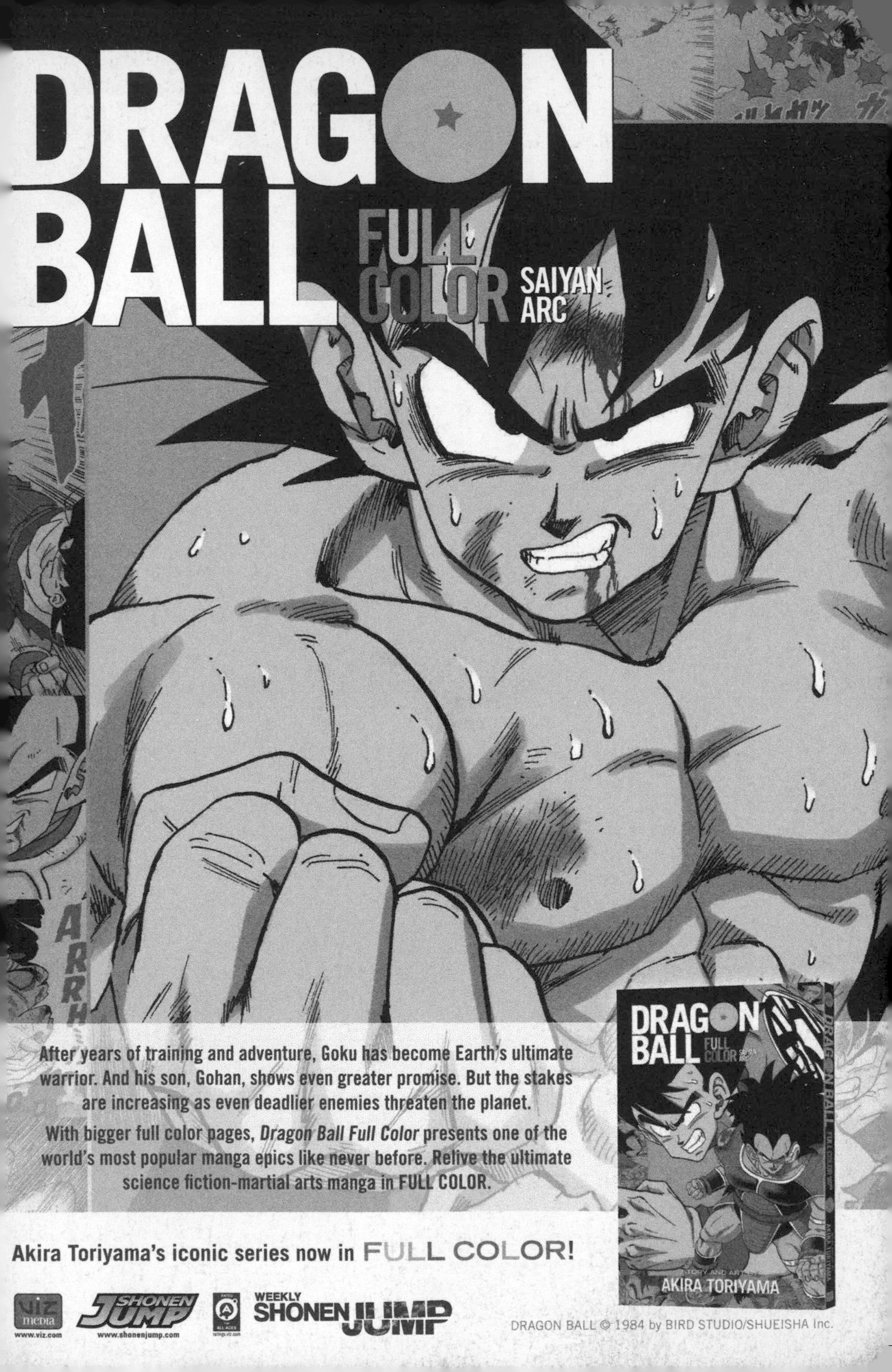
DRAGON BALL
FULL COLOR
SAIYAN ARC
After years of training and adventure, Goku has become Earth's ultimate warrior. And his son, Gohan, shows even greater promise. But the stakes are increasing as even deadlier enemies threaten the planet.
With bigger full color pages, *Dragon Ball Full Color* presents one of the world's most popular manga epics like never before. Relive the ultimate science fiction-martial arts manga in FULL COLOR.
DRAGON BALL FULL COLOR SAIYAN ARC
AKIRA TORIYAMA
Akira Toriyama's iconic series now in FULL COLOR!
www.viz.com
www.shonenjump.com
WEEKLY SHONEN JUMP
DRAGON BALL © 1984 by BIRD STUDIO/SHUEISHA Inc.

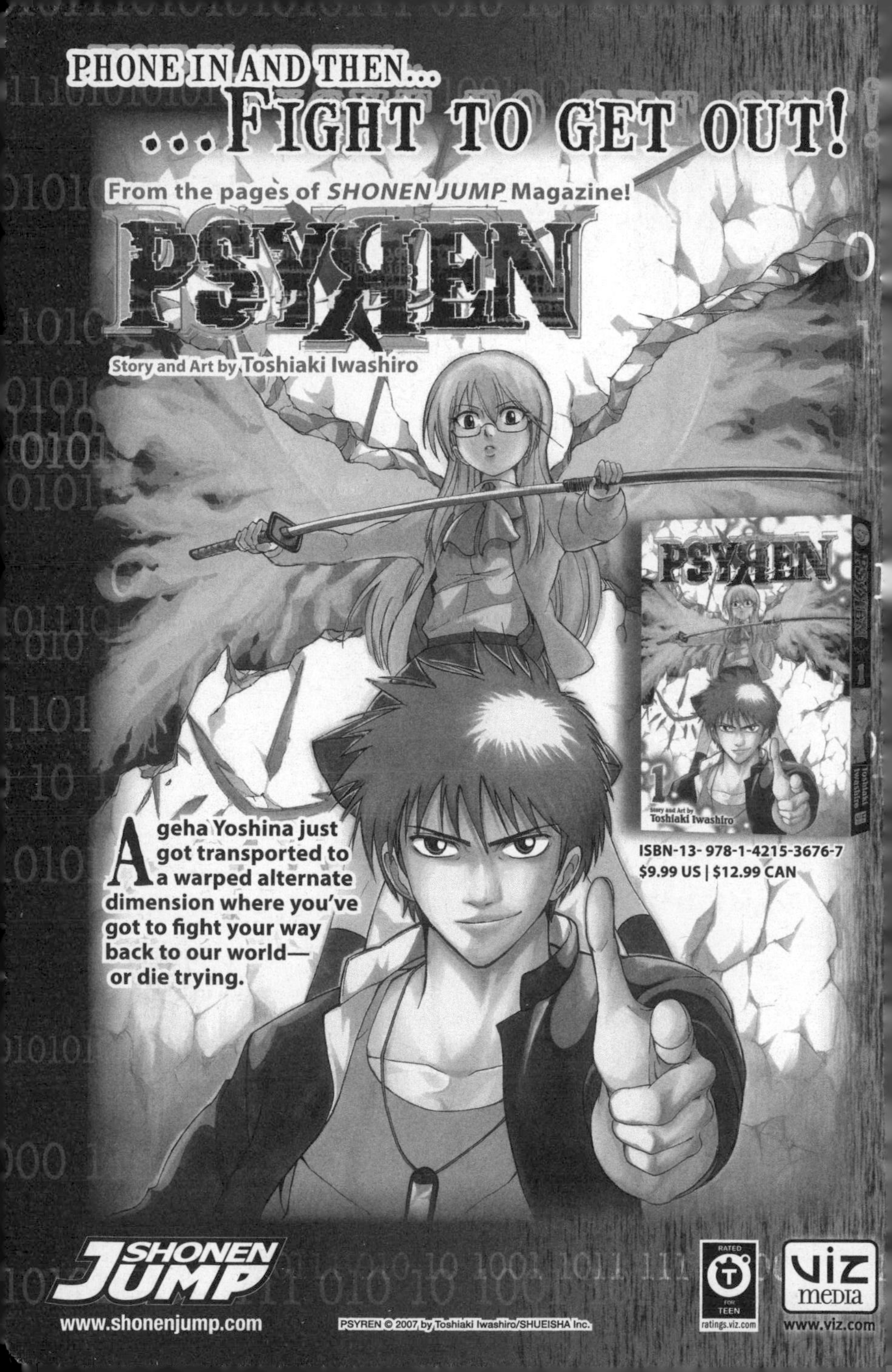
PHONE IN AND THEN...
...FIGHT TO GET OUT!
From the pages of SHONEN JUMP Magazine!
PSYREN
Story and Art by Toshiaki Iwashiro
Ageha Yoshina just got transported to a warped alternate dimension where you've got to fight your way back to our world— or die trying.
PSYREN
1
Story and Art by Toshiaki Iwashiro
ISBN-13- 978-1-4215-3676-7
$9.99 US | $12.99 CAN
SHONEN JUMP
www.shonenjump.com
PSYREN © 2007 by Toshiaki Iwashiro/SHUEISHA Inc.
RATED T FOR TEEN
ratings.viz.com
VIZ media
www.viz.com

Story by YUMI HOTTA
Art by TAKESHI OBATA

The breakthrough series by Takeshi Obata, the artist of *Death Note!*

Hikaru Shindo is like any sixth-grader in Japan: a pretty normal schoolboy with a penchant for antics. One day, he finds an old bloodstained Go board in his grandfather's attic. Trapped inside the Go board is Fujiwara-no-Sai, the ghost of an ancient Go master. In one fateful moment, Sai becomes a part of Hikaru's consciousness and together, through thick and thin, they make an unstoppable Go-playing team.

Will they be able to defeat Go players who have dedicated their lives to the game? And will Sai achieve the "Divine Move" so he'll finally be able to rest in peace? Find out in this *Shonen Jump* classic!

www.shonenjump.com

www.viz.com

BAKUMAN。

STORY BY TSUGUMI OHBA
ART BY TAKESHI OBATA

From the creators of *Death Note*

The mystery behind manga making REVEALED!

Average student Moritaka Mashiro enjoys drawing for fun. When his classmate and aspiring writer Akito Takagi discovers his talent, he begs to team up. But what exactly does it take to make it in the manga-publishing world?

Bakuman。 Vol. 1
ISBN: 978-1-4215-3513-5
$9.99 US / $12.99 CAN *

YOU ARE READING IN THE WRONG DIRECTION!!

Whoops! Guess what?
You're starting at the wrong end of the comic!

...It's true! In keeping with the original Japanese format, *Yu-Gi-Oh! 5Ds* is meant to be read from right to left, starting in the upper-right corner.

Unlike English, which is read from left to right, Japanese is read from right to left, meaning that action, sound effects and word-balloon order are completely reversed... something which can make readers unfamiliar with Japanese feel pretty backwards themselves. For this reason, manga or Japanese comics published in the U.S. in English have sometimes been published "flopped"—that is, printed in exact reverse order, as though seen from the other side of a mirror.

By flopping pages, U.S. publishers can avoid confusing readers, but the compromise is not without its downside. For one thing, a character in a flopped manga series who once wore in the original Japanese version a T-shirt emblazoned with "M A Y" (as in "the merry month of") now wears one which reads "Y A M"! Additionally, many manga creators in Japan are themselves unhappy with the process, as some feel the mirror-imaging of their art alters their original intentions.

We are proud to bring you Masahiro Hikokubo and Masashi Sato's *Yu-Gi-Oh! 5D's* in the original unflopped format. For now, though, turn to the other side of the book and let the duel begin...!

—Editor